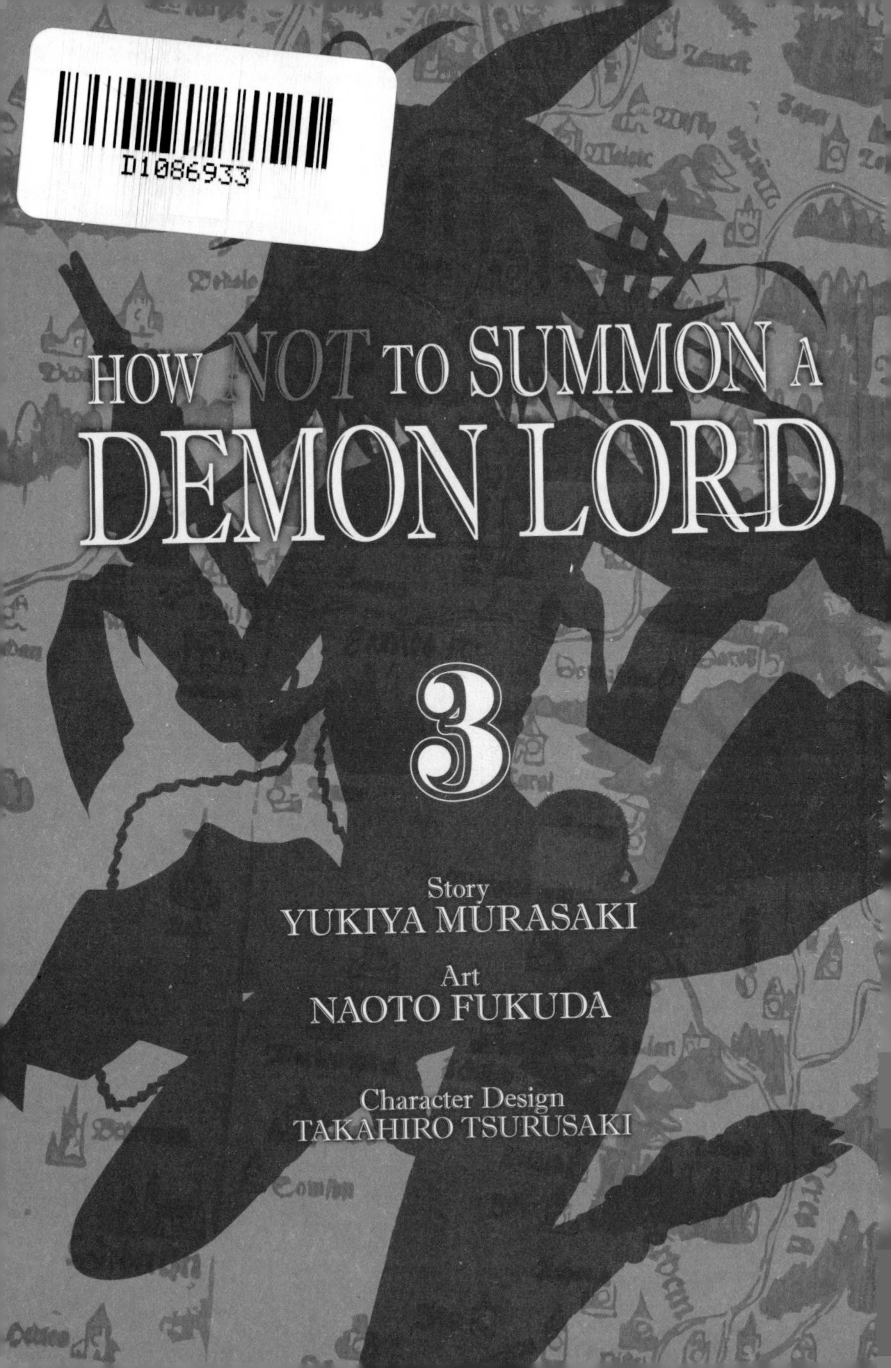

HOW NOT TO SUMMON A DEMON LORD

3

Story
YUKIYA MURASAKI

Art
NAOTO FUKUDA

Character Design
TAKAHIRO TSURUSAKI

HOW NOT TO SUMMON A DEMON LORD

CHARACTERS

INTRODUCTIONS

Race: Demon
Level: 150

Self-proclaimed Demon Lord from another world.

Thanks to "Magic Deflection," an effect of the Demon Lord's Ring he received in-game, Rem and Shera were stuck with Enslavement Collars instead of him when they attempted an Enslavement Ritual. In the real world, Diablo was unpopular, didn't have a way with words, and couldn't interact with other people to save his life. But in this world, he's tall, handsome, and practically invincible! He still doesn't have a way with words, but he manages to make it through tough situations by acting like a Demon Lord.

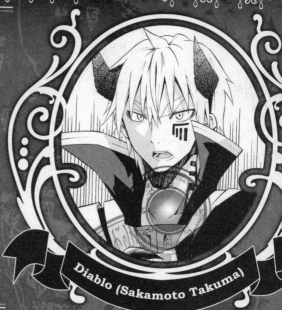

Diablo (Sakamoto Takuma)

STORY

Sakamoto Takuma is so overwhelmingly strong at the MMO *Cross Reverie* that he is known as the "Demon Lord." One day, he is summoned to another world practically identical to the game by two girls: Shera, an Elf, and Rem, a Pantherian. Thanks to a pair of Enslavement Collars, Sakamoto Takuma--now Diablo--has control over the two girls...but he really sucks at talking to other people!! To hide this, Diablo begins behaving like his Demon Lord persona from the game. After demonstrating his power, built up through skills he acquired by playing *Cross Reverie,* Diablo, Rem, and Shera set out on an adventure together. Along the way, Diablo and Shera are sent by the Adventurer's Guild to the Bridge of Ulug...only to find an army of over one hundred Fallen has gathered to march on the Bridge of Ulug! If the fortress falls, so does the town...

Rem Galleu

Race: Pantherian   Level: 40
A Summoner and an Adventurer.
Trapped within her is the soul of the Demon
Lord Krebskulm, which will be released
upon her death. She became an Adventurer
in order to search for a way to free herself
from this curse. She has a small body, is
adorable and catlike with fluffy ears and a
tail. She's also flat as a board.

Shera L. Greenwood

Race: Elf   Level: 30
A Summoner, she is an expert archer, as one
would expect of an Elf. She is slender and
elegant, but also has an impressively large
bosom that is at odds with the rest of her
body. Her innocent and naive personality
calms everyone around her. She's actually
the princess of the Kingdom of Greenwood,
but has left home in order to live freely.

Celestine Baudelaire

Race: Human
Leader of the Mages Association in Faltra.
Uses her magic energy to power the
barrier protecting the town of Faltra from
the Fallen. Has a kind personality and is
concerned for Rem.

Sylvie

Race: Grasswalker
Guildmaster of the Adventurer's Guild
in Faltra. As is typical for Grasswalkers,
she looks extremely young. Her age is
unknown. Wears skimpy outfits, keeping
things pretty risqué. Sends Diablo and the
others out on quests.

Emile Bichelberger

Race: Human   Level: 50
A Warrior of the Adventurer's Guild in Faltra.
Calls himself the "Protector of All Women," and uses sword-
based martial arts to do battle. Has sworn an oath to never
fall while in front of women and has appointed himself an
ally to all of womankind. He sometimes takes things a little
too far. A nice guy, but is not without his faults.

HOW NOT TO SUMMON A DEMON LORD

3

CONTENTS

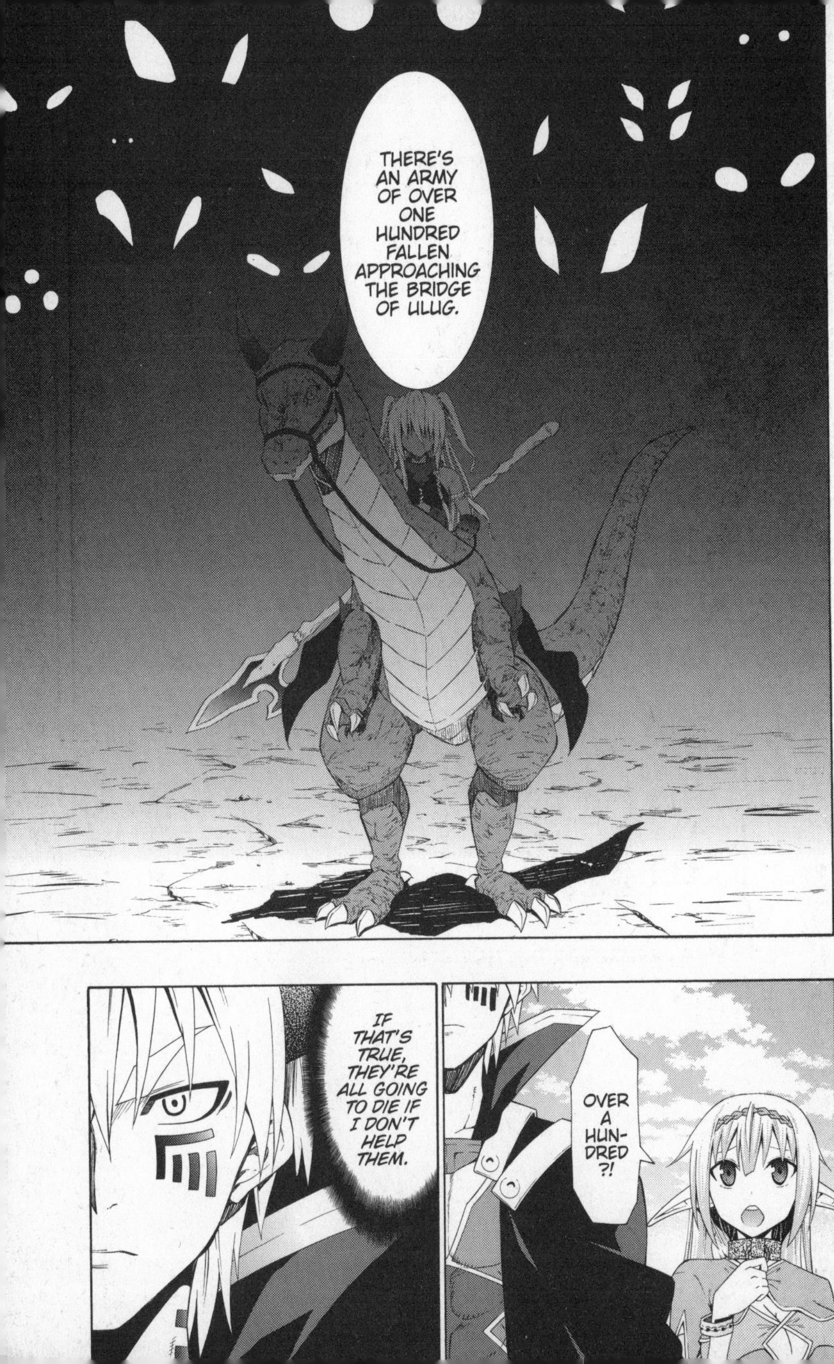
THERE'S AN ARMY OF OVER ONE HUNDRED FALLEN APPROACHING THE BRIDGE OF ULUG.
OVER A HUN-DRED?!
IF THAT'S TRUE, THEY'RE ALL GOING TO DIE IF I DON'T HELP THEM.

10 TRYING TO SAVE THE WORLD II

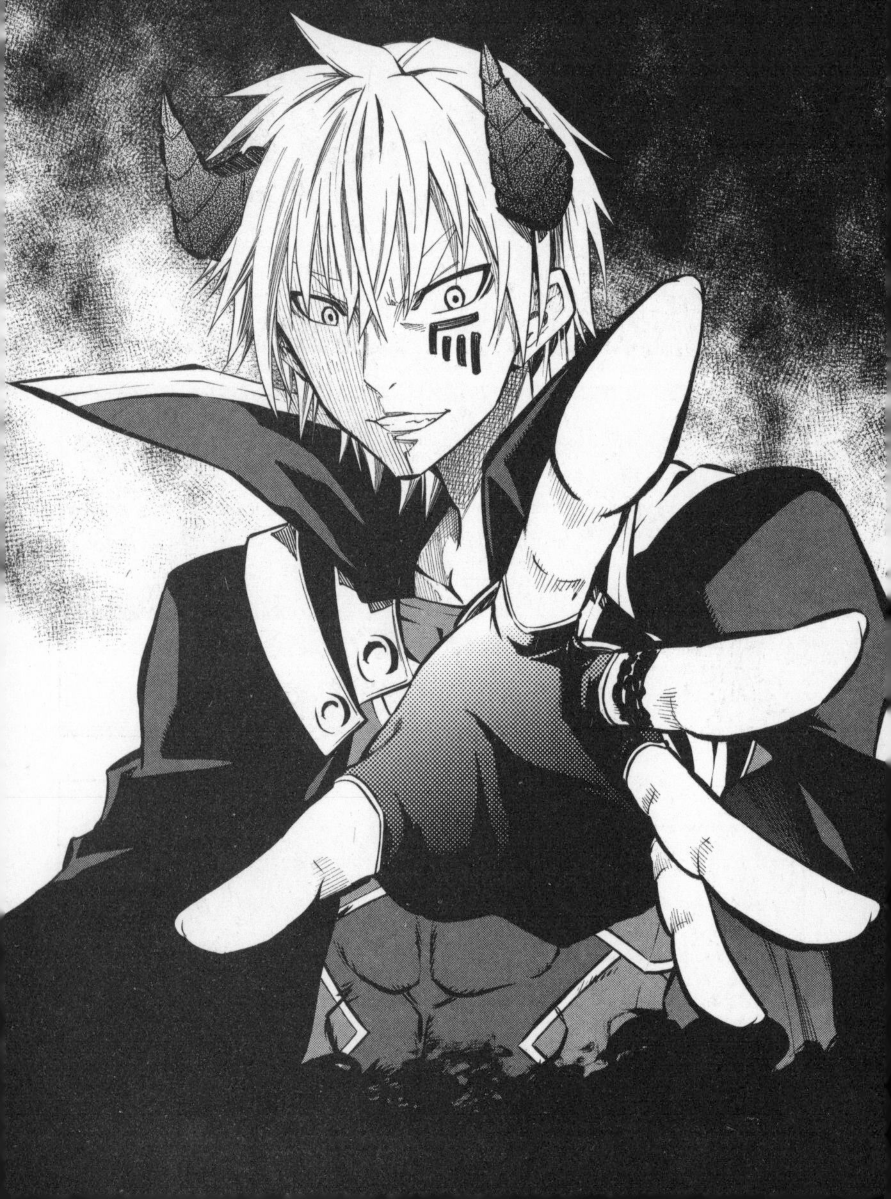

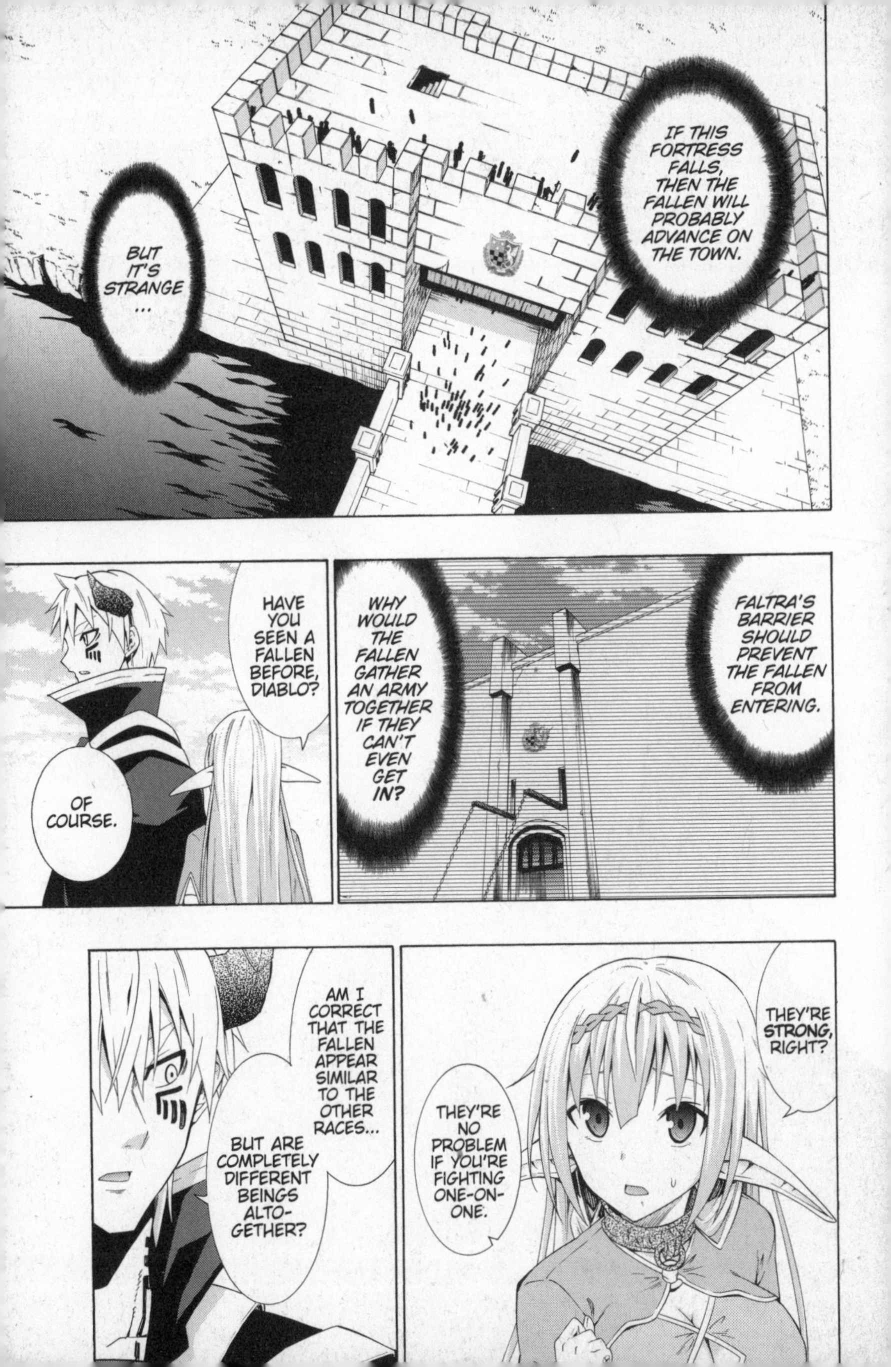
IF THIS FORTRESS FALLS, THEN THE FALLEN WILL PROBABLY ADVANCE ON THE TOWN.
BUT IT'S STRANGE...
FALTRA'S BARRIER SHOULD PREVENT THE FALLEN FROM ENTERING.
WHY WOULD THE FALLEN GATHER AN ARMY TOGETHER IF THEY CAN'T EVEN GET IN?
HAVE YOU SEEN A FALLEN BEFORE, DIABLO?
OF COURSE.
THEY'RE STRONG, RIGHT?
THEY'RE NO PROBLEM IF YOU'RE FIGHTING ONE-ON-ONE.
AM I CORRECT THAT THE FALLEN APPEAR SIMILAR TO THE OTHER RACES...
BUT ARE COMPLETELY DIFFERENT BEINGS ALTO-GETHER?

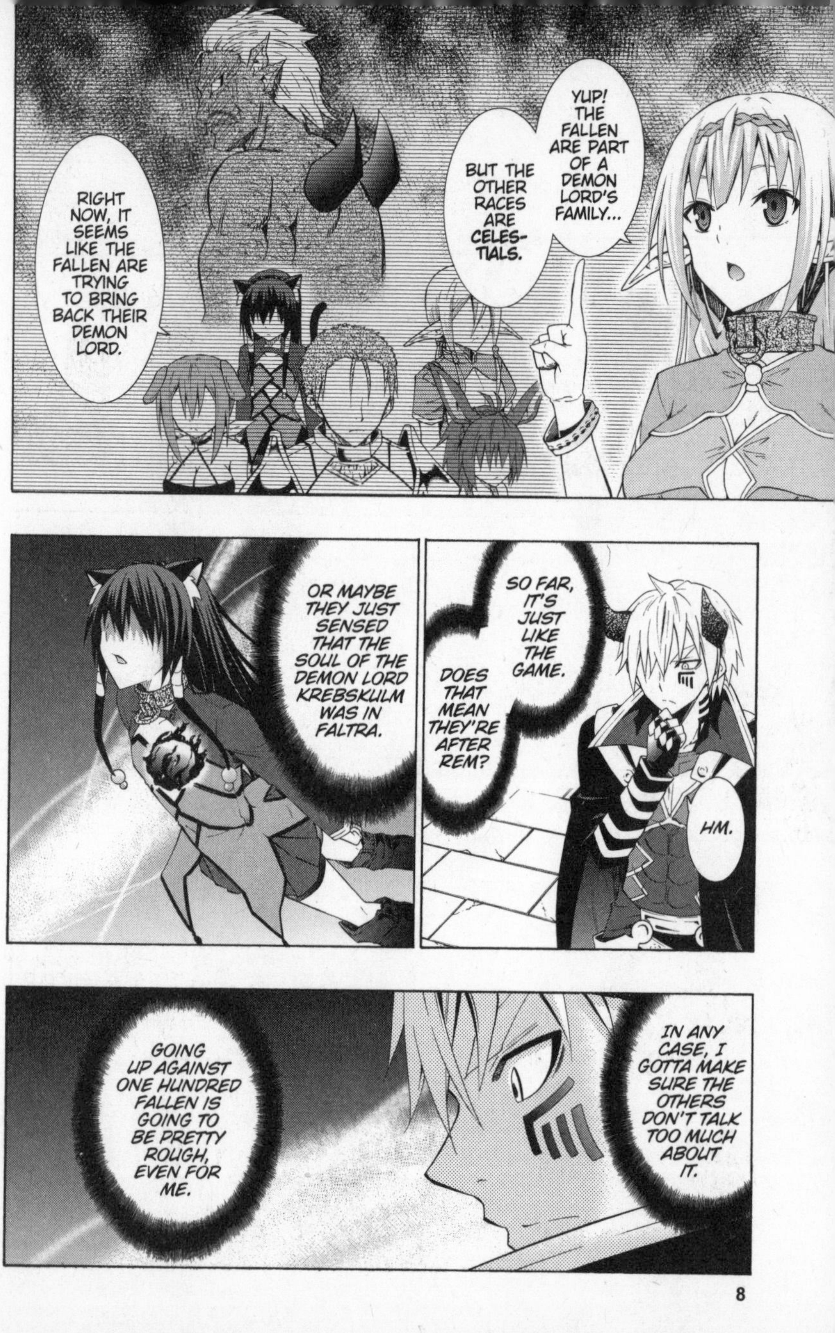
YUP! THE FALLEN ARE PART OF A DEMON LORD'S FAMILY...
BUT THE OTHER RACES ARE CELES-TIALS.
RIGHT NOW, IT SEEMS LIKE THE FALLEN ARE TRYING TO BRING BACK THEIR DEMON LORD.
SO FAR, IT'S JUST LIKE THE GAME.
DOES THAT MEAN THEY'RE AFTER REM?
HM.
OR MAYBE THEY JUST SENSED THAT THE SOUL OF THE DEMON LORD KREBSKULM WAS IN FALTRA.
IN ANY CASE, I GOTTA MAKE SURE THE OTHERS DON'T TALK TOO MUCH ABOUT IT.
GOING UP AGAINST ONE HUNDRED FALLEN IS GOING TO BE PRETTY ROUGH, EVEN FOR ME.

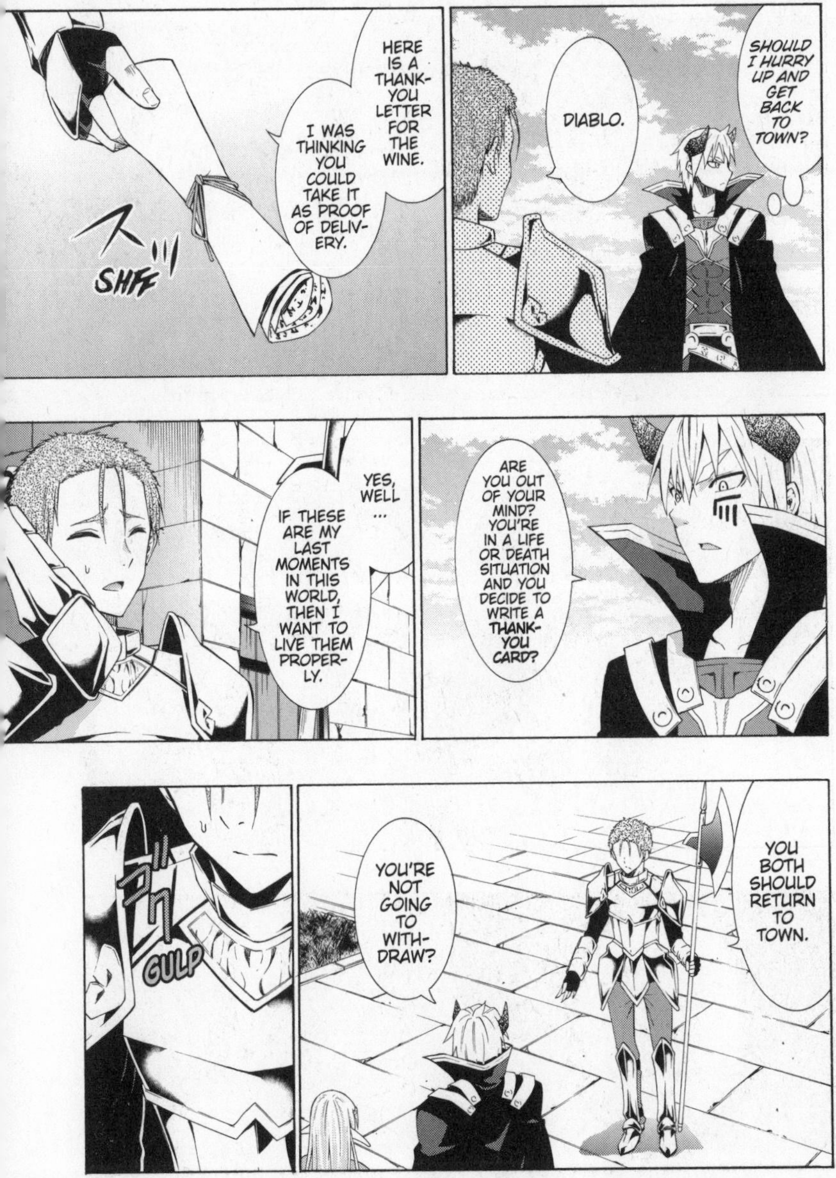
SHOULD I HURRY UP AND GET BACK TO TOWN?
DIABLO.
HERE IS A THANK-YOU LETTER FOR THE WINE.
I WAS THINKING YOU COULD TAKE IT AS PROOF OF DELIVERY.
SHFF
ARE YOU OUT OF YOUR MIND? YOU'RE IN A LIFE OR DEATH SITUATION AND YOU DECIDE TO WRITE A THANK-YOU CARD?
YES, WELL ...
IF THESE ARE MY LAST MOMENTS IN THIS WORLD, THEN I WANT TO LIVE THEM PROPERLY.
YOU BOTH SHOULD RETURN TO TOWN.
YOU'RE NOT GOING TO WITHDRAW?
GULP

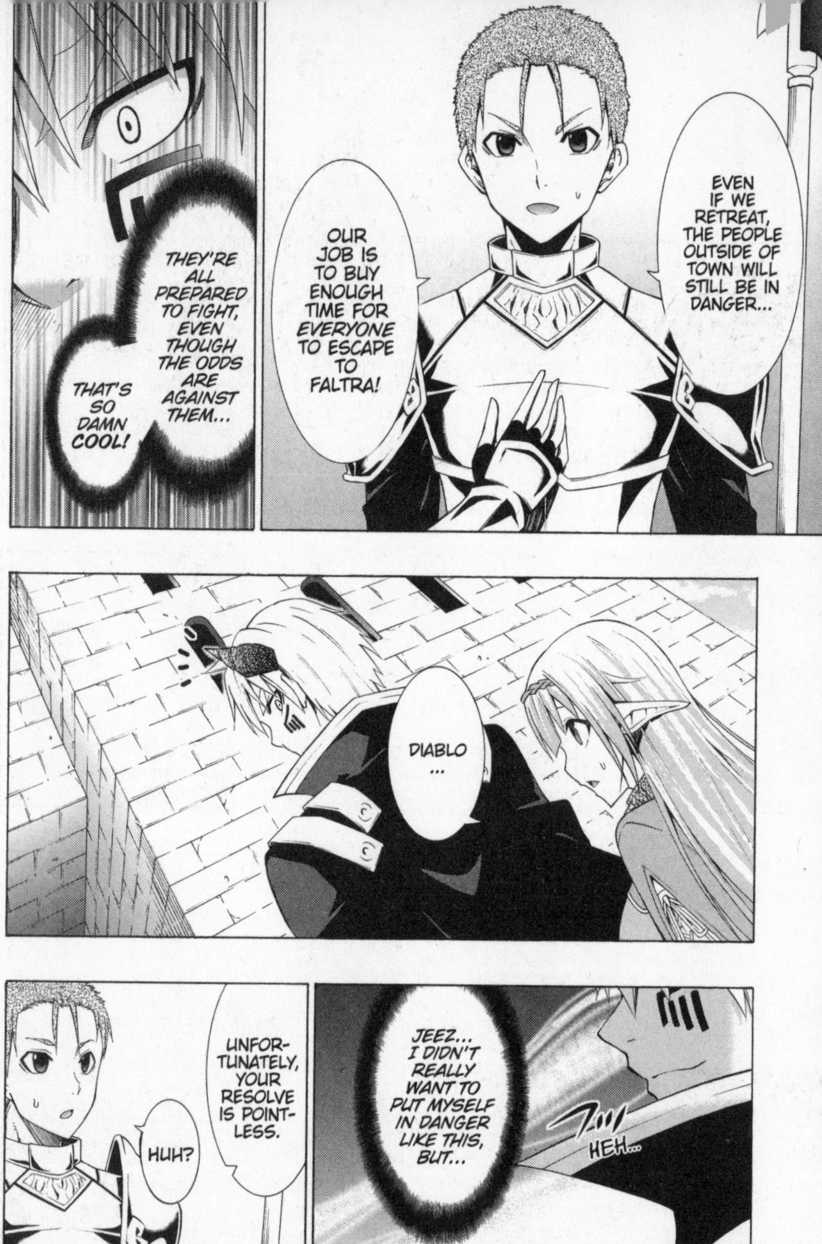
EVEN IF WE RETREAT, THE PEOPLE OUTSIDE OF TOWN WILL STILL BE IN DANGER...
OUR JOB IS TO BUY ENOUGH TIME FOR EVERYONE TO ESCAPE TO FALTRA!
THEY'RE ALL PREPARED TO FIGHT, EVEN THOUGH THE ODDS ARE AGAINST THEM...
THAT'S SO DAMN COOL!
DIABLO...
JEEZ... I DIDN'T REALLY WANT TO PUT MYSELF IN DANGER LIKE THIS, BUT...
HEH...
UNFORTUNATELY, YOUR RESOLVE IS POINTLESS.
HUH?

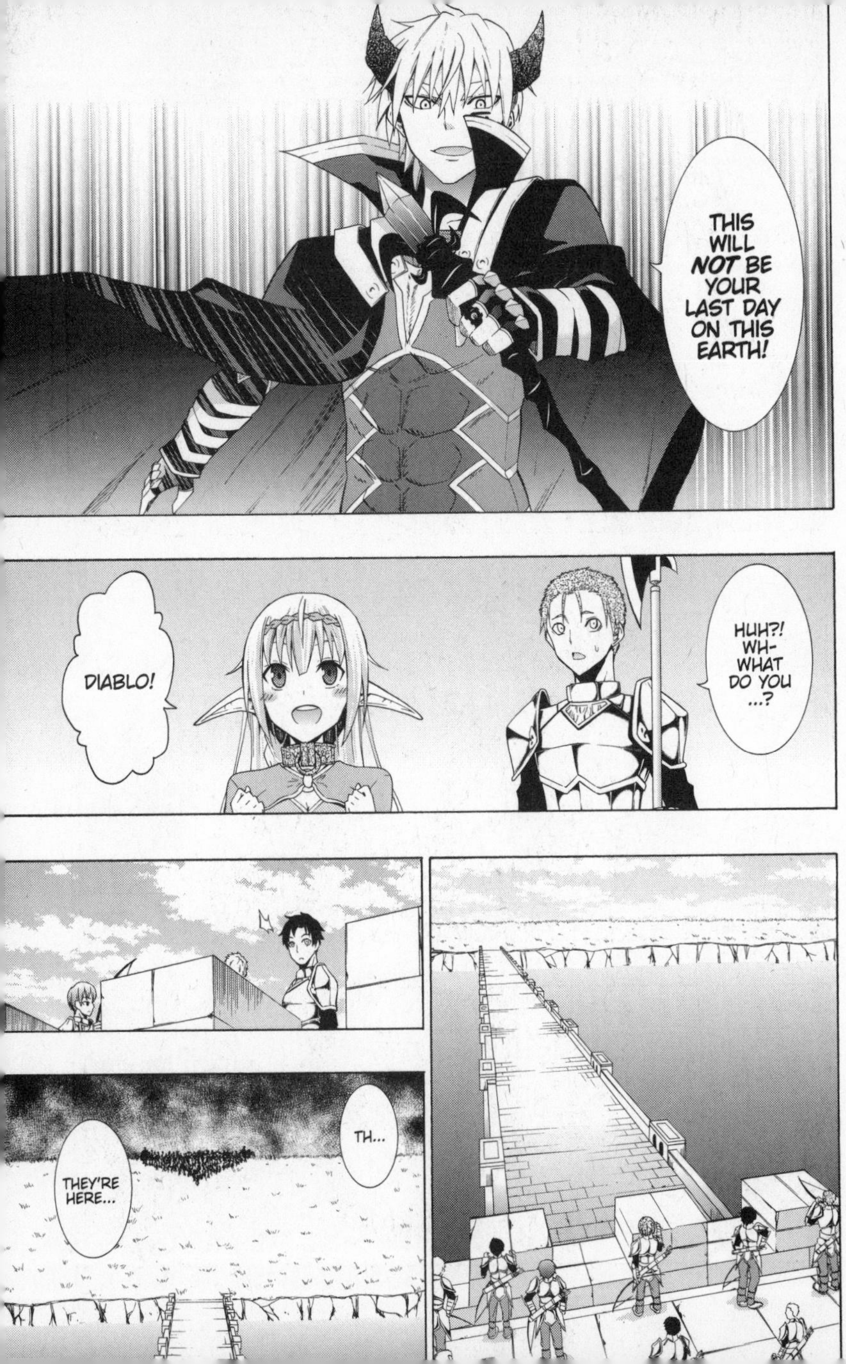
THIS WILL ***NOT*** BE YOUR LAST DAY ON THIS EARTH!
HUH?! WH-WHAT DO YOU ...?
DIABLO!
TH...
THEY'RE HERE...

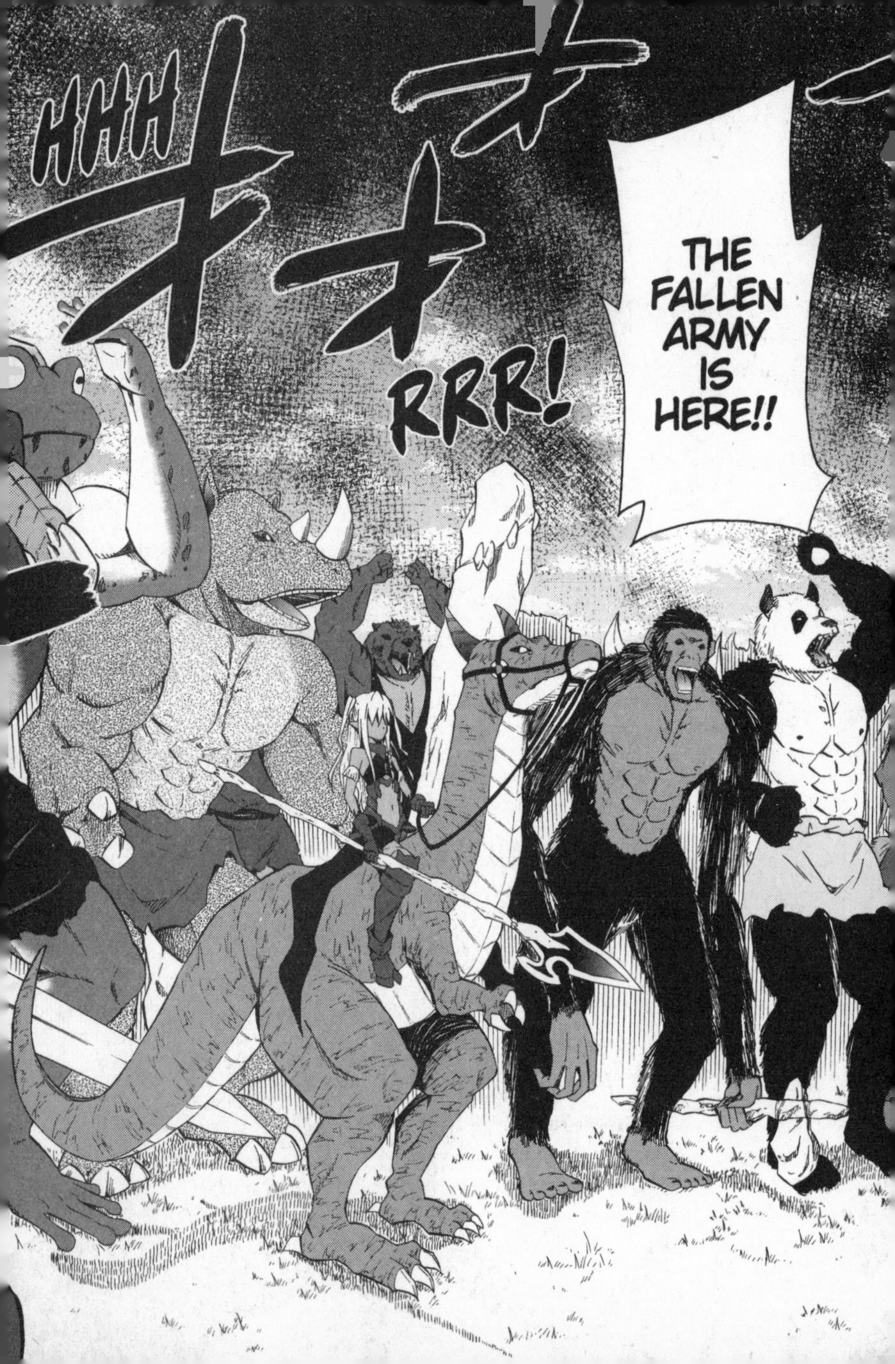
HHH
RRR!
THE FALLEN ARMY IS HERE!!

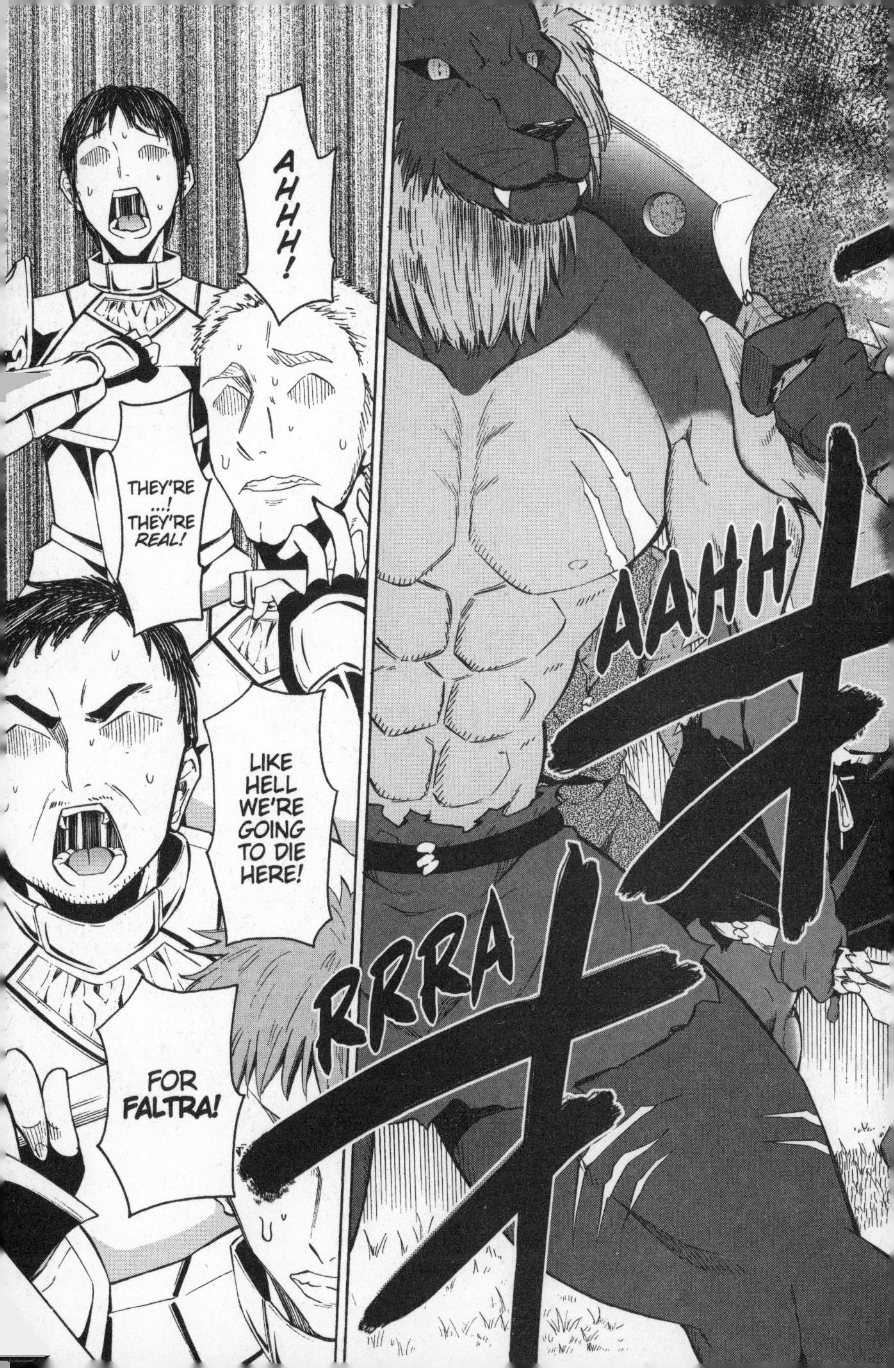
RRRA
AAHH
AHHH!
THEY'RE ...! THEY'RE *REAL!*
LIKE HELL WE'RE GOING TO DIE HERE!
FOR FALTRA!

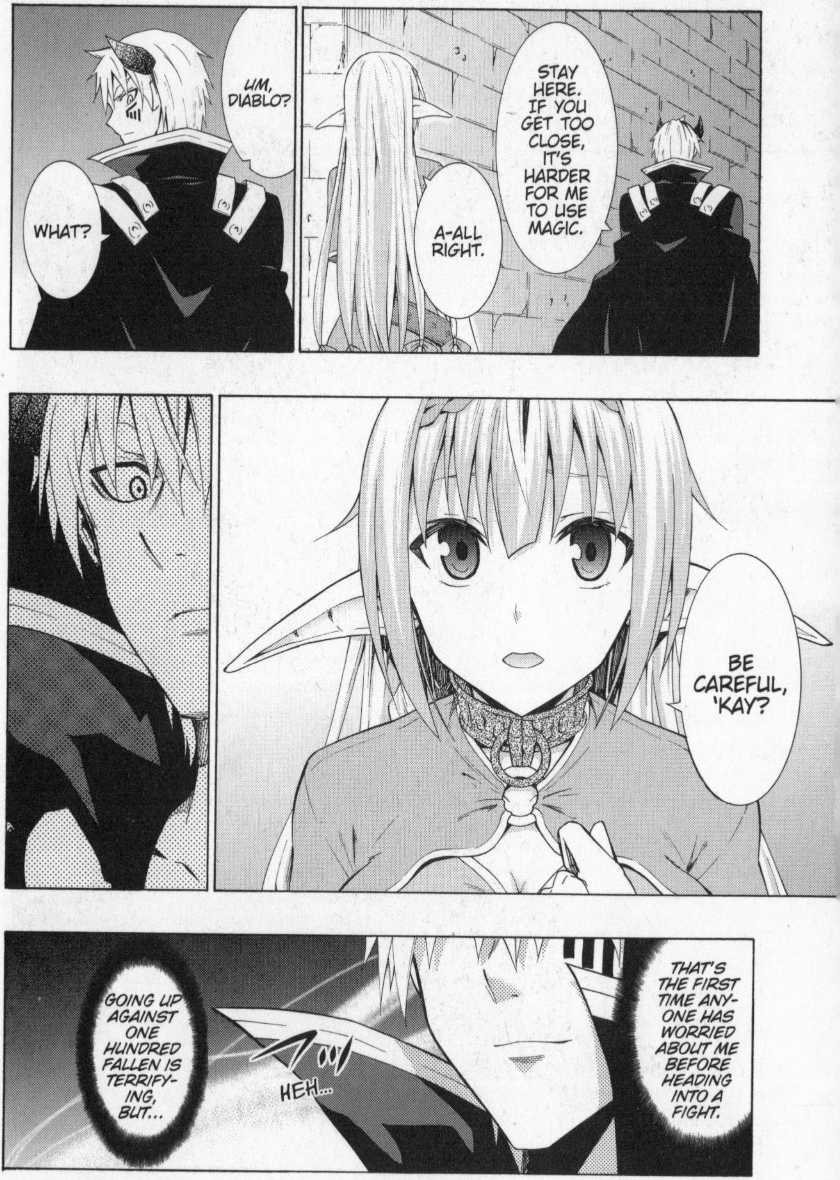
STAY HERE. IF YOU GET TOO CLOSE, IT'S HARDER FOR ME TO USE MAGIC.
A-ALL RIGHT.
UM, DIABLO?
WHAT?
BE CAREFUL, 'KAY?
THAT'S THE FIRST TIME ANY-ONE HAS WORRIED ABOUT ME BEFORE HEADING INTO A FIGHT.
HEH...
GOING UP AGAINST ONE HUNDRED FALLEN IS TERRIFY-ING, BUT...

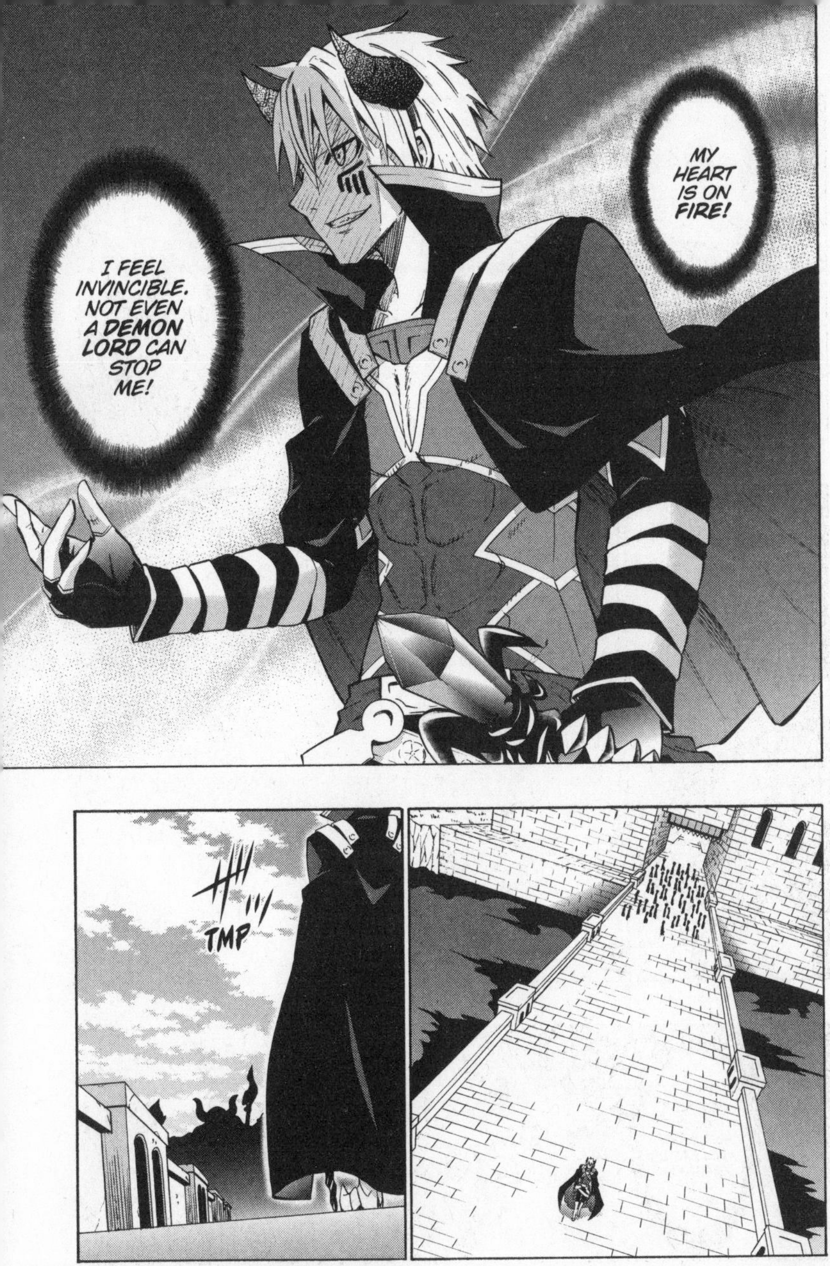
MY HEART IS ON FIRE!
I FEEL INVINCIBLE. NOT EVEN A DEMON LORD CAN STOP ME!
TMP

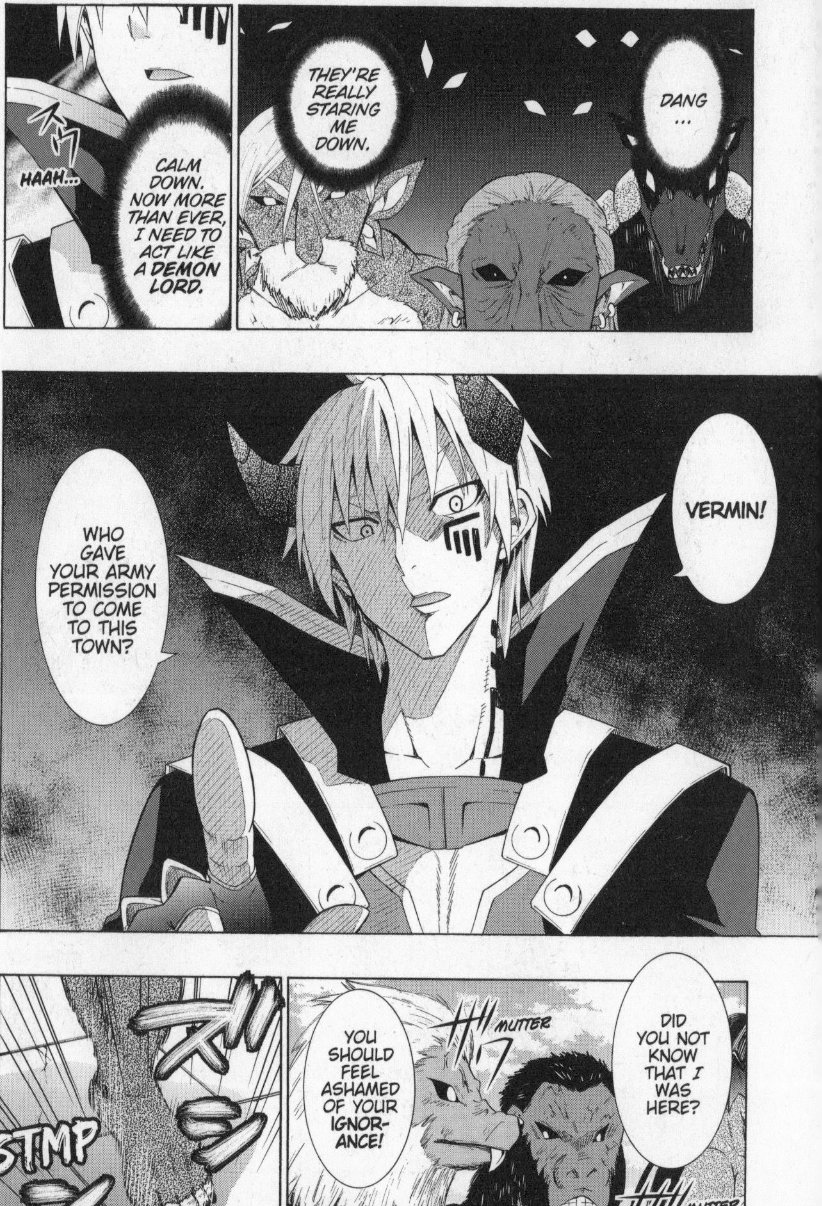
DANG ...
THEY'RE REALLY STARING ME DOWN.
HAAH...
CALM DOWN. NOW MORE THAN EVER, I NEED TO ACT LIKE A DEMON LORD.
VERMIN!
WHO GAVE YOUR ARMY PERMISSION TO COME TO THIS TOWN?
DID YOU NOT KNOW THAT I WAS HERE?
MUTTER
YOU SHOULD FEEL ASHAMED OF YOUR IGNOR-ANCE!
MUTTER
STMP

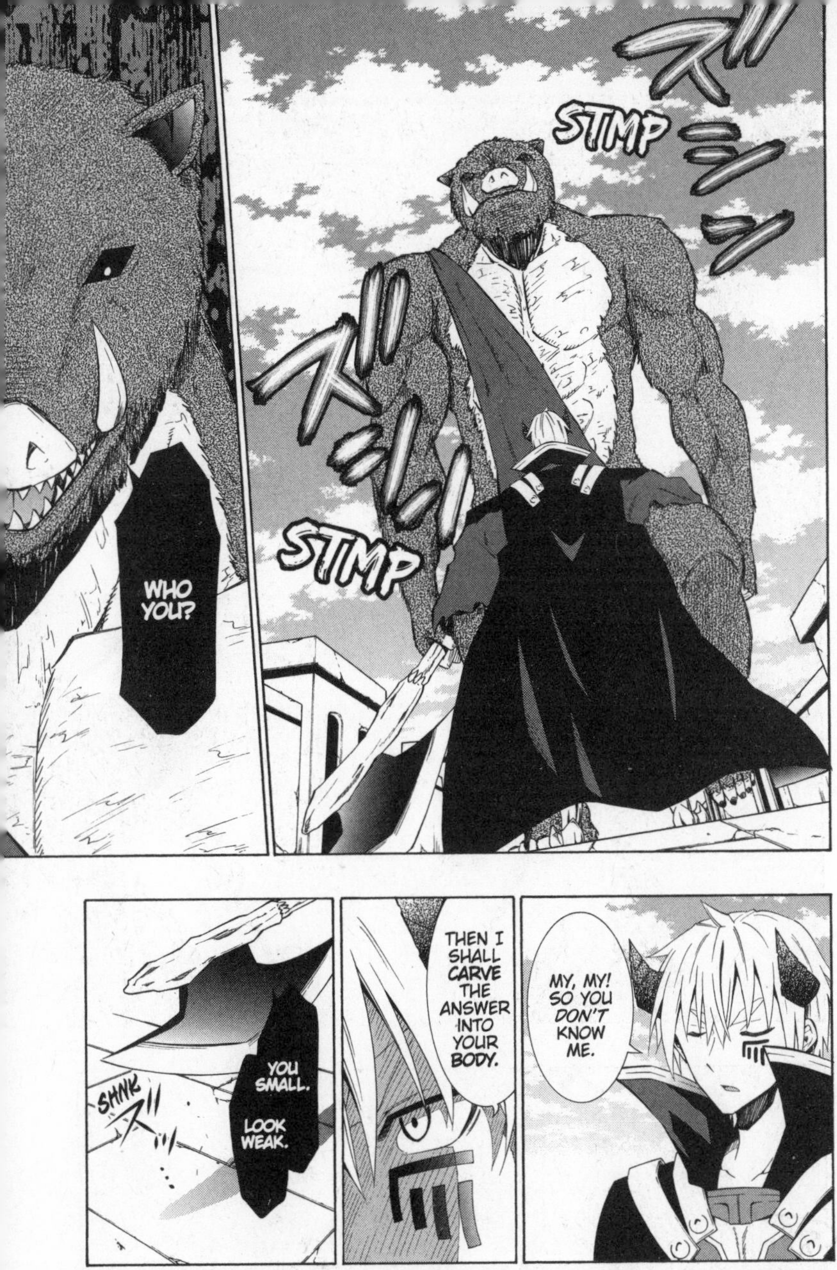
STMP
STMP
WHO YOU?
MY, MY! SO YOU DON'T KNOW ME.
THEN I SHALL CARVE THE ANSWER INTO YOUR BODY.
YOU SMALL.
LOOK WEAK.
SHNK

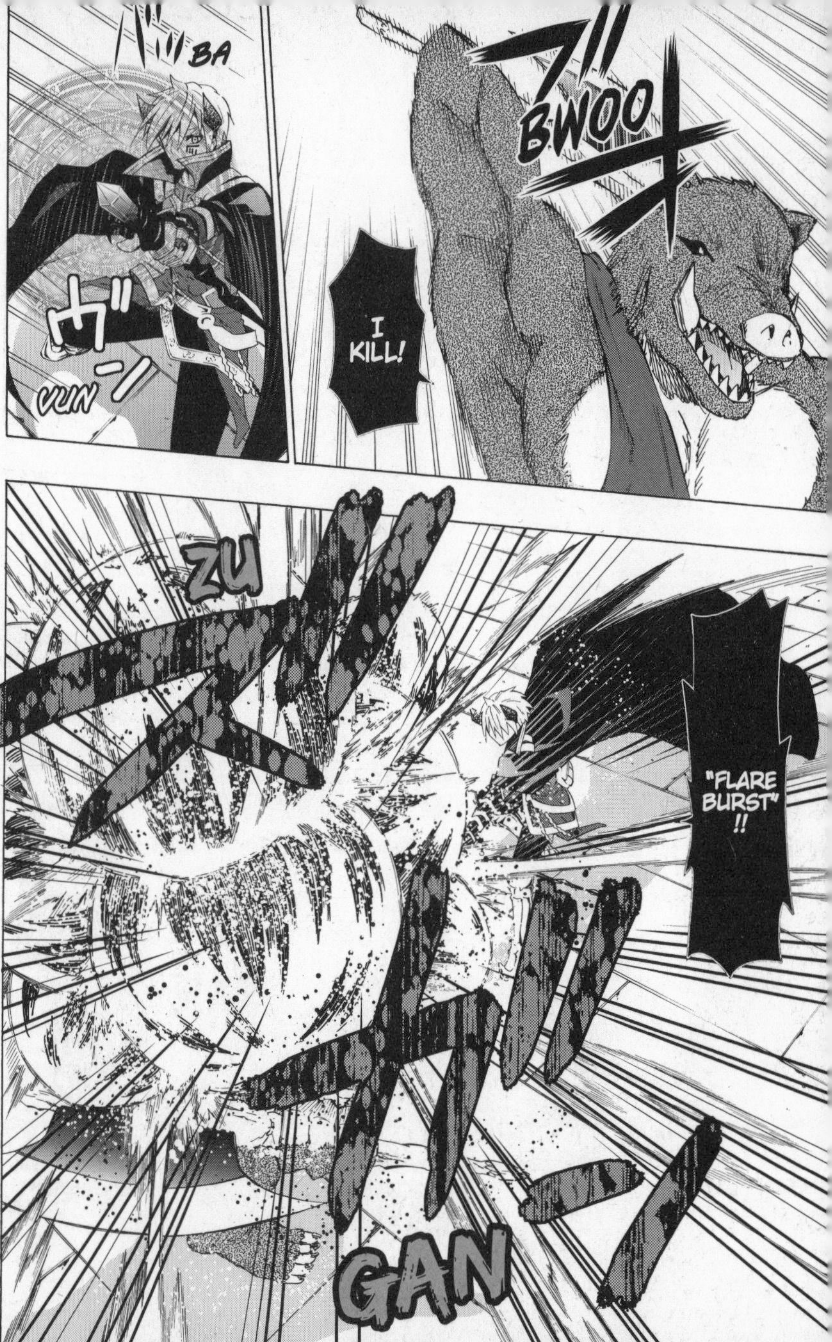
BWOO
I KILL!
BA
VUN
"FLARE BURST"!!
ZU
GAN

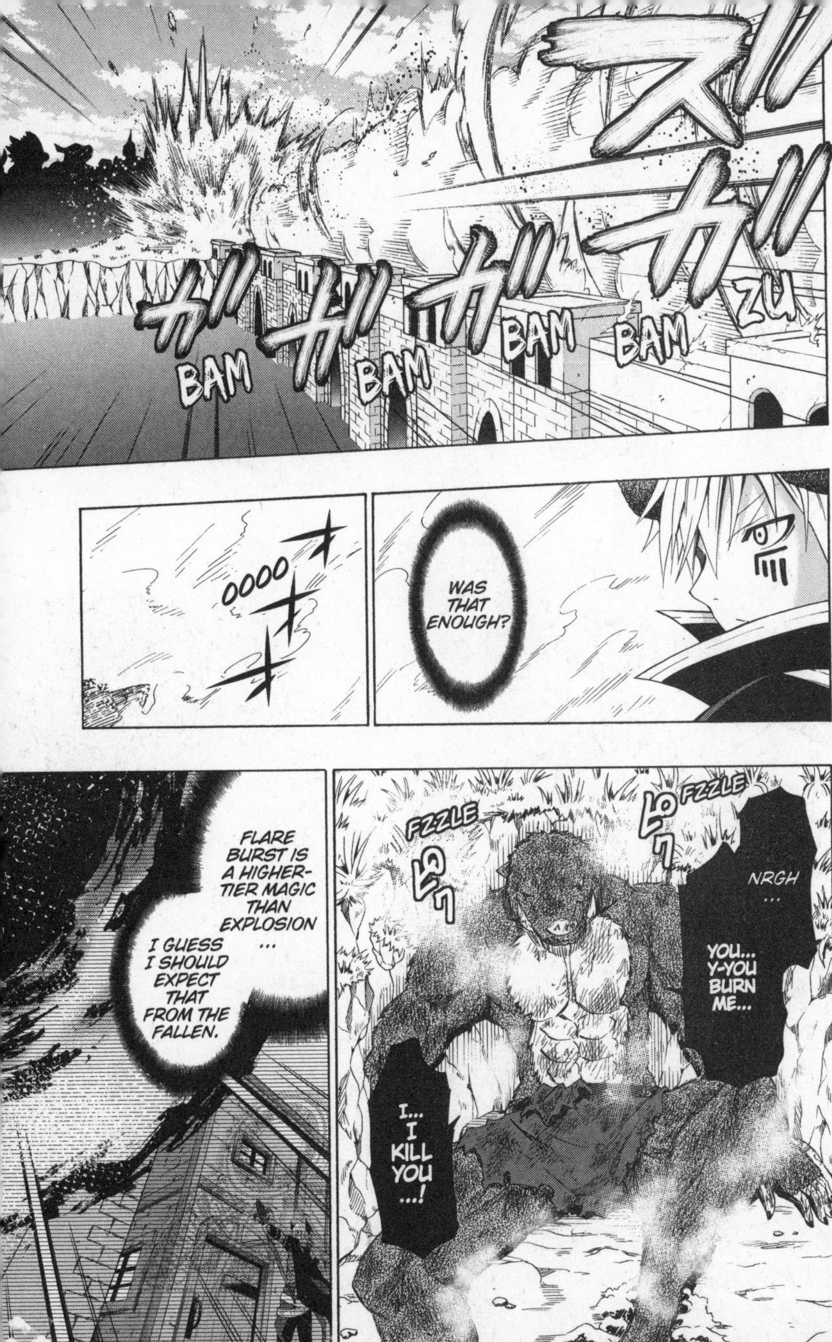
ZU
BAM
BAM
BAM
BAM
WAS THAT ENOUGH?
OOOO
FZZLE
FZZLE
NRGH...
YOU... Y-YOU BURN ME...
I... I KILL YOU...!
FLARE BURST IS A HIGHER-TIER MAGIC THAN EXPLOSION...
I GUESS I SHOULD EXPECT THAT FROM THE FALLEN.

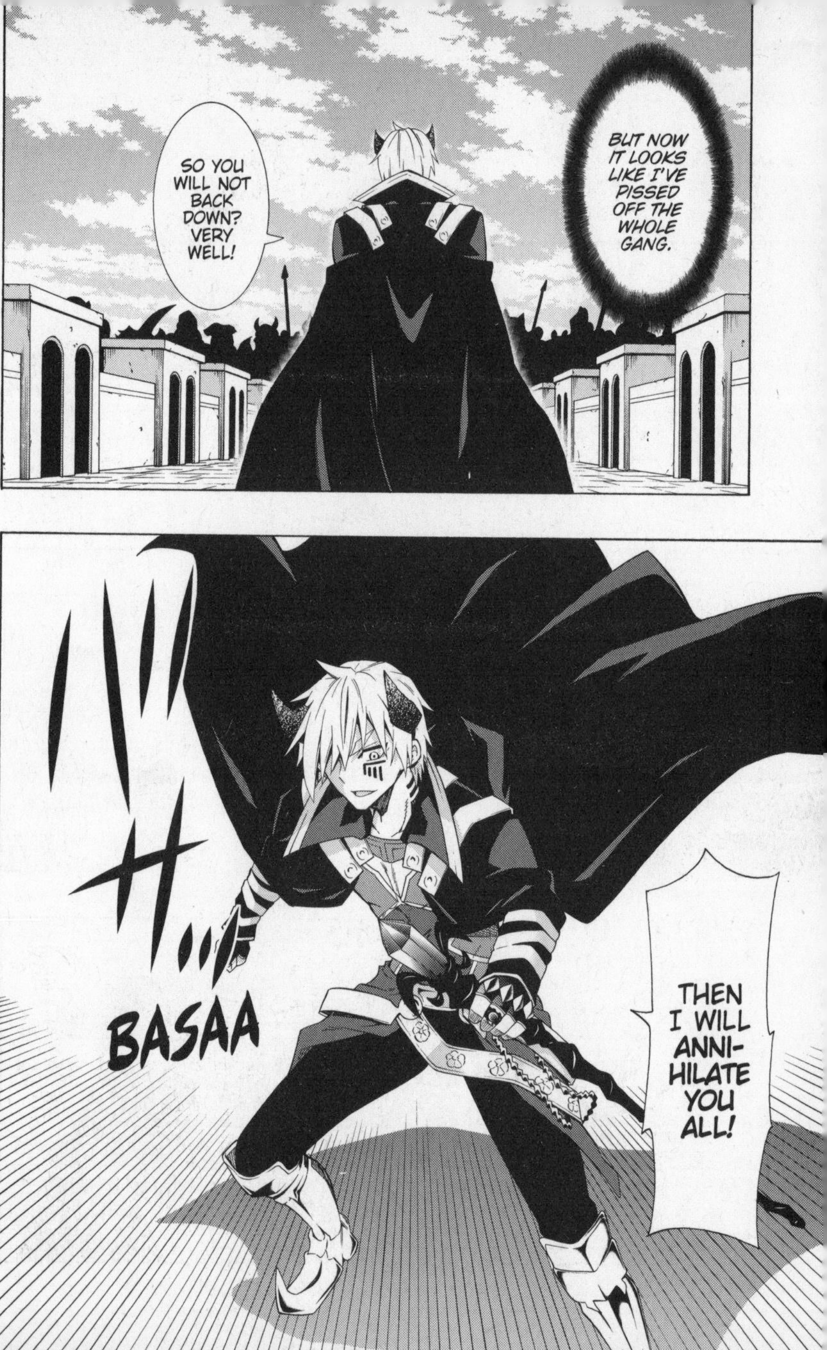
BUT NOW IT LOOKS LIKE I'VE PISSED OFF THE WHOLE GANG.
SO YOU WILL NOT BACK DOWN? VERY WELL!
THEN I WILL ANNI-HILATE YOU ALL!
BASAA

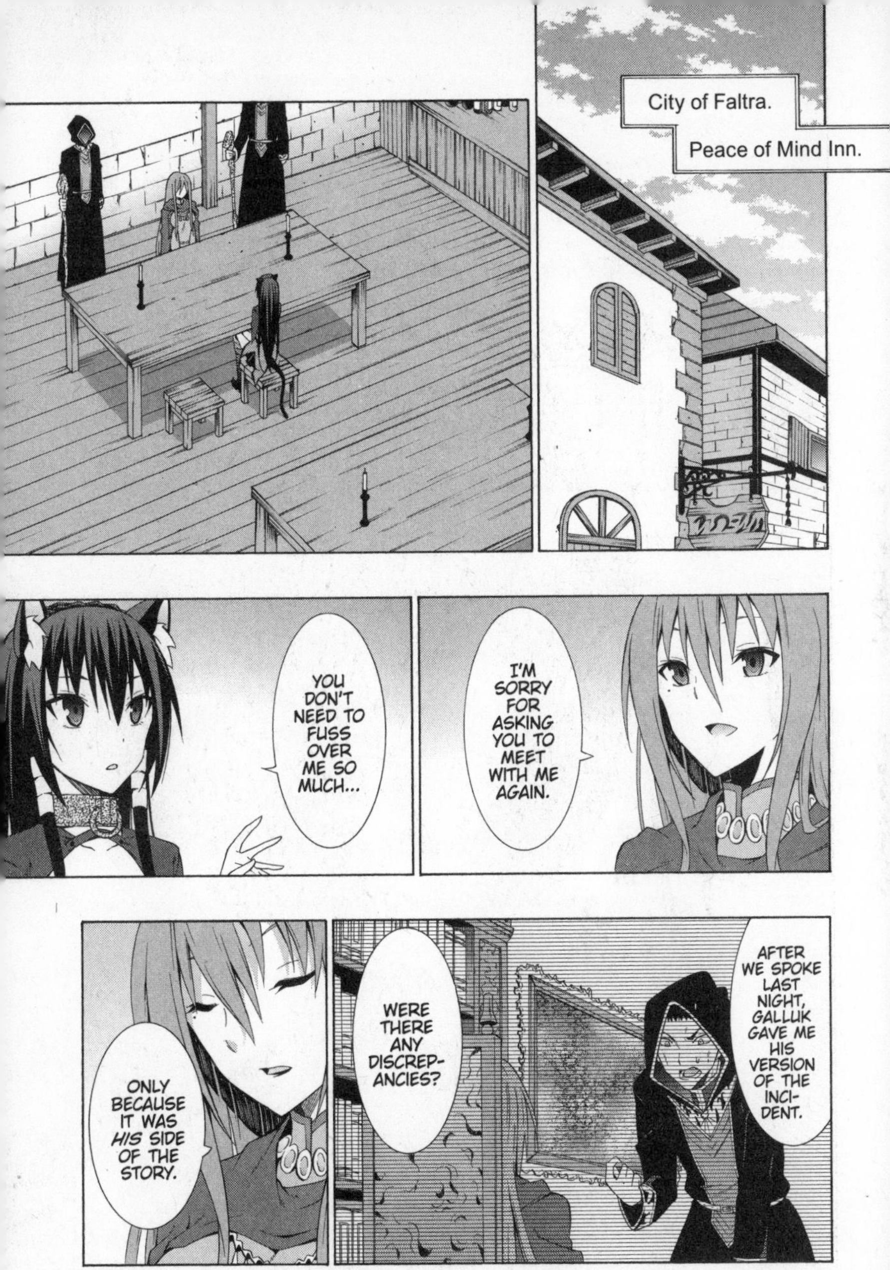
City of Faltra.
Peace of Mind Inn.
I'M SORRY FOR ASKING YOU TO MEET WITH ME AGAIN.
YOU DON'T NEED TO FUSS OVER ME SO MUCH...
AFTER WE SPOKE LAST NIGHT, GALLUK GAVE ME HIS VERSION OF THE INCIDENT.
WERE THERE ANY DISCREP-ANCIES?
ONLY BECAUSE IT WAS *HIS* SIDE OF THE STORY.

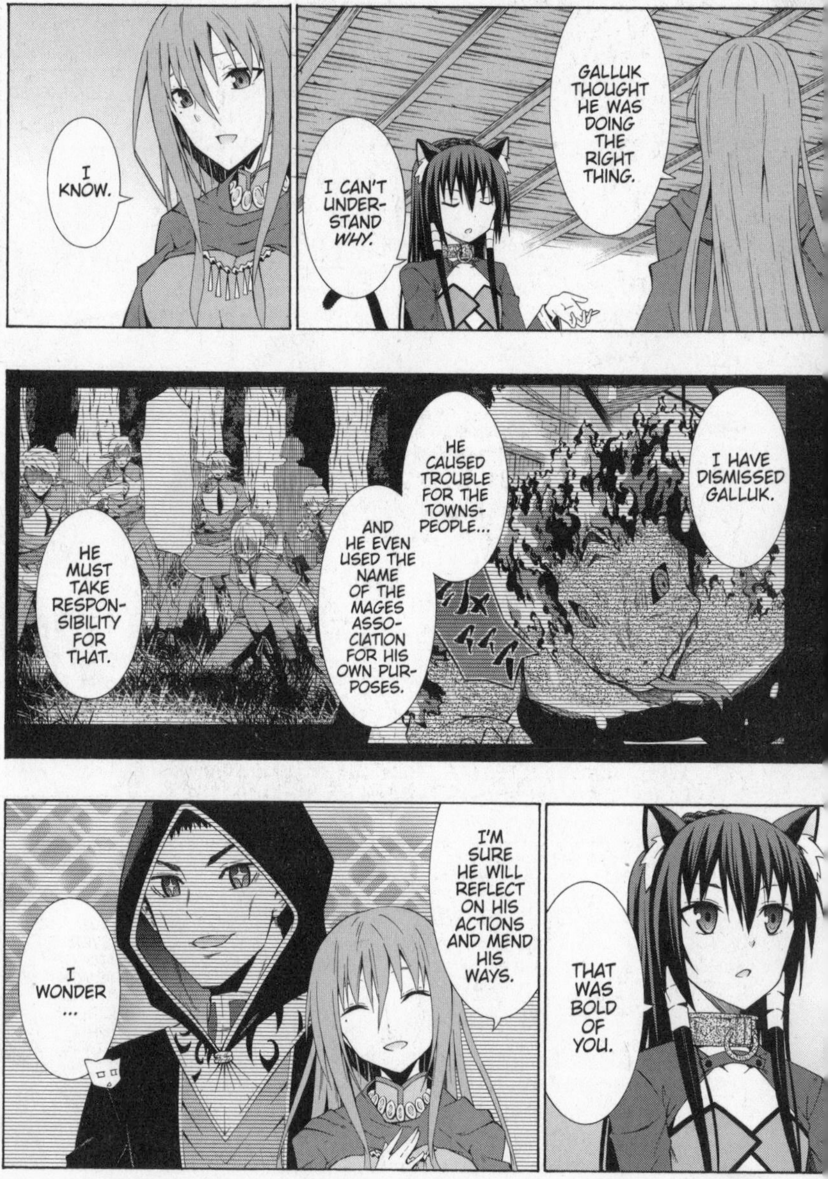
GALLUK THOUGHT HE WAS DOING THE RIGHT THING.
I CAN'T UNDERSTAND *WHY*.
I KNOW.
I HAVE DISMISSED GALLUK.
HE CAUSED TROUBLE FOR THE TOWNSPEOPLE...
AND HE EVEN USED THE NAME OF THE MAGES ASSOCIATION FOR HIS OWN PURPOSES.
HE MUST TAKE RESPONSIBILITY FOR THAT.
THAT WAS BOLD OF YOU.
I'M SURE HE WILL REFLECT ON HIS ACTIONS AND MEND HIS WAYS.
I WONDER ...

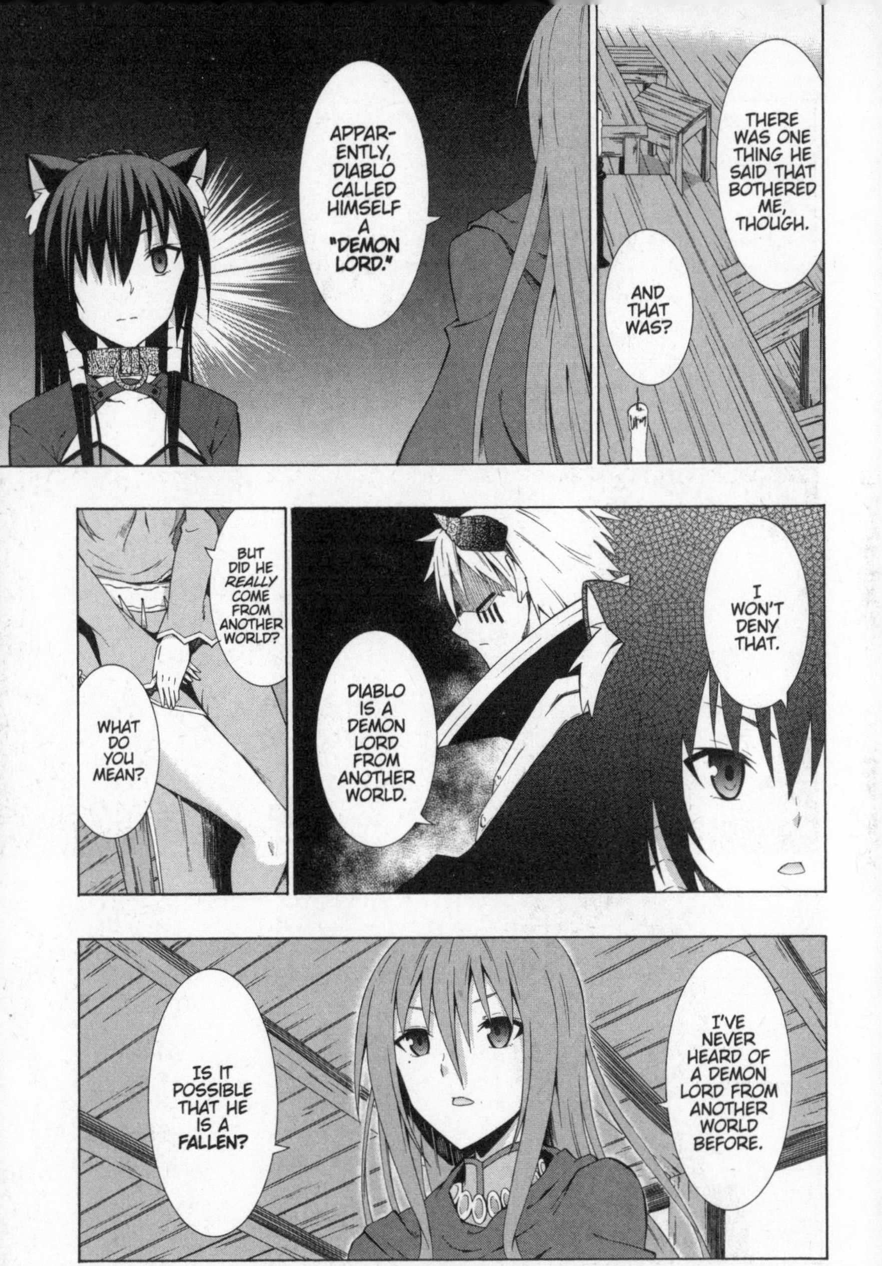
THERE WAS ONE THING HE SAID THAT BOTHERED ME, THOUGH.
AND THAT WAS?
APPAR-ENTLY, DIABLO CALLED HIMSELF A "DEMON LORD."
I WON'T DENY THAT.
DIABLO IS A DEMON LORD FROM ANOTHER WORLD.
BUT DID HE *REALLY* COME FROM ANOTHER WORLD?
WHAT DO YOU MEAN?
I'VE NEVER HEARD OF A DEMON LORD FROM ANOTHER WORLD BEFORE.
IS IT POSSIBLE THAT HE IS A FALLEN?

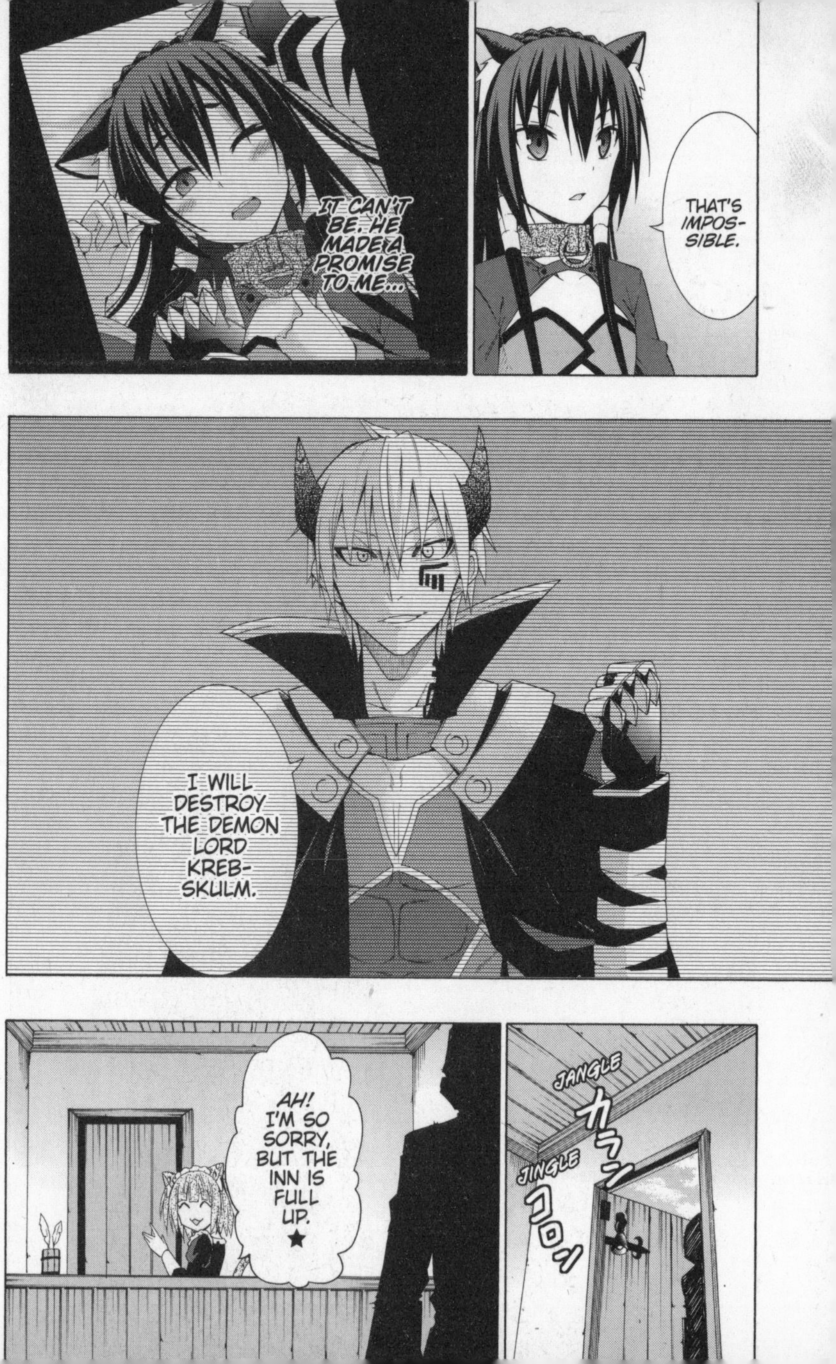
THAT'S IMPOSSIBLE.
IT CAN'T BE. HE MADE A PROMISE TO ME...
I WILL DESTROY THE DEMON LORD KREBSKULM.
JANGLE
カラン
JINGLE
コロン
AH! I'M SO SORRY, BUT THE INN IS FULL UP. ★

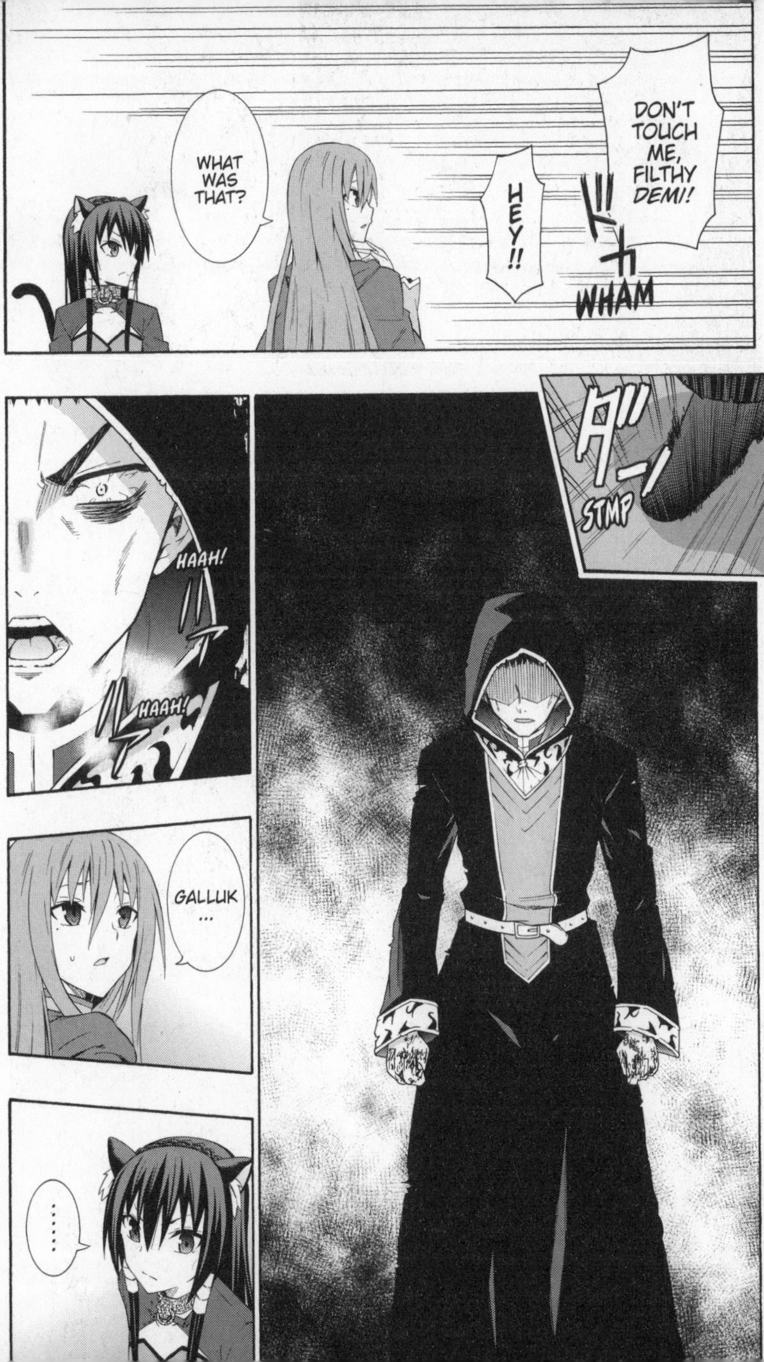
DON'T TOUCH ME, FILTHY DEMI!
WHAM
HEY!!
WHAT WAS THAT?
STMP
HAAH!
HAAH!
GALLUK ...
......

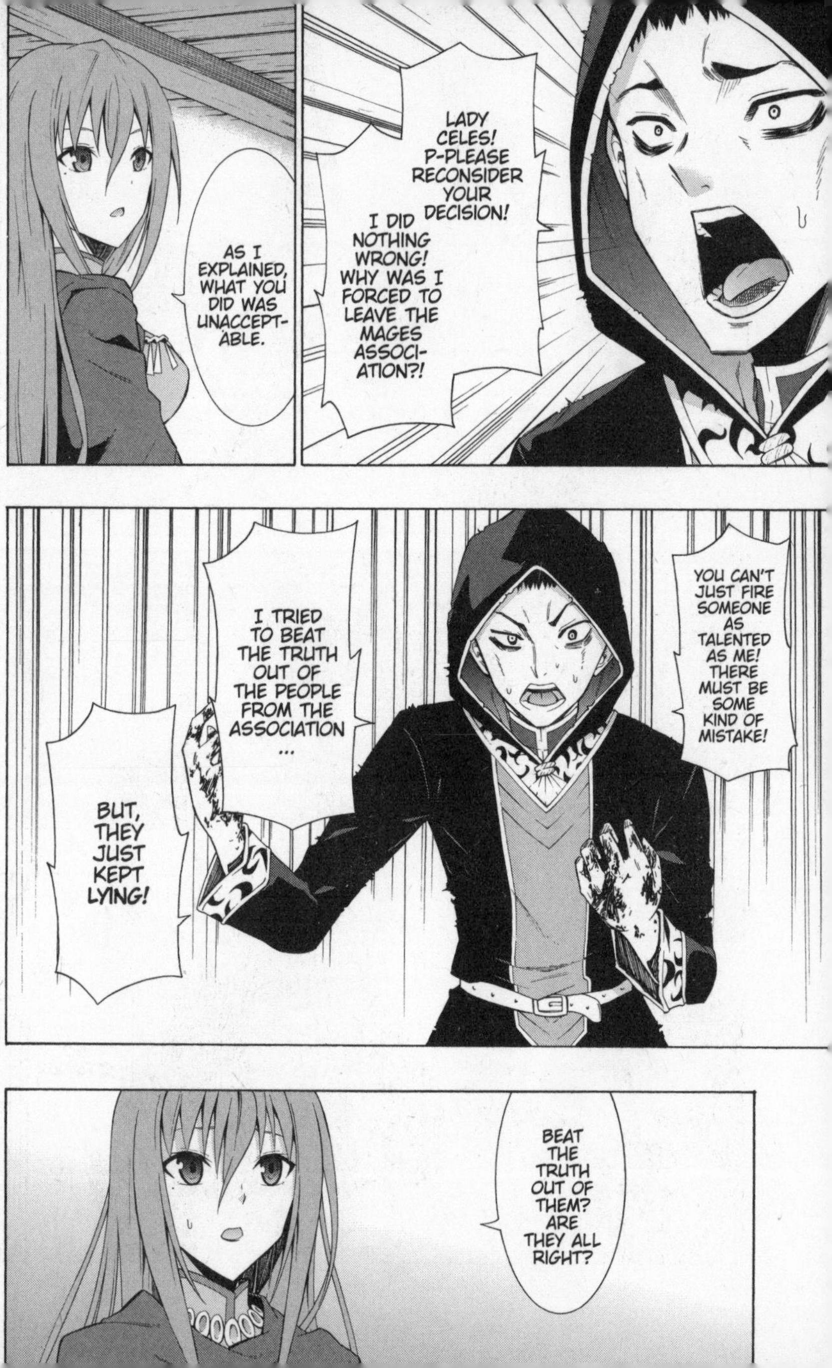
LADY CELES! P-PLEASE RECONSIDER YOUR DECISION!
I DID NOTHING WRONG! WHY WAS I FORCED TO LEAVE THE MAGES ASSOCIATION?!
AS I EXPLAINED, WHAT YOU DID WAS UNACCEPTABLE.
YOU CAN'T JUST FIRE SOMEONE AS TALENTED AS ME! THERE MUST BE SOME KIND OF MISTAKE!
I TRIED TO BEAT THE TRUTH OUT OF THE PEOPLE FROM THE ASSOCIATION ...
BUT, THEY JUST KEPT LYING!
BEAT THE TRUTH OUT OF THEM? ARE THEY ALL RIGHT?

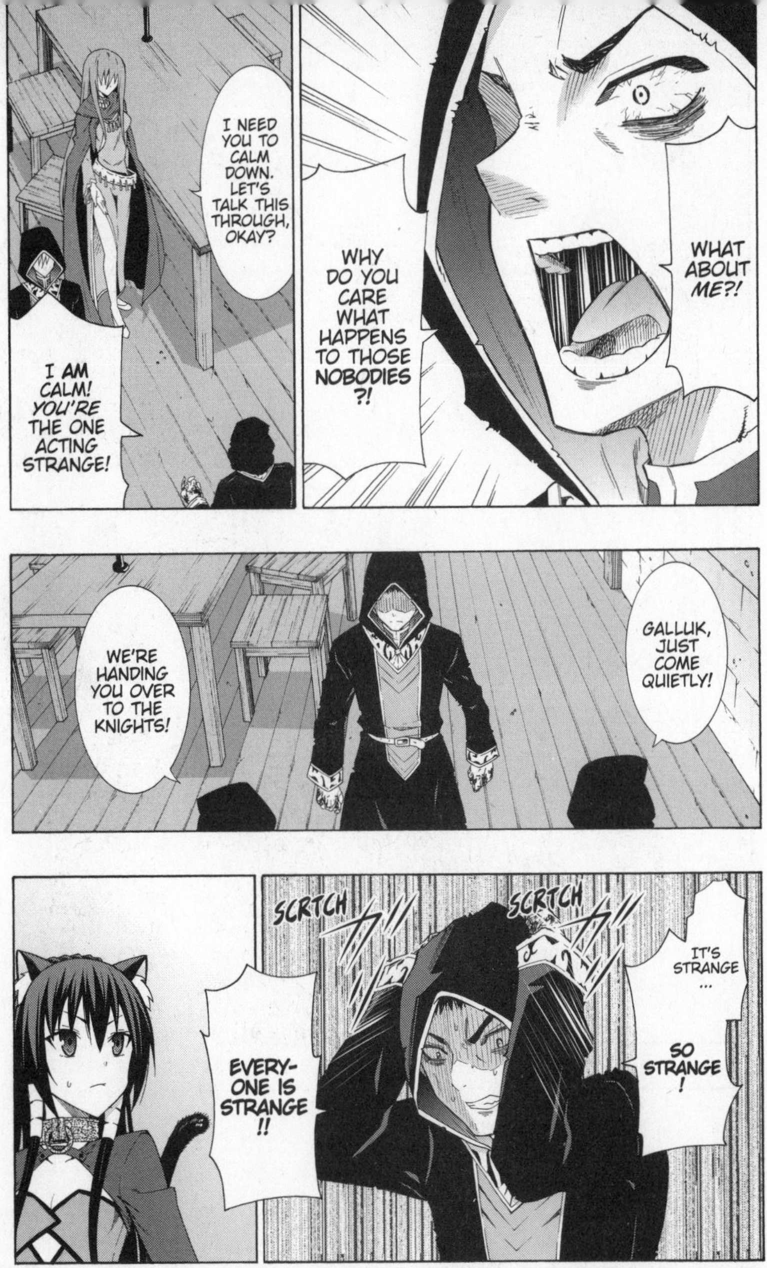
WHAT ABOUT ME?!
WHY DO YOU CARE WHAT HAPPENS TO THOSE NOBODIES ?!
I NEED YOU TO CALM DOWN. LET'S TALK THIS THROUGH, OKAY?
I AM CALM! YOU'RE THE ONE ACTING STRANGE!
GALLUK, JUST COME QUIETLY!
WE'RE HANDING YOU OVER TO THE KNIGHTS!
IT'S STRANGE ...
SCRTCH
SCRTCH
SO STRANGE !
EVERY-ONE IS STRANGE !!

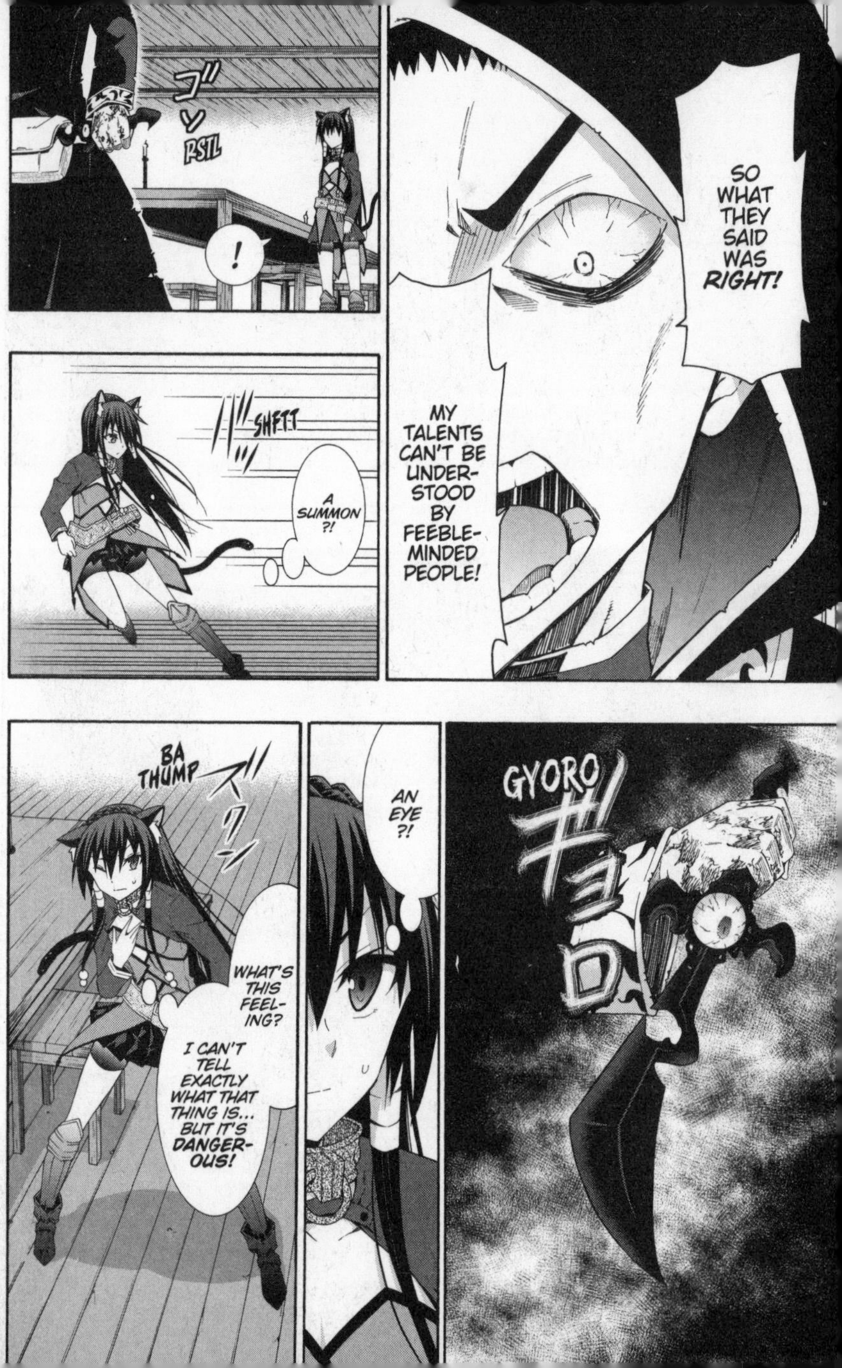
SO WHAT THEY SAID WAS RIGHT!
MY TALENTS CAN'T BE UNDER-STOOD BY FEEBLE-MINDED PEOPLE!
ゴソ
RSTL
!
SHFTT
A SUMMON?!
GYORO
ギョロ
AN EYE?!
BA THUMP
WHAT'S THIS FEEL-ING?
I CAN'T TELL EXACTLY WHAT THAT THING IS... BUT IT'S DANGER-OUS!

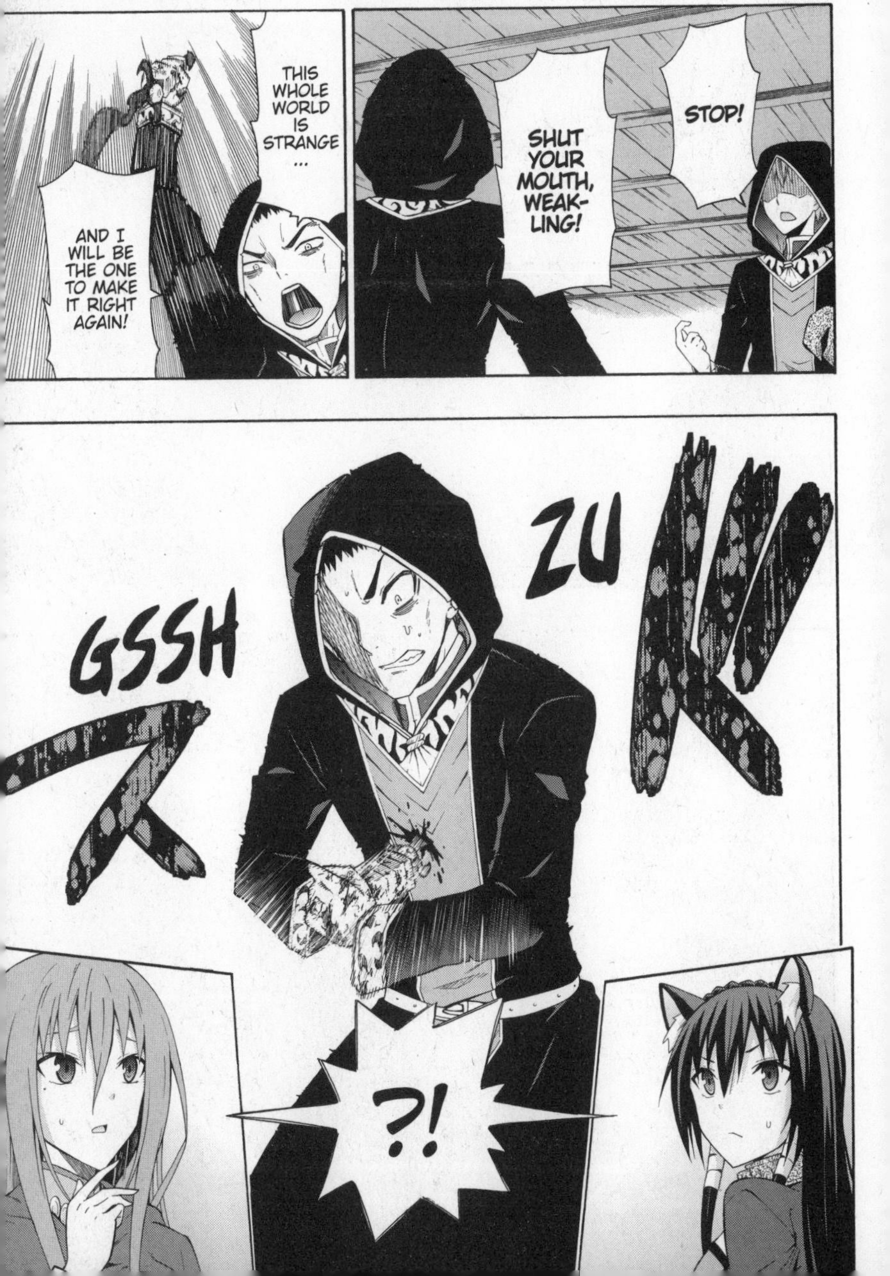
STOP!
SHUT YOUR MOUTH, WEAK-LING!
THIS WHOLE WORLD IS STRANGE ...
AND I WILL BE THE ONE TO MAKE IT RIGHT AGAIN!
ZU
GSSH
?!

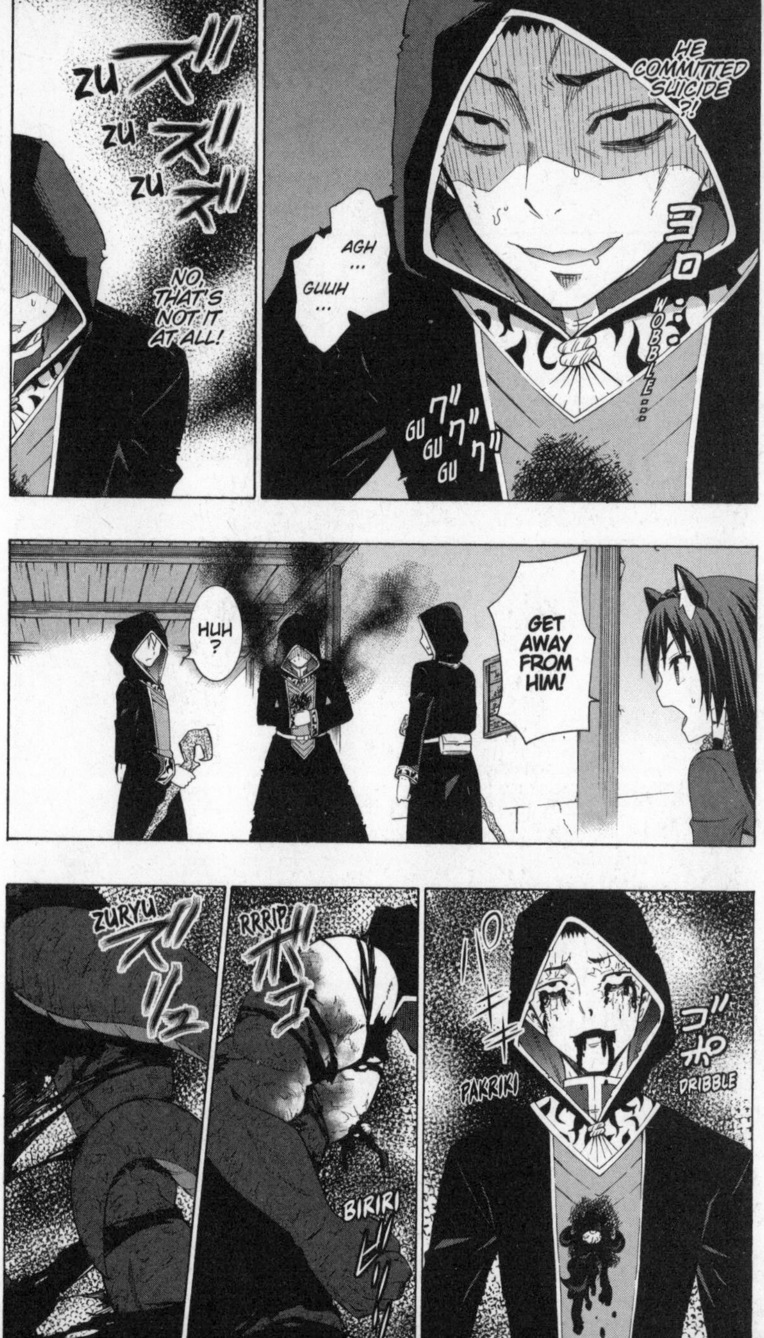
HE COMMITTED SUICIDE?!
WOBBLE...
AGH... GUUH...
GU GU GU
ZU ZU ZU
NO, THAT'S NOT IT AT ALL!
GET AWAY FROM HIM!
HUH?
PAKRIKI
DRIBBLE
RRRIP
BIRIRI
ZURYU

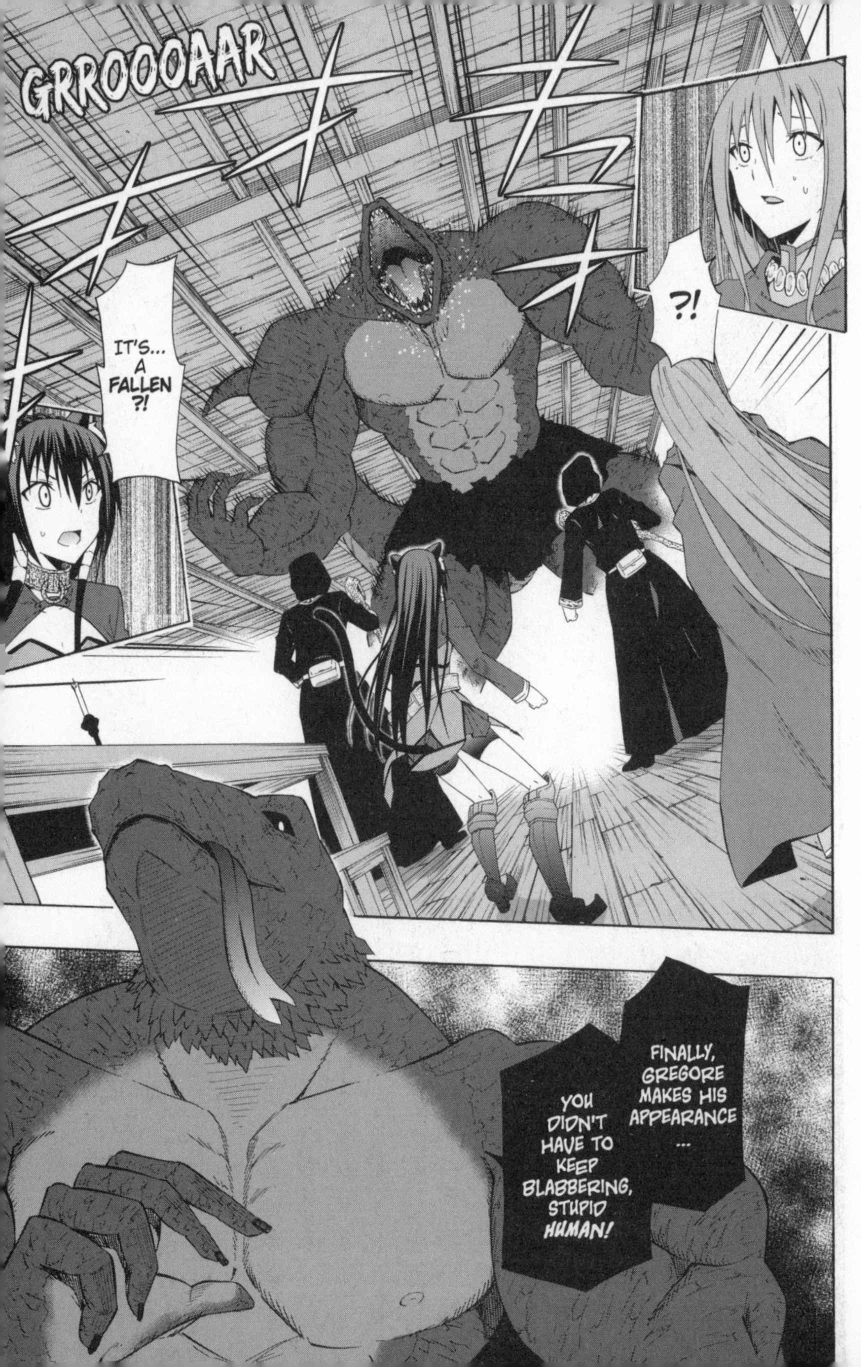
GRROOOAAR
?!
IT'S... A FALLEN ?!
FINALLY, GREGORE MAKES HIS APPEARANCE ...
YOU DIDN'T HAVE TO KEEP BLABBERING, STUPID HUMAN!

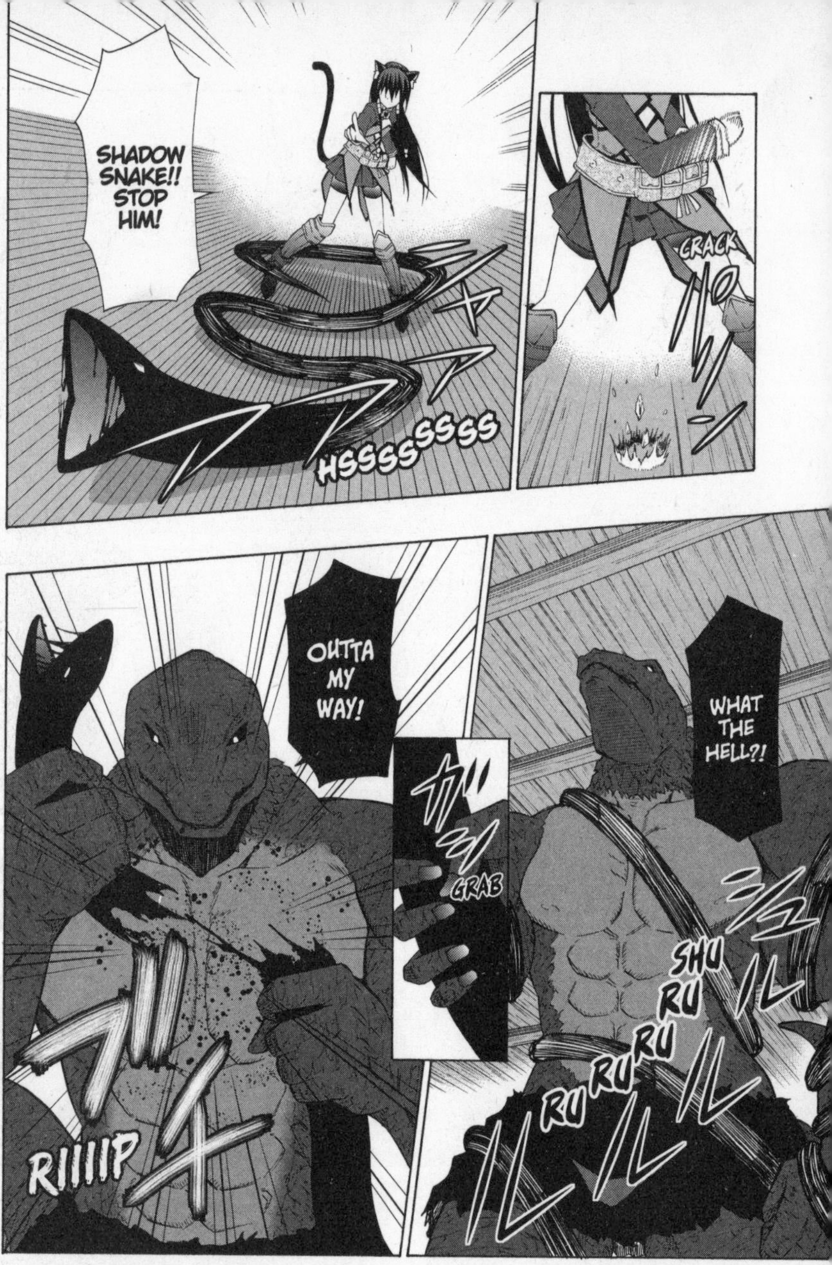
CRACK
SHADOW SNAKE!! STOP HIM!
HSSSSSSSS
WHAT THE HELL?!
SHU RU RU RU RU RU RU
OUTTA MY WAY!
GRAB
RIIIIP

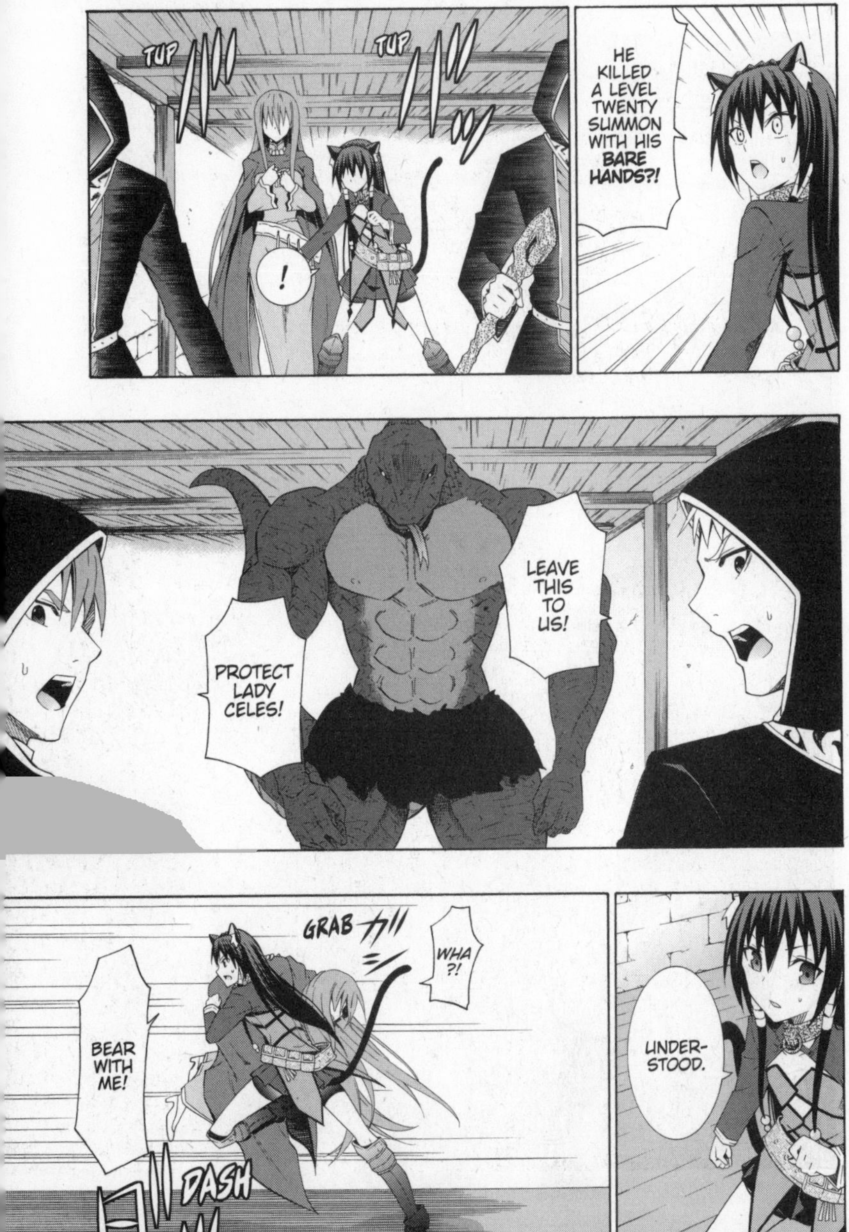
HE KILLED A LEVEL TWENTY SUMMON WITH HIS BARE HANDS?!
TUP
TUP
!
LEAVE THIS TO US!
PROTECT LADY CELES!
UNDER-STOOD.
GRAB
WHA ?!
BEAR WITH ME!
DASH

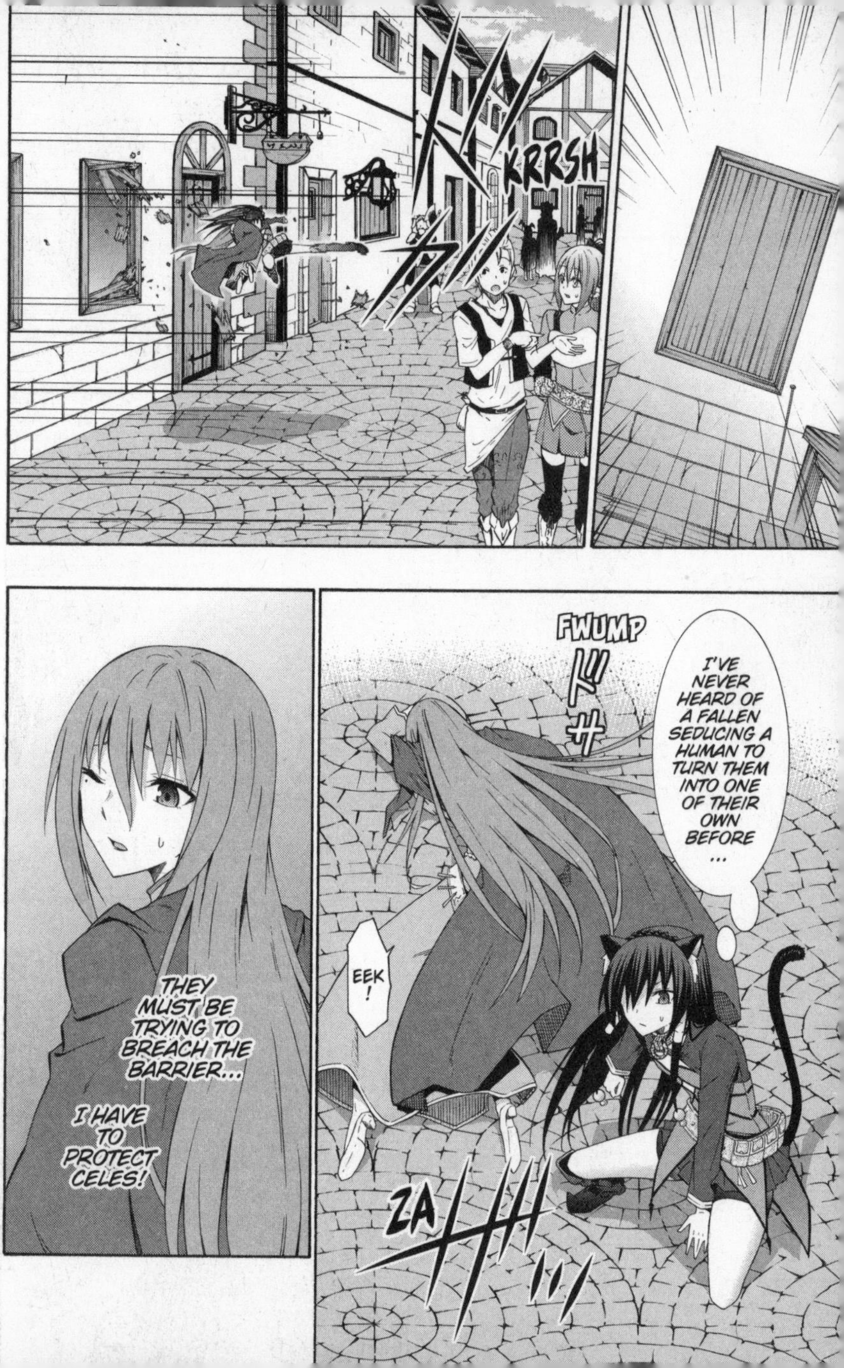
KRRSH
FWUMP
I'VE NEVER HEARD OF A FALLEN SEDUCING A HUMAN TO TURN THEM INTO ONE OF THEIR OWN BEFORE ...
EEK!
ZA
THEY MUST BE TRYING TO BREACH THE BARRIER...
I HAVE TO PROTECT CELES!

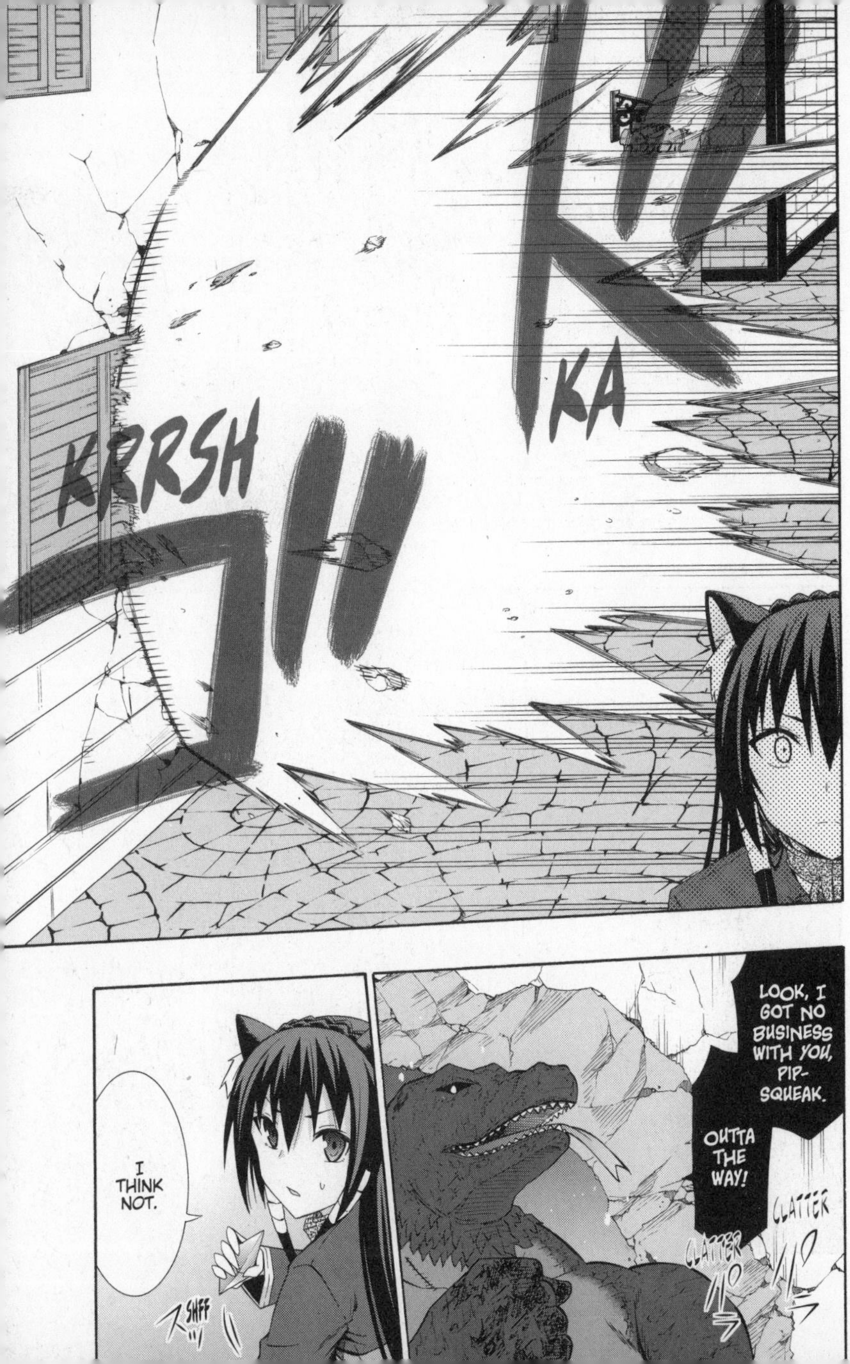
KA
KRRSH
LOOK, I GOT NO BUSINESS WITH YOU, PIP-SQUEAK.
OUTTA THE WAY!
CLATTER
CLATTER
I THINK NOT.
SHFF

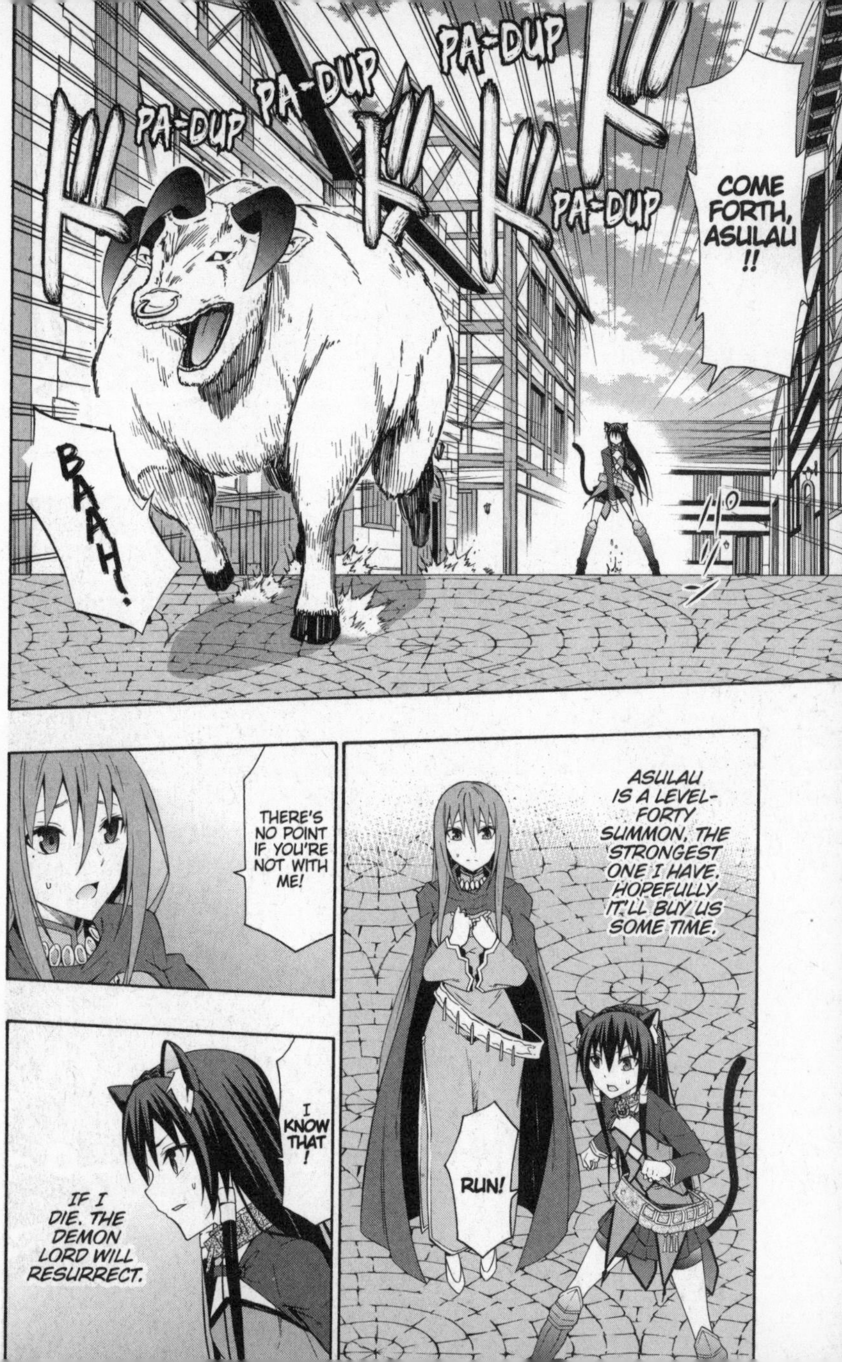
COME FORTH, ASULAU !!
PA-DUP
PA-DUP
PA-DUP
PA-DUP
BAAH!
ASULAU IS A LEVEL-FORTY SUMMON, THE STRONGEST ONE I HAVE. HOPEFULLY IT'LL BUY US SOME TIME.
RUN!
THERE'S NO POINT IF YOU'RE NOT WITH ME!
I KNOW THAT!
IF I DIE, THE DEMON LORD WILL RESURRECT.

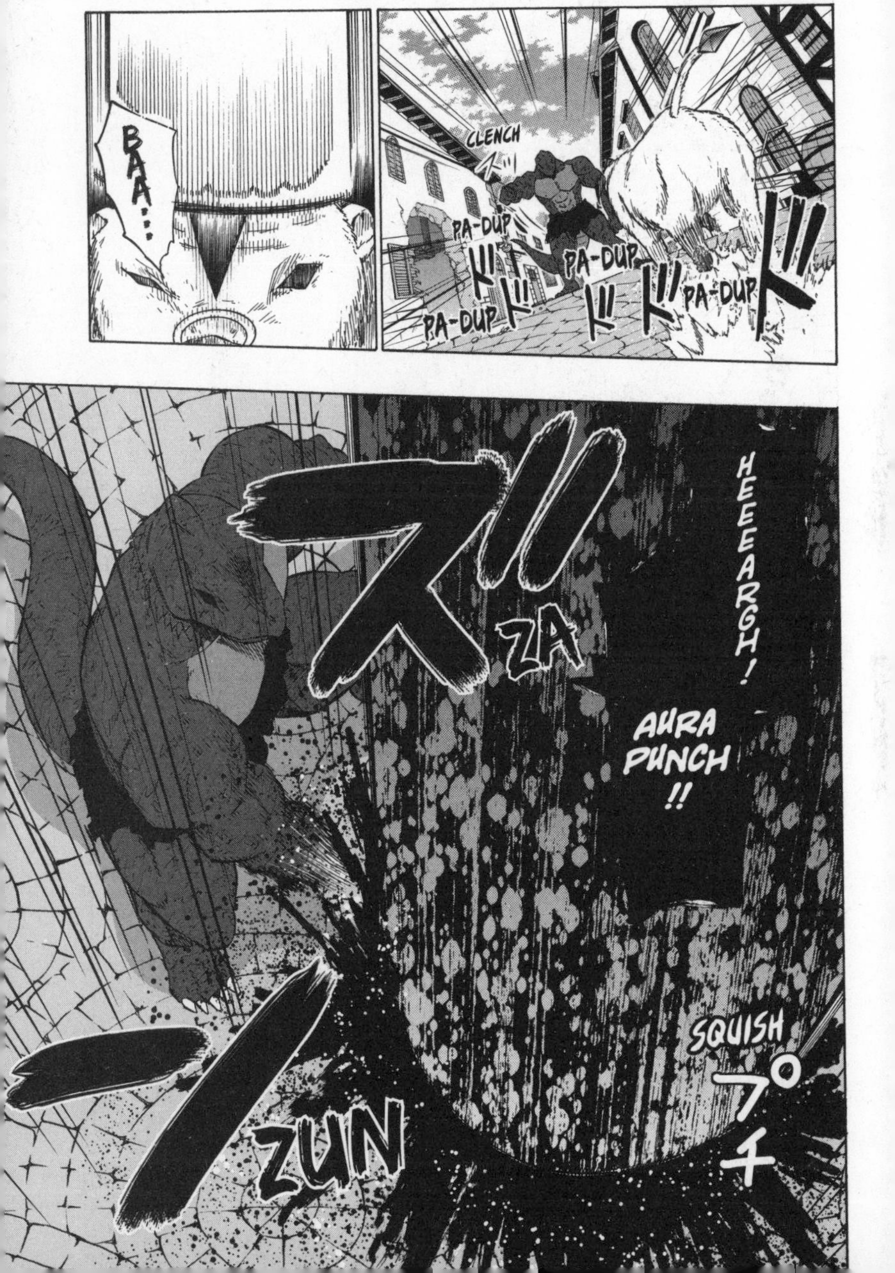
CLENCH
PA-DUP
PA-DUP
PA-DUP
PA-DUP
BAA...
HEEEEARGH!
AURA PUNCH!!
ズ
ZA
ZUN
SQUISH
プチ

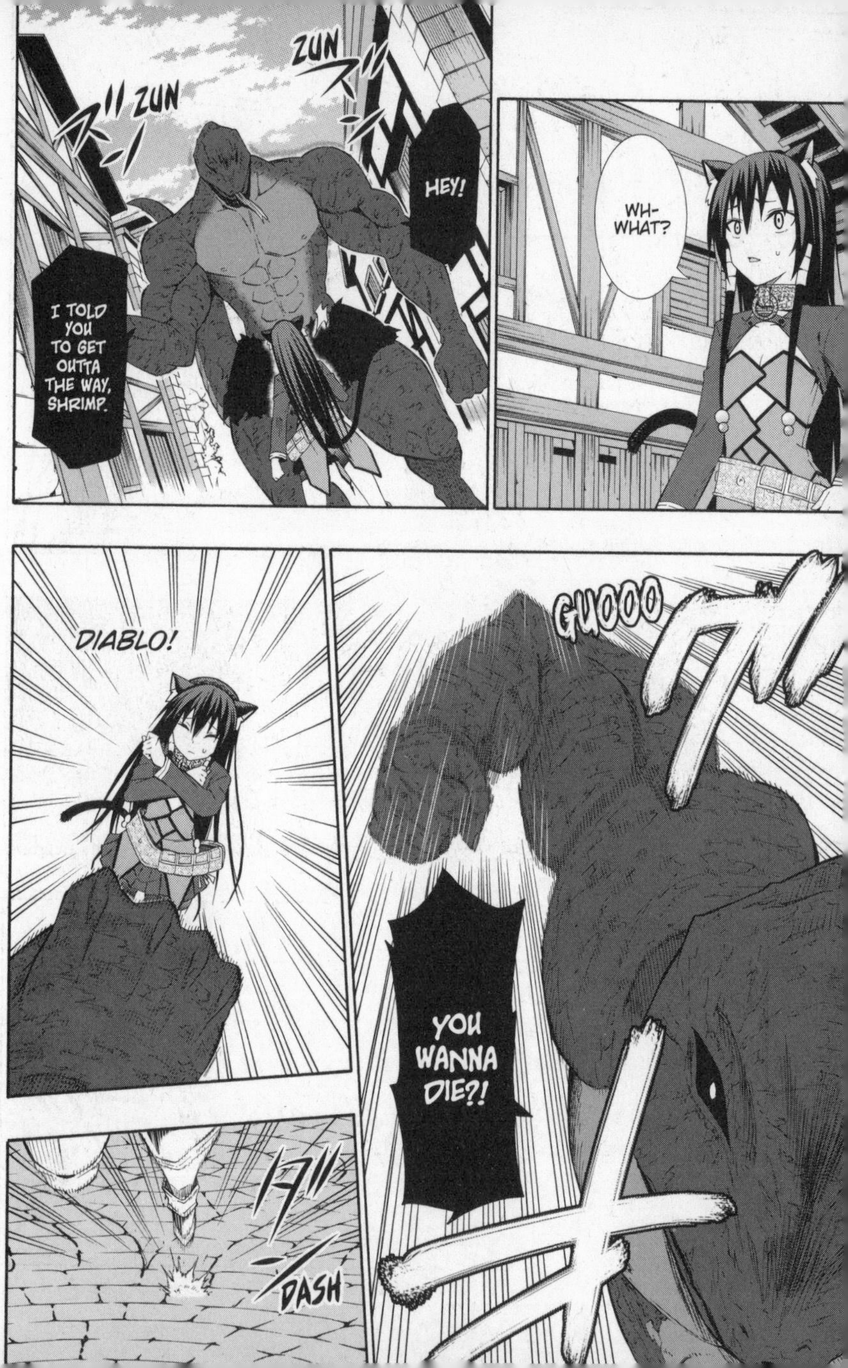
WH-WHAT?
ZUN
HEY!
ZUN
I TOLD YOU TO GET OUTTA THE WAY, SHRIMP.
GUOOO
YOU WANNA DIE?!
DIABLO!
DASH

CLANG

?!

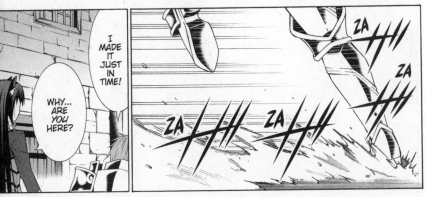

I MADE IT JUST IN TIME!

WHY... ARE YOU HERE?

ZA

ZA

ZA

ZA

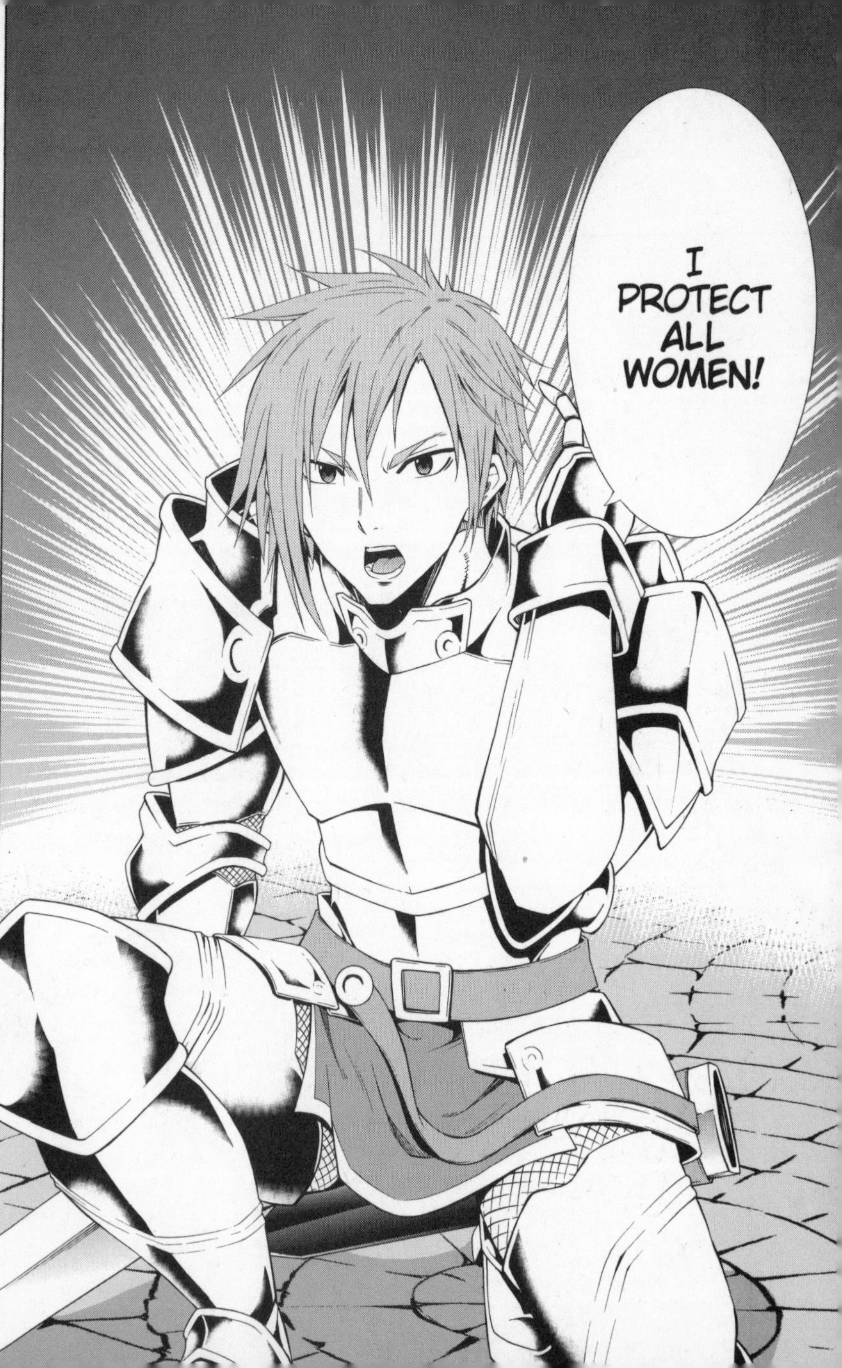
I PROTECT ALL WOMEN!

HOW NOT
TO SUMMON A
DEMON LORD

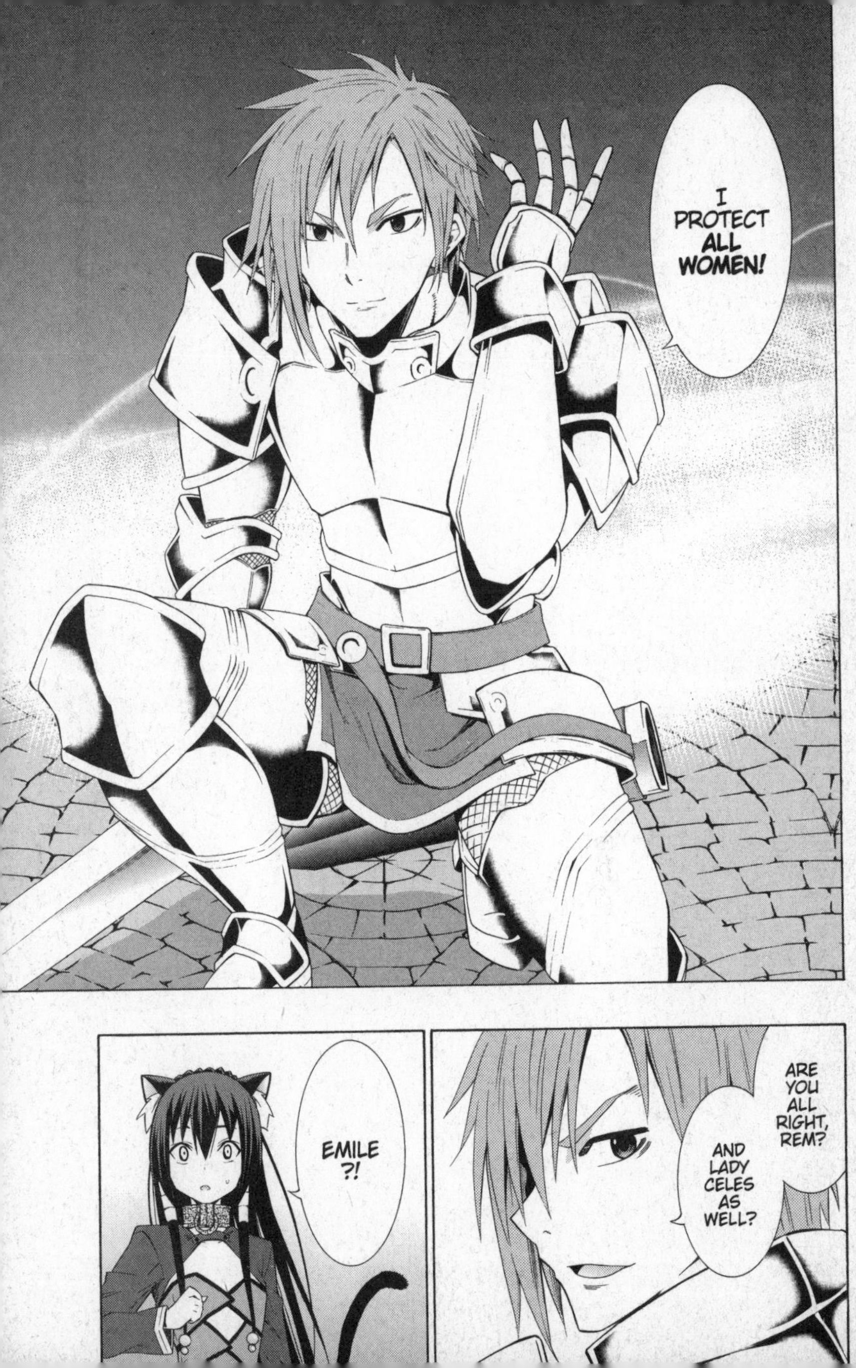
I PROTECT ALL WOMEN!
ARE YOU ALL RIGHT, REM?
AND LADY CELES AS WELL?
EMILE ?!

11 TRYING TO SAVE THE WORLD III

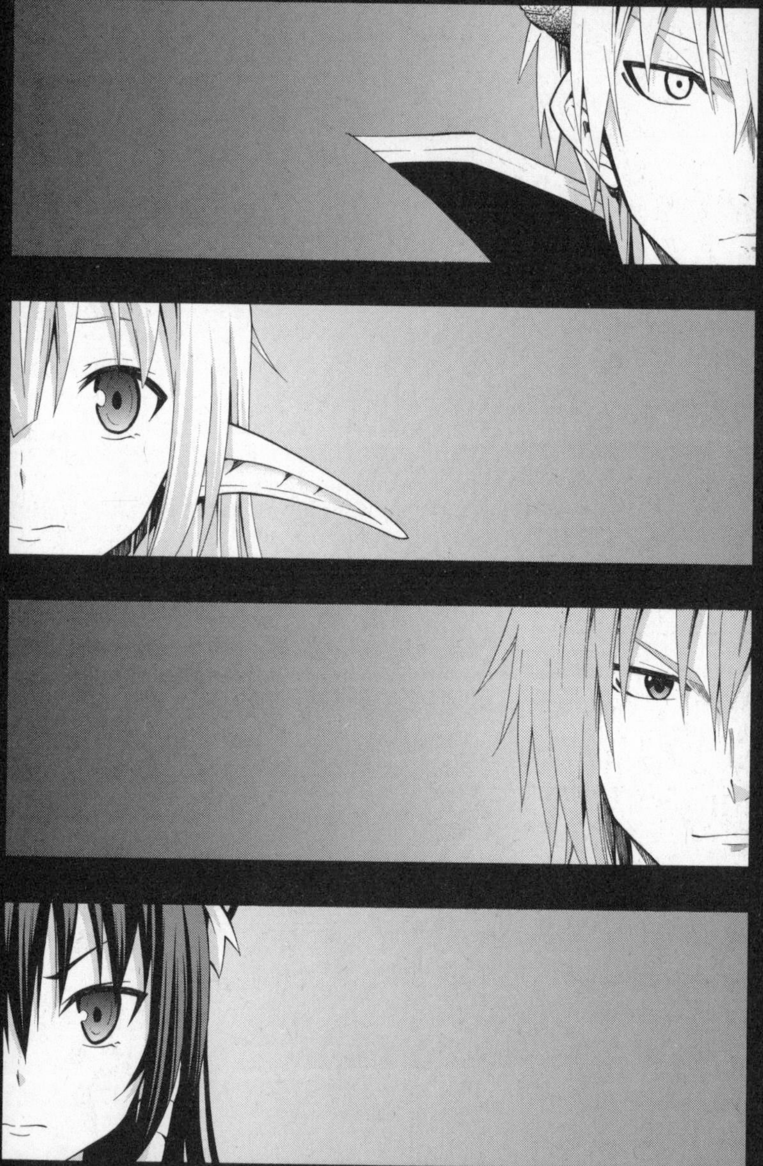

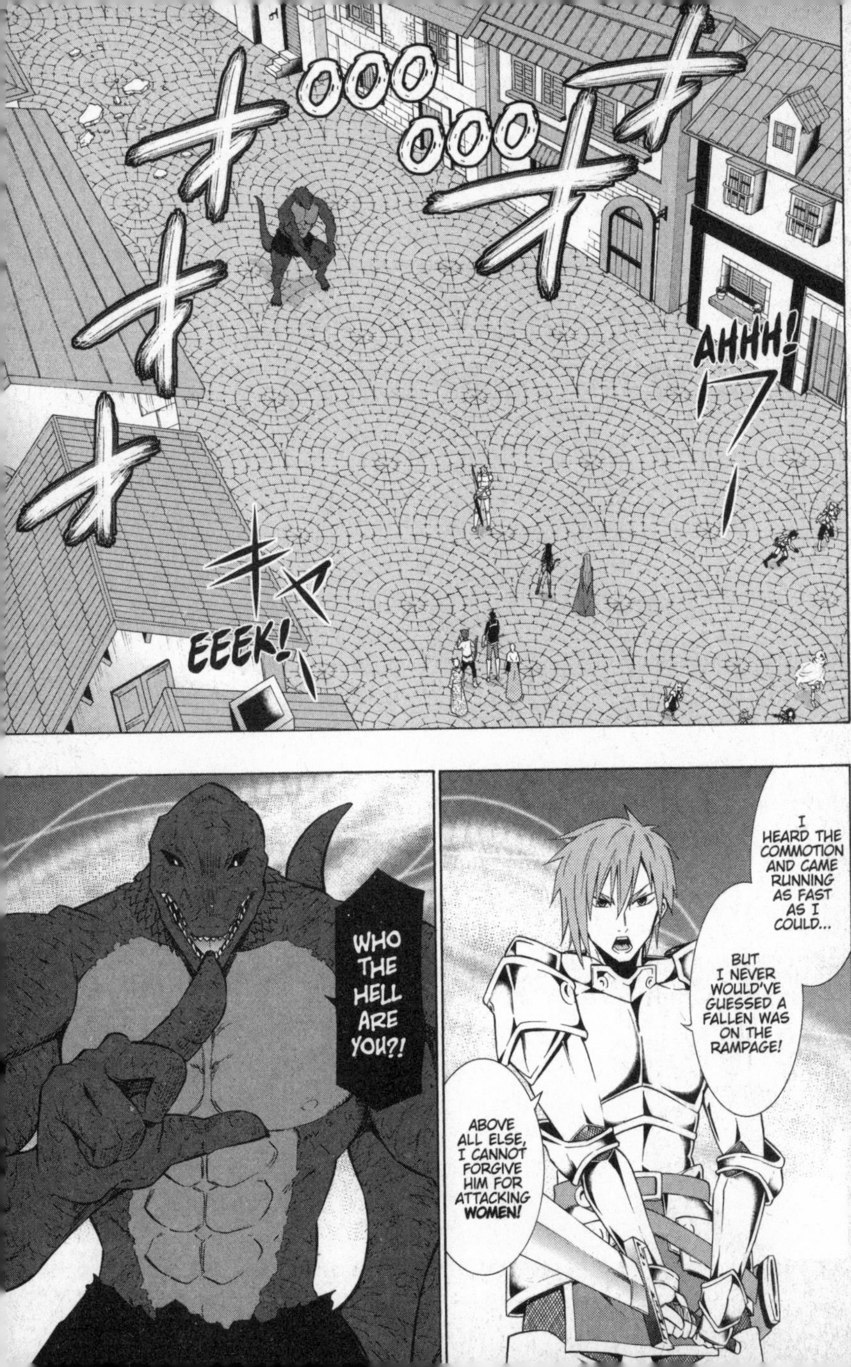

OOOO
OOOO
AHHH!
EEEK!
I HEARD THE COMMOTION AND CAME RUNNING AS FAST AS I COULD...
BUT I NEVER WOULD'VE GUESSED A FALLEN WAS ON THE RAMPAGE!
ABOVE ALL ELSE, I CANNOT FORGIVE HIM FOR ATTACKING WOMEN!
WHO THE HELL ARE YOU?!

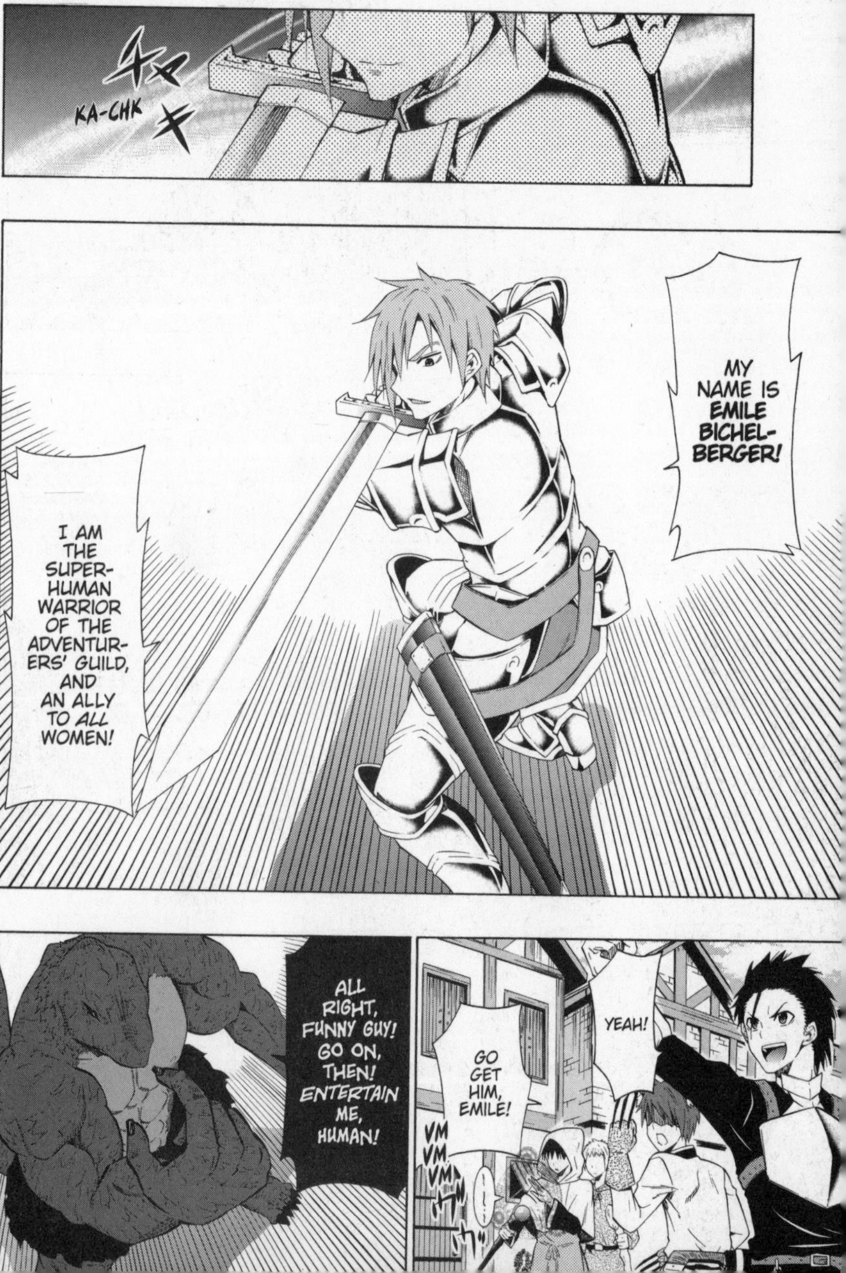
KA-CHK
MY NAME IS EMILE BICHEL-BERGER!
I AM THE SUPER-HUMAN WARRIOR OF THE ADVENTURER-ERS' GUILD, AND AN ALLY TO ALL WOMEN!
YEAH!
GO GET HIM, EMILE!
VM VM VM
ALL RIGHT, FUNNY GUY! GO ON, THEN! ENTERTAIN ME, HUMAN!

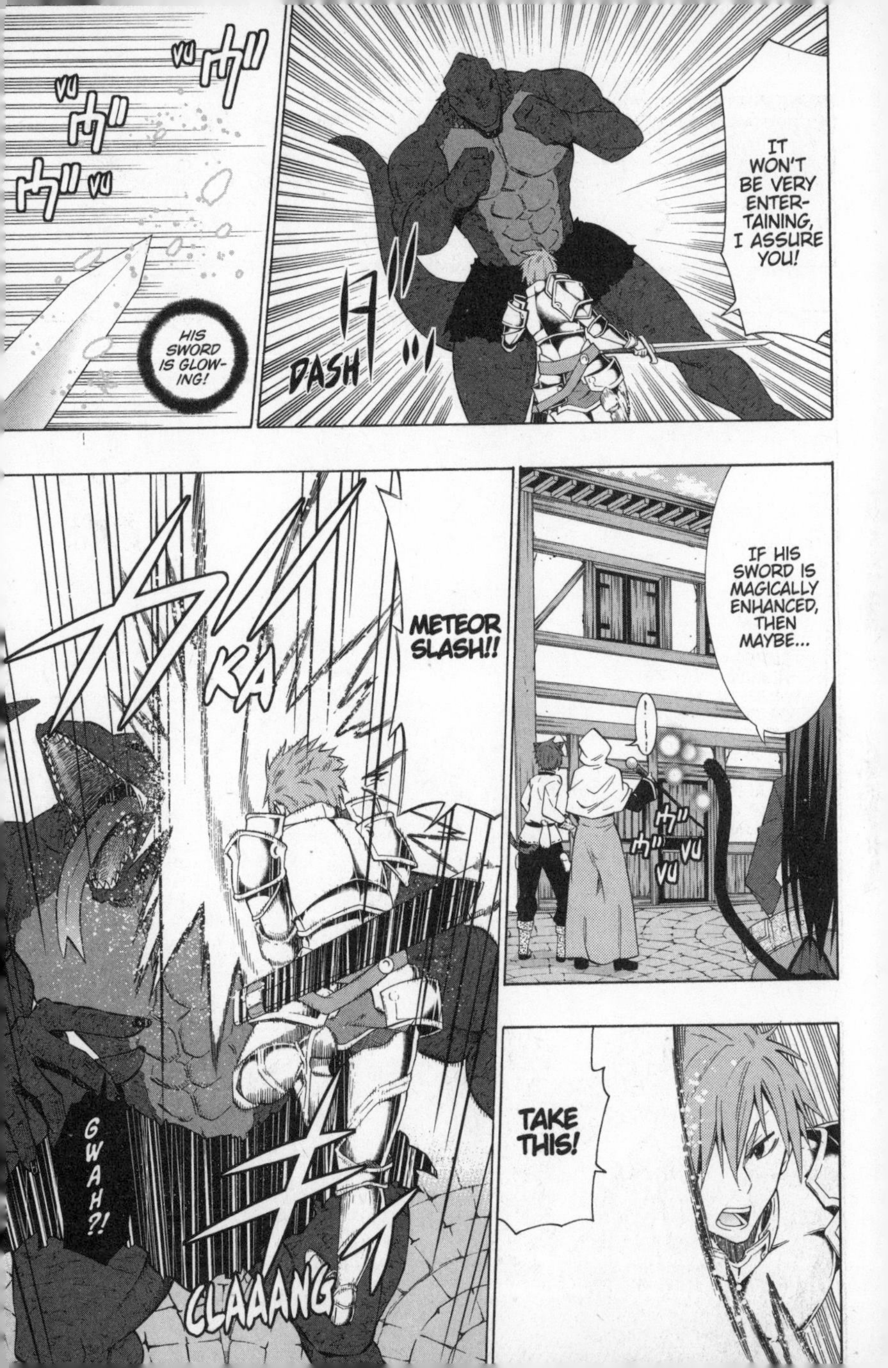
IT WON'T BE VERY ENTERTAINING, I ASSURE YOU!
DASH
VU VU VU
HIS SWORD IS GLOWING!
IF HIS SWORD IS MAGICALLY ENHANCED, THEN MAYBE...
!
VU VU
TAKE THIS!
METEOR SLASH!!
KA
GWAH?!
CLAAANG

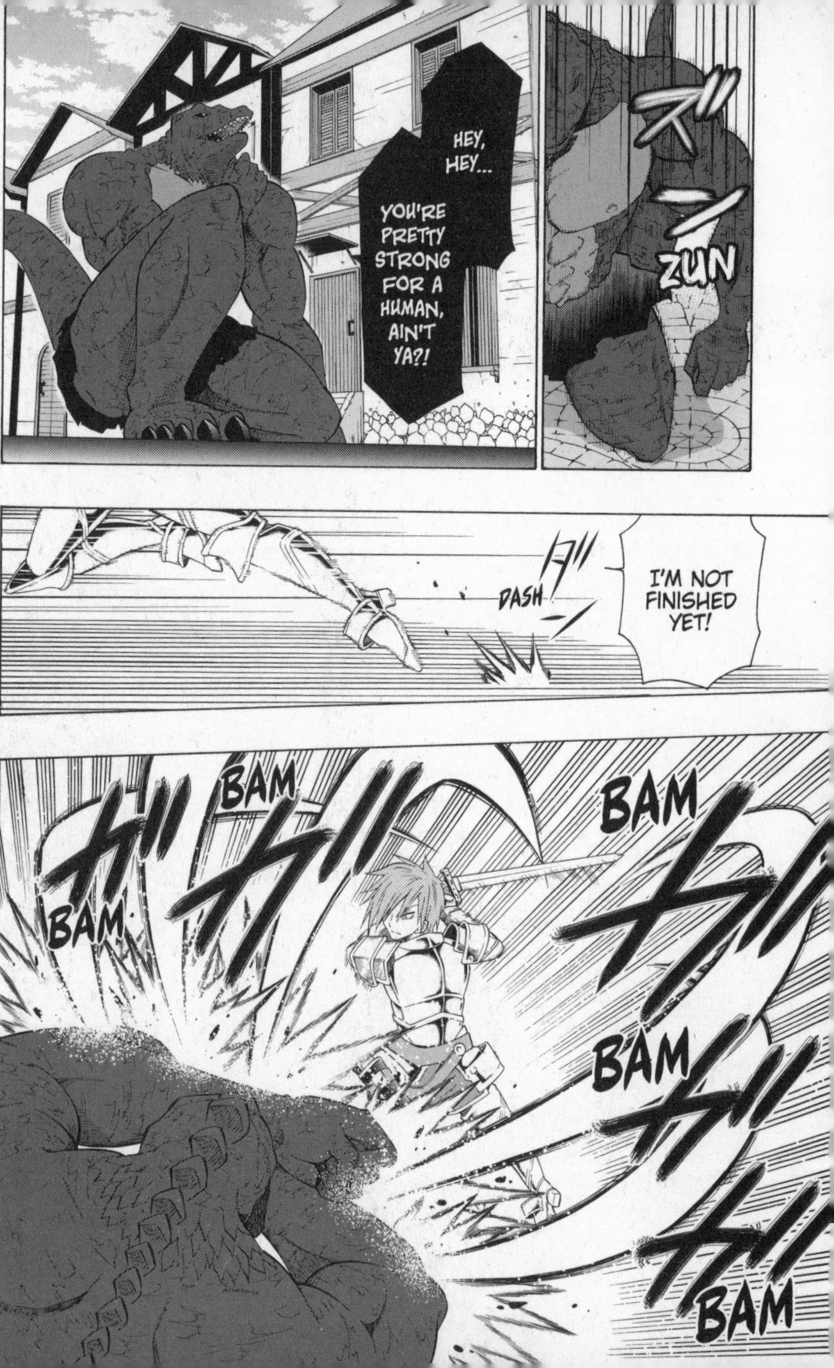
ZUN
HEY, HEY...
YOU'RE PRETTY STRONG FOR A HUMAN, AIN'T YA?!
I'M NOT FINISHED YET!
DASH
BAM
BAM
BAM
BAM
BAM

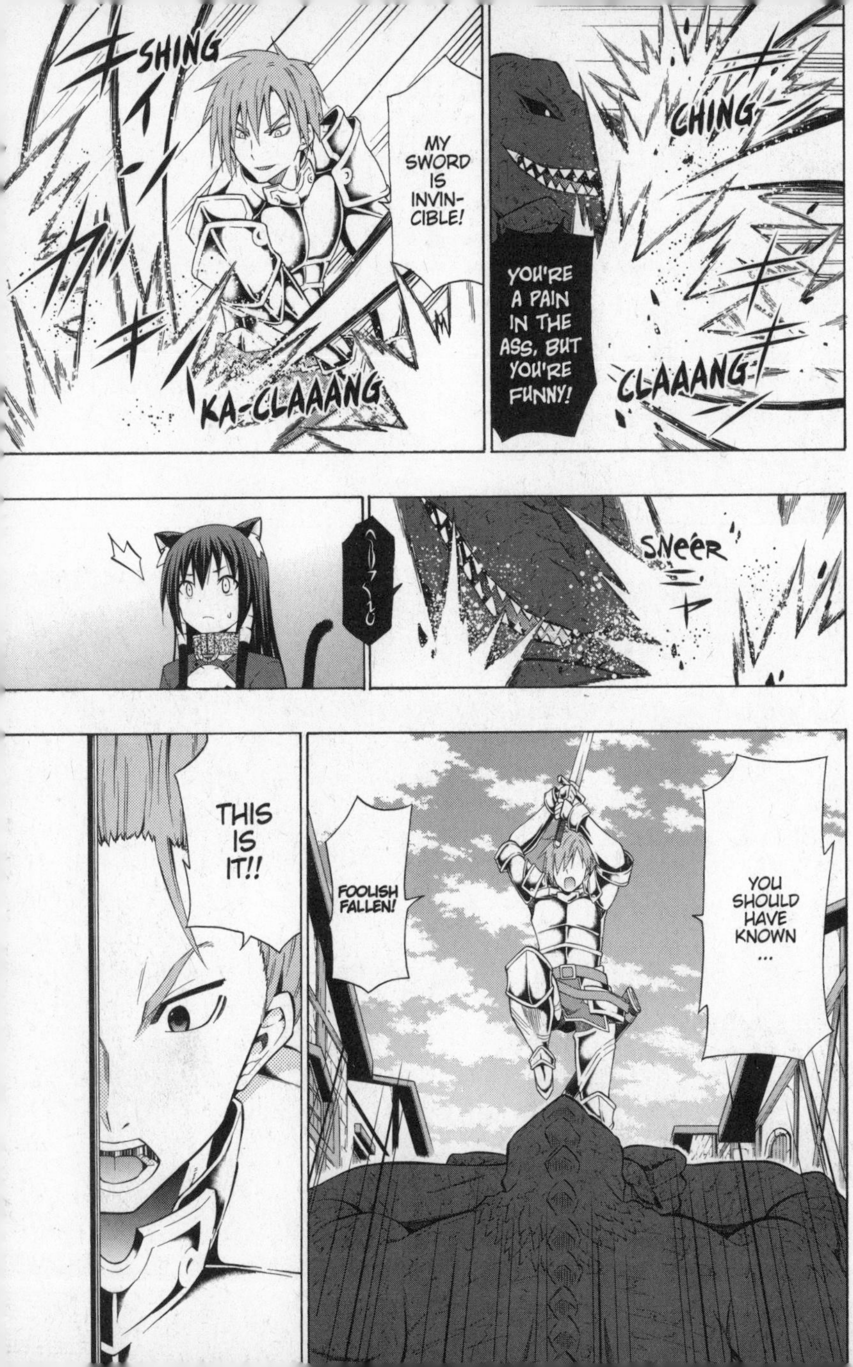
CHING
YOU'RE A PAIN IN THE ASS, BUT YOU'RE FUNNY!
CLAAANG
SHING
MY SWORD IS INVINCIBLE!
KA-CLAAANG
SNEER
YOU SHOULD HAVE KNOWN...
FOOLISH FALLEN!
THIS IS IT!!

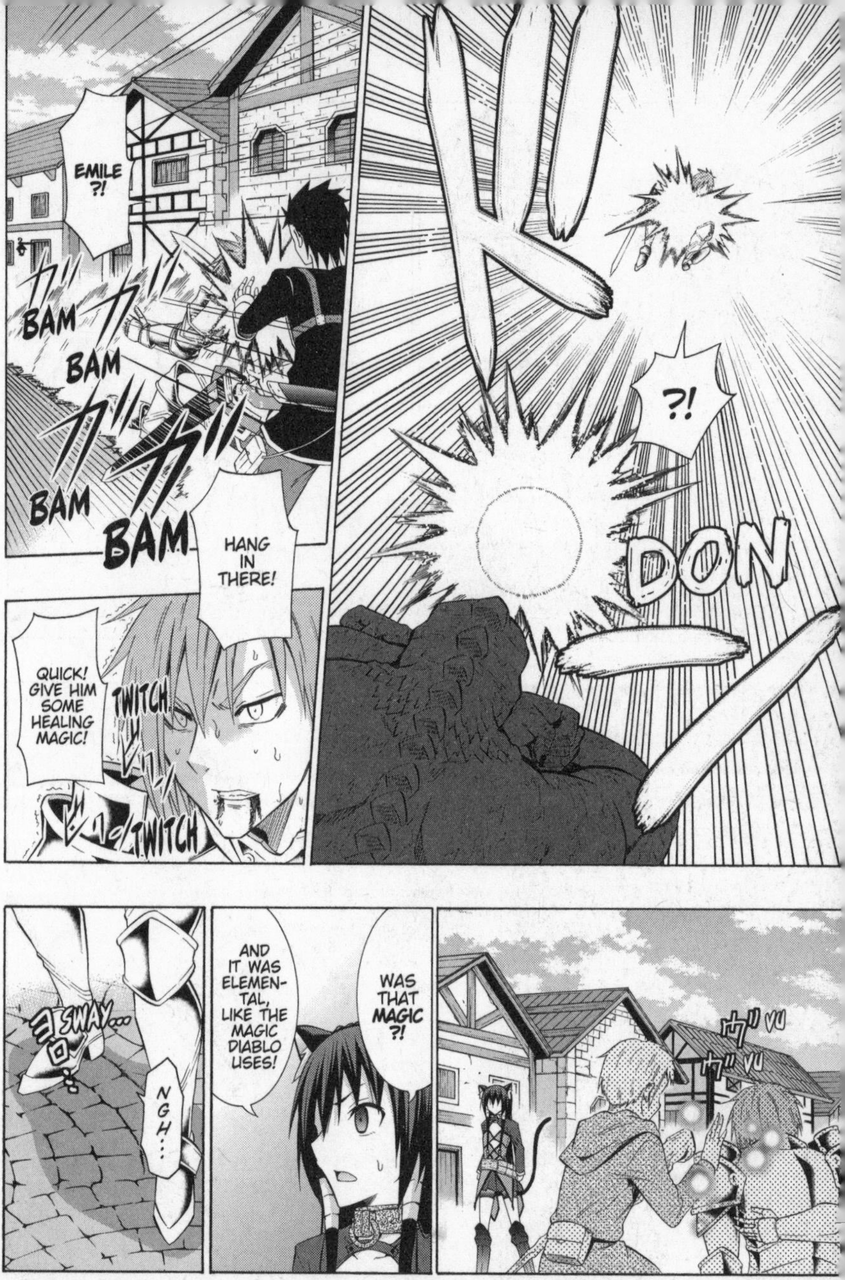
?!
DON
EMILE ?!
BAM
BAM
BAM
BAM
HANG IN THERE!
QUICK! GIVE HIM SOME HEALING MAGIC!
TWITCH
TWITCH
VU
VU
WAS THAT MAGIC?!
AND IT WAS ELEMENTAL, LIKE THE MAGIC DIABLO USES!
SWAY...
NGH...

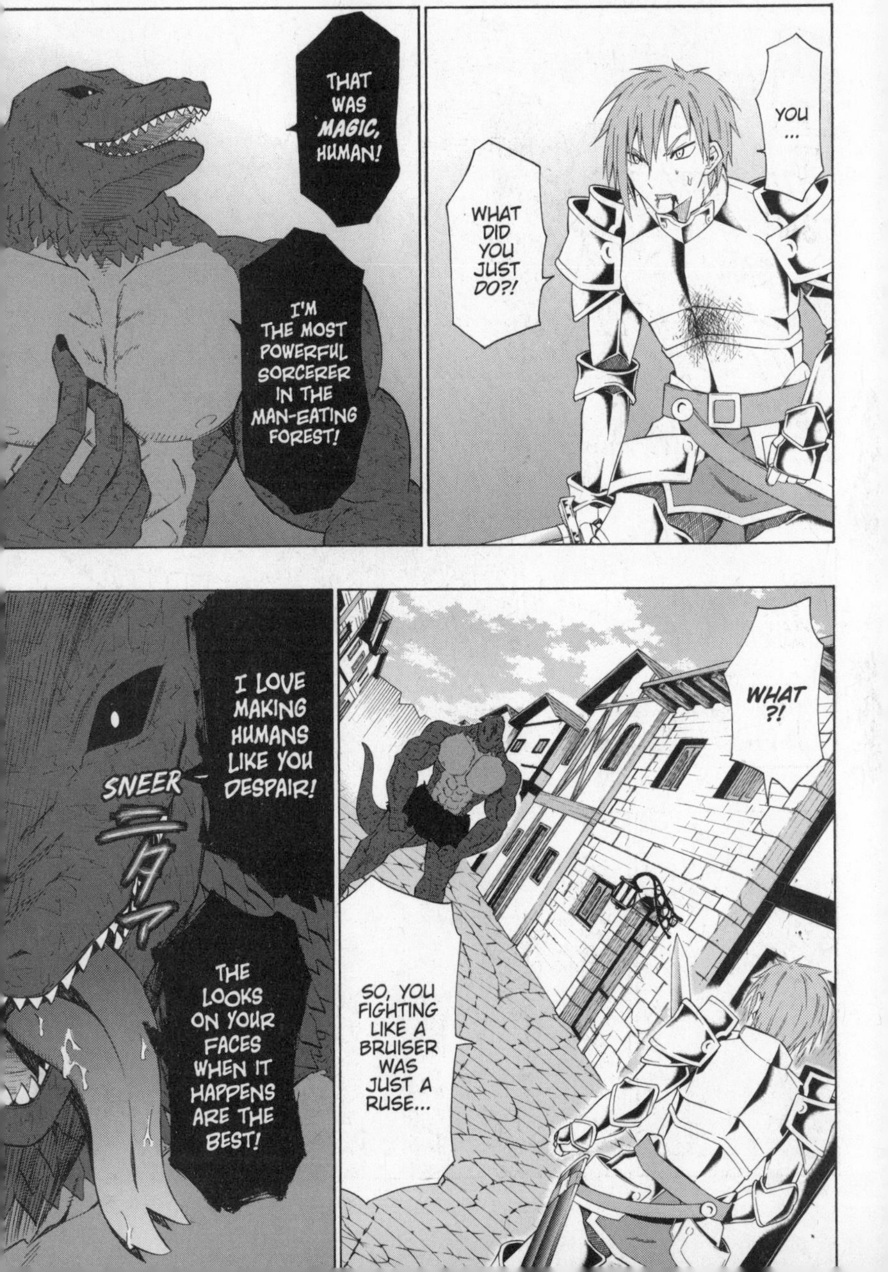
YOU ...
WHAT DID YOU JUST DO?!
THAT WAS MAGIC, HUMAN!
I'M THE MOST POWERFUL SORCERER IN THE MAN-EATING FOREST!
WHAT ?!
SO, YOU FIGHTING LIKE A BRUISER WAS JUST A RUSE...
I LOVE MAKING HUMANS LIKE YOU DESPAIR!
SNEER
THE LOOKS ON YOUR FACES WHEN IT HAPPENS ARE THE BEST!

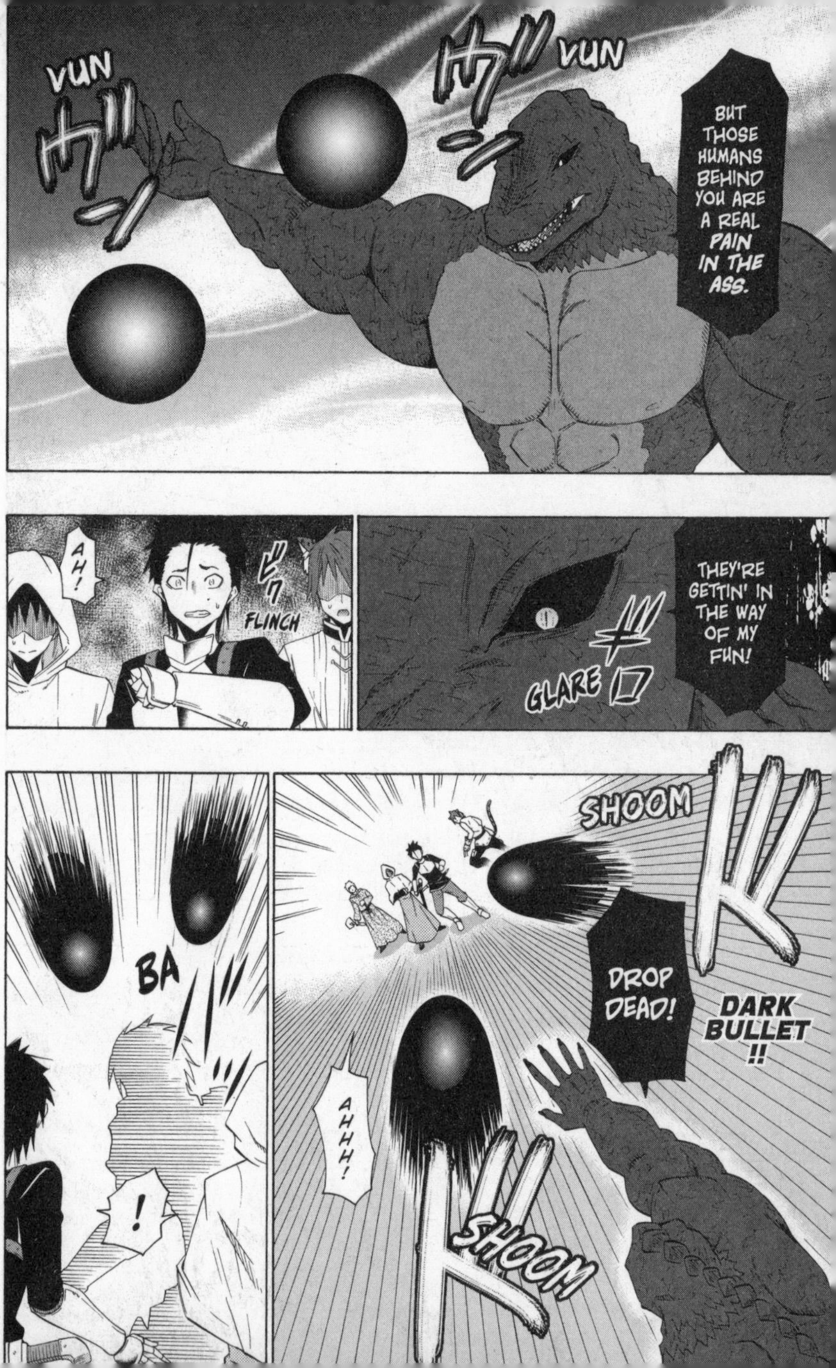
BUT THOSE HUMANS BEHIND YOU ARE A REAL PAIN IN THE ASS.
VUN
VUN
THEY'RE GETTIN' IN THE WAY OF MY FUN!
GLARE
FLINCH
AH!
SHOOM
DARK BULLET!!
DROP DEAD!
AHHH!
SHOOM
BA
!

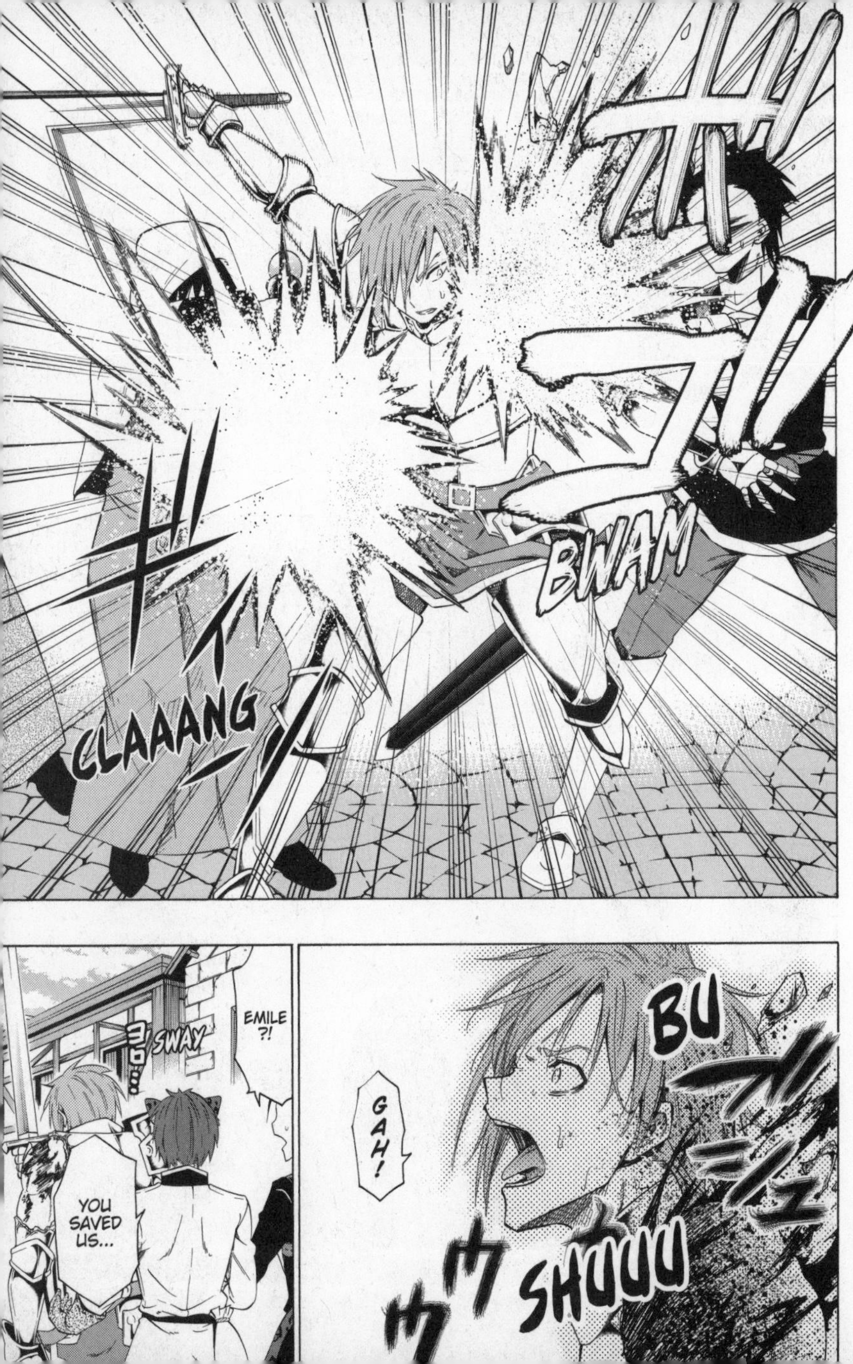
BWAM
CLAAANG
BU
GAH!
SHUUU
EMILE?!
SWAY
YOU SAVED US...

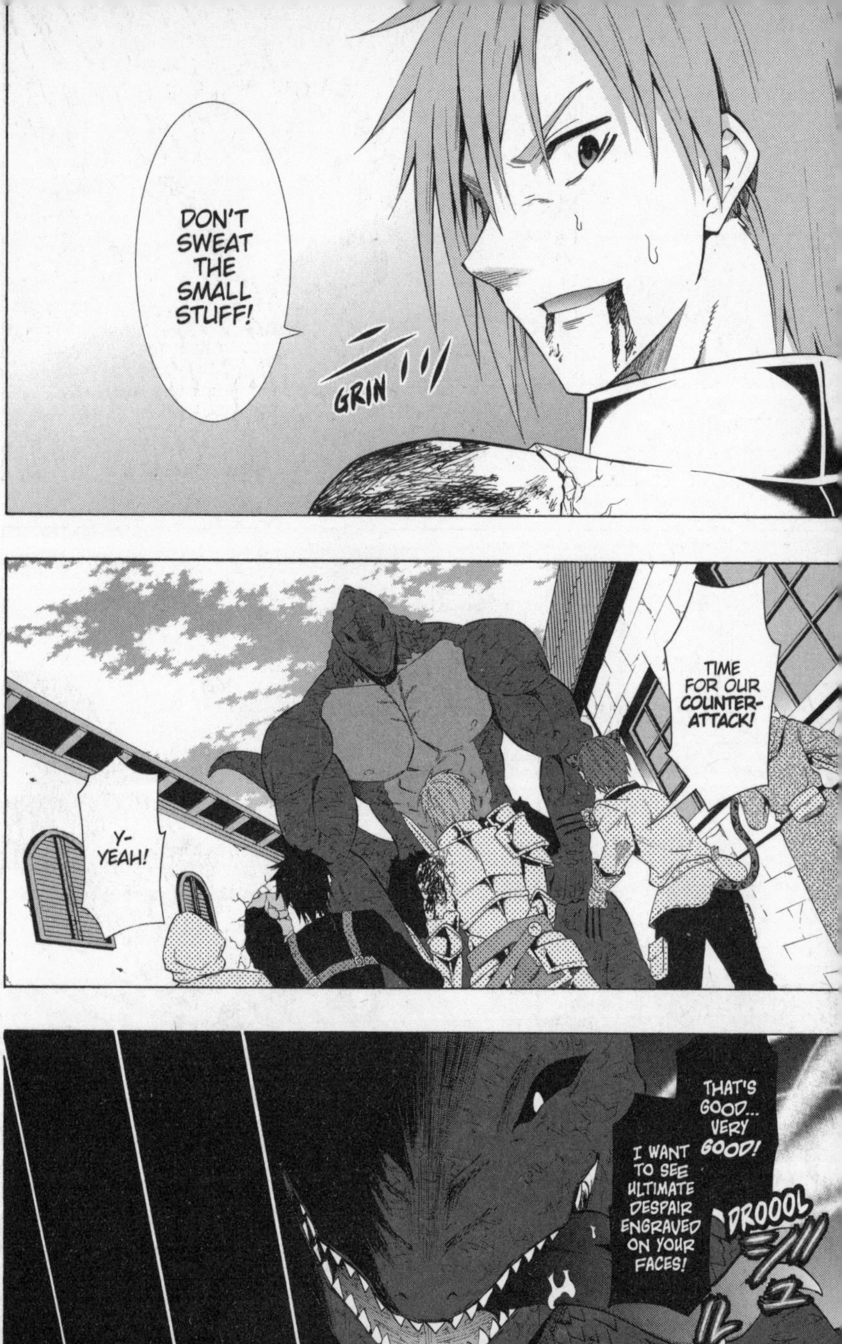
DON'T SWEAT THE SMALL STUFF!
GRIN
TIME FOR OUR COUNTER-ATTACK!
Y-YEAH!
THAT'S GOOD... VERY GOOD!
I WANT TO SEE ULTIMATE DESPAIR ENGRAVED ON YOUR FACES!
DROOOL

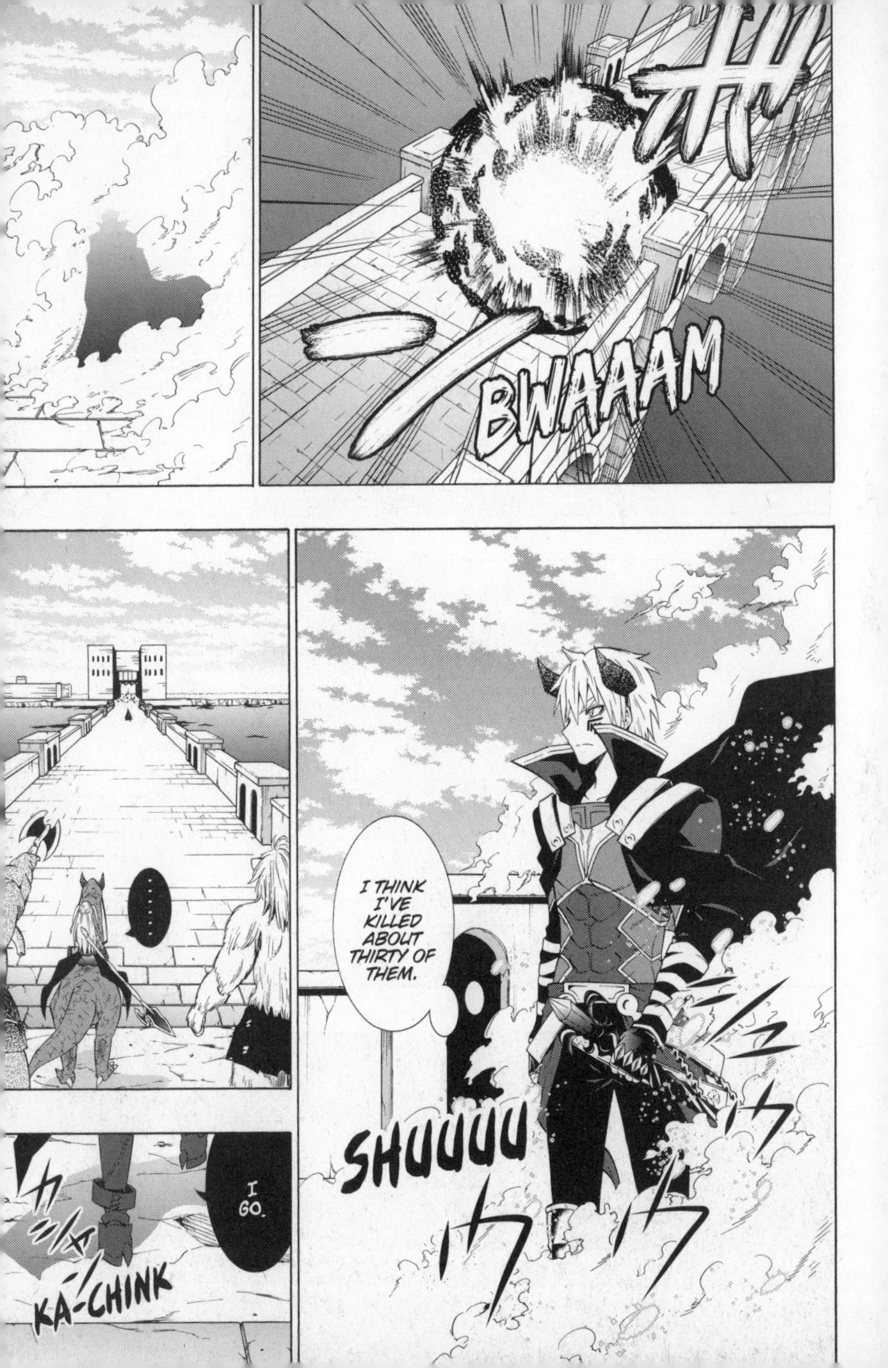
BWAAAM
I THINK I'VE KILLED ABOUT THIRTY OF THEM.
SHUUUU
......
I GO.
KA-CHINK

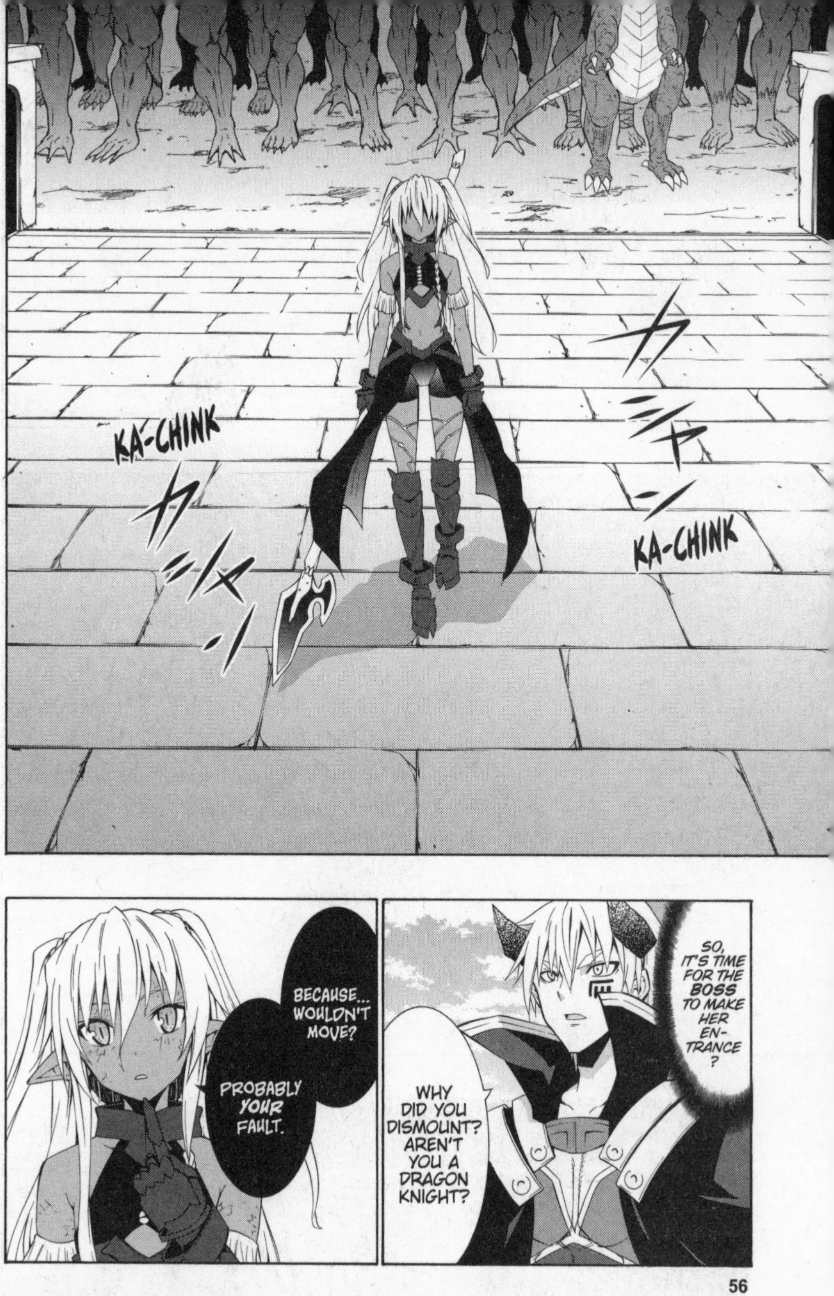
KA-CHINK
KA-CHINK
SO, IT'S TIME FOR THE BOSS TO MAKE HER EN-TRANCE?
WHY DID YOU DISMOUNT? AREN'T YOU A DRAGON KNIGHT?
BECAUSE... WOULDN'T MOVE?
PROBABLY YOUR FAULT.

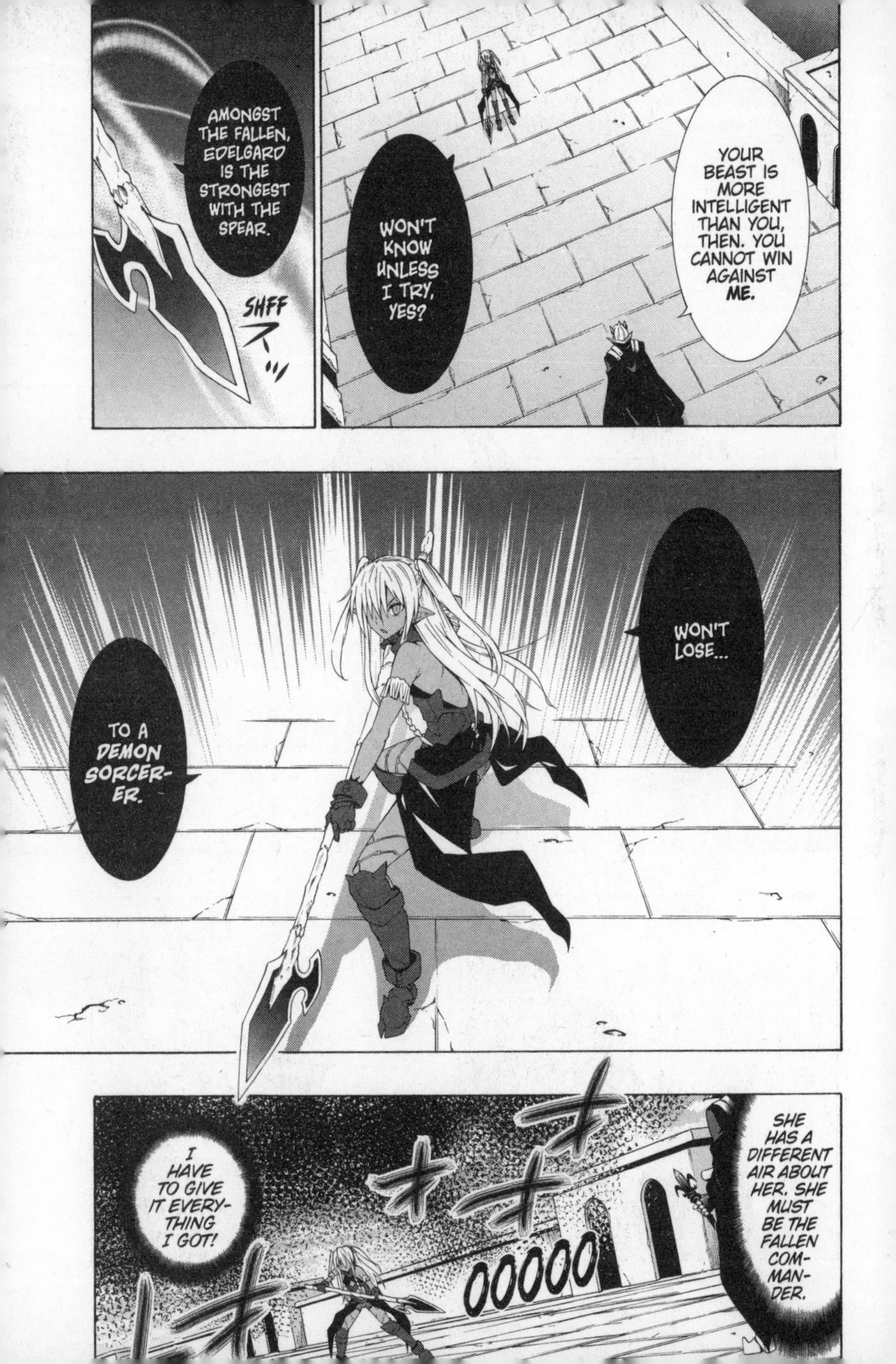
YOUR BEAST IS MORE INTELLIGENT THAN YOU, THEN. YOU CANNOT WIN AGAINST **ME.**
WON'T KNOW UNLESS I TRY, YES?
AMONGST THE FALLEN, EDELGARD IS THE STRONGEST WITH THE SPEAR.
SHFF
WON'T LOSE...
TO A **DEMON SORCERER.**
SHE HAS A DIFFERENT AIR ABOUT HER. SHE MUST BE THE FALLEN COMMANDER.
I HAVE TO GIVE IT EVERYTHING I GOT!
OOOOO

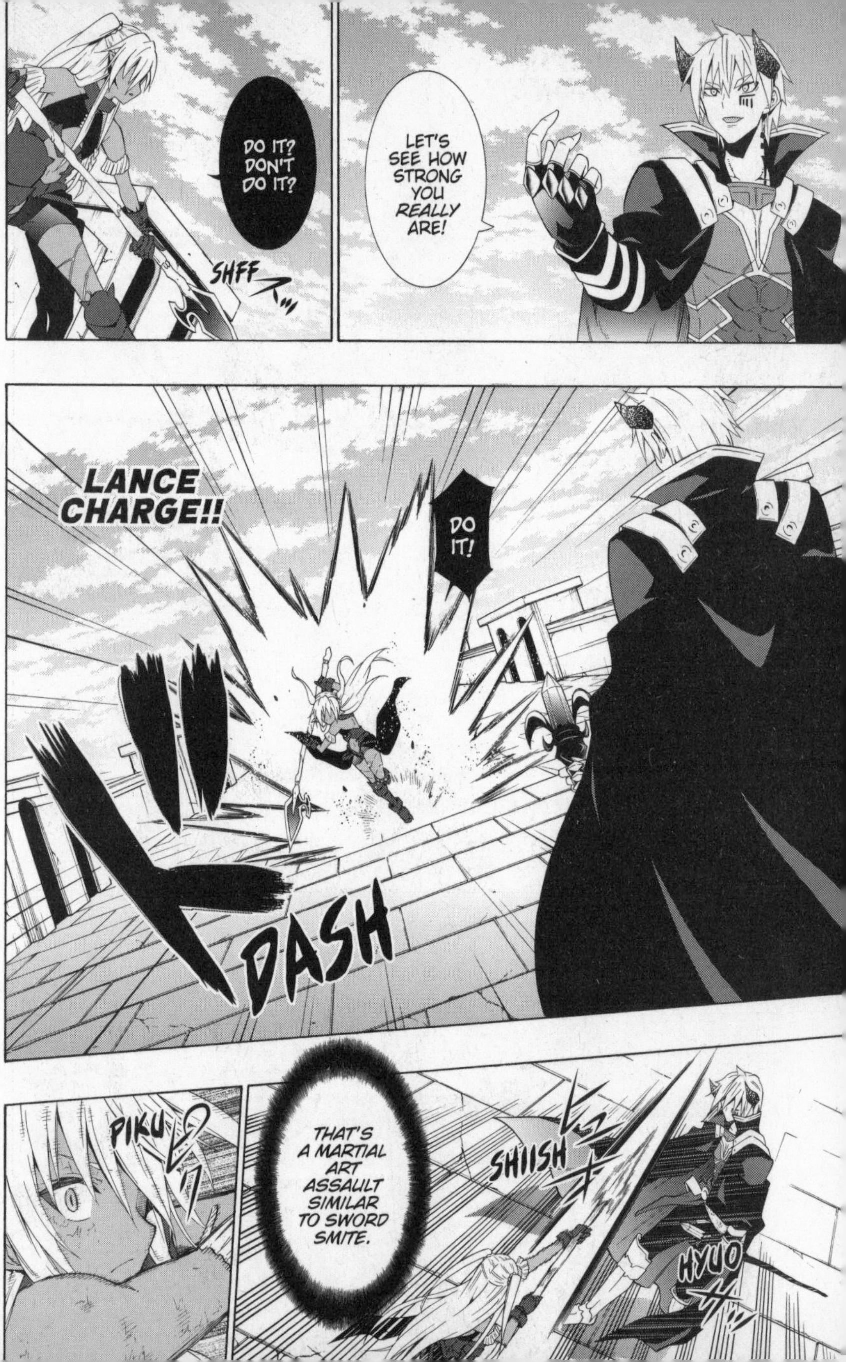
LET'S SEE HOW STRONG YOU REALLY ARE!
DO IT? DON'T DO IT?
SHFF
DO IT!
LANCE CHARGE!!
DASH
SHIISH
HYUO
THAT'S A MARTIAL ART ASSAULT SIMILAR TO SWORD SMITE.
PIKU

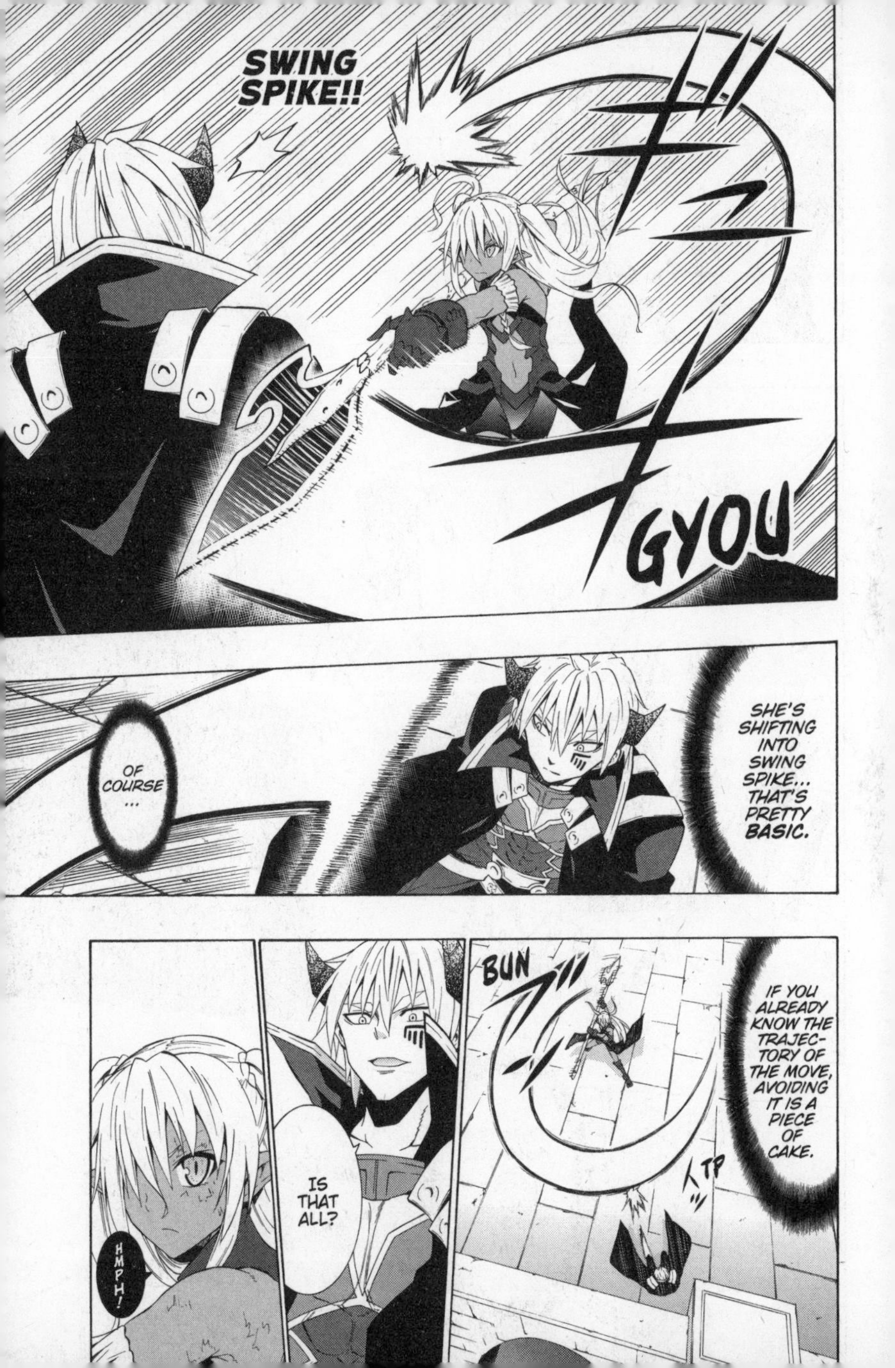
SWING SPIKE!!
GYOU
SHE'S SHIFTING INTO SWING SPIKE... THAT'S PRETTY BASIC.
OF COURSE...
IF YOU ALREADY KNOW THE TRAJEC-TORY OF THE MOVE, AVOIDING IT IS A PIECE OF CAKE.
BUN
TP
IS THAT ALL?
HMPH!

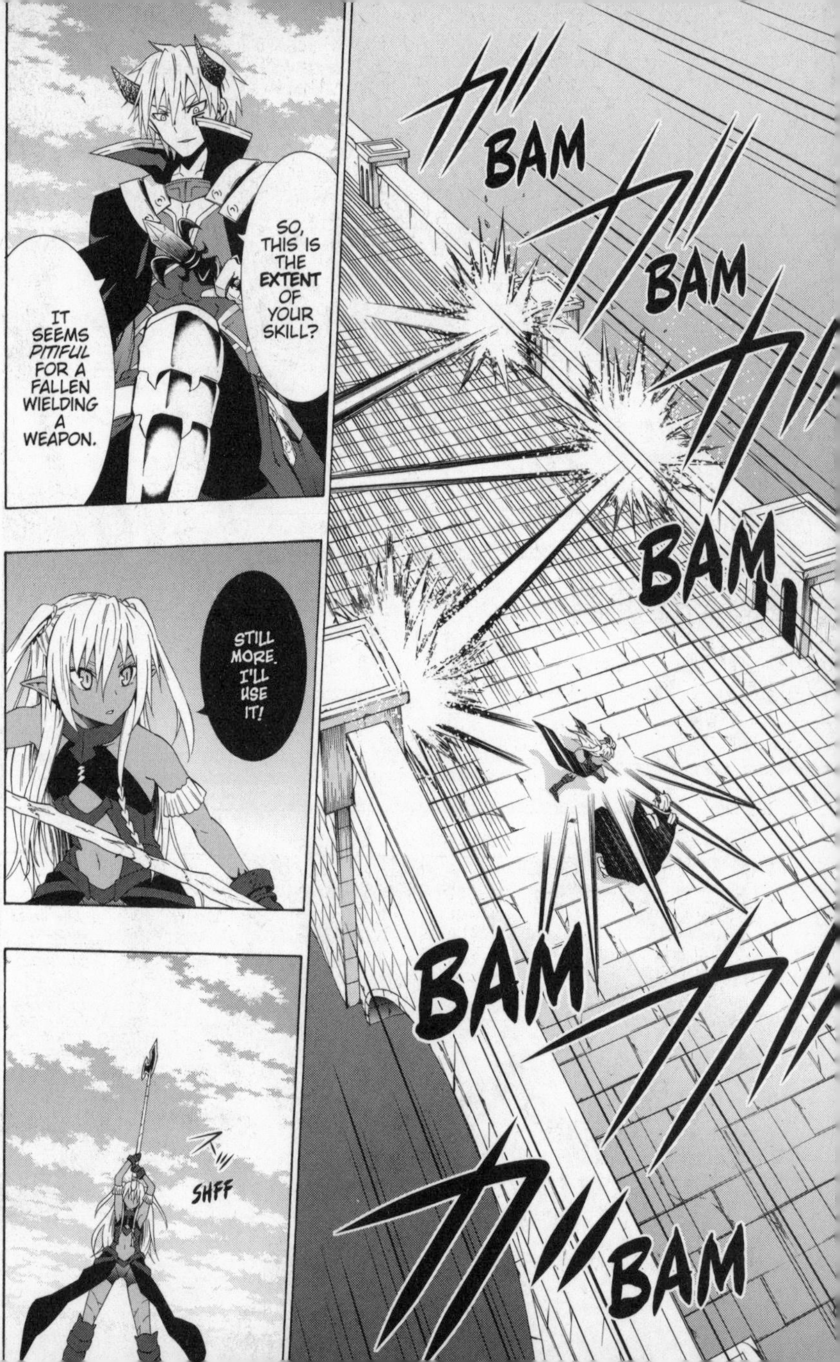
BAM
BAM
BAM
BAM
BAM
SO, THIS IS THE EXTENT OF YOUR SKILL?
IT SEEMS *PITIFUL* FOR A FALLEN WIELDING A WEAPON.
STILL MORE. I'LL USE IT!
SHFF

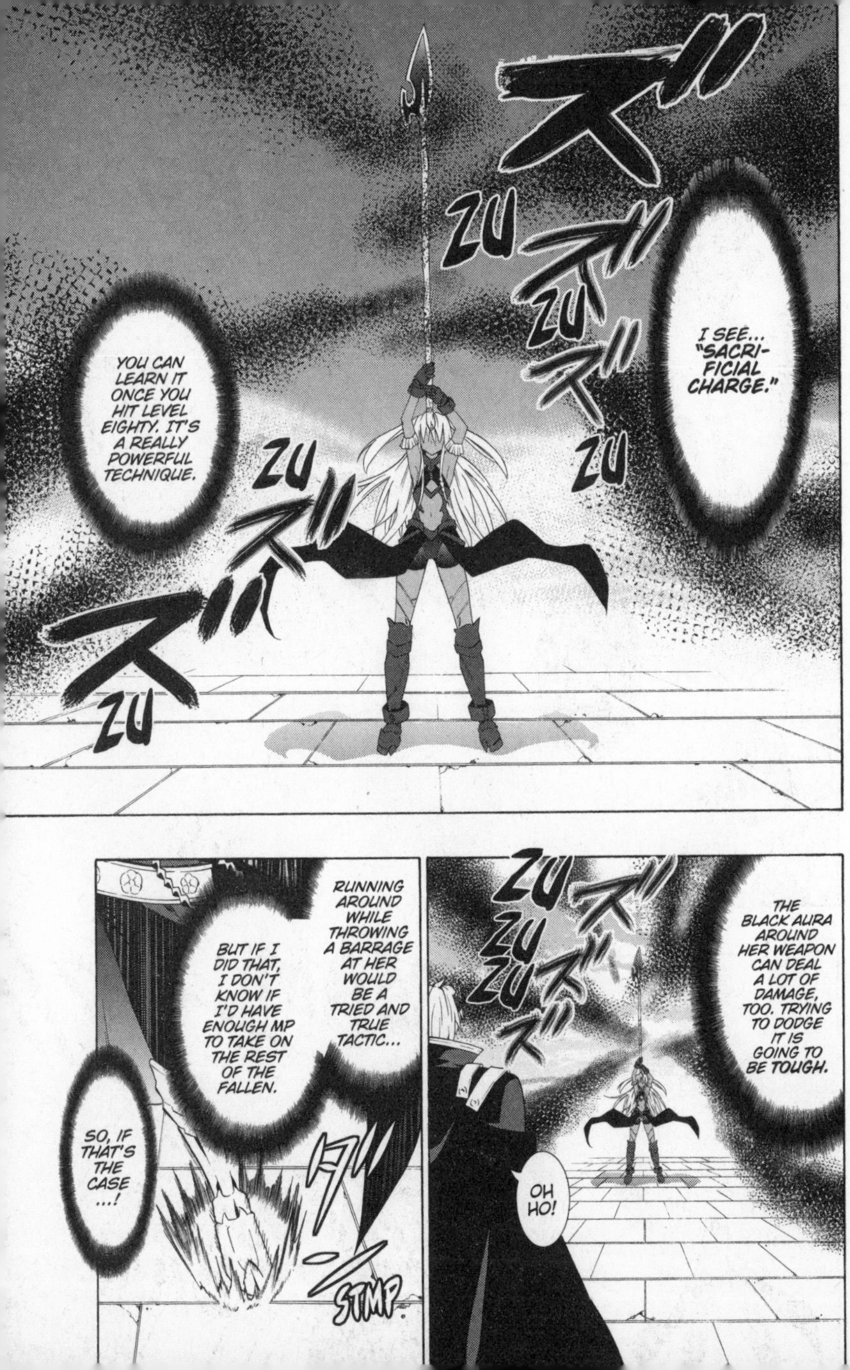

ZU
ZU
I SEE... "SACRIFICIAL CHARGE."
ZU
YOU CAN LEARN IT ONCE YOU HIT LEVEL EIGHTY. IT'S A REALLY POWERFUL TECHNIQUE.
ZU
ZU
ZU ZU ZU
THE BLACK AURA AROUND HER WEAPON CAN DEAL A LOT OF DAMAGE, TOO. TRYING TO DODGE IT IS GOING TO BE TOUGH.
OH HO!
RUNNING AROUND WHILE THROWING A BARRAGE AT HER WOULD BE A TRIED AND TRUE TACTIC...
BUT IF I DID THAT, I DON'T KNOW IF I'D HAVE ENOUGH MP TO TAKE ON THE REST OF THE FALLEN.
SO, IF THAT'S THE CASE...!
STMP

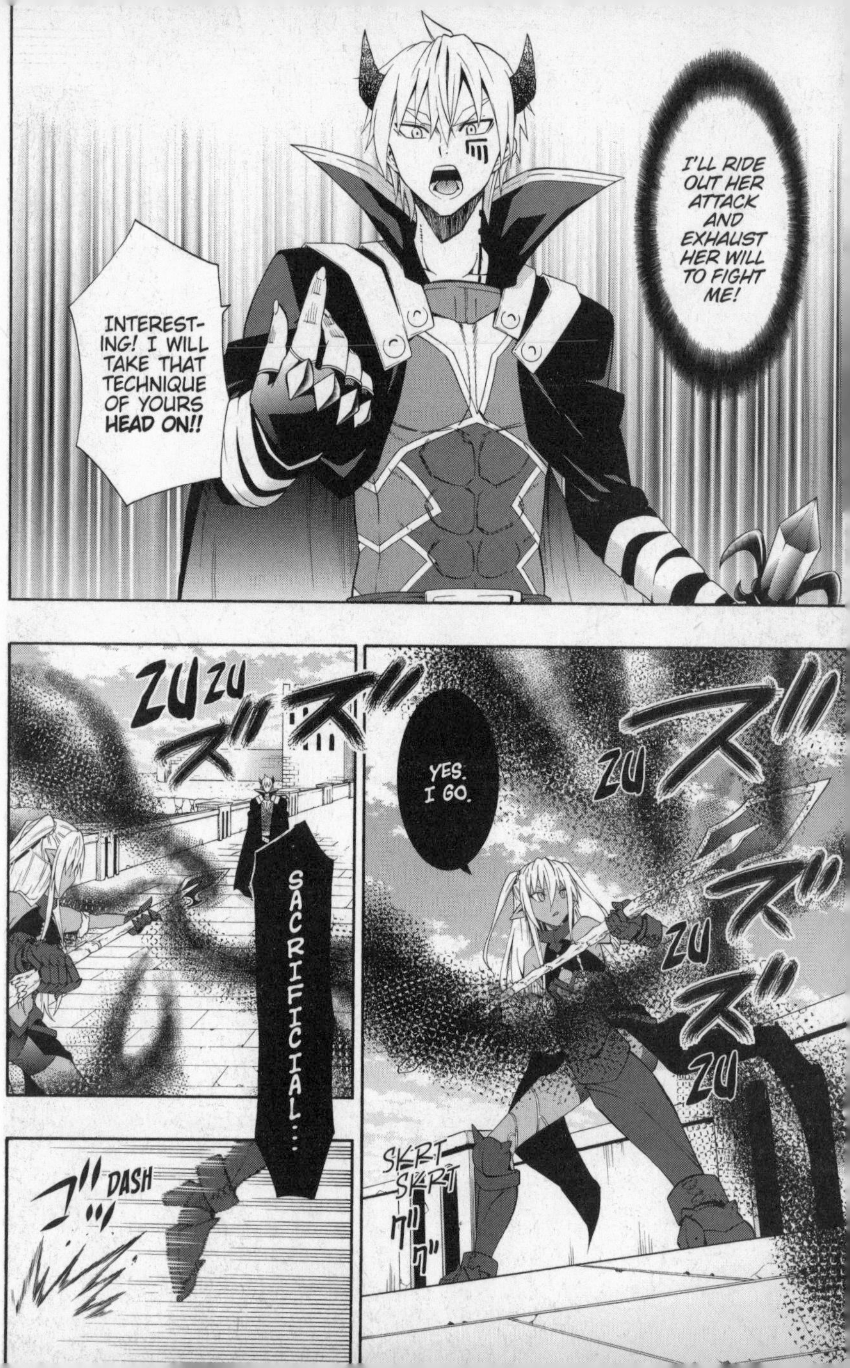
I'LL RIDE OUT HER ATTACK AND EXHAUST HER WILL TO FIGHT ME!
INTEREST-ING! I WILL TAKE THAT TECHNIQUE OF YOURS HEAD ON!!
ZU
YES. I GO.
ZU
ZU
ZU
ZUZU
SACRIFICIAL...
SKRT SKRT
DASH

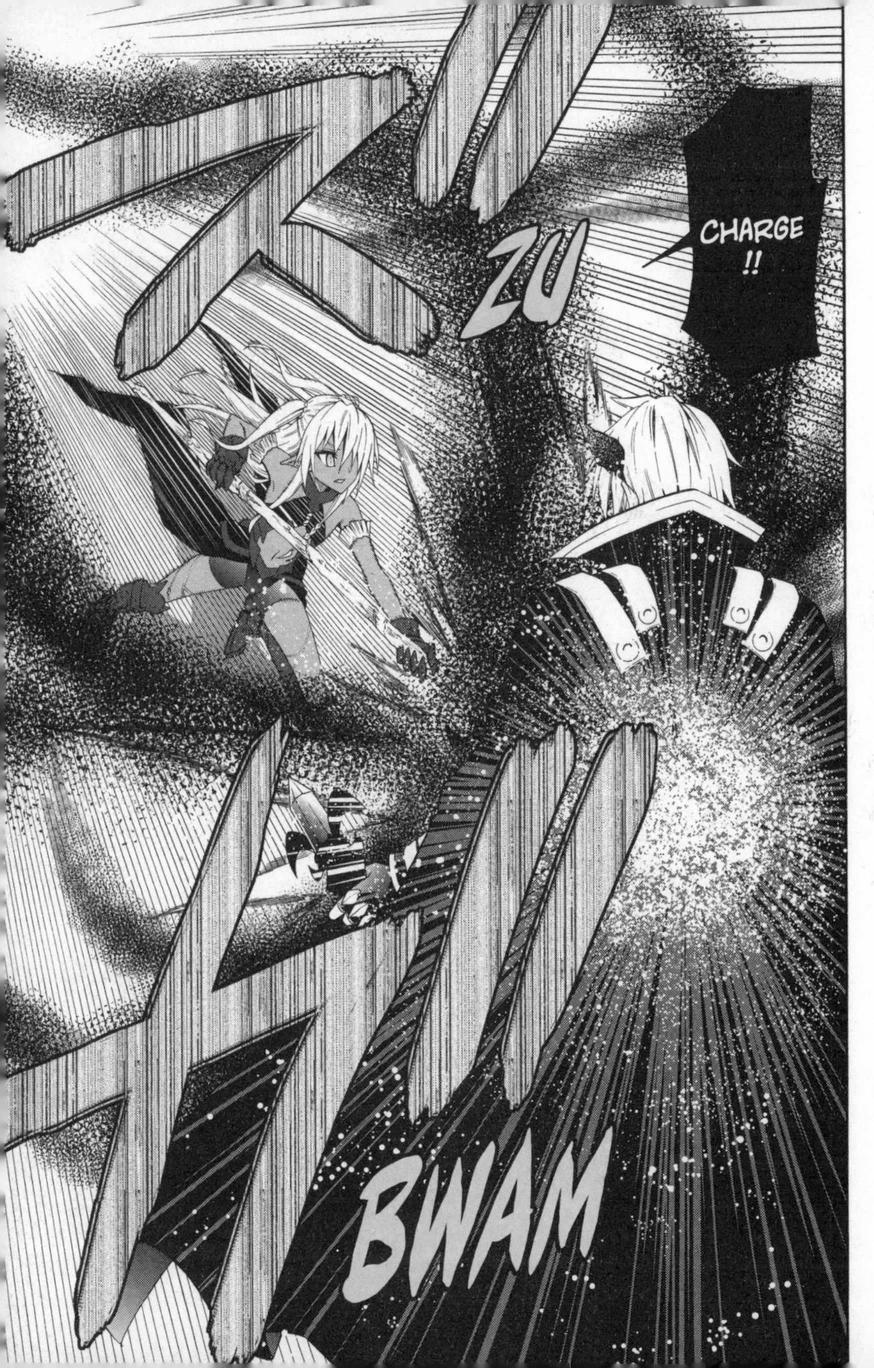
CHARGE !!
ZU
BWAM

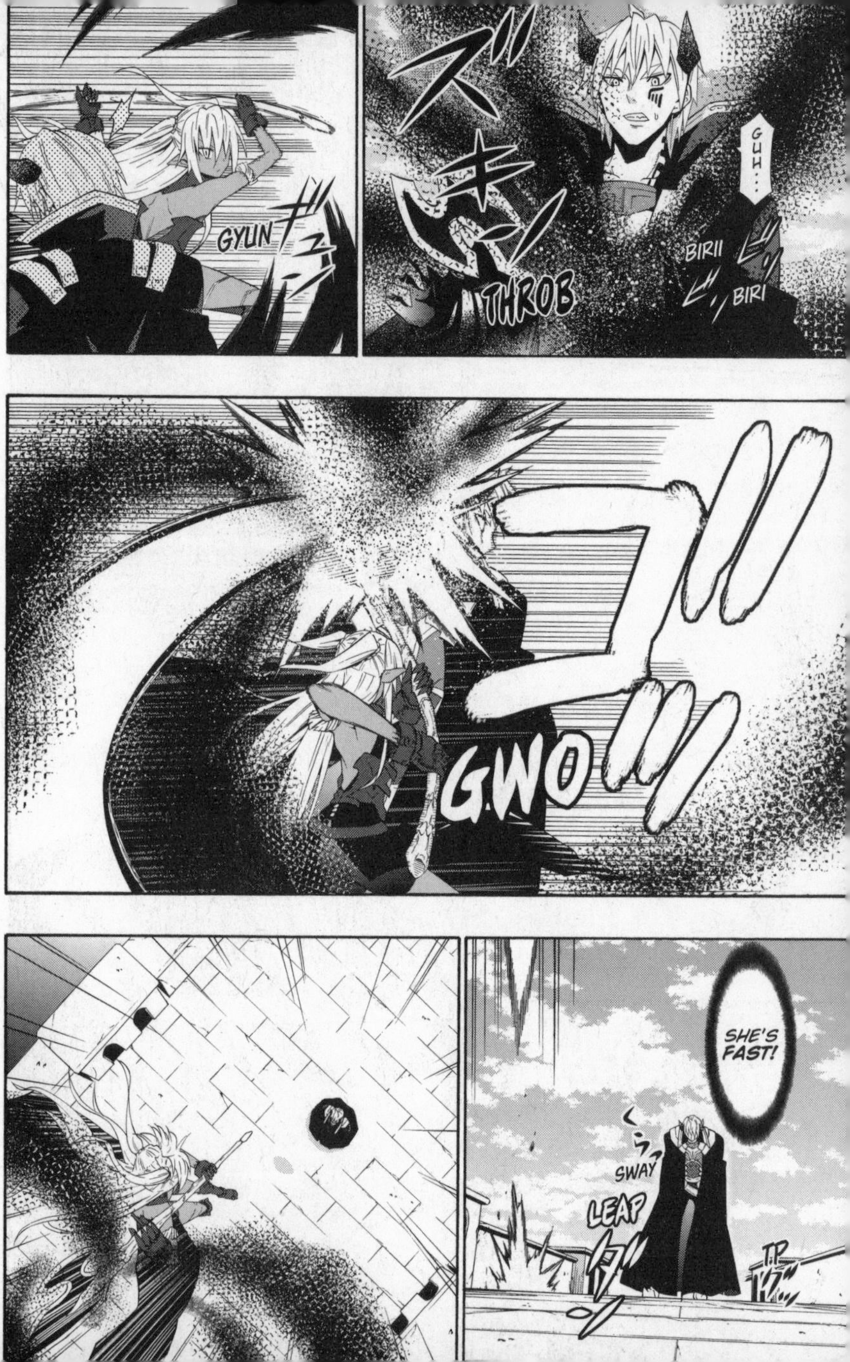
GUH...
BIRII
BIRI
THROB
GYUN
GWO
SHE'S FAST!
SWAY
LEAP
T.P

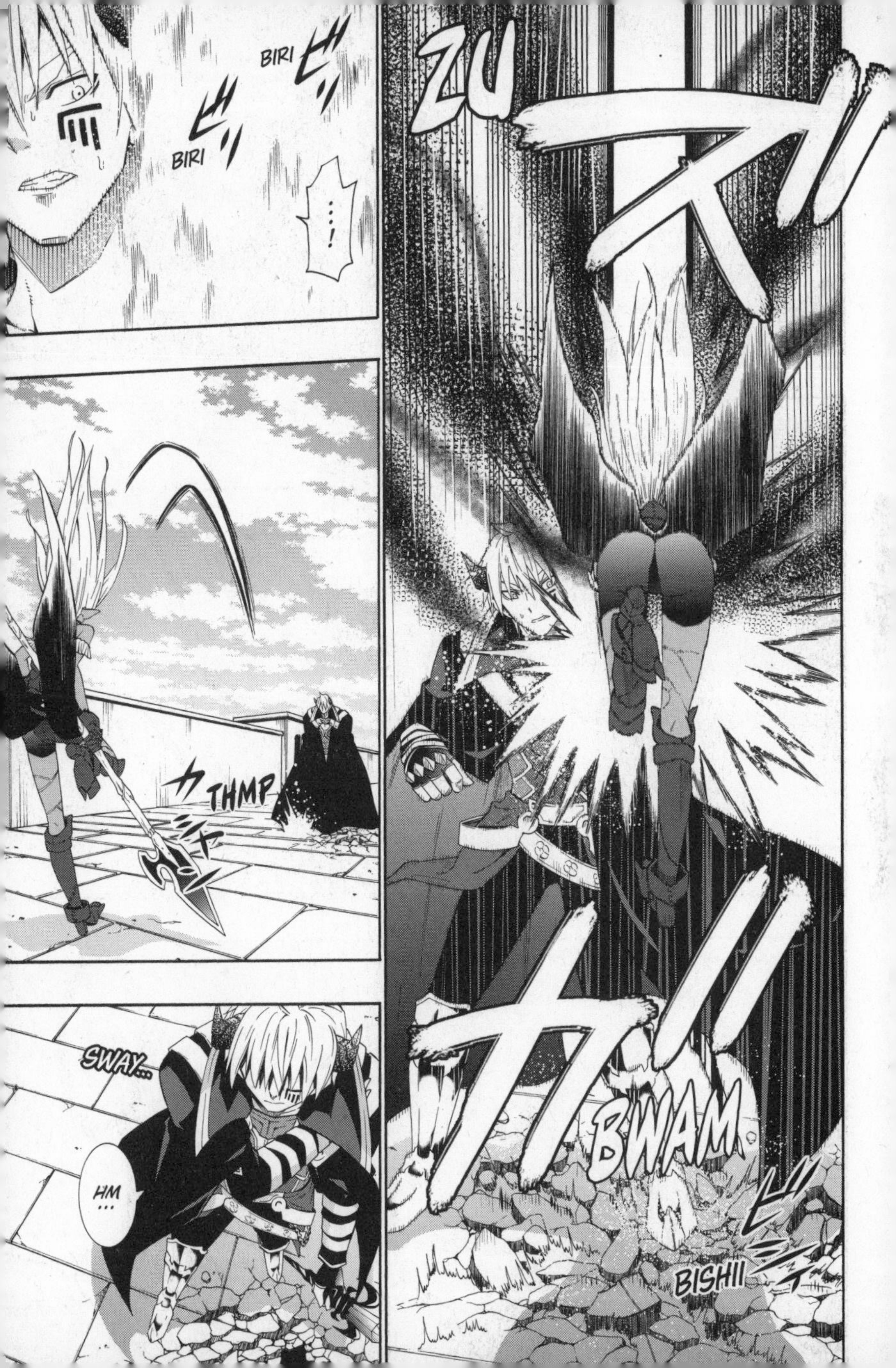
ZU
BWAM
BISHII
BIRI
BIRI
...!
THMP
SWAY...
HM...

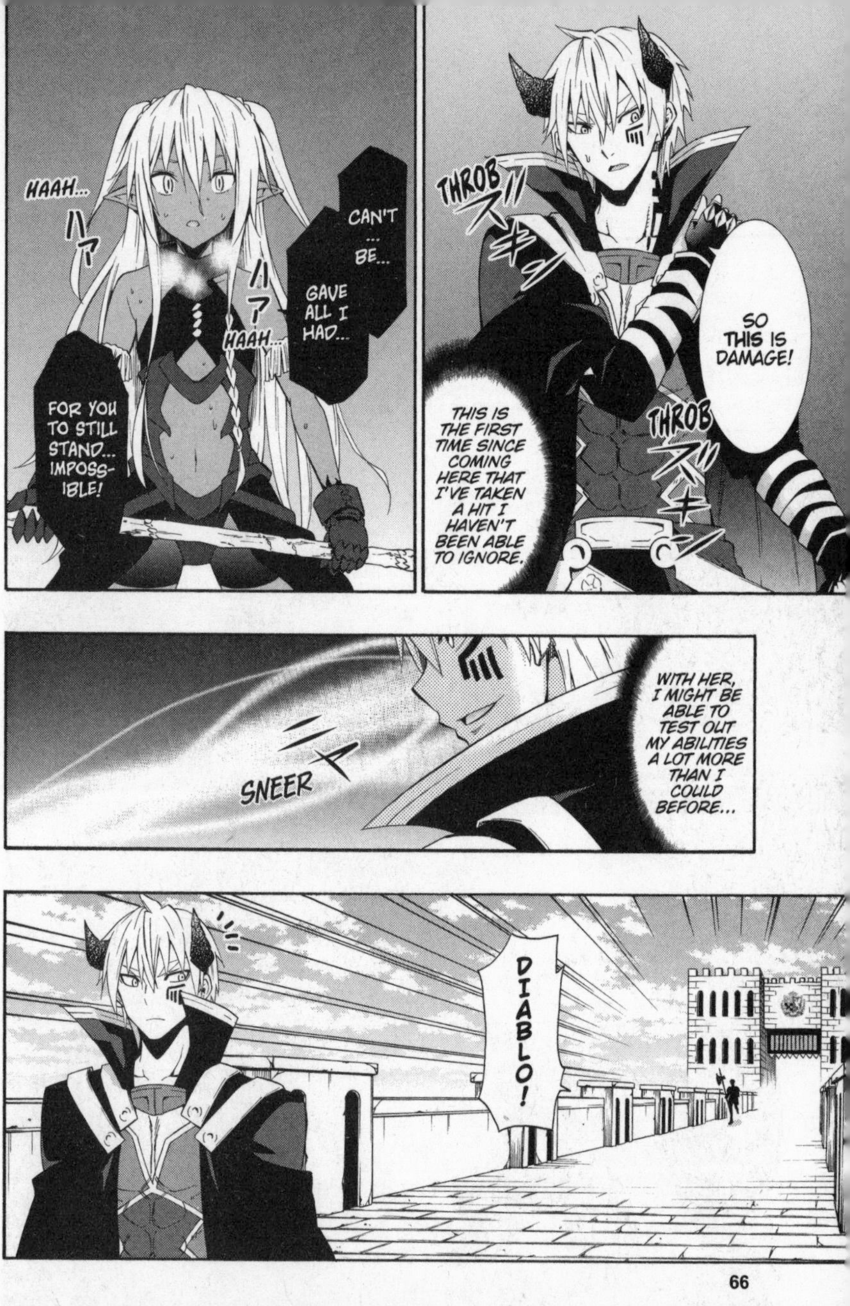

THROB ズキッ
SO THIS IS DAMAGE!
THIS IS THE FIRST TIME SINCE COMING HERE THAT I'VE TAKEN A HIT I HAVEN'T BEEN ABLE TO IGNORE.
THROB ズキッ
CAN'T ... BE...
GAVE ALL I HAD...
HAAH... ハァ
HAAH... ハァ
FOR YOU TO STILL STAND... IMPOSS-IBLE!
WITH HER, I MIGHT BE ABLE TO TEST OUT MY ABILITIES A LOT MORE THAN I COULD BEFORE...
SNEER ニヤ
DIABLO!

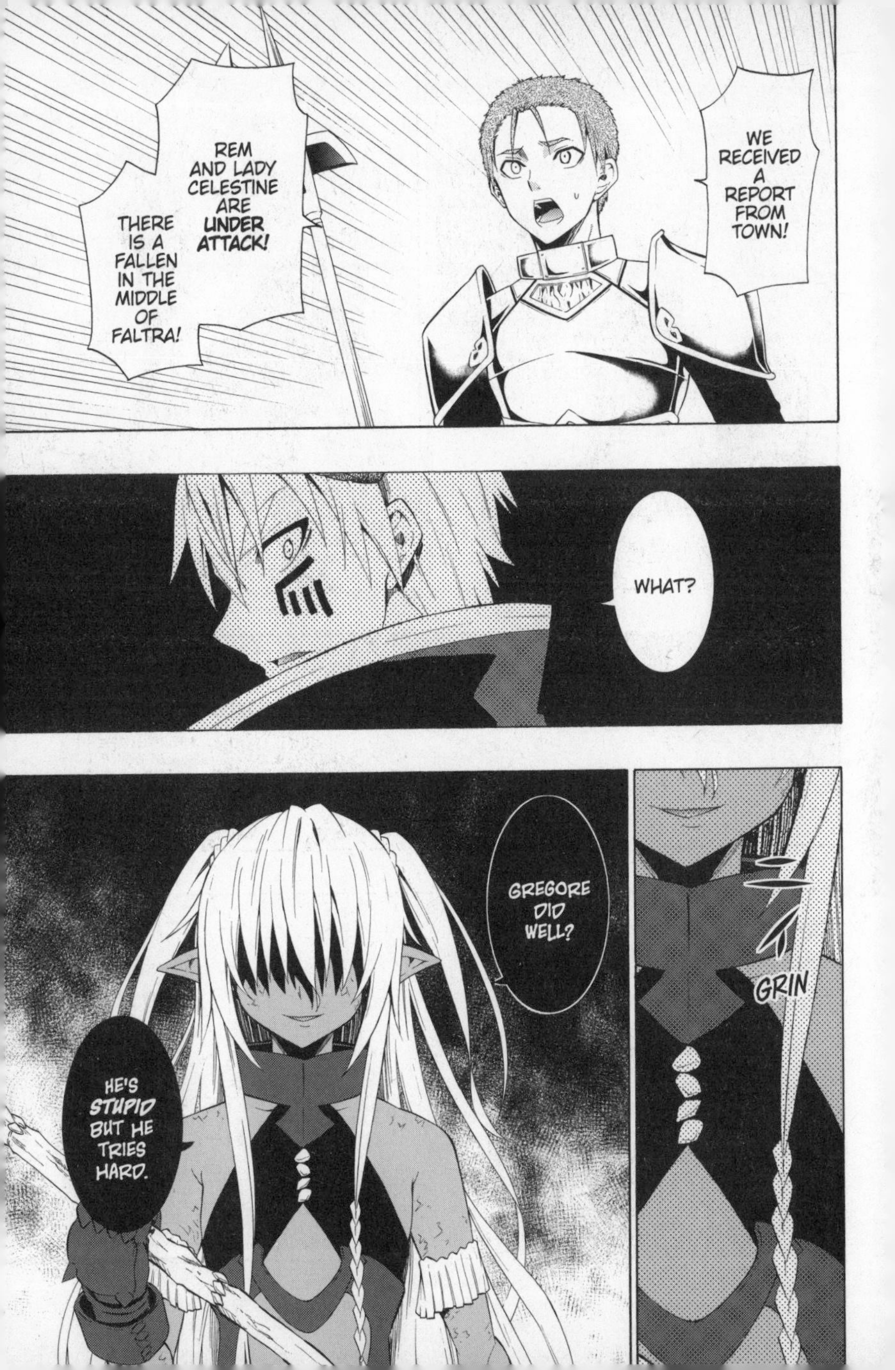
WE RECEIVED A REPORT FROM TOWN!
REM AND LADY CELESTINE ARE UNDER ATTACK!
THERE IS A FALLEN IN THE MIDDLE OF FALTRA!
WHAT?
GRIN
GREGORE DID WELL?
HE'S STUPID BUT HE TRIES HARD.

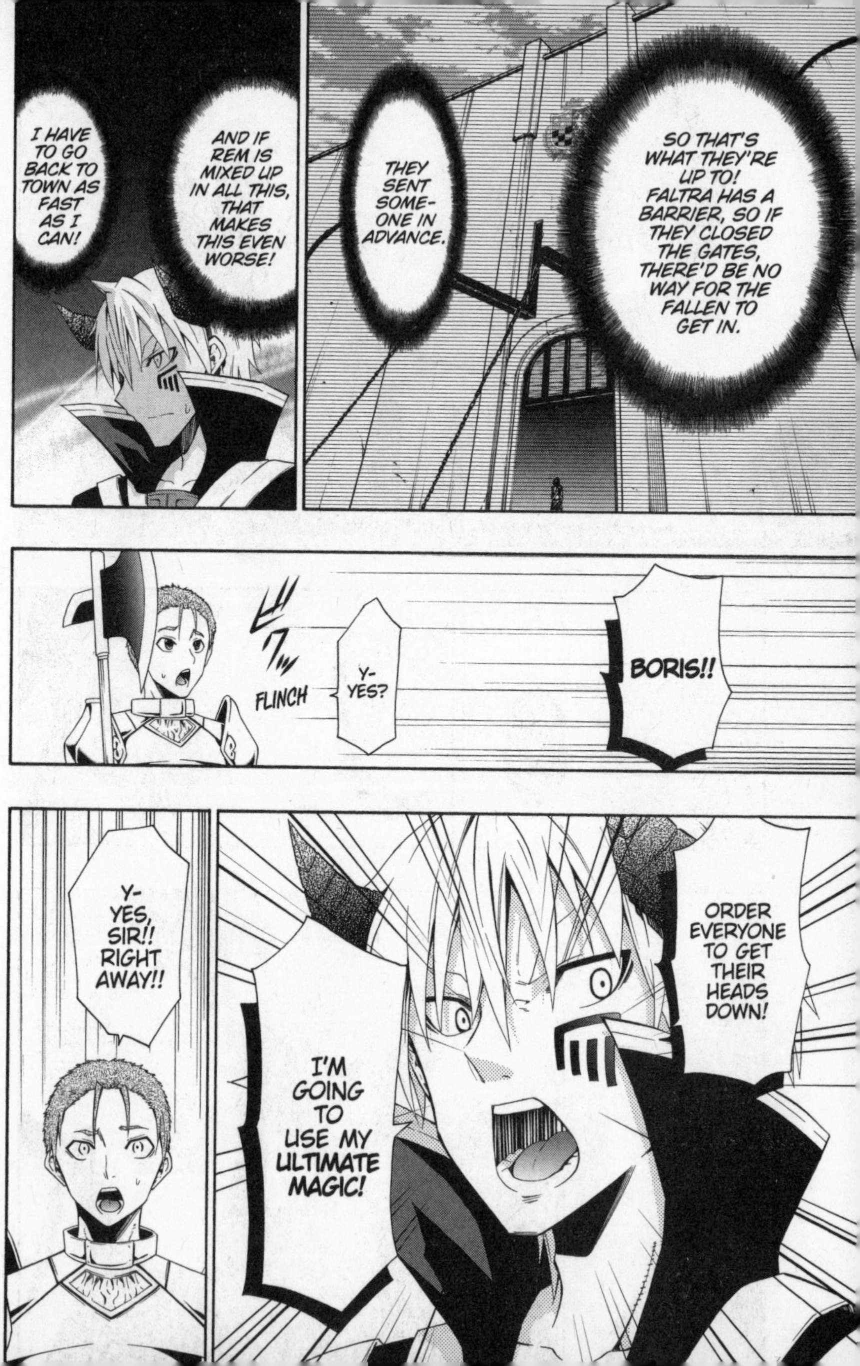
SO THAT'S WHAT THEY'RE UP TO! FALTRA HAS A BARRIER, SO IF THEY CLOSED THE GATES, THERE'D BE NO WAY FOR THE FALLEN TO GET IN.
THEY SENT SOME-ONE IN ADVANCE.
AND IF REM IS MIXED UP IN ALL THIS, THAT MAKES THIS EVEN WORSE!
I HAVE TO GO BACK TO TOWN AS FAST AS I CAN!
BORIS!!
Y-YES?
FLINCH
ORDER EVERYONE TO GET THEIR HEADS DOWN!
I'M GOING TO USE MY ULTIMATE MAGIC!
Y-YES, SIR!! RIGHT AWAY!!

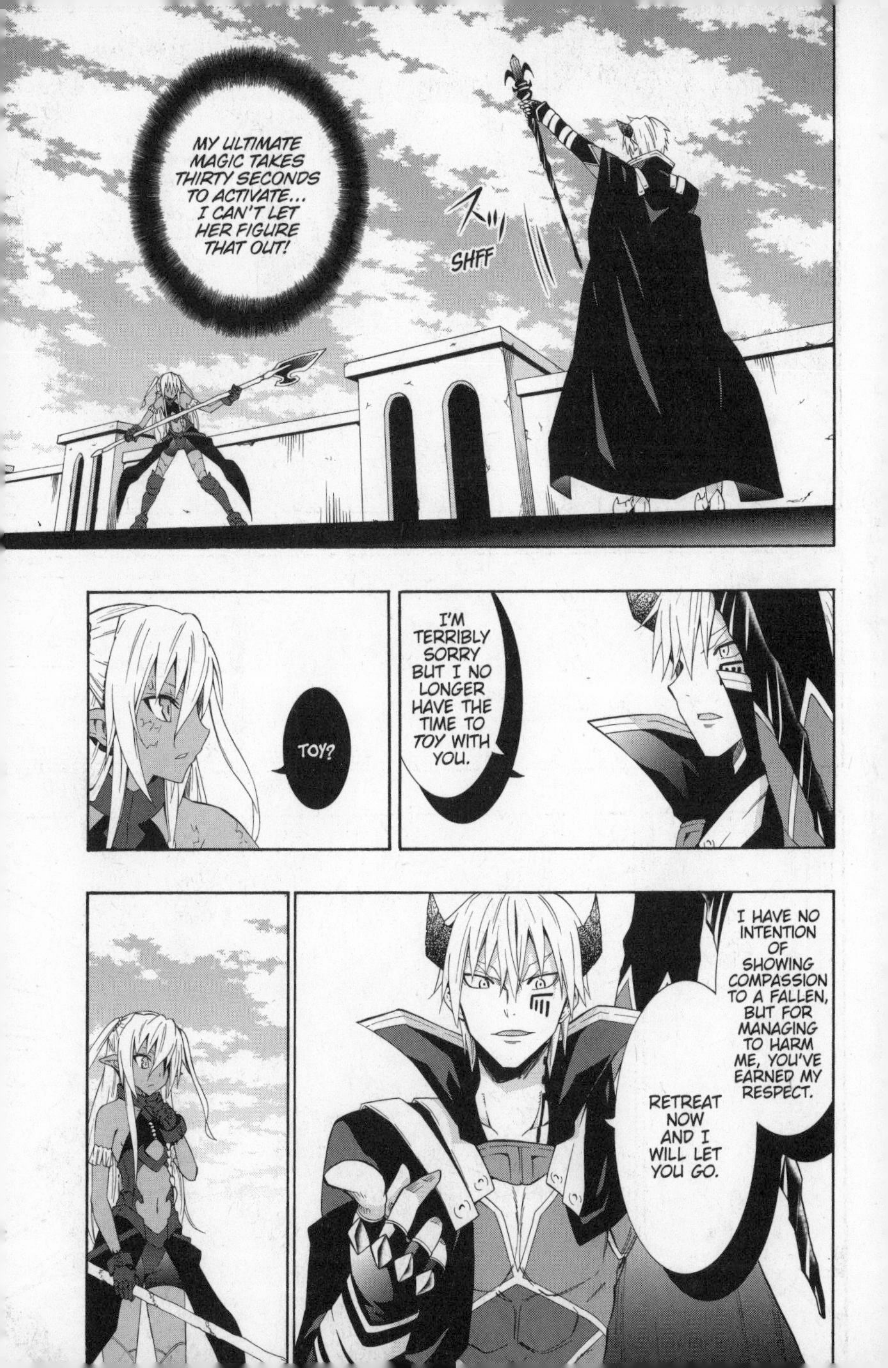
MY ULTIMATE MAGIC TAKES THIRTY SECONDS TO ACTIVATE... I CAN'T LET HER FIGURE THAT OUT!
スッ
SHFF
I'M TERRIBLY SORRY BUT I NO LONGER HAVE THE TIME TO TOY WITH YOU.
TOY?
I HAVE NO INTENTION OF SHOWING COMPASSION TO A FALLEN, BUT FOR MANAGING TO HARM ME, YOU'VE EARNED MY RESPECT.
RETREAT NOW AND I WILL LET YOU GO.

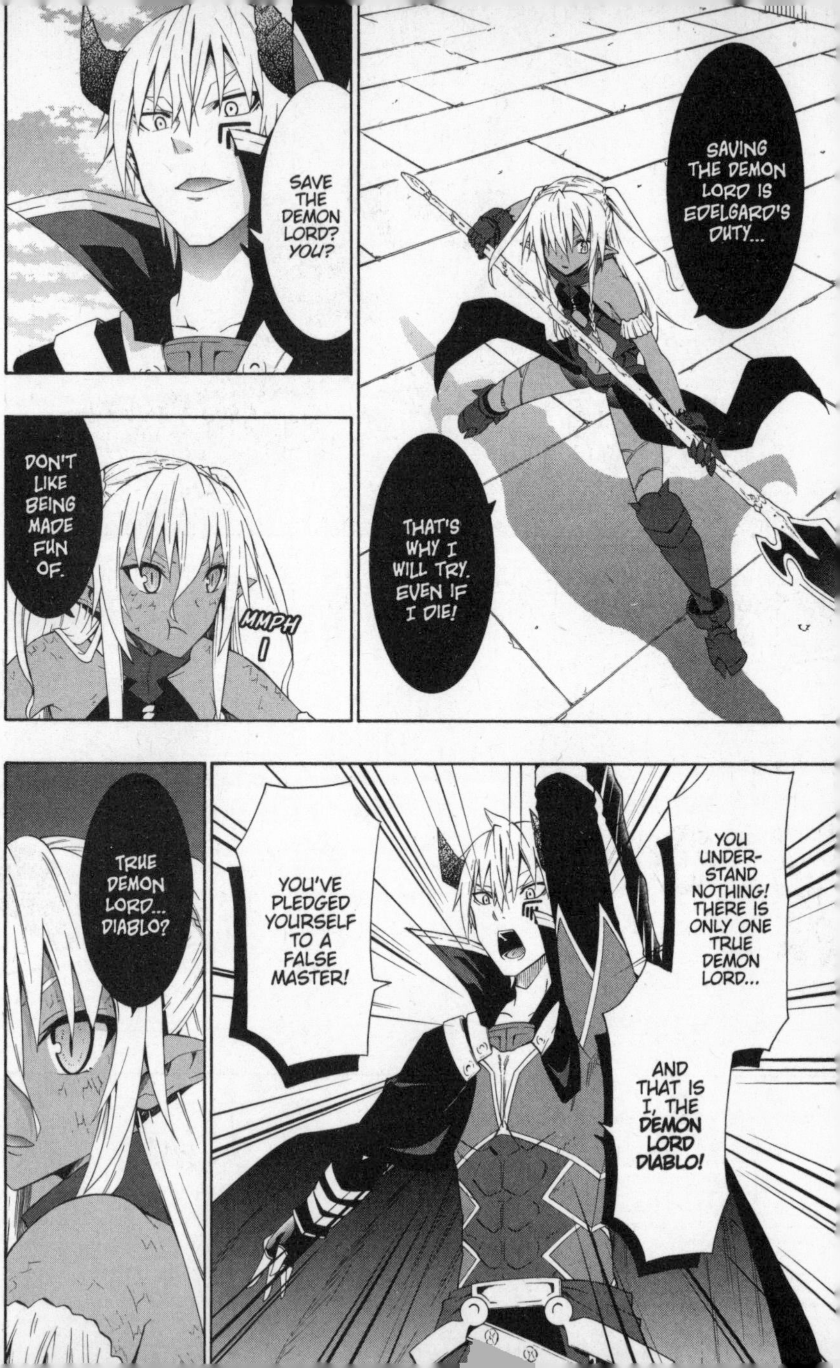
SAVING THE DEMON LORD IS EDELGARD'S DUTY...
THAT'S WHY I WILL TRY. EVEN IF I DIE!
SAVE THE DEMON LORD? YOU?
DON'T LIKE BEING MADE FUN OF.
MMPH
YOU UNDERSTAND NOTHING! THERE IS ONLY ONE TRUE DEMON LORD...
YOU'VE PLEDGED YOURSELF TO A FALSE MASTER!
AND THAT IS I, THE DEMON LORD DIABLO!
TRUE DEMON LORD... DIABLO?

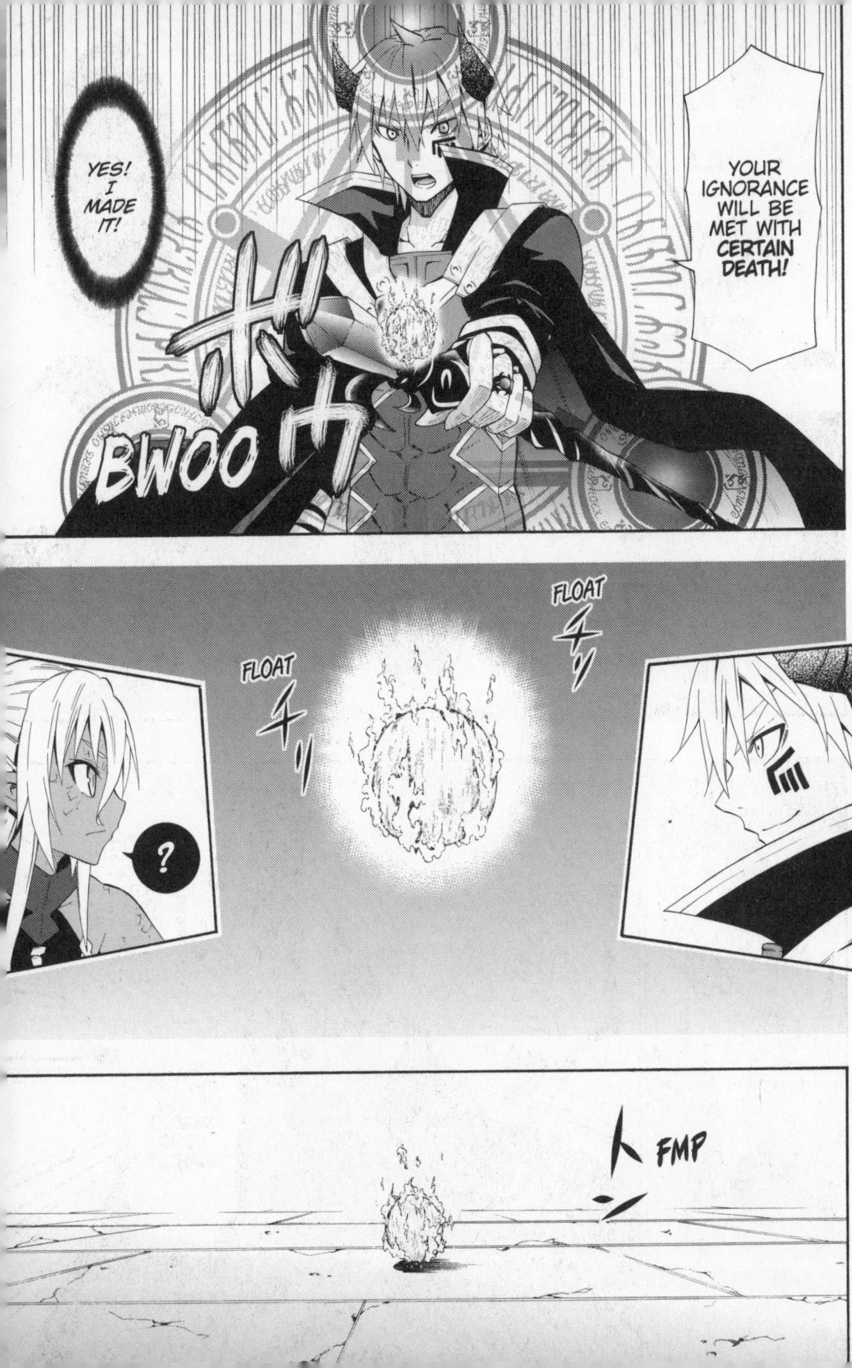
YOUR IGNORANCE WILL BE MET WITH CERTAIN DEATH!
YES! I MADE IT!
BWOO
FLOAT
FLOAT
?
FMP

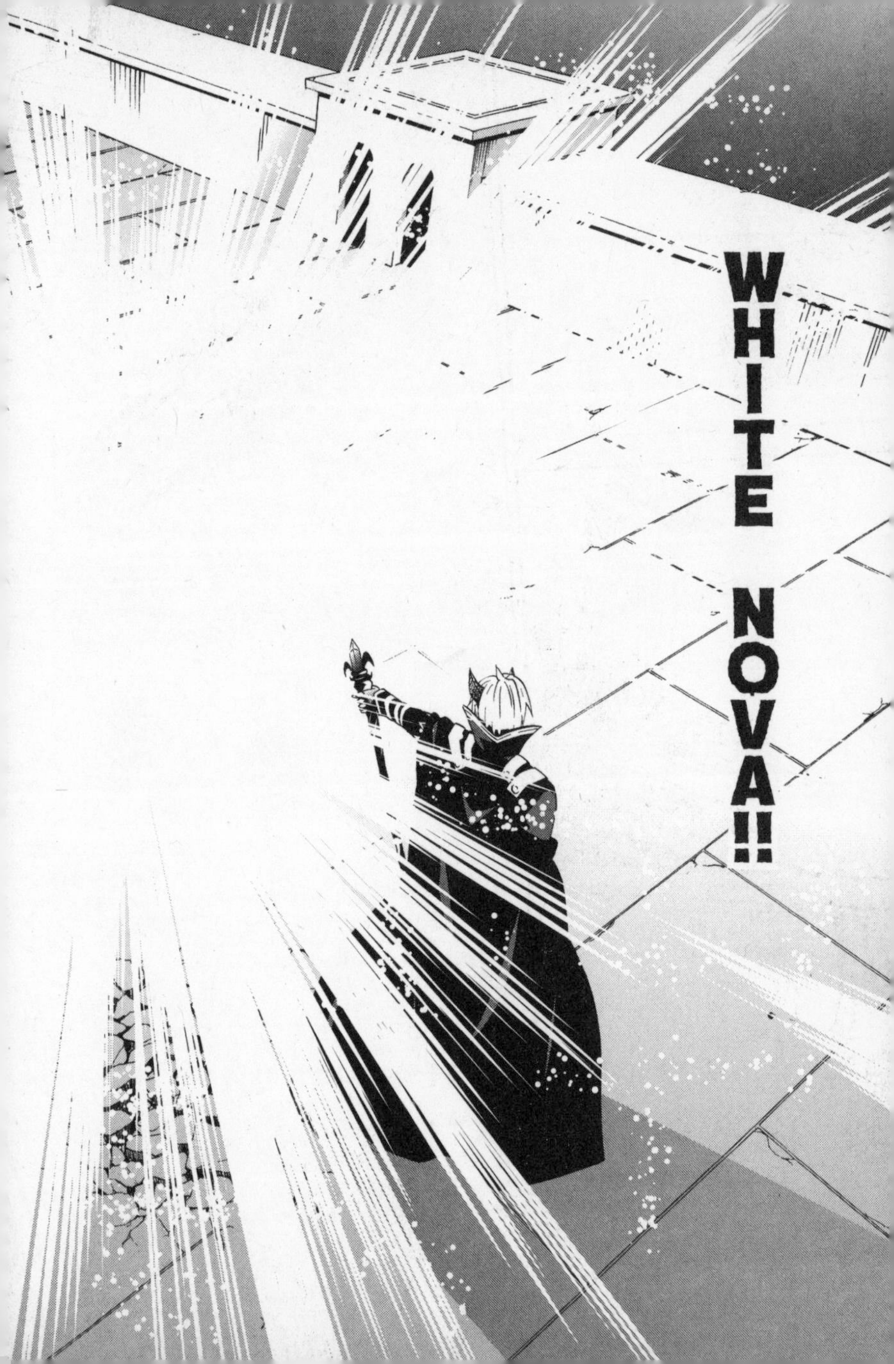
WHITE NOVA!!

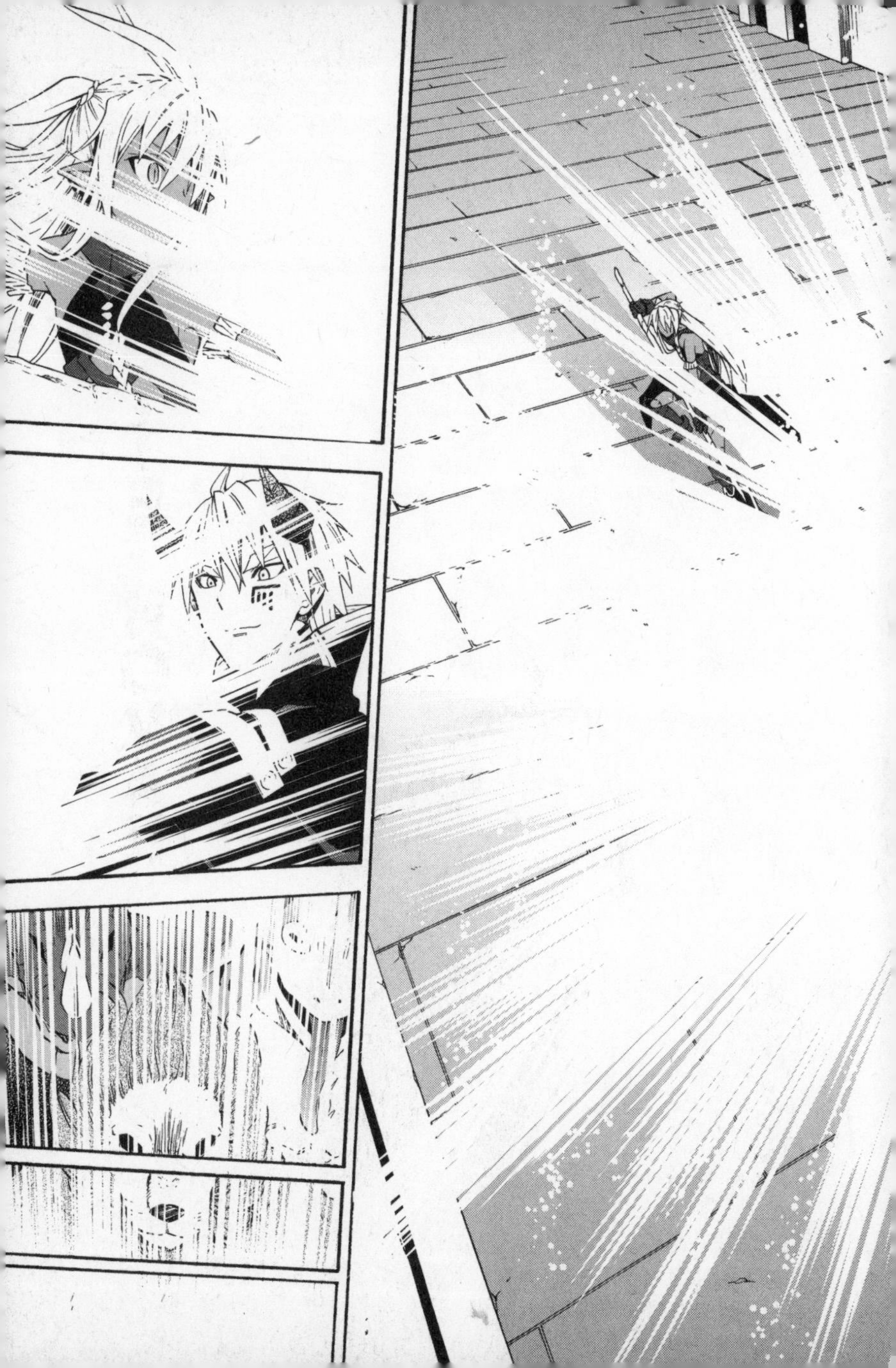

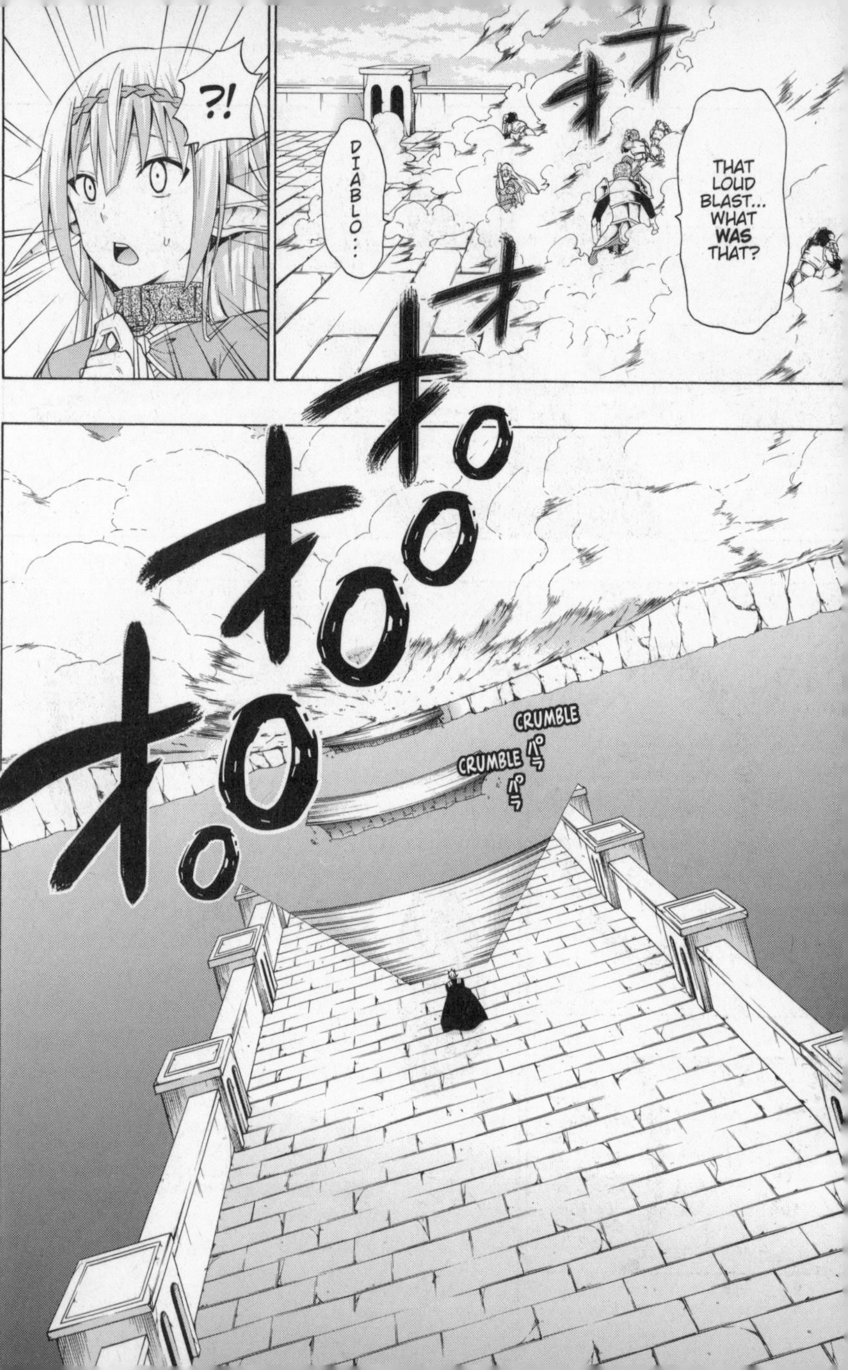
THAT LOUD BLAST... WHAT WAS THAT?
DIABLO...
?!
CRUMBLE パラ
CRUMBLE パラ

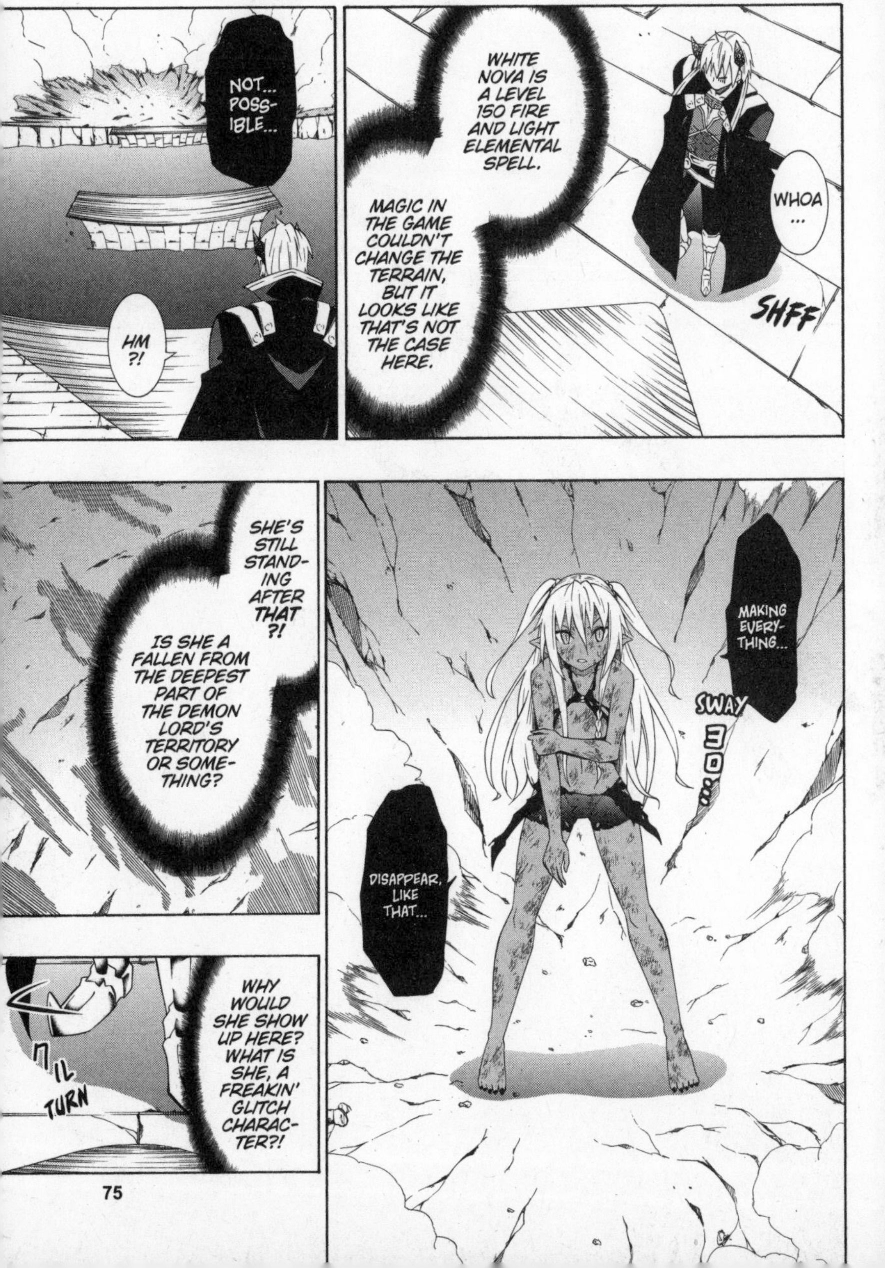
WHITE NOVA IS A LEVEL 150 FIRE AND LIGHT ELEMENTAL SPELL.
MAGIC IN THE GAME COULDN'T CHANGE THE TERRAIN, BUT IT LOOKS LIKE THAT'S NOT THE CASE HERE.
WHOA ...
SHFF
NOT... POSS-IBLE...
HM ?!
MAKING EVERY-THING...
SWAY
DISAPPEAR, LIKE THAT...
SHE'S STILL STAND-ING AFTER THAT ?!
IS SHE A FALLEN FROM THE DEEPEST PART OF THE DEMON LORD'S TERRITORY OR SOME-THING?
WHY WOULD SHE SHOW UP HERE? WHAT IS SHE, A FREAKIN' GLITCH CHARAC-TER?!
TURN

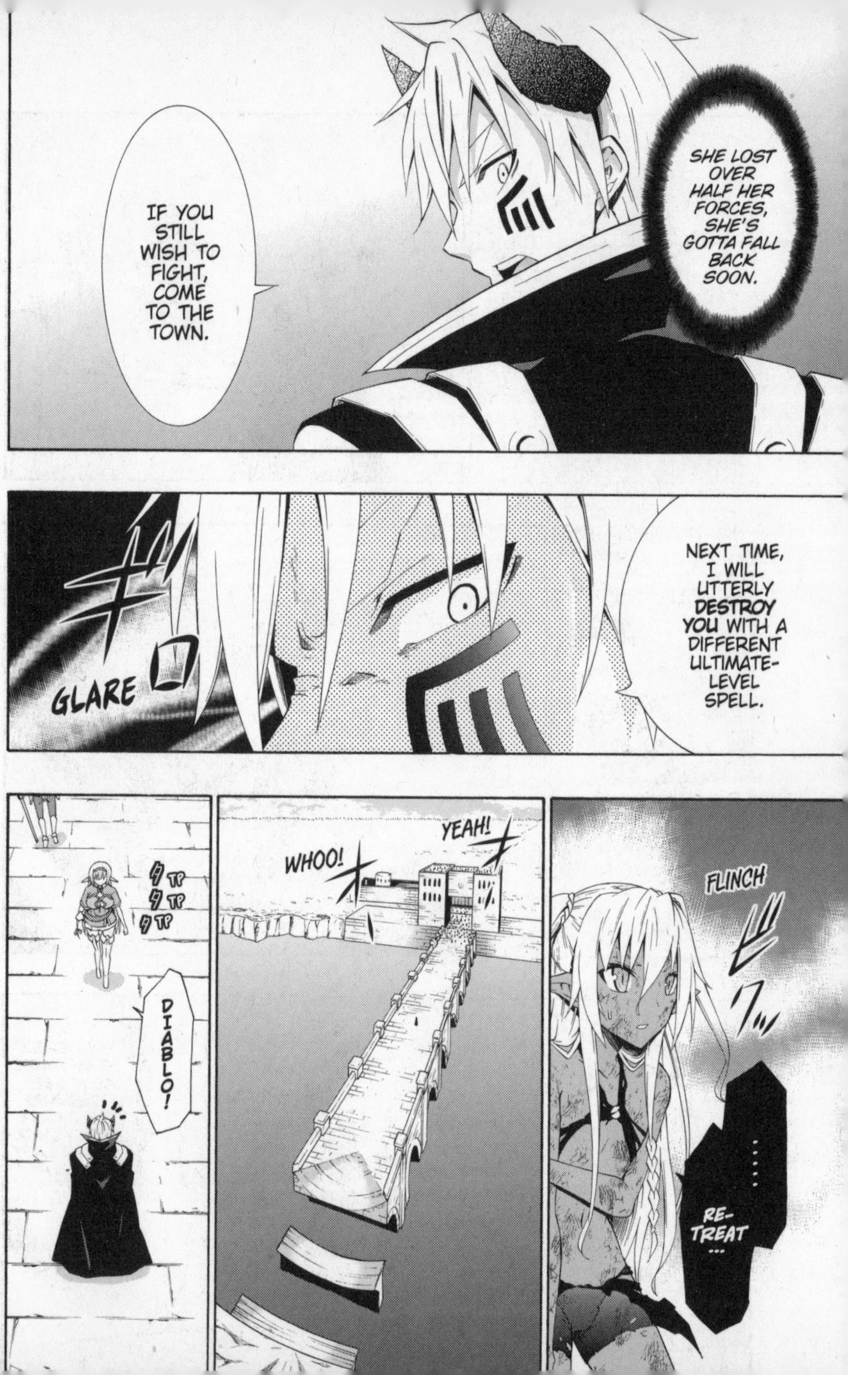
SHE LOST OVER HALF HER FORCES, SHE'S GOTTA FALL BACK SOON.
IF YOU STILL WISH TO FIGHT, COME TO THE TOWN.
NEXT TIME, I WILL UTTERLY **DESTROY YOU** WITH A DIFFERENT ULTIMATE-LEVEL SPELL.
GLARE
FLINCH
......
RE-TREAT...
YEAH!
WHOO!
TP
TP
TP
DIABLO!

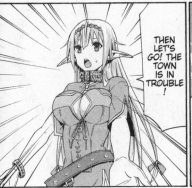

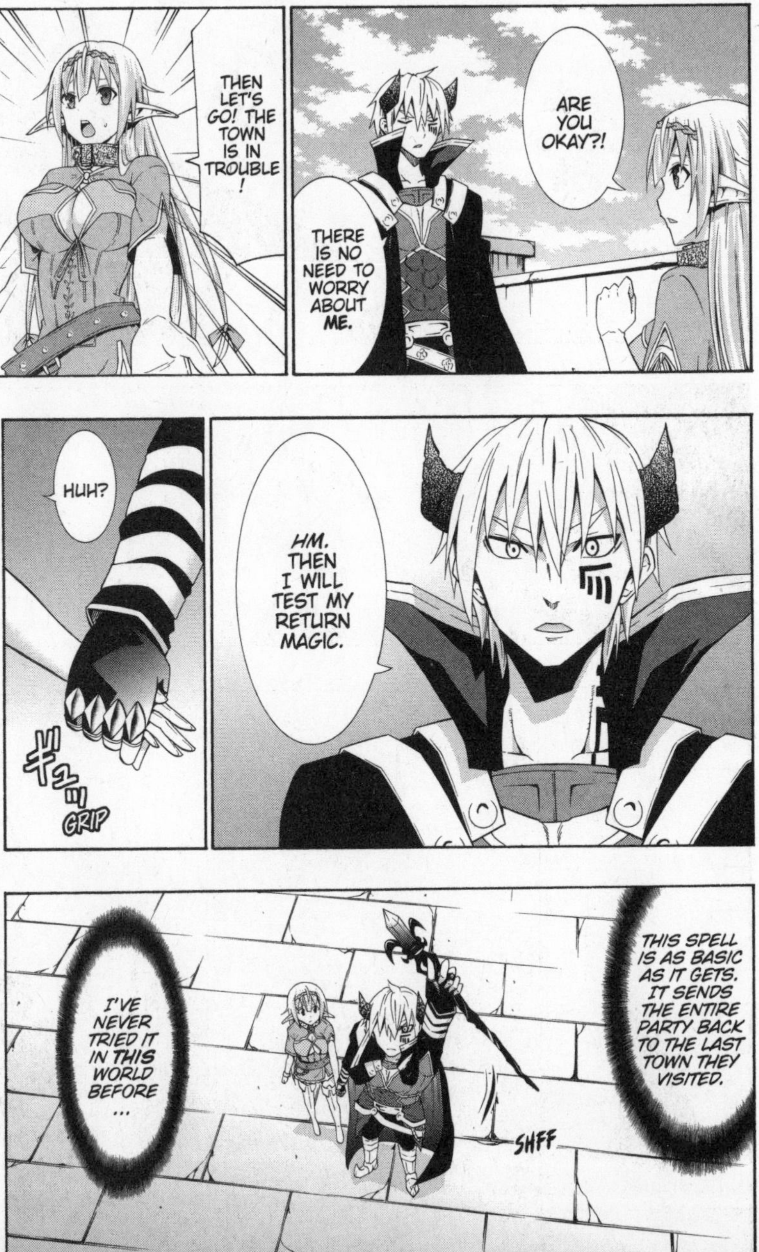
ARE YOU OKAY?!
THERE IS NO NEED TO WORRY ABOUT ME.
THEN LET'S GO! THE TOWN IS IN TROUBLE!
HM. THEN I WILL TEST MY RETURN MAGIC.
HUH?
ギュッ
GRIP
THIS SPELL IS AS BASIC AS IT GETS. IT SENDS THE ENTIRE PARTY BACK TO THE LAST TOWN THEY VISITED.
SHFF
I'VE NEVER TRIED IT IN THIS WORLD BEFORE...

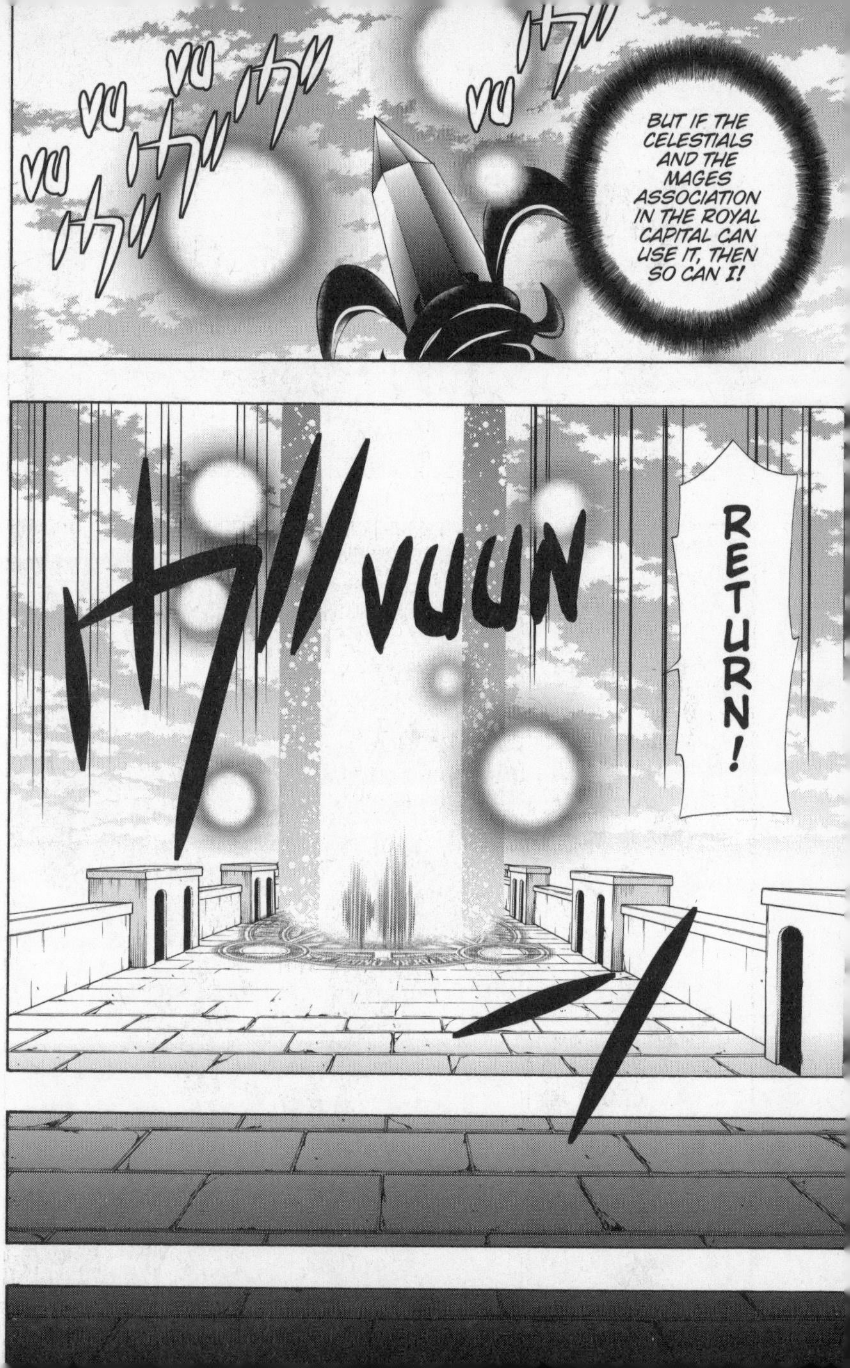
BUT IF THE CELESTIALS AND THE MAGES ASSOCIATION IN THE ROYAL CAPITAL CAN USE IT, THEN SO CAN I!
VU VU VU VU
VUUN
RETURN!

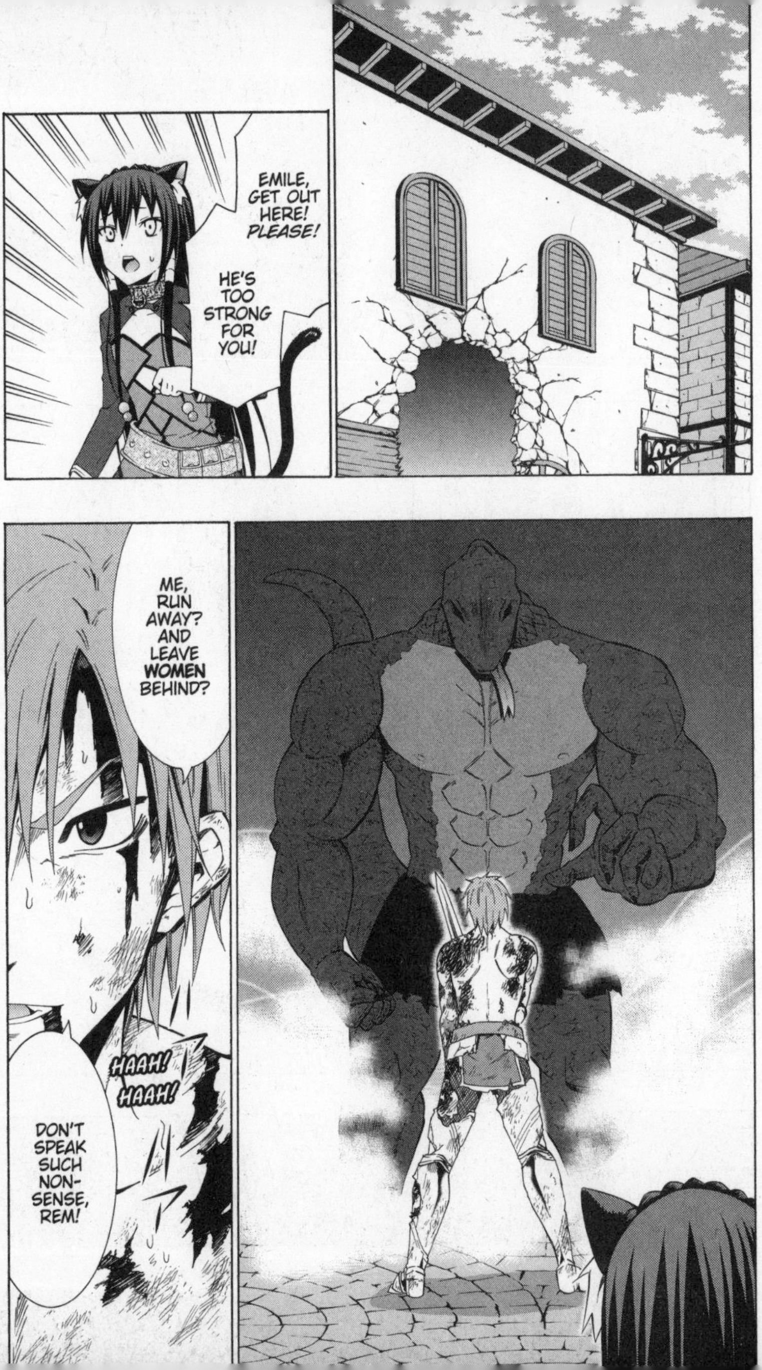
EMILE, GET OUT HERE! PLEASE!
HE'S TOO STRONG FOR YOU!
ME, RUN AWAY? AND LEAVE WOMEN BEHIND?
HAAH! HAAH!
DON'T SPEAK SUCH NON-SENSE, REM!

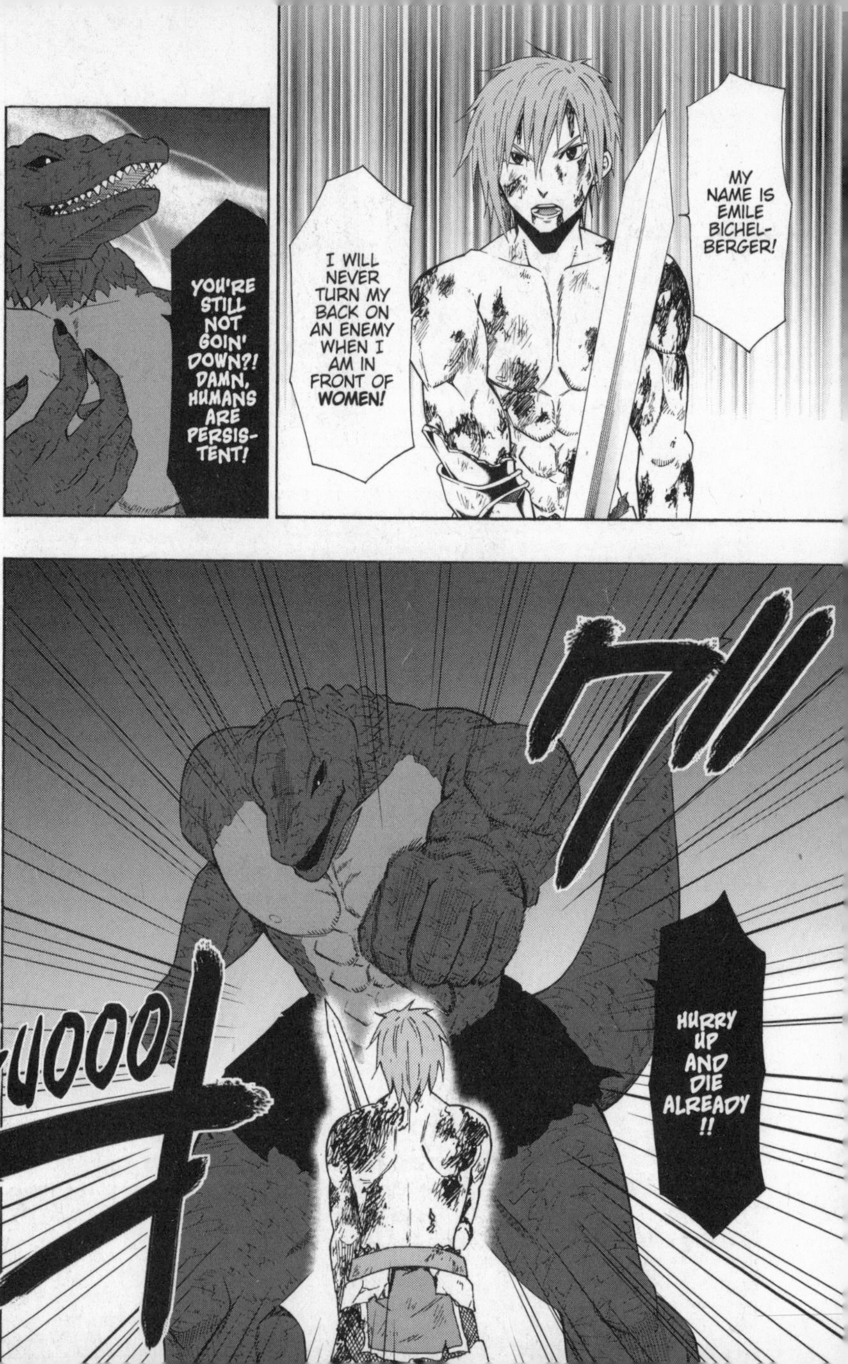
MY NAME IS EMILE BICHEL-BERGER!
I WILL NEVER TURN MY BACK ON AN ENEMY WHEN I AM IN FRONT OF WOMEN!
YOU'RE STILL NOT GOIN' DOWN?! DAMN, HUMANS ARE PERSIS-TENT!
HURRY UP AND DIE ALREADY!!
GUOOO

HOW NOT
TO SUMMON A
DEMON LORD

12 TRYING TO SAVE THE WORLD IV

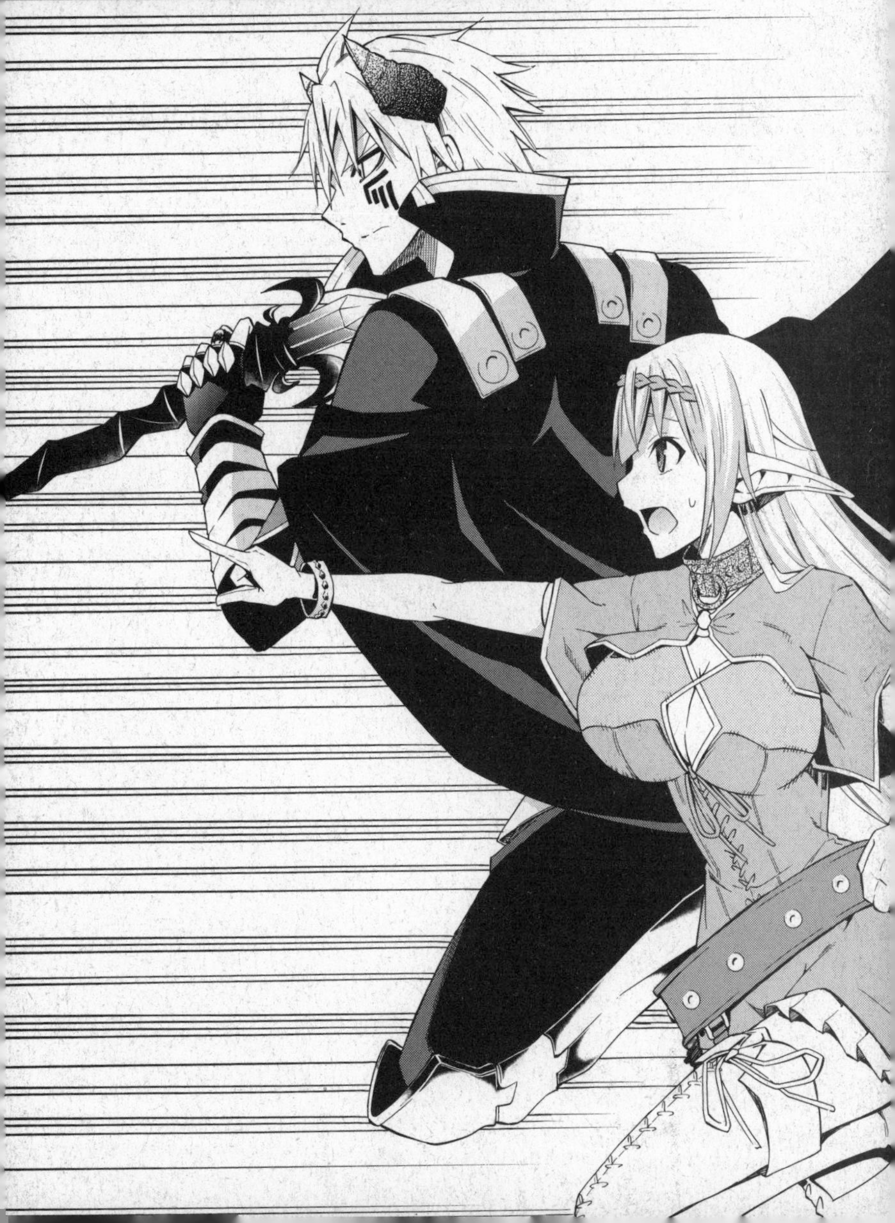

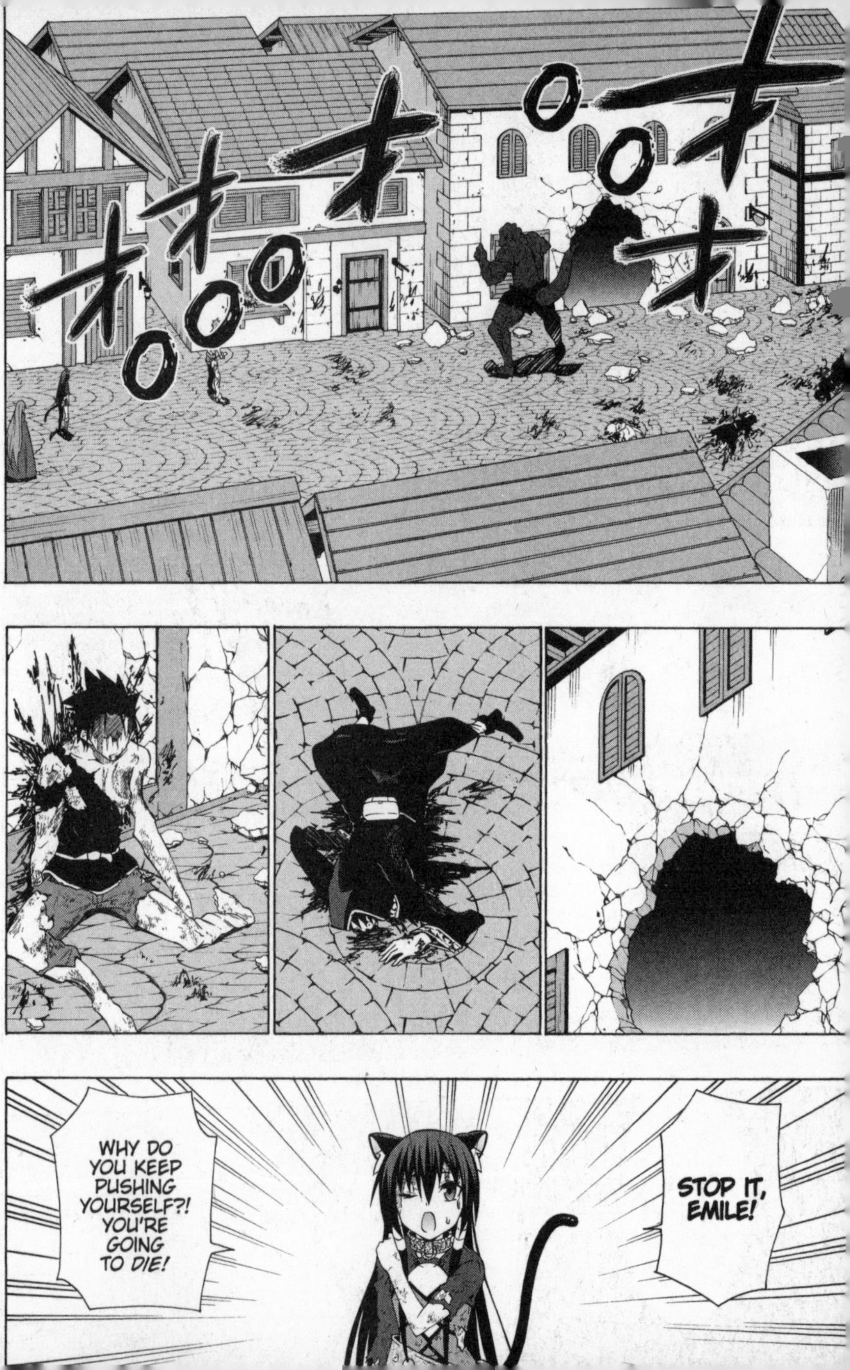
STOP IT, EMILE!
WHY DO YOU KEEP PUSHING YOURSELF?! YOU'RE GOING TO DIE!

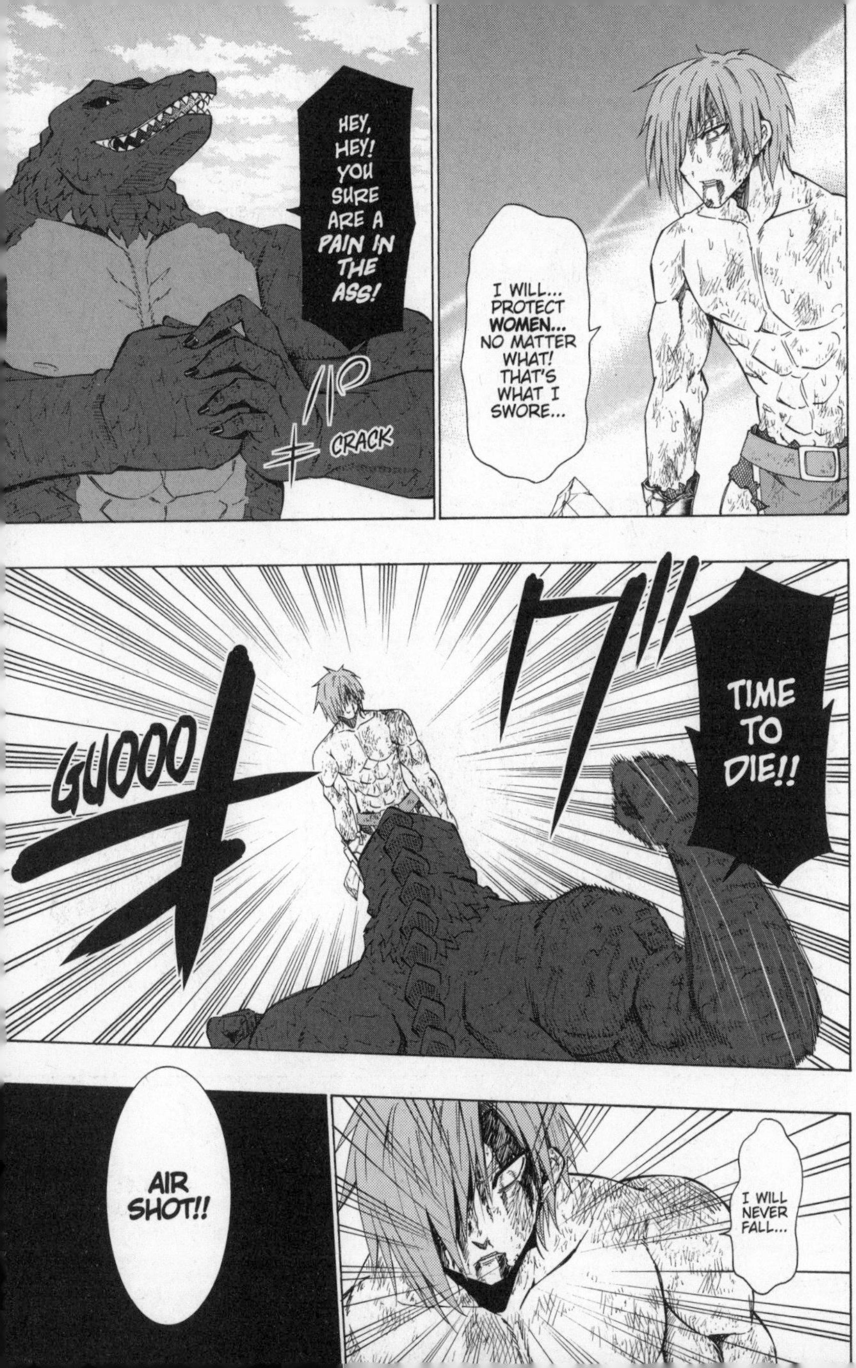
I WILL... PROTECT WOMEN... NO MATTER WHAT! THAT'S WHAT I SWORE...
HEY, HEY! YOU SURE ARE A PAIN IN THE ASS!
CRACK
TIME TO DIE!!
GUOOO
I WILL NEVER FALL...
AIR SHOT!!

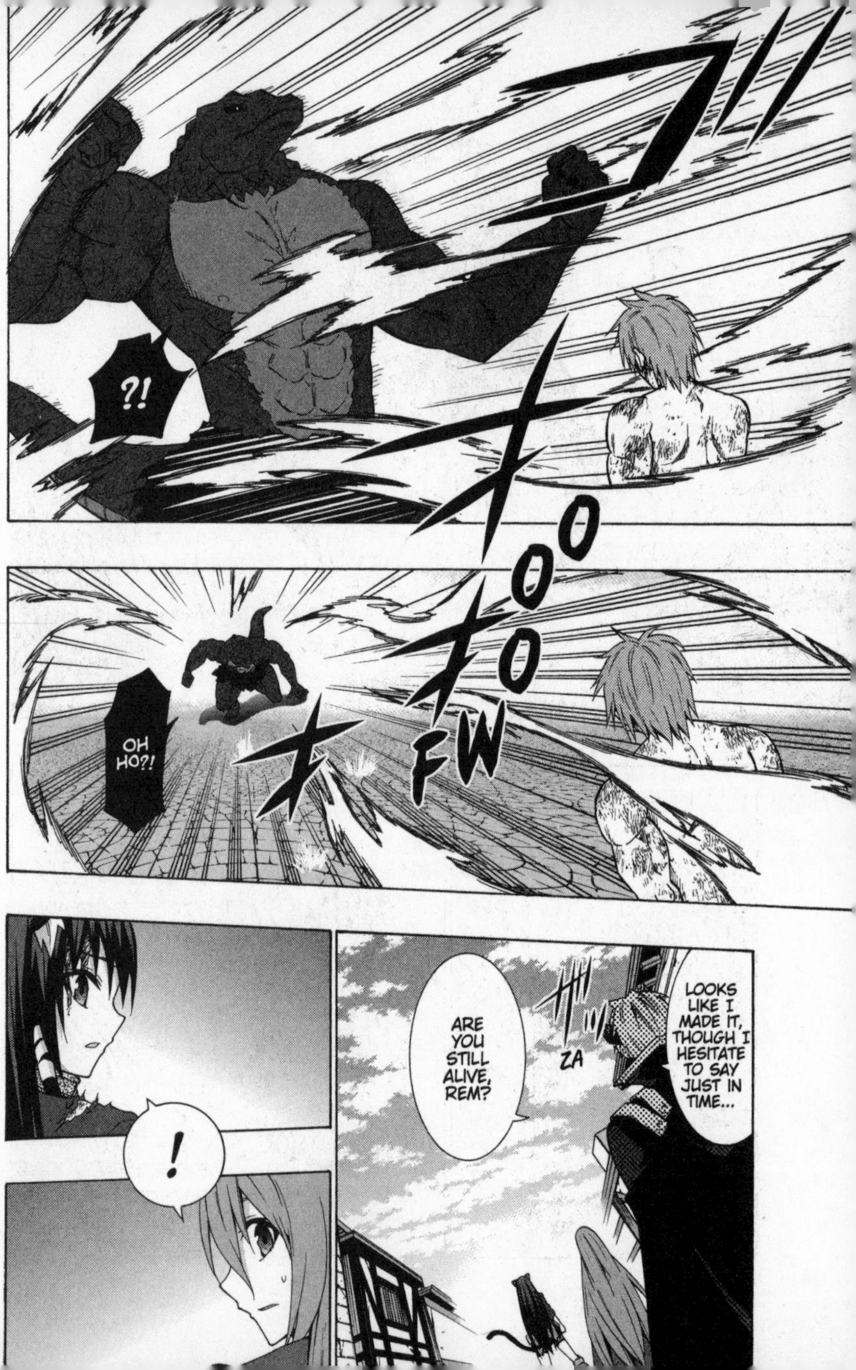
?!
FWOOO
OH HO?!
LOOKS LIKE I MADE IT, THOUGH I HESITATE TO SAY JUST IN TIME...
ZA
ARE YOU STILL ALIVE, REM?
!

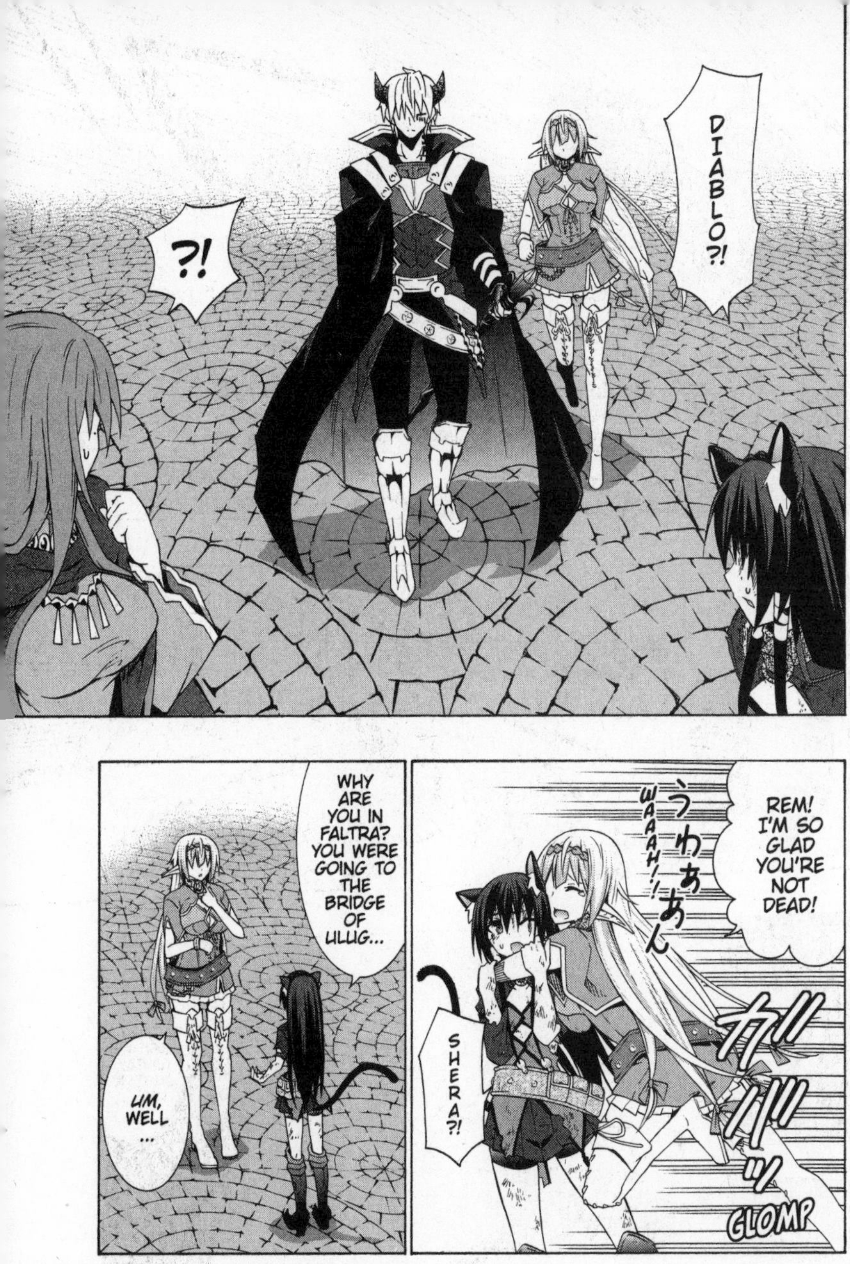
DIABLO?!
?!
REM! I'M SO GLAD YOU'RE NOT DEAD!
うわぁあん
WAAAH!!
SHERA?!
GLOMP
WHY ARE YOU IN FALTRA? YOU WERE GOING TO THE BRIDGE OF ULUG...
UM, WELL...

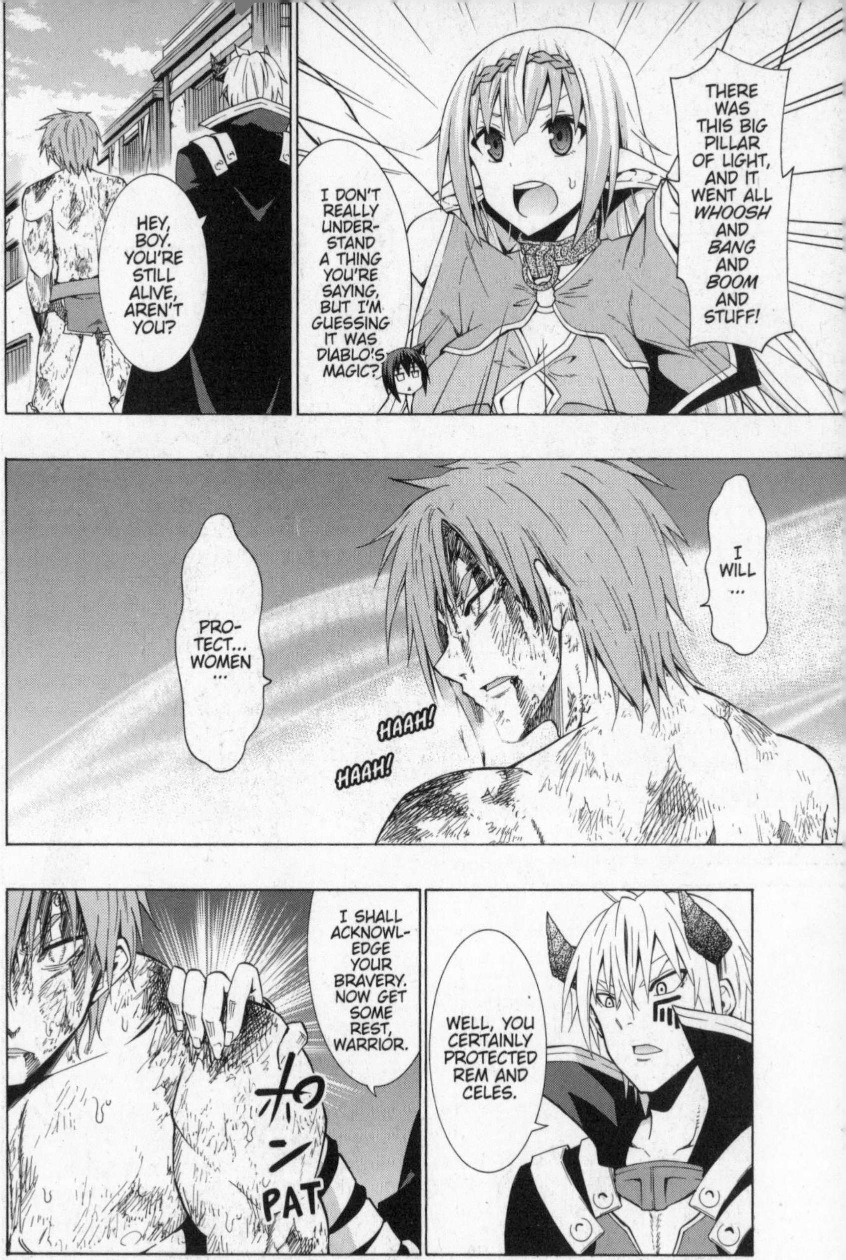
THERE WAS THIS BIG PILLAR OF LIGHT, AND IT WENT ALL *WHOOSH* AND *BANG* AND *BOOM* AND STUFF!
I DON'T REALLY UNDERSTAND A THING YOU'RE SAYING, BUT I'M GUESSING IT WAS DIABLO'S MAGIC?
HEY, BOY. YOU'RE STILL ALIVE, AREN'T YOU?
I WILL ...
PROTECT... WOMEN ...
HAAH!
HAAH!
WELL, YOU CERTAINLY PROTECTED REM AND CELES.
I SHALL ACKNOWLEDGE YOUR BRAVERY. NOW GET SOME REST, WARRIOR.
PAT

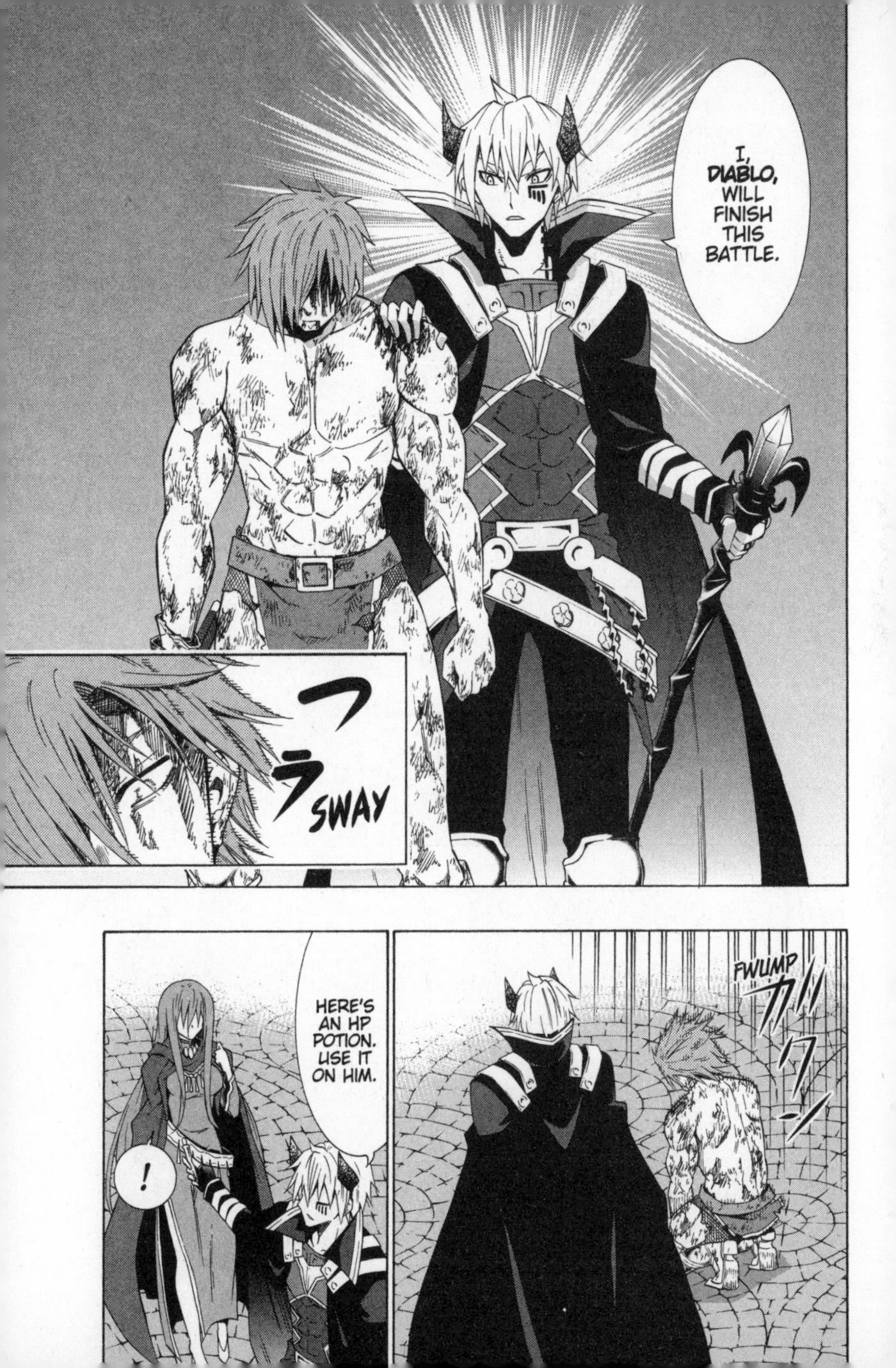
I, DIABLO, WILL FINISH THIS BATTLE.
フラ
SWAY
FWUMP
HERE'S AN HP POTION. USE IT ON HIM.
!

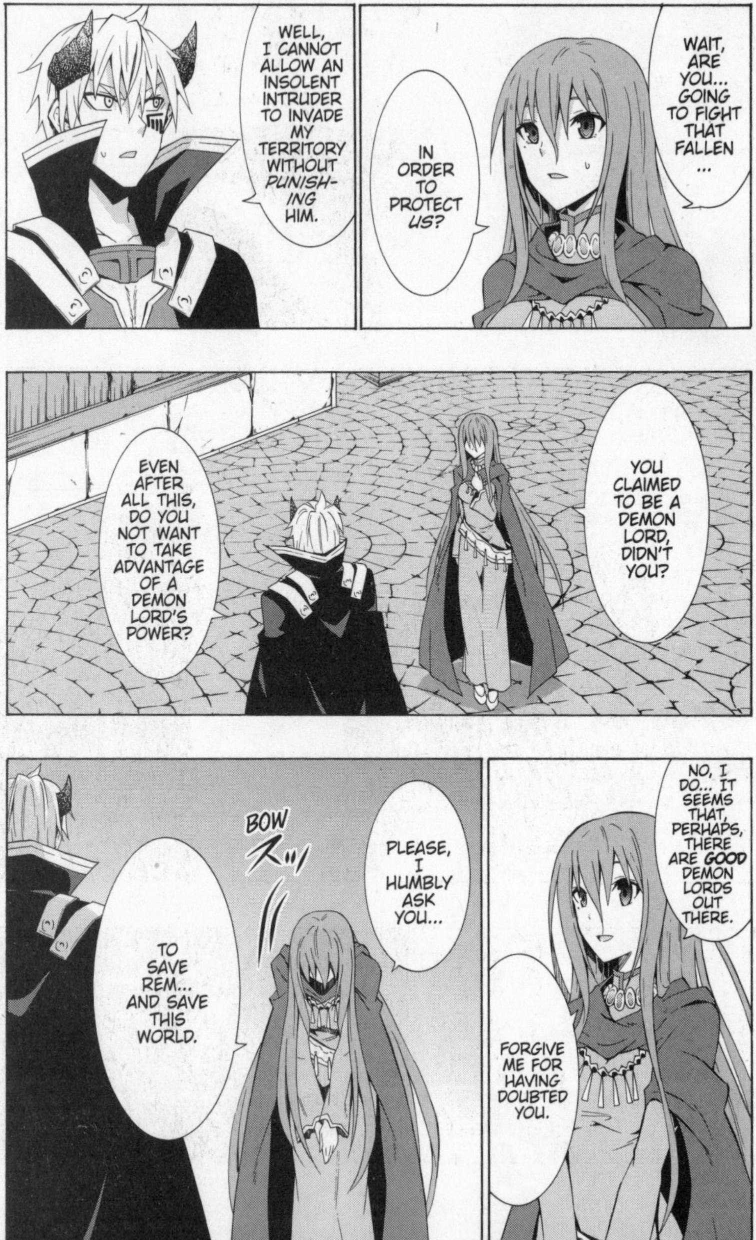
WAIT, ARE YOU... GOING TO FIGHT THAT FALLEN ...
IN ORDER TO PROTECT *US*?
WELL, I CANNOT ALLOW AN INSOLENT INTRUDER TO INVADE MY TERRITORY WITHOUT *PUNISHING* HIM.
YOU CLAIMED TO BE A DEMON LORD, DIDN'T YOU?
EVEN AFTER ALL THIS, DO YOU NOT WANT TO TAKE ADVANTAGE OF A DEMON LORD'S POWER?
NO, I DO... IT SEEMS THAT, PERHAPS, THERE ARE **GOOD** DEMON LORDS OUT THERE.
FORGIVE ME FOR HAVING DOUBTED YOU.
BOW
スッ
PLEASE, I HUMBLY ASK YOU...
TO SAVE REM... AND SAVE THIS WORLD.

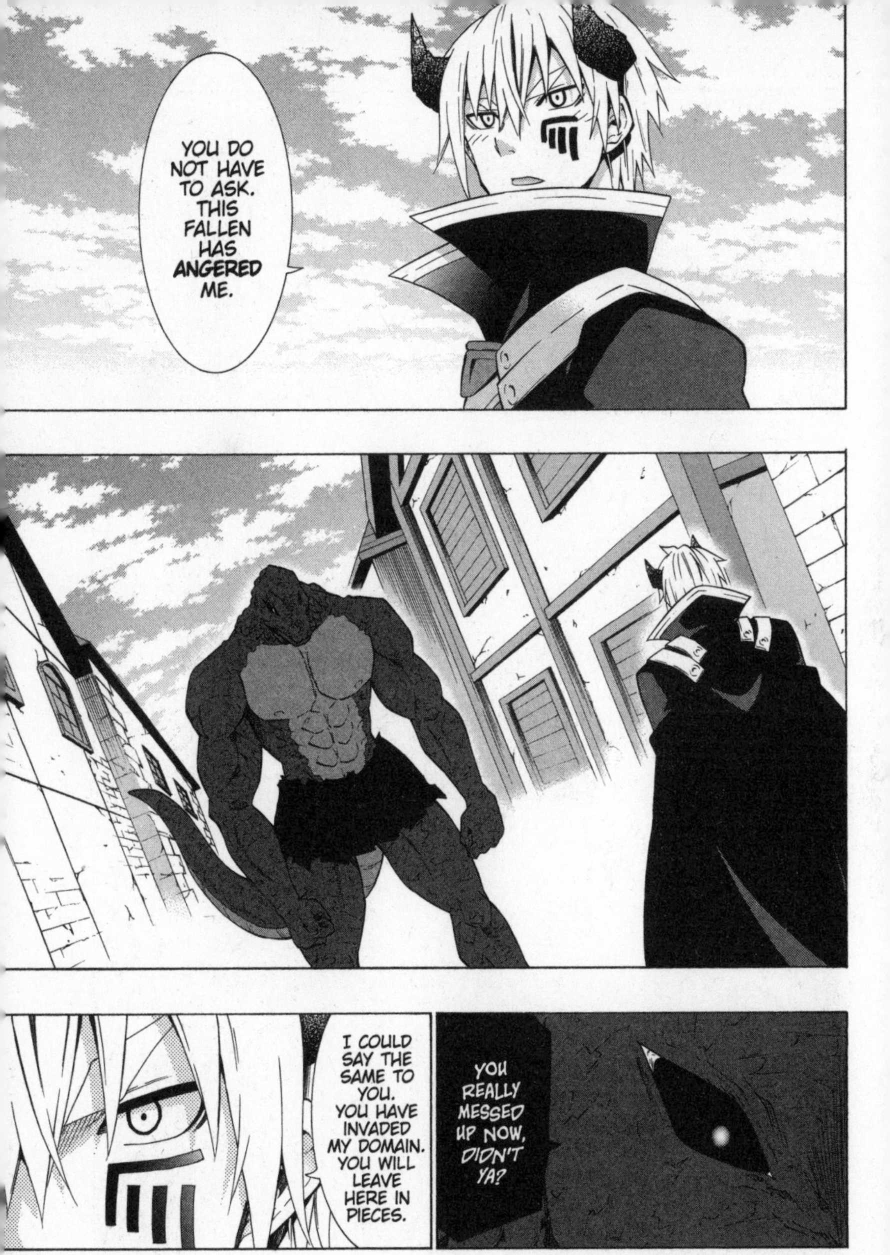
YOU DO NOT HAVE TO ASK. THIS FALLEN HAS ANGERED ME.
YOU REALLY MESSED UP NOW, DIDN'T YA?
I COULD SAY THE SAME TO YOU. YOU HAVE INVADED MY DOMAIN. YOU WILL LEAVE HERE IN PIECES.

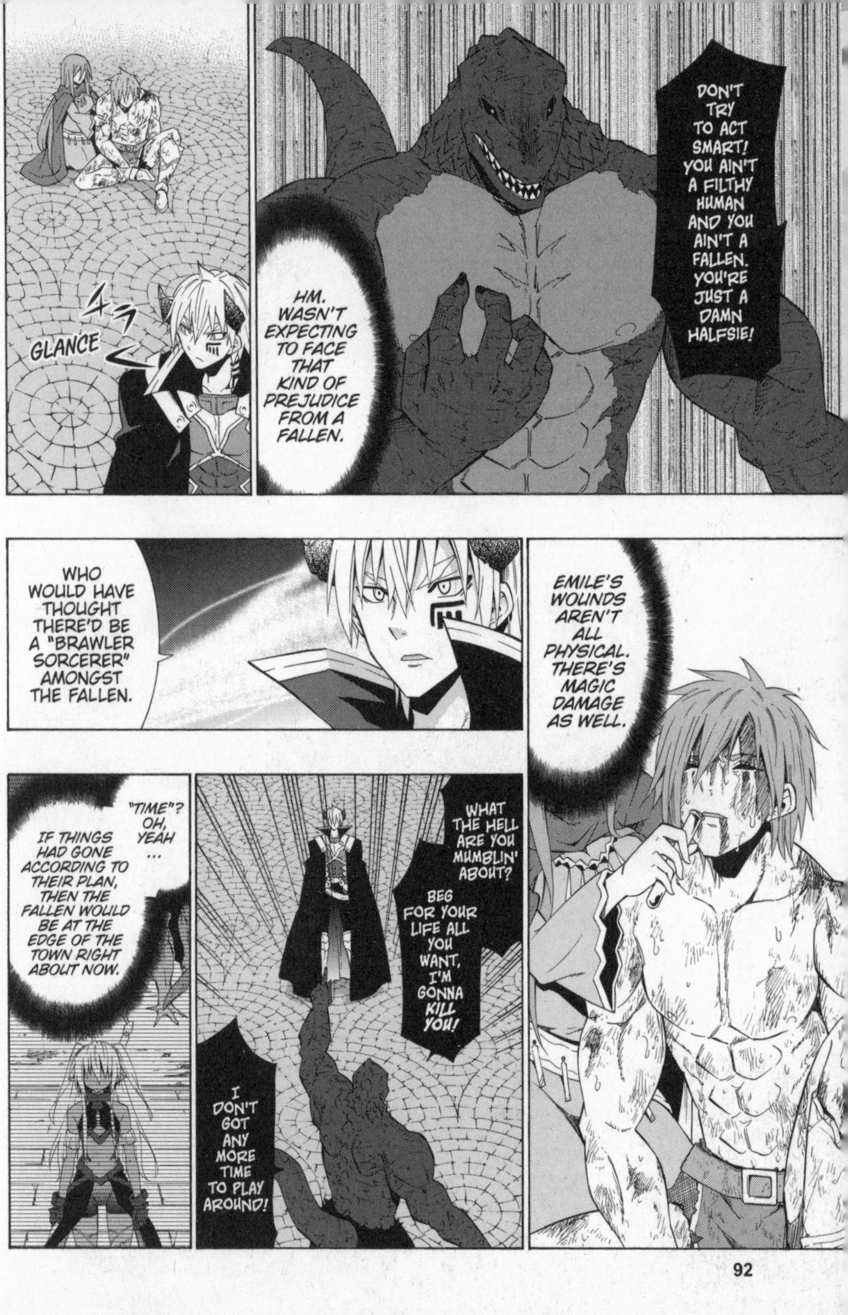
DON'T TRY TO ACT SMART! YOU AIN'T A FILTHY HUMAN AND YOU AIN'T A FALLEN. YOU'RE JUST A DAMN HALFSIE!
HM. WASN'T EXPECTING TO FACE THAT KIND OF PREJUDICE FROM A FALLEN.
GLANCE
EMILE'S WOUNDS AREN'T ALL PHYSICAL. THERE'S MAGIC DAMAGE AS WELL.
WHO WOULD HAVE THOUGHT THERE'D BE A "BRAWLER SORCERER" AMONGST THE FALLEN.
WHAT THE HELL ARE YOU MUMBLIN' ABOUT?
BEG FOR YOUR LIFE ALL YOU WANT, I'M GONNA KILL YOU!
I DON'T GOT ANY MORE TIME TO PLAY AROUND!
"TIME"? OH, YEAH ...
IF THINGS HAD GONE ACCORDING TO THEIR PLAN, THEN THE FALLEN WOULD BE AT THE EDGE OF THE TOWN RIGHT ABOUT NOW.

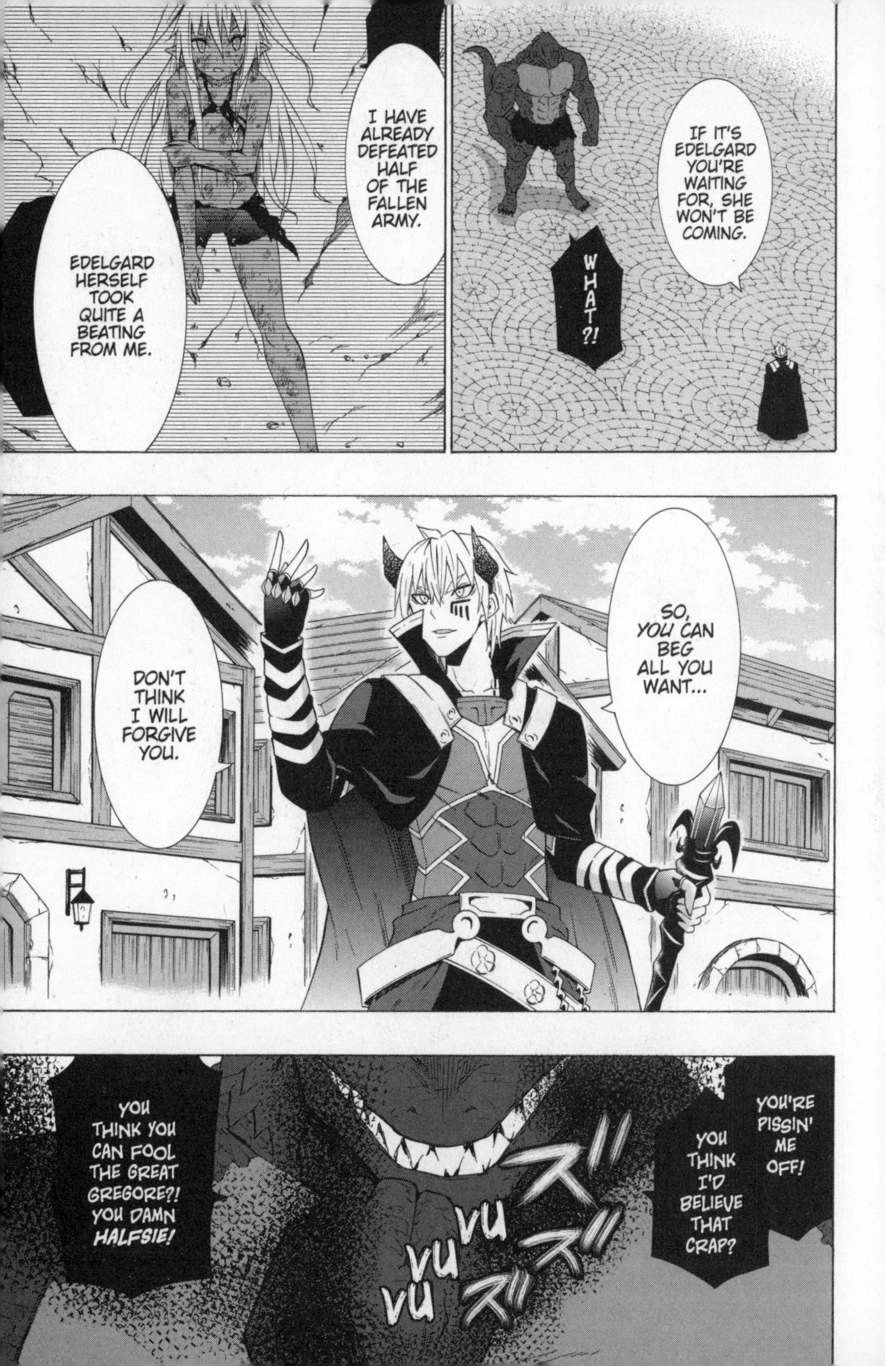

IF IT'S EDELGARD YOU'RE WAITING FOR, SHE WON'T BE COMING.
WHAT?!
I HAVE ALREADY DEFEATED HALF OF THE FALLEN ARMY.
EDELGARD HERSELF TOOK QUITE A BEATING FROM ME.
SO, YOU CAN BEG ALL YOU WANT...
DON'T THINK I WILL FORGIVE YOU.
YOU'RE PISSIN' ME OFF!
YOU THINK I'D BELIEVE THAT CRAP?
VU VU VU VU
YOU THINK YOU CAN FOOL THE GREAT GREGORE?! YOU DAMN HALFSIE!

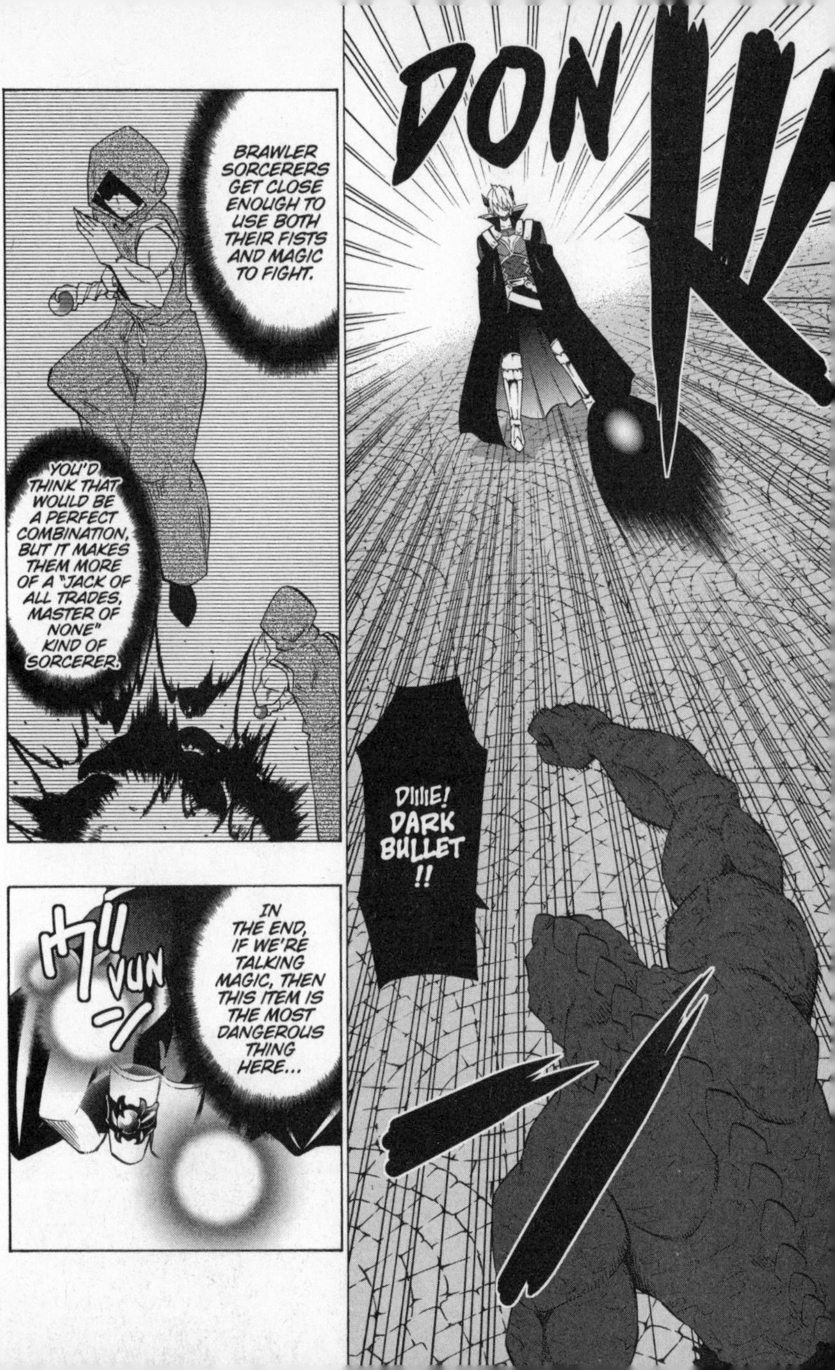
DON
DIIIE! DARK BULLET!!
BRAWLER SORCERERS GET CLOSE ENOUGH TO USE BOTH THEIR FISTS AND MAGIC TO FIGHT.
YOU'D THINK THAT WOULD BE A PERFECT COMBINATION, BUT IT MAKES THEM MORE OF A "JACK OF ALL TRADES, MASTER OF NONE" KIND OF SORCERER.
IN THE END, IF WE'RE TALKING MAGIC, THEN THIS ITEM IS THE MOST DANGEROUS THING HERE...
VUN

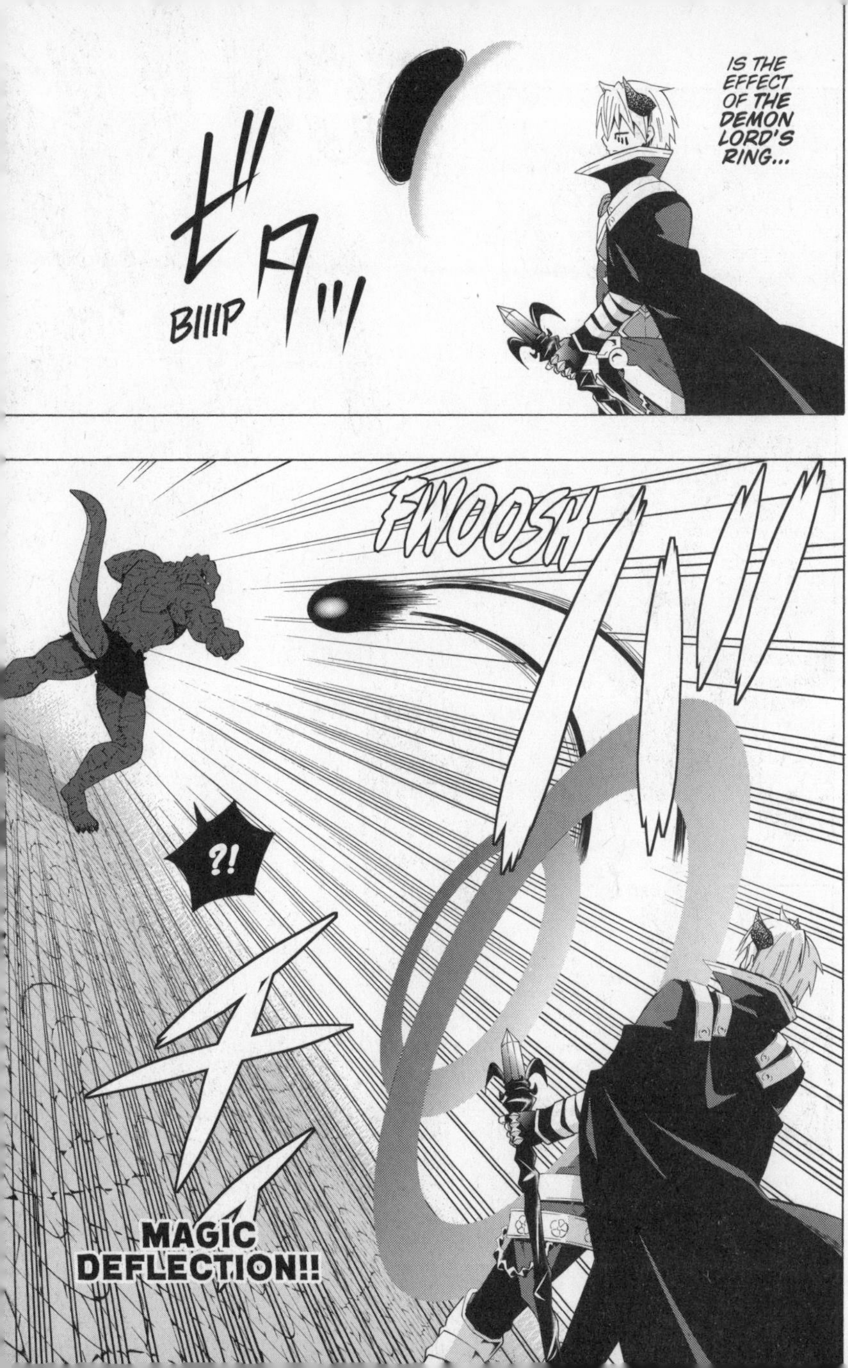
IS THE EFFECT OF THE DEMON LORD'S RING...
ゼタッ
BIIIP
FWOOSH
?!
MAGIC DEFLECTION!!

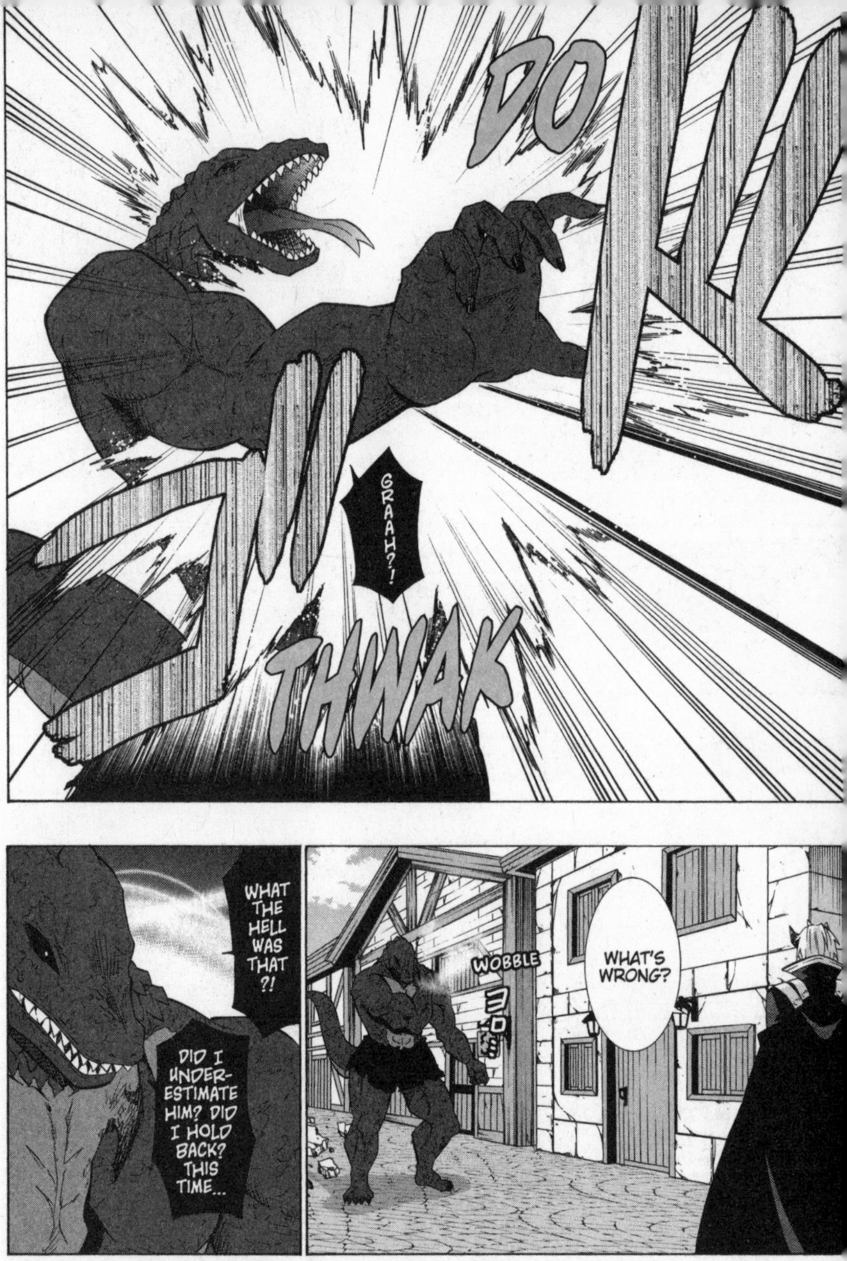

DO
GRAAH?!
THWAK
WHAT'S WRONG?
WOBBLE
ヨロ
WHAT THE HELL WAS THAT?!
DID I UNDER-ESTIMATE HIM? DID I HOLD BACK? THIS TIME...

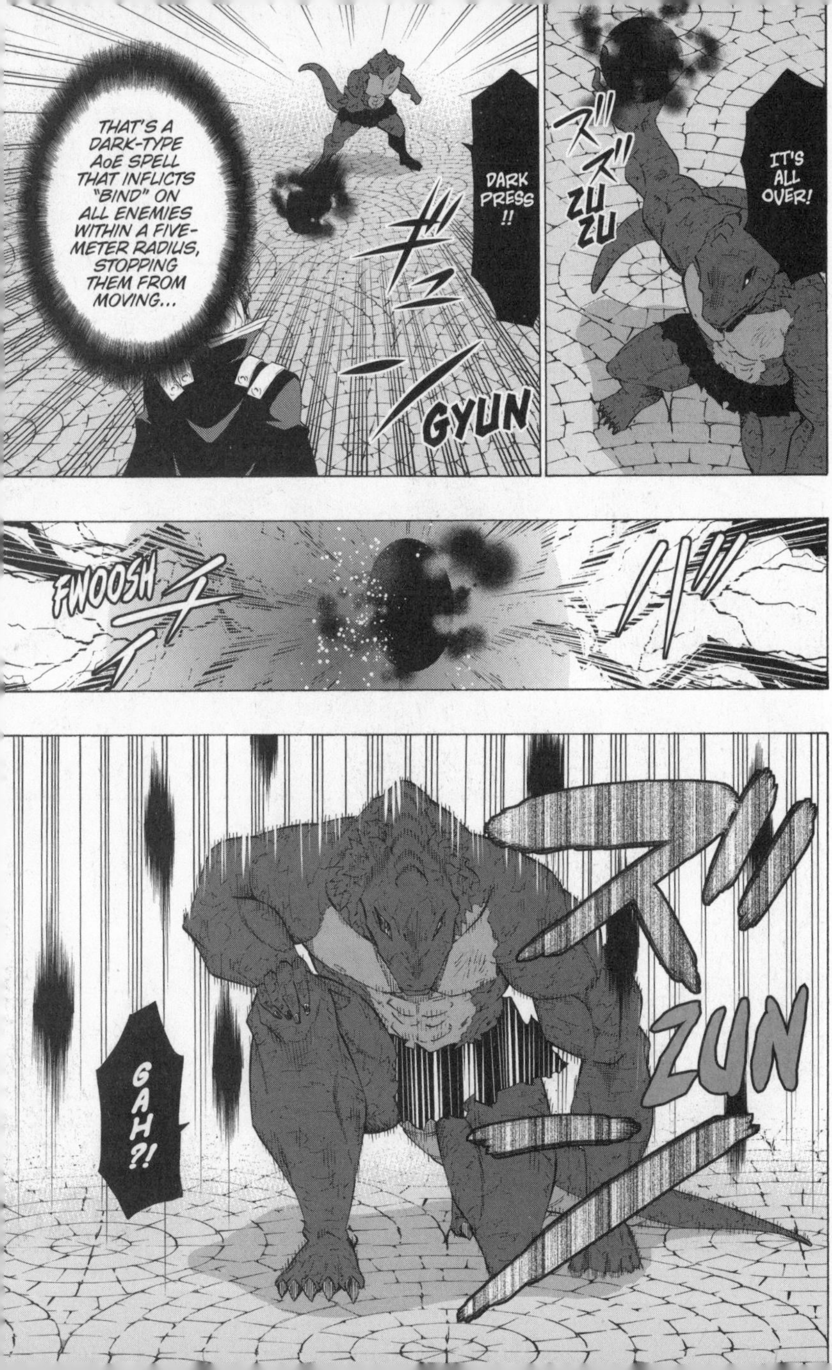
IT'S ALL OVER!
ZUZU ZUZU
DARK PRESS !!
THAT'S A DARK-TYPE AoE SPELL THAT INFLICTS "BIND" ON ALL ENEMIES WITHIN A FIVE-METER RADIUS, STOPPING THEM FROM MOVING...
GYUN
FWOOSH
ZUN
GAH?!

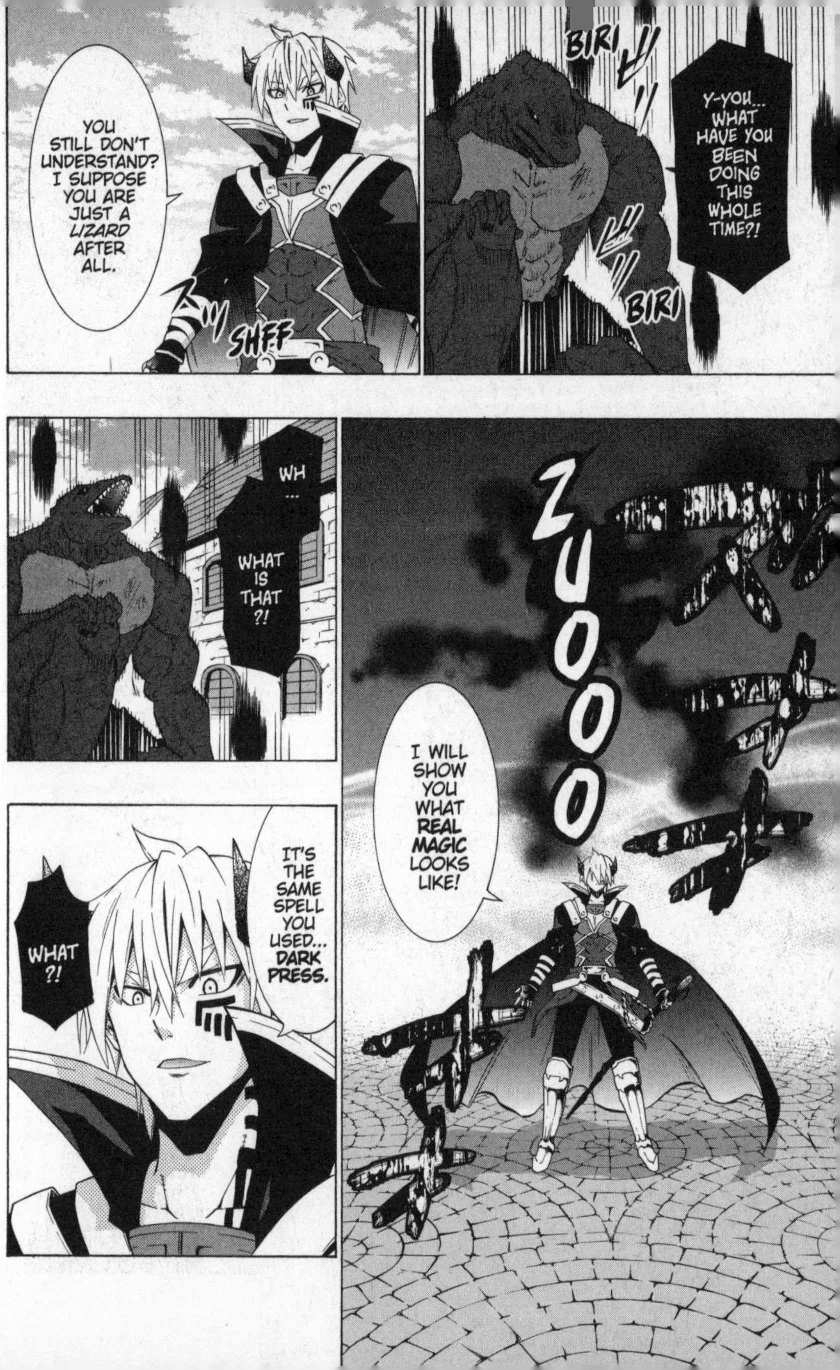
BIRI
Y-YOU... WHAT HAVE YOU BEEN DOING THIS WHOLE TIME?!
BIRI
YOU STILL DON'T UNDERSTAND? I SUPPOSE YOU ARE JUST A LIZARD AFTER ALL.
SHFF
ZUOOO
I WILL SHOW YOU WHAT REAL MAGIC LOOKS LIKE!
WH... WHAT IS THAT?!
IT'S THE SAME SPELL YOU USED... DARK PRESS.
WHAT?!

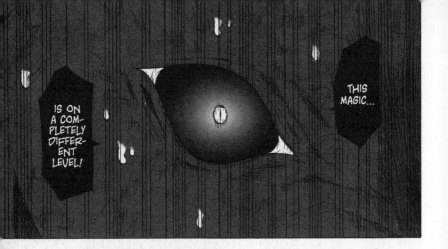

THIS MAGIC...

IS ON A COMPLETELY DIFFERENT LEVEL!

DARK PRESS!!

GUHH!!

HYUUU

THERE.

ZUN

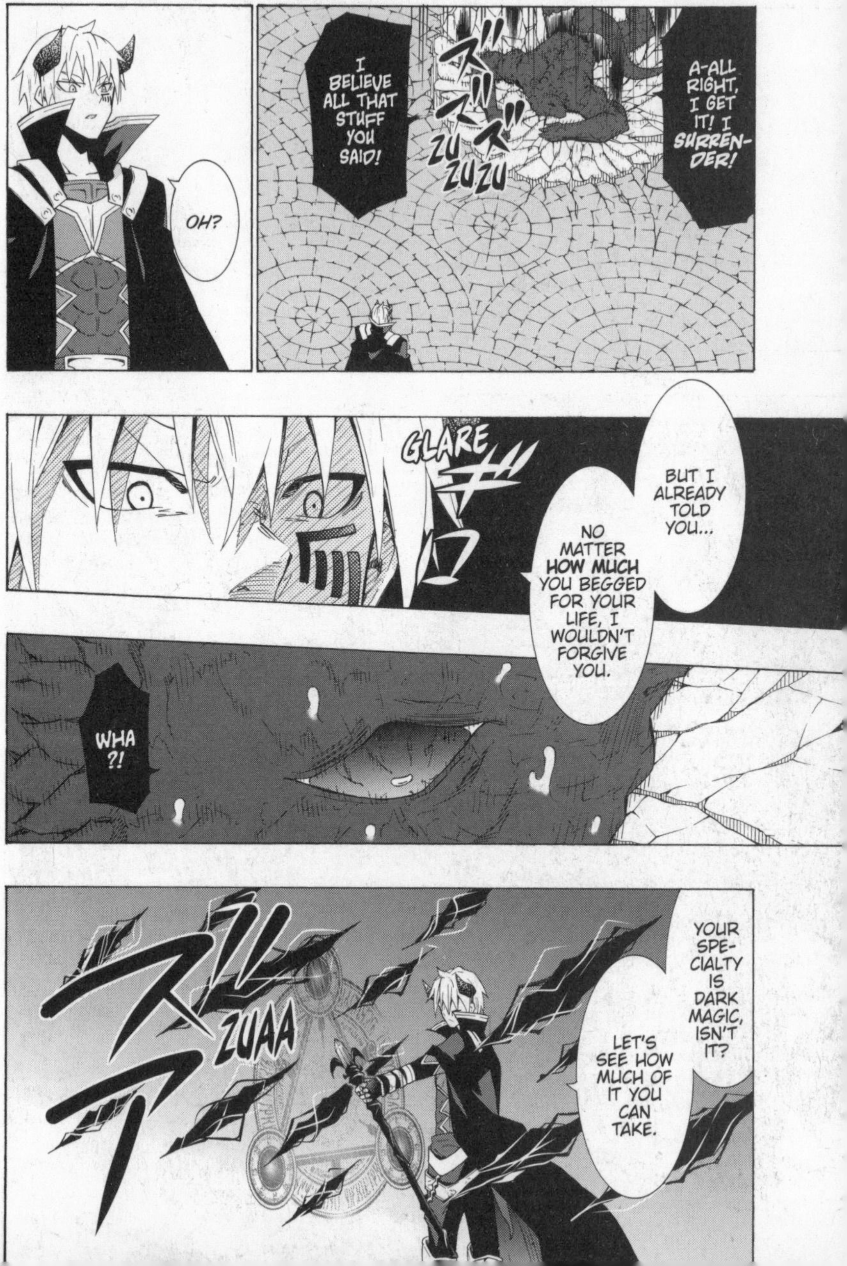
A-ALL RIGHT, I GET IT! I SURRENDER!
ZU ZU ZU
I BELIEVE ALL THAT STUFF YOU SAID!
OH?
BUT I ALREADY TOLD YOU...
NO MATTER HOW MUCH YOU BEGGED FOR YOUR LIFE, I WOULDN'T FORGIVE YOU.
GLARE
WHA?!
YOUR SPECIALTY IS DARK MAGIC, ISN'T IT?
LET'S SEE HOW MUCH OF IT YOU CAN TAKE.
ZUAA

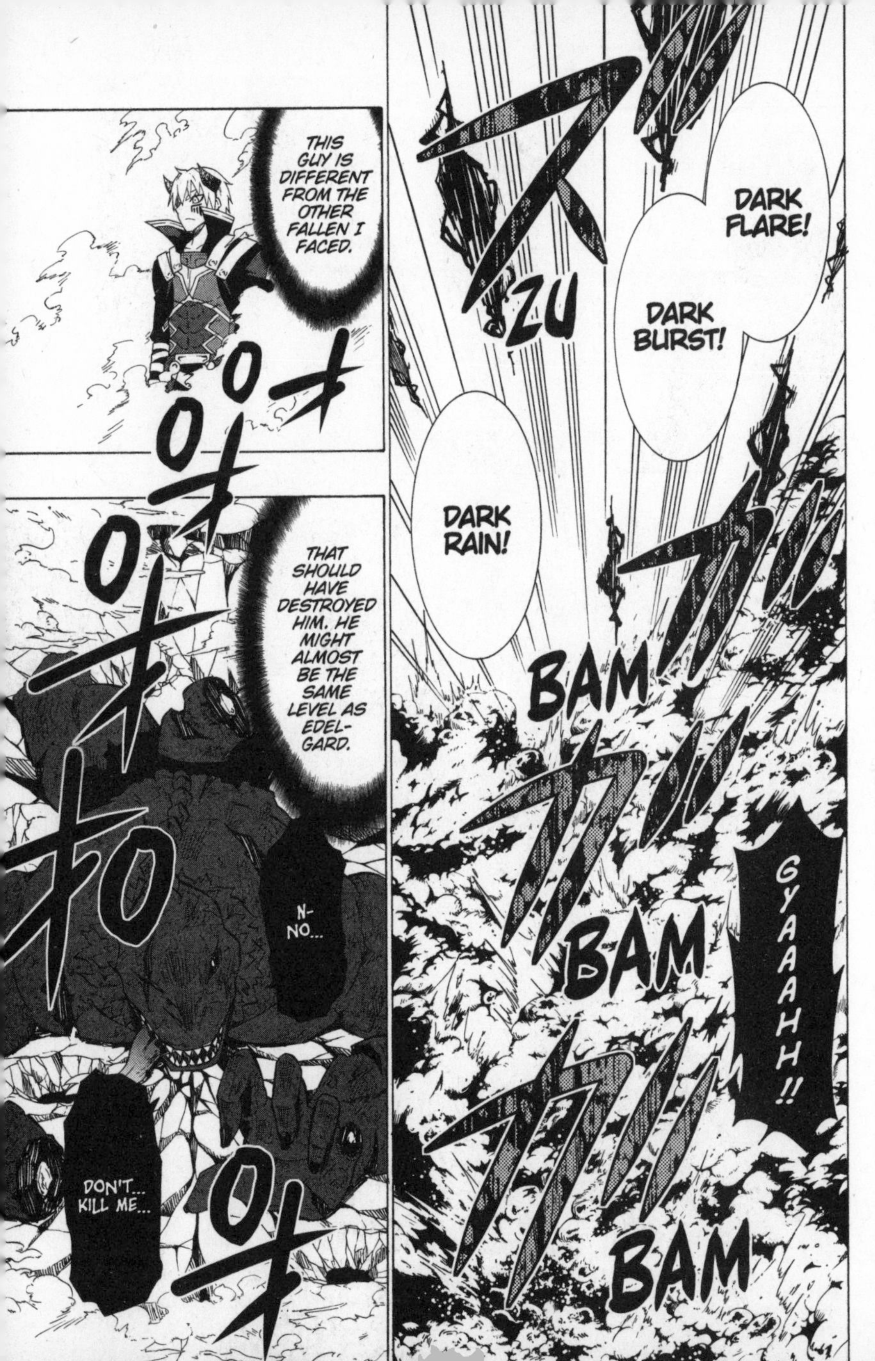
DARK FLARE!
DARK BURST!
ZU
DARK RAIN!
BAM
BAM
BAM
GYAAAAHH!!
THIS GUY IS DIFFERENT FROM THE OTHER FALLEN I FACED.
THAT SHOULD HAVE DESTROYED HIM. HE MIGHT ALMOST BE THE SAME LEVEL AS EDEL-GARD.
N-NO...
DON'T... KILL ME...

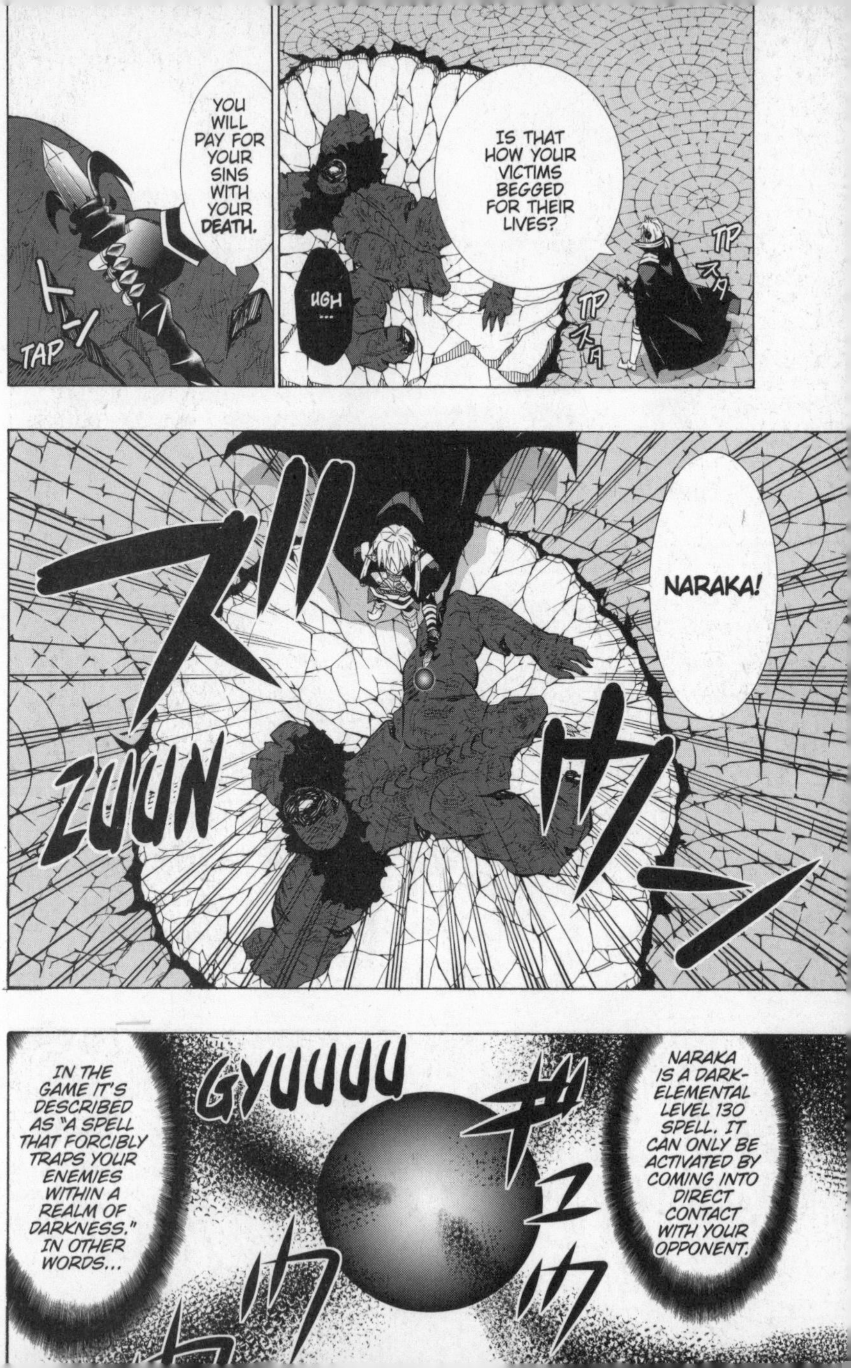

IS THAT HOW YOUR VICTIMS BEGGED FOR THEIR LIVES?
TP
TP
UGH...
YOU WILL PAY FOR YOUR SINS WITH YOUR DEATH.
TAP
NARAKA!
ZUUN
NARAKA IS A DARK-ELEMENTAL LEVEL 130 SPELL. IT CAN ONLY BE ACTIVATED BY COMING INTO DIRECT CONTACT WITH YOUR OPPONENT.
GYUUUU
IN THE GAME IT'S DESCRIBED AS "A SPELL THAT FORCIBLY TRAPS YOUR ENEMIES WITHIN A REALM OF DARKNESS." IN OTHER WORDS...

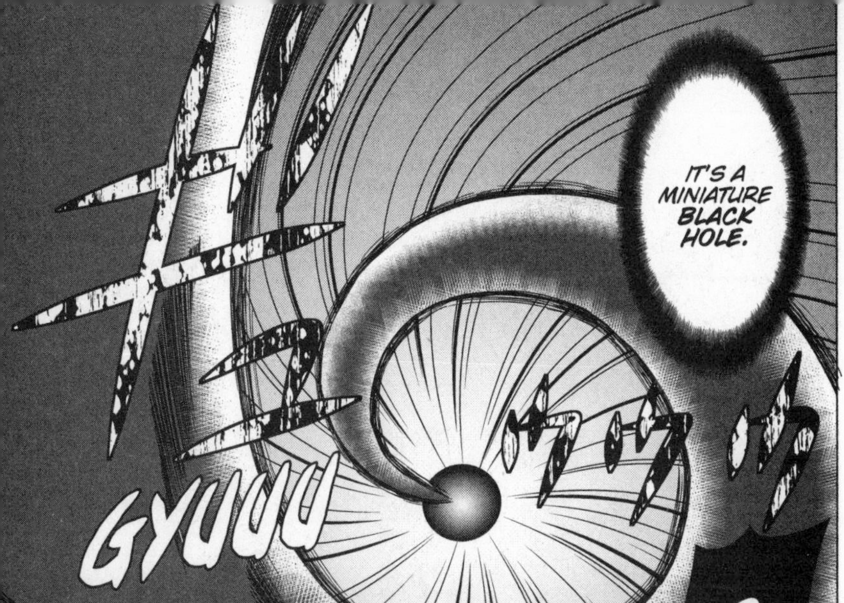
IT'S A MINIATURE BLACK HOLE.
GYUUU
GWAAAAAH!!

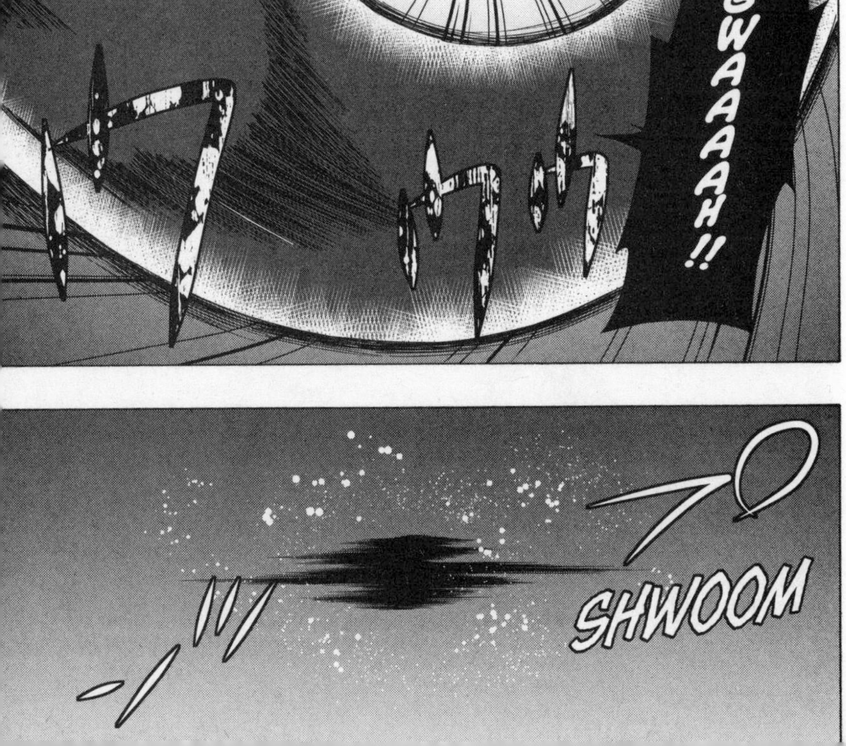
SHWOOM

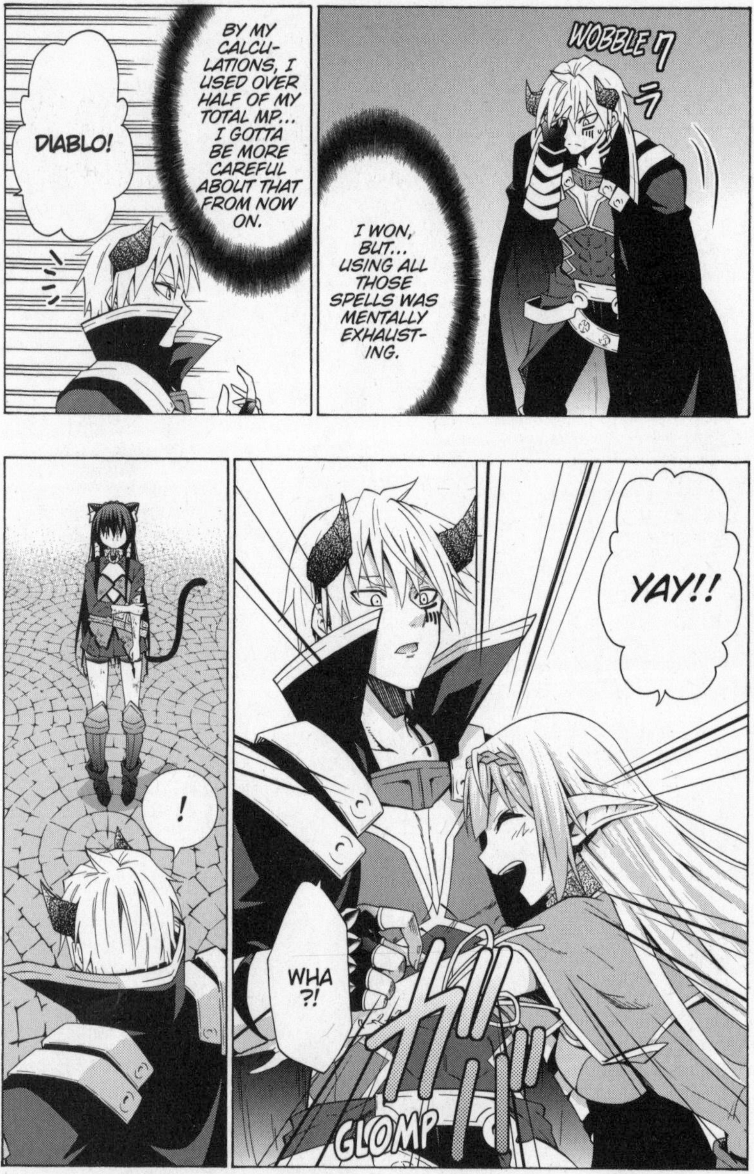
WOBBLE
I WON, BUT... USING ALL THOSE SPELLS WAS MENTALLY EXHAUST-ING.
BY MY CALCU-LATIONS, I USED OVER HALF OF MY TOTAL MP... I GOTTA BE MORE CAREFUL ABOUT THAT FROM NOW ON.
DIABLO!
YAY!!
WHA ?!
GLOMP
!

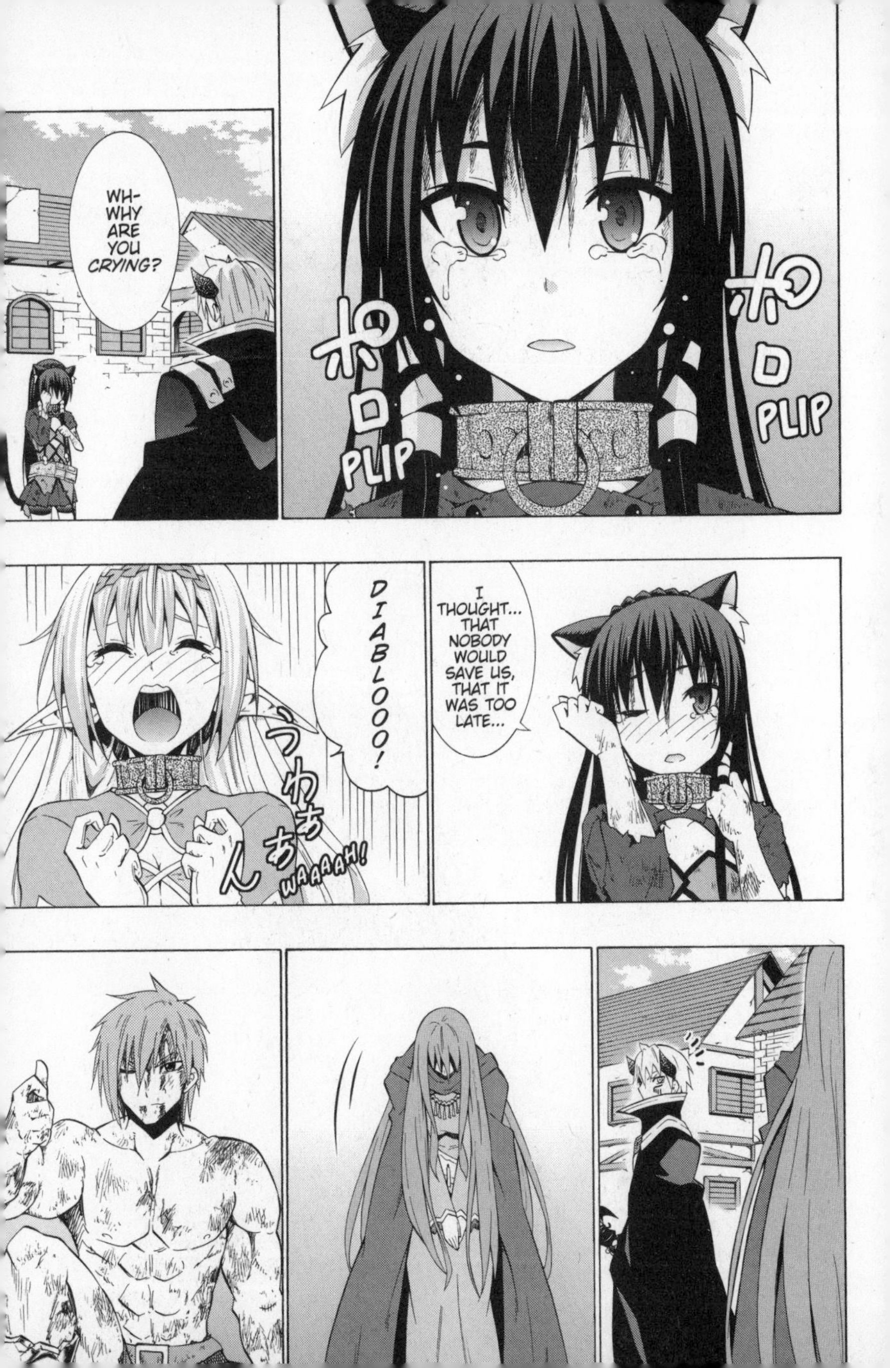
ポロ
PLIP
ポロ
PLIP
WH-WHY ARE YOU CRYING?
I THOUGHT... THAT NOBODY WOULD SAVE US, THAT IT WAS TOO LATE...
DIABLOOOO!
うわああん
WAAAAH!

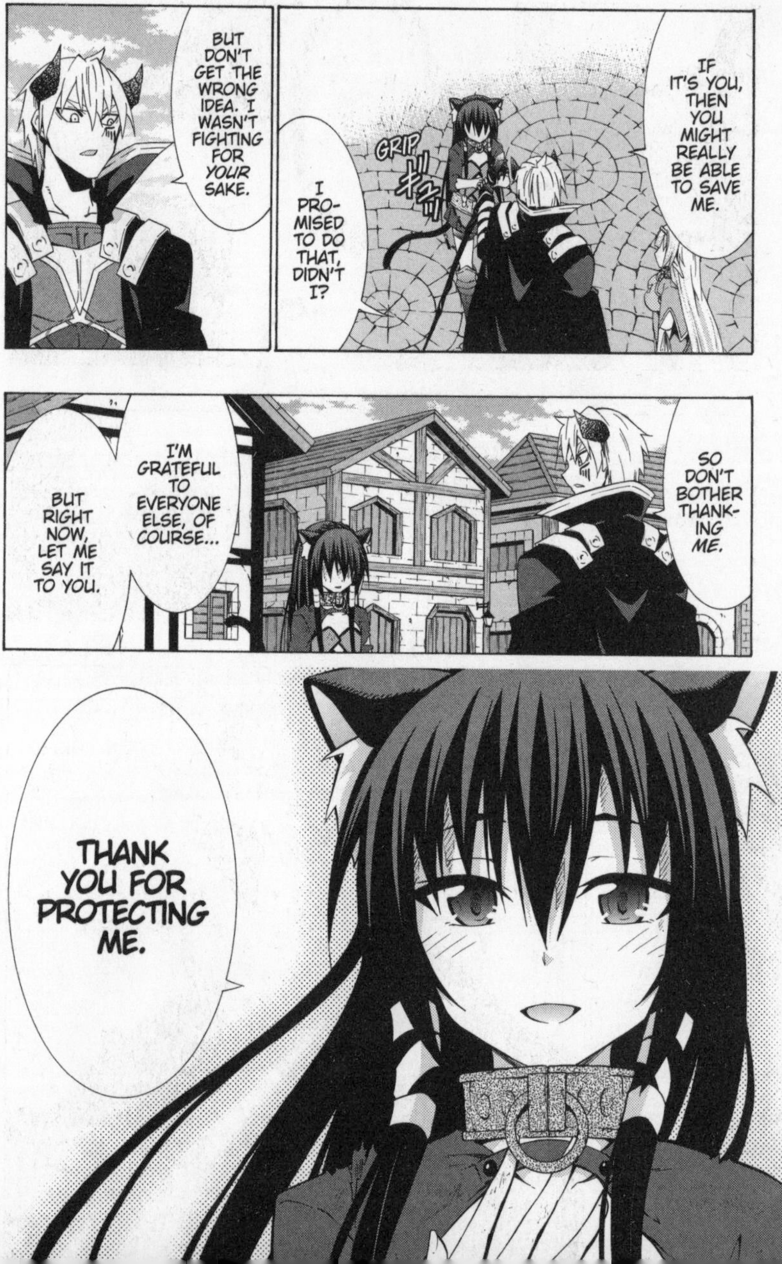
IF IT'S YOU, THEN YOU MIGHT REALLY BE ABLE TO SAVE ME.
GRIP
I PROMISED TO DO THAT, DIDN'T I?
BUT DON'T GET THE WRONG IDEA. I WASN'T FIGHTING FOR *YOUR* SAKE.
SO DON'T BOTHER THANKING ME.
I'M GRATEFUL TO EVERYONE ELSE, OF COURSE...
BUT RIGHT NOW, LET ME SAY IT TO YOU.
THANK YOU FOR PROTECTING ME.

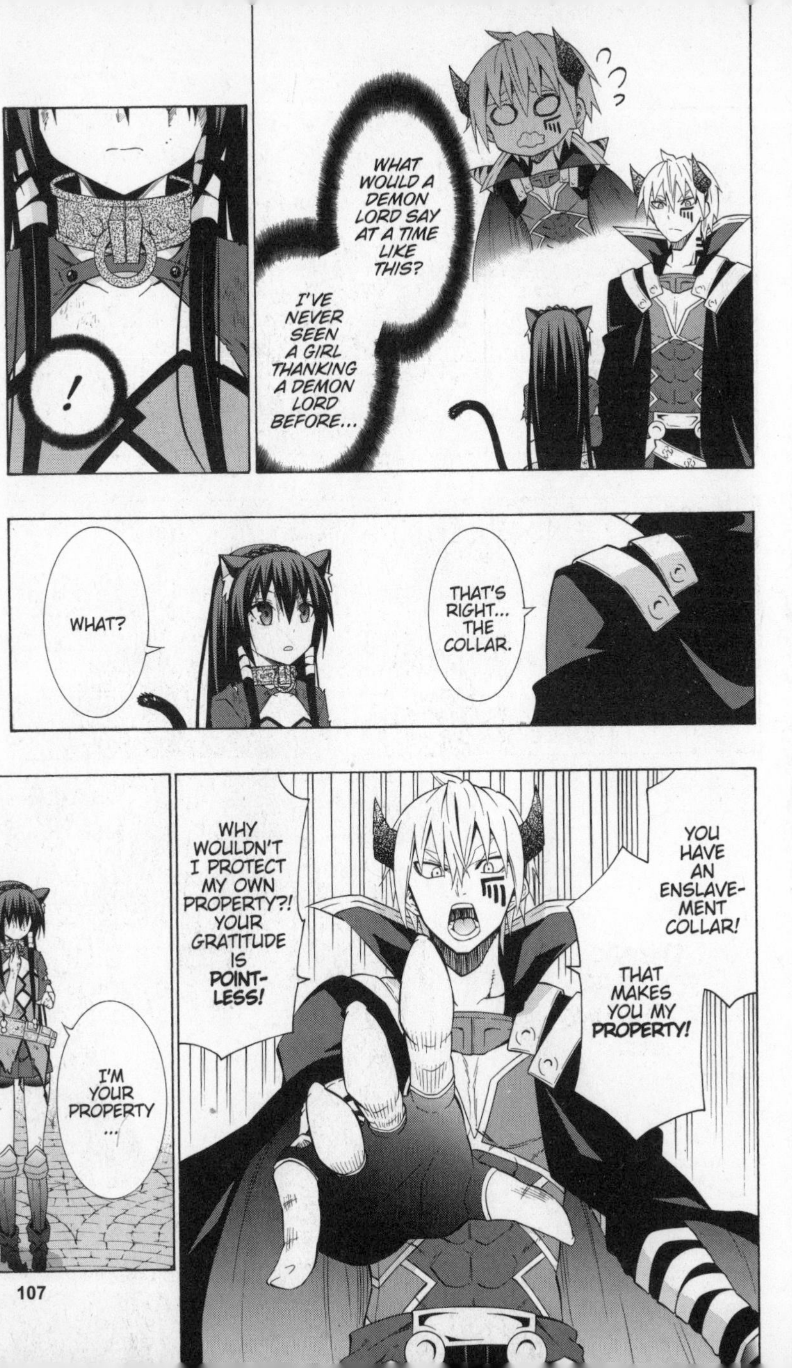
WHAT WOULD A DEMON LORD SAY AT A TIME LIKE THIS?
I'VE NEVER SEEN A GIRL THANKING A DEMON LORD BEFORE...
!
THAT'S RIGHT... THE COLLAR.
WHAT?
YOU HAVE AN ENSLAVE-MENT COLLAR!
THAT MAKES YOU MY **PROPERTY**!
WHY WOULDN'T I PROTECT MY OWN PROPERTY?! YOUR GRATITUDE IS **POINT-LESS**!
I'M YOUR PROPERTY...

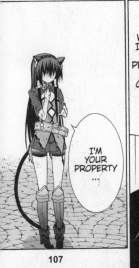

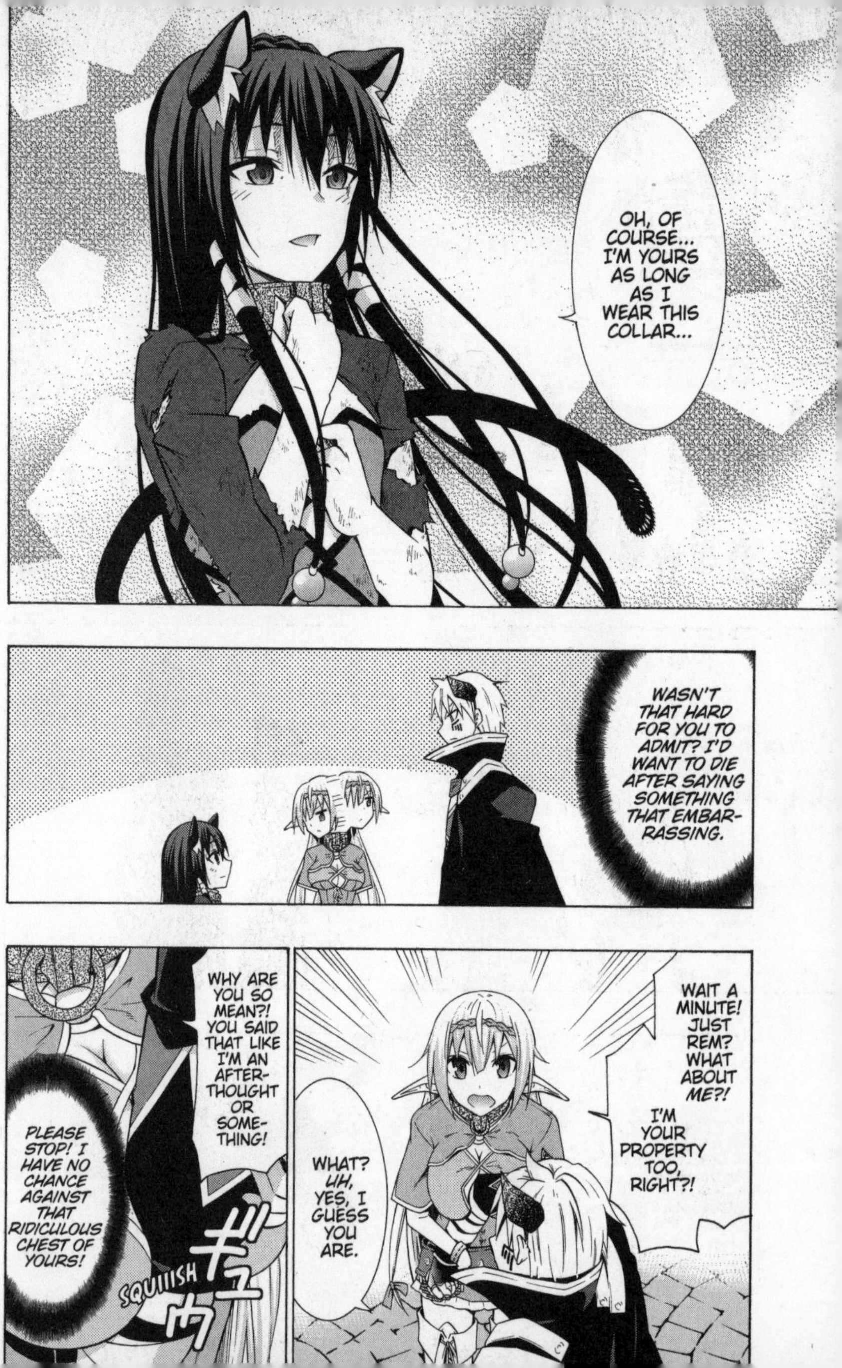
OH, OF COURSE... I'M YOURS AS LONG AS I WEAR THIS COLLAR...
WASN'T THAT HARD FOR YOU TO ADMIT? I'D WANT TO DIE AFTER SAYING SOMETHING THAT EMBAR-RASSING.
WAIT A MINUTE! JUST REM? WHAT ABOUT ME?!
I'M YOUR PROPERTY TOO, RIGHT?!
WHAT? UH, YES, I GUESS YOU ARE.
WHY ARE YOU SO MEAN?! YOU SAID THAT LIKE I'M AN AFTER-THOUGHT OR SOME-THING!
PLEASE STOP! I HAVE NO CHANCE AGAINST THAT RIDICULOUS CHEST OF YOURS!
ギュ
SQUIIISH

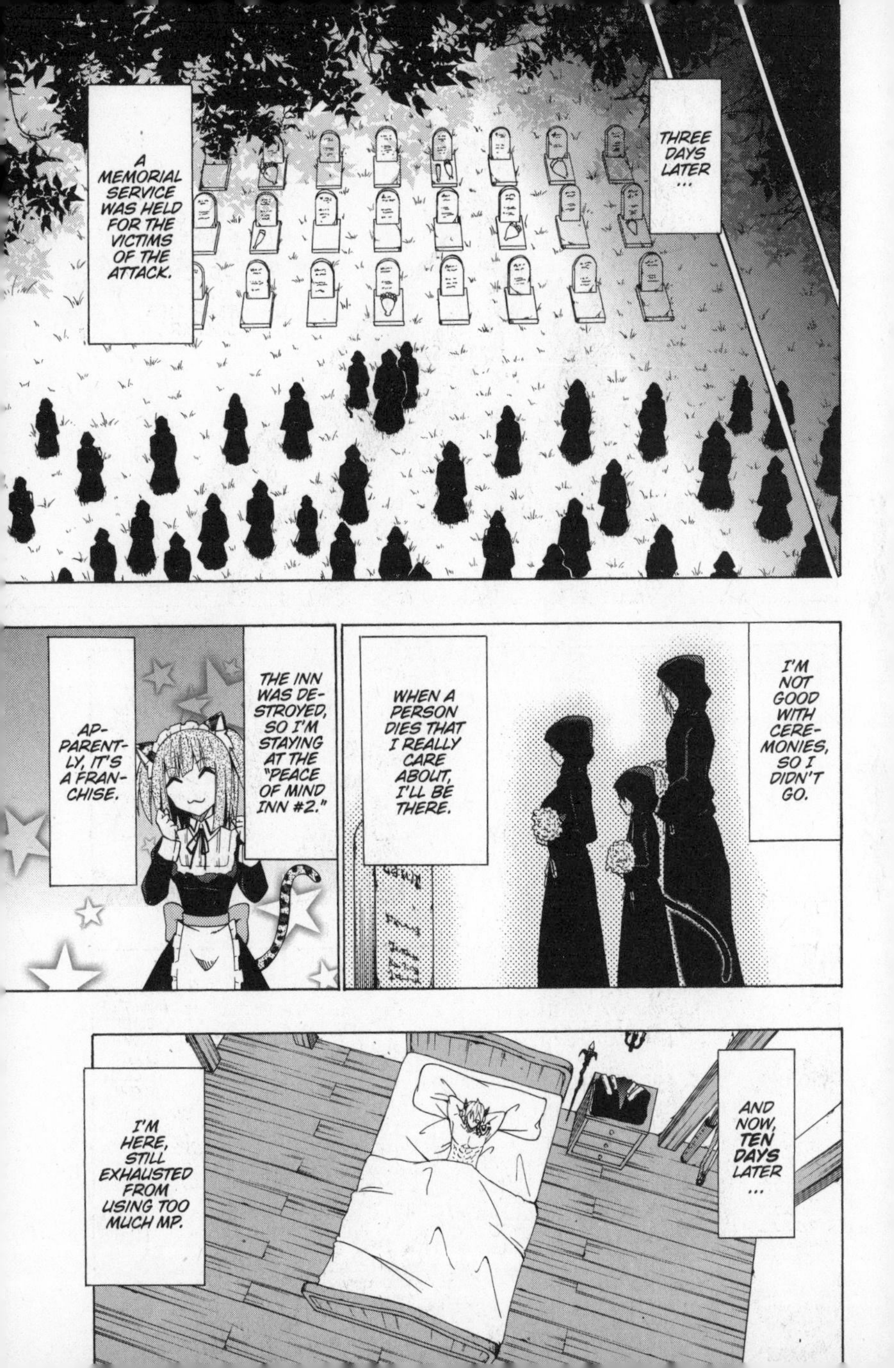
THREE DAYS LATER ...
A MEMORIAL SERVICE WAS HELD FOR THE VICTIMS OF THE ATTACK.
I'M NOT GOOD WITH CEREMONIES, SO I DIDN'T GO.
WHEN A PERSON DIES THAT I REALLY CARE ABOUT, I'LL BE THERE.
THE INN WAS DESTROYED, SO I'M STAYING AT THE "PEACE OF MIND INN #2."
APPARENTLY, IT'S A FRANCHISE.
AND NOW, TEN DAYS LATER ...
I'M HERE, STILL EXHAUSTED FROM USING TOO MUCH MP.

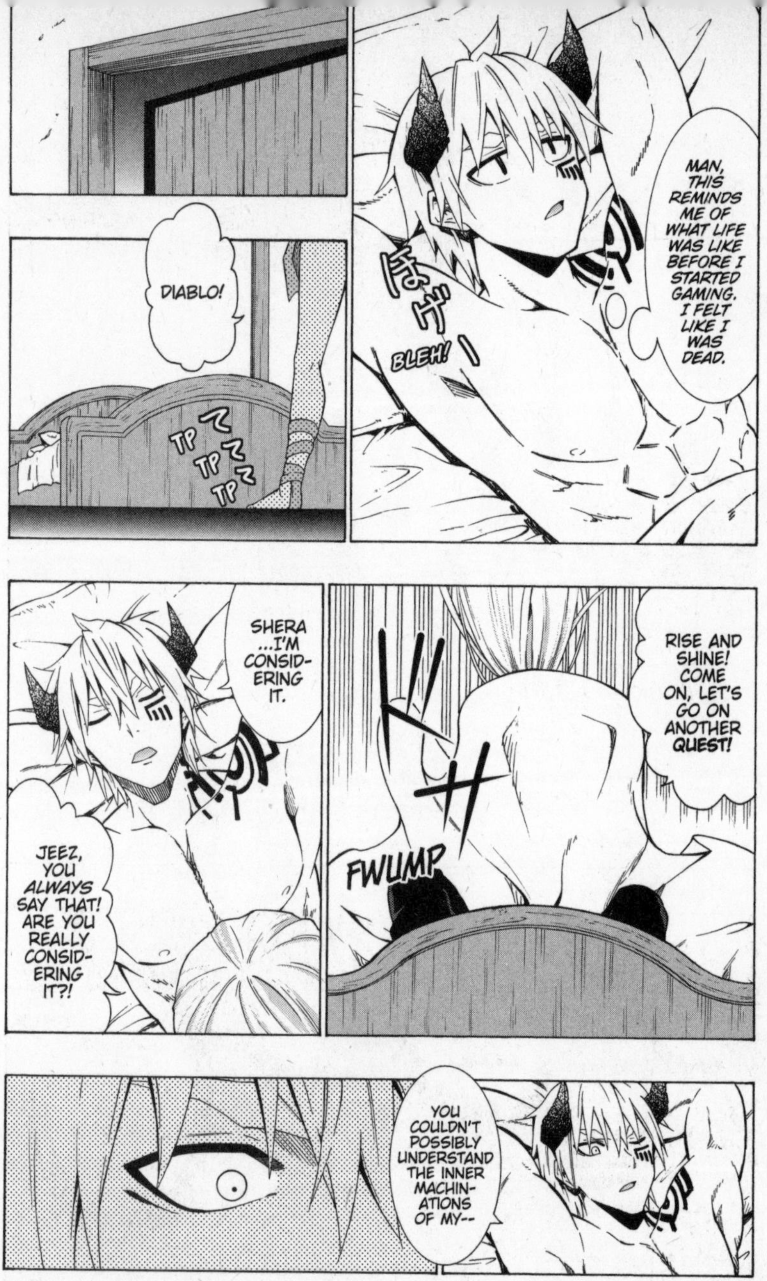
MAN, THIS REMINDS ME OF WHAT LIFE WAS LIKE BEFORE I STARTED GAMING. I FELT LIKE I WAS DEAD.
BLEH!
DIABLO!
TP TP TP
RISE AND SHINE! COME ON, LET'S GO ON ANOTHER QUEST!
FWUMP
SHERA ...I'M CONSIDERING IT.
JEEZ, YOU ALWAYS SAY THAT! ARE YOU REALLY CONSIDERING IT?!
YOU COULDN'T POSSIBLY UNDERSTAND THE INNER MACHINATIONS OF MY--

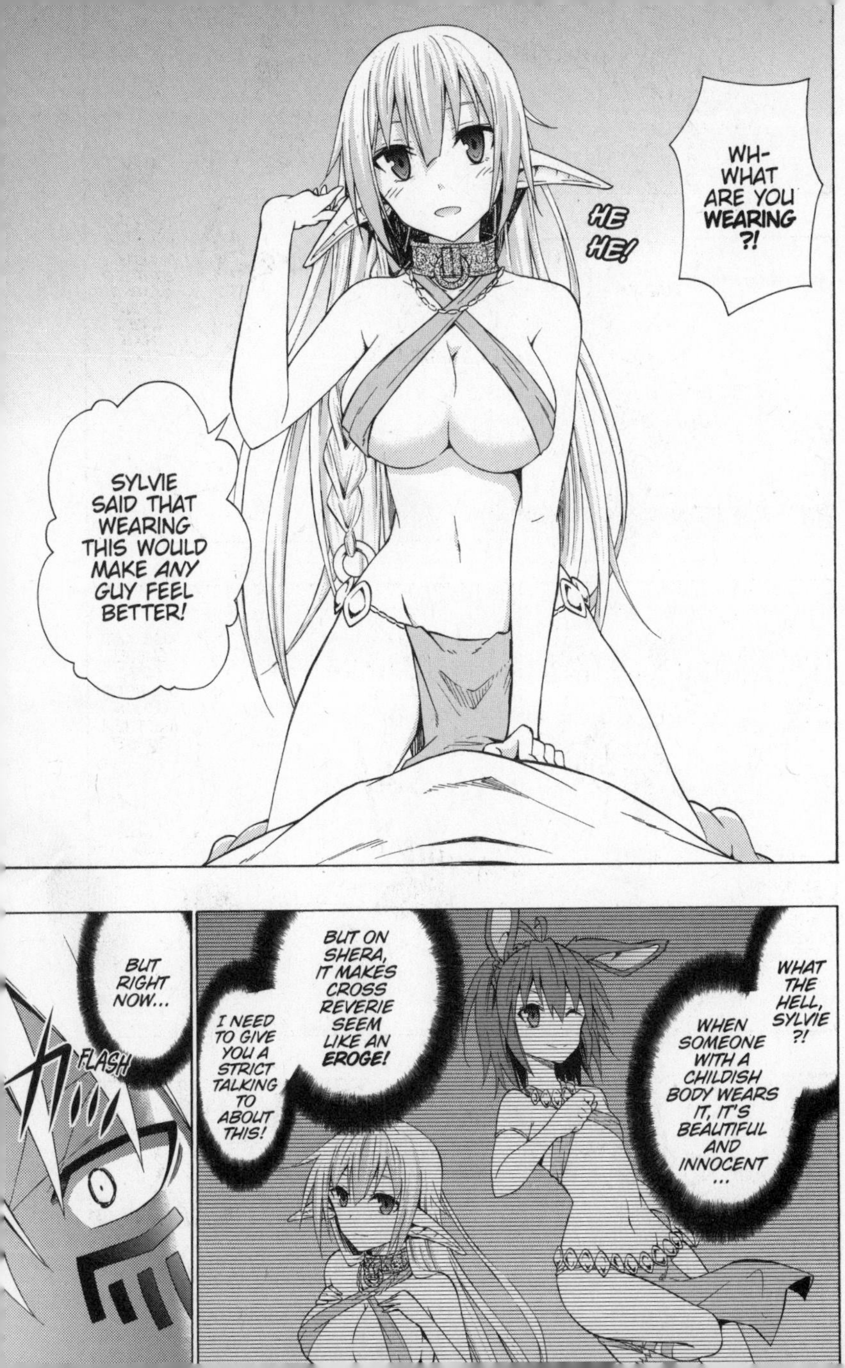
WH- WHAT ARE YOU WEARING ?!
HE HE!
SYLVIE SAID THAT WEARING THIS WOULD MAKE ANY GUY FEEL BETTER!
WHAT THE HELL, SYLVIE ?!
WHEN SOMEONE WITH A CHILDISH BODY WEARS IT, IT'S BEAUTIFUL AND INNOCENT ...
BUT ON SHERA, IT MAKES CROSS REVERIE SEEM LIKE AN EROGE!
I NEED TO GIVE YOU A STRICT TALKING TO ABOUT THIS!
BUT RIGHT NOW...
FLASH

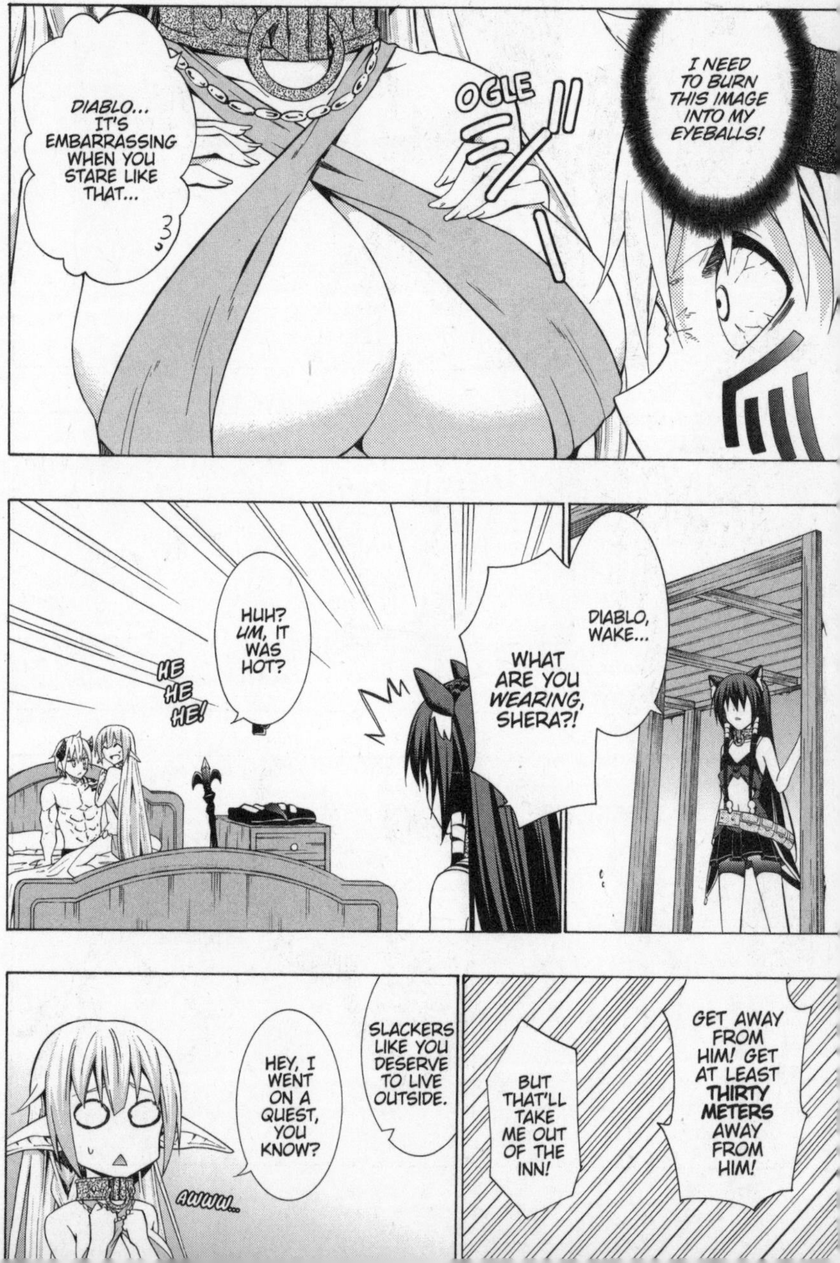
I NEED TO BURN THIS IMAGE INTO MY EYEBALLS!
OGLE
DIABLO... IT'S EMBARRASSING WHEN YOU STARE LIKE THAT...
DIABLO, WAKE...
WHAT ARE YOU WEARING, SHERA?!
HUH? UM, IT WAS HOT?
HE HE HE!
GET AWAY FROM HIM! GET AT LEAST THIRTY METERS AWAY FROM HIM!
BUT THAT'LL TAKE ME OUT OF THE INN!
SLACKERS LIKE YOU DESERVE TO LIVE OUTSIDE.
HEY, I WENT ON A QUEST, YOU KNOW?
AWWW...

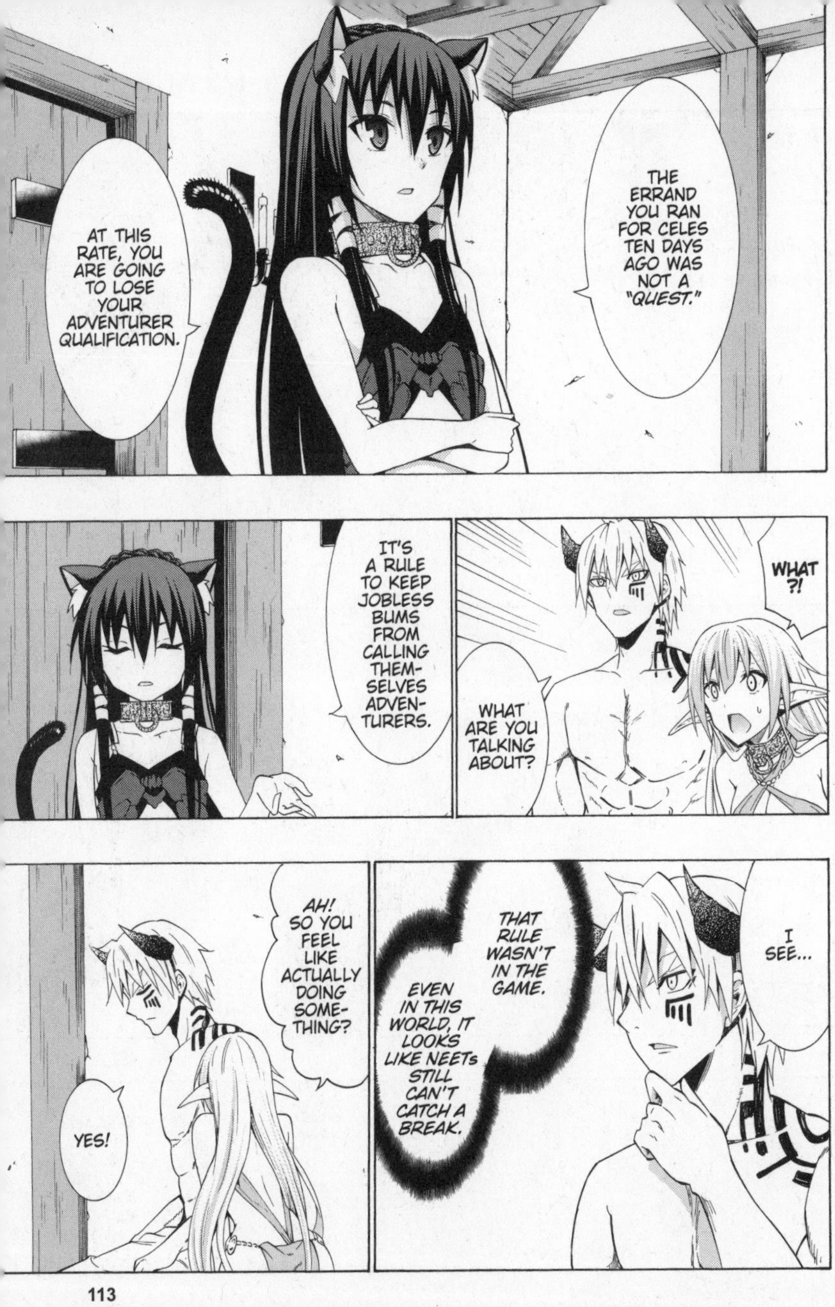

THE ERRAND YOU RAN FOR CELES TEN DAYS AGO WAS NOT A "QUEST."
AT THIS RATE, YOU ARE GOING TO LOSE YOUR ADVENTURER QUALIFICATION.
WHAT ?!
WHAT ARE YOU TALKING ABOUT?
IT'S A RULE TO KEEP JOBLESS BUMS FROM CALLING THEM-SELVES ADVEN-TURERS.
I SEE...
THAT RULE WASN'T IN THE GAME.
EVEN IN THIS WORLD, IT LOOKS LIKE NEETs STILL CAN'T CATCH A BREAK.
AH! SO YOU FEEL LIKE ACTUALLY DOING SOME-THING?
YES!

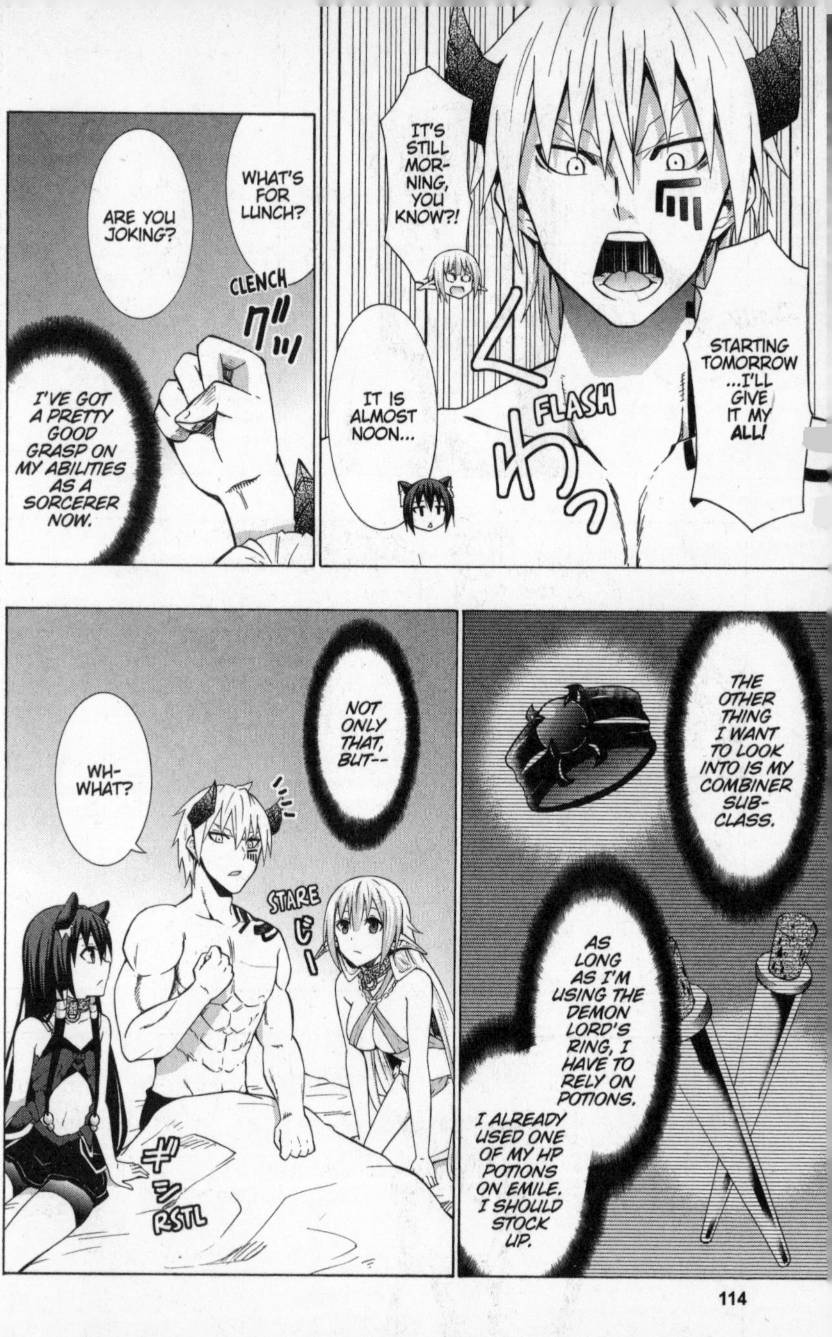
STARTING TOMORROW ...I'LL GIVE IT MY ALL!
IT'S STILL MORN-NING, YOU KNOW?!
IT IS ALMOST NOON...
FLASH
WHAT'S FOR LUNCH?
ARE YOU JOKING?
CLENCH
I'VE GOT A PRETTY GOOD GRASP ON MY ABILITIES AS A SORCERER NOW.
THE OTHER THING I WANT TO LOOK INTO IS MY COMBINER SUB-CLASS.
AS LONG AS I'M USING THE DEMON LORD'S RING, I HAVE TO RELY ON POTIONS.
I ALREADY USED ONE OF MY HP POTIONS ON EMILE. I SHOULD STOCK UP.
NOT ONLY THAT, BUT--
WH-WHAT?
STARE
RSTL

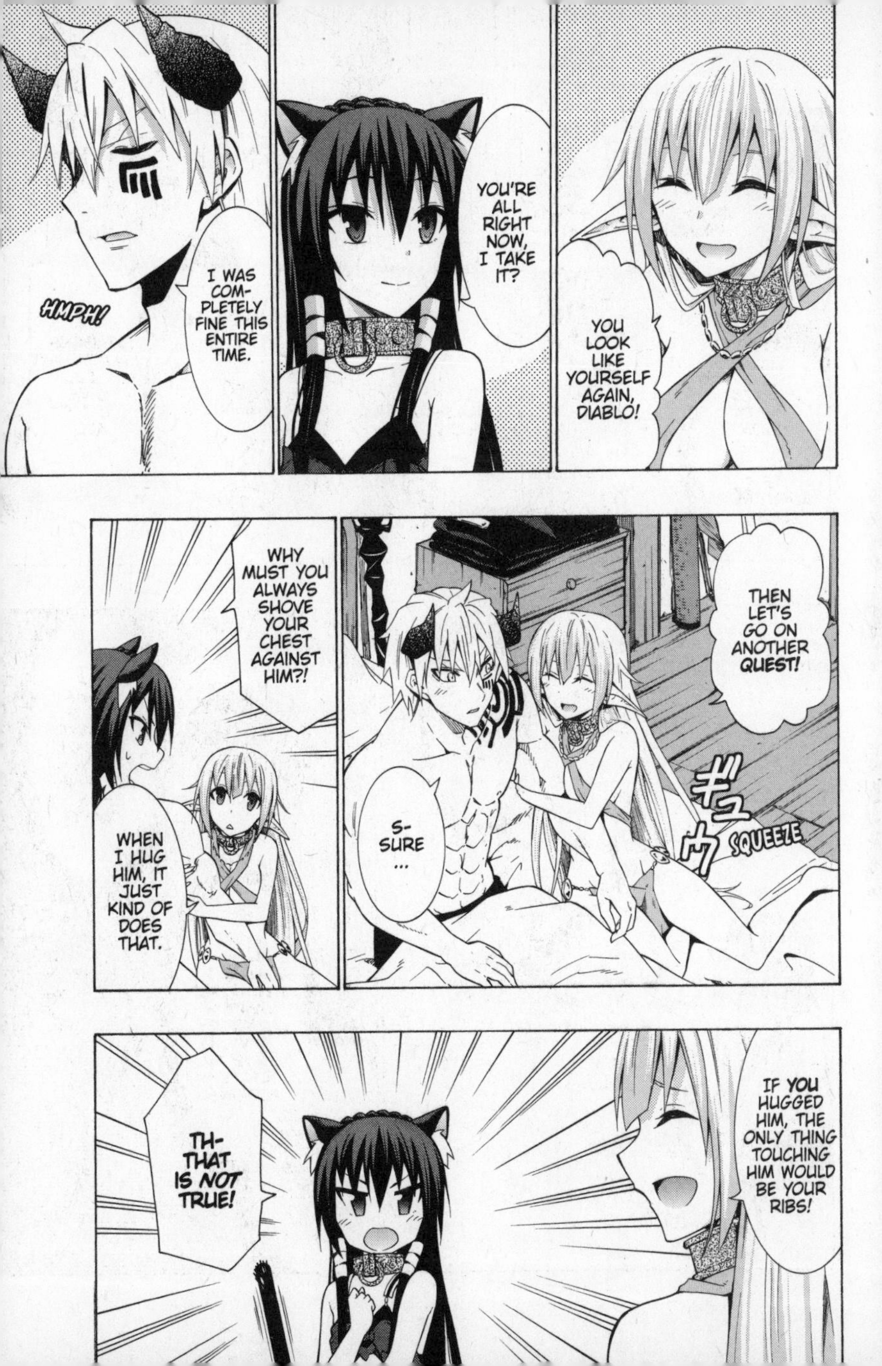
YOU LOOK LIKE YOURSELF AGAIN, DIABLO!
YOU'RE ALL RIGHT NOW, I TAKE IT?
I WAS COM-PLETELY FINE THIS ENTIRE TIME.
HMPH!
THEN LET'S GO ON ANOTHER QUEST!
ギュウ SQUEEZE
S-SURE ...
WHY MUST YOU ALWAYS SHOVE YOUR CHEST AGAINST HIM?!
WHEN I HUG HIM, IT JUST KIND OF DOES THAT.
IF YOU HUGGED HIM, THE ONLY THING TOUCHING HIM WOULD BE YOUR RIBS!
TH-THAT IS NOT TRUE!

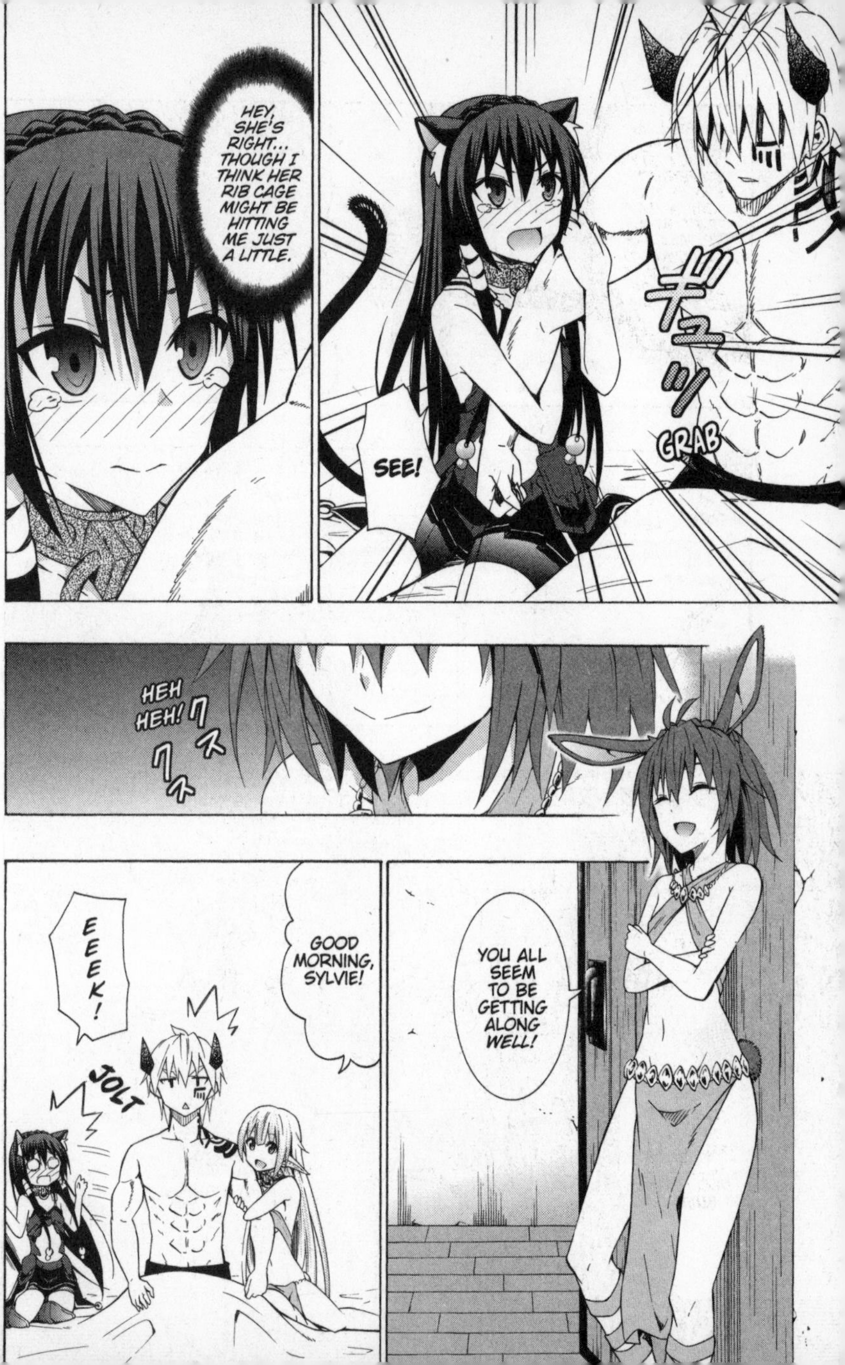
ギュッ
GRAB
SEE!
HEY, SHE'S RIGHT... THOUGH I THINK HER RIB CAGE MIGHT BE HITTING ME JUST A LITTLE.
HEH HEH! クスクス
YOU ALL SEEM TO BE GETTING ALONG WELL!
GOOD MORNING, SYLVIE!
EEEK!
JOLT

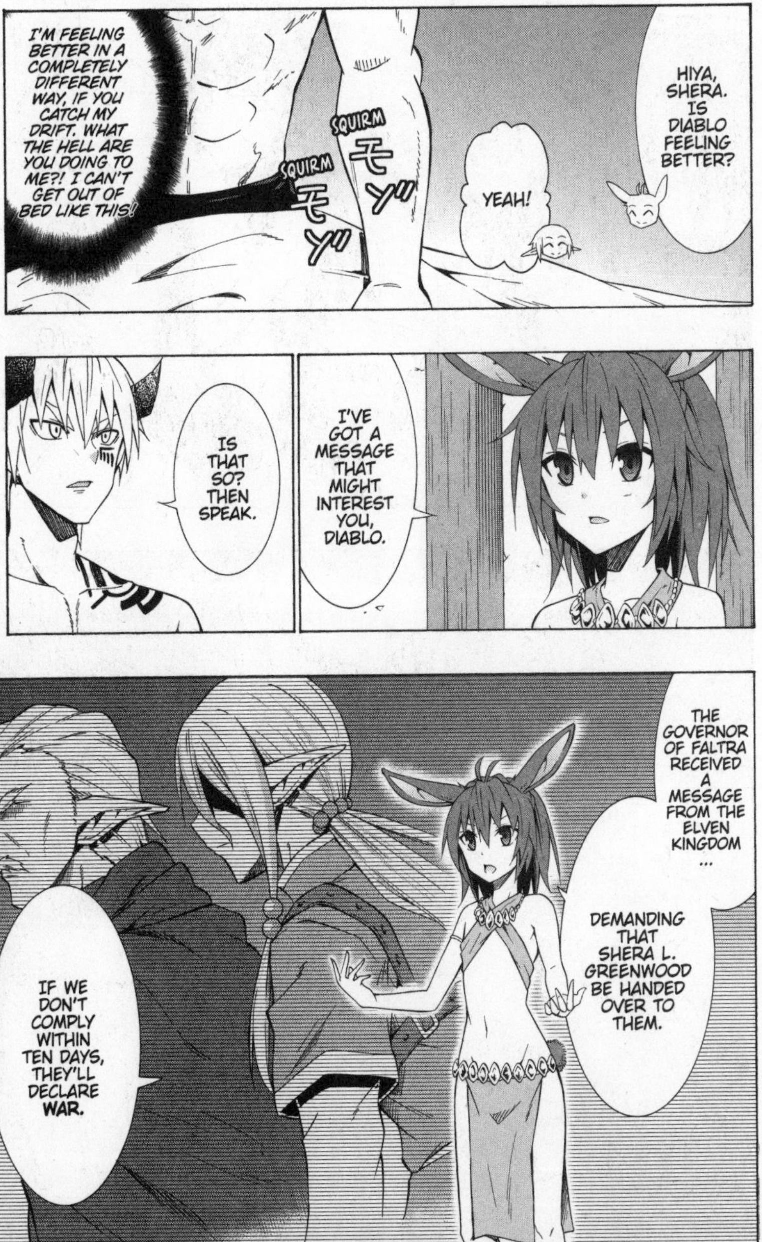
HIYA, SHERA. IS DIABLO FEELING BETTER?
YEAH!
SQUIRM
モゾ
SQUIRM
モゾ
I'M FEELING BETTER IN A COMPLETELY DIFFERENT WAY, IF YOU CATCH MY DRIFT. WHAT THE HELL ARE YOU DOING TO ME?! I CAN'T GET OUT OF BED LIKE THIS!
I'VE GOT A MESSAGE THAT MIGHT INTEREST YOU, DIABLO.
IS THAT SO? THEN SPEAK.
THE GOVERNOR OF FALTRA RECEIVED A MESSAGE FROM THE ELVEN KINGDOM ...
DEMANDING THAT SHERA L. GREENWOOD BE HANDED OVER TO THEM.
IF WE DON'T COMPLY WITHIN TEN DAYS, THEY'LL DECLARE WAR.

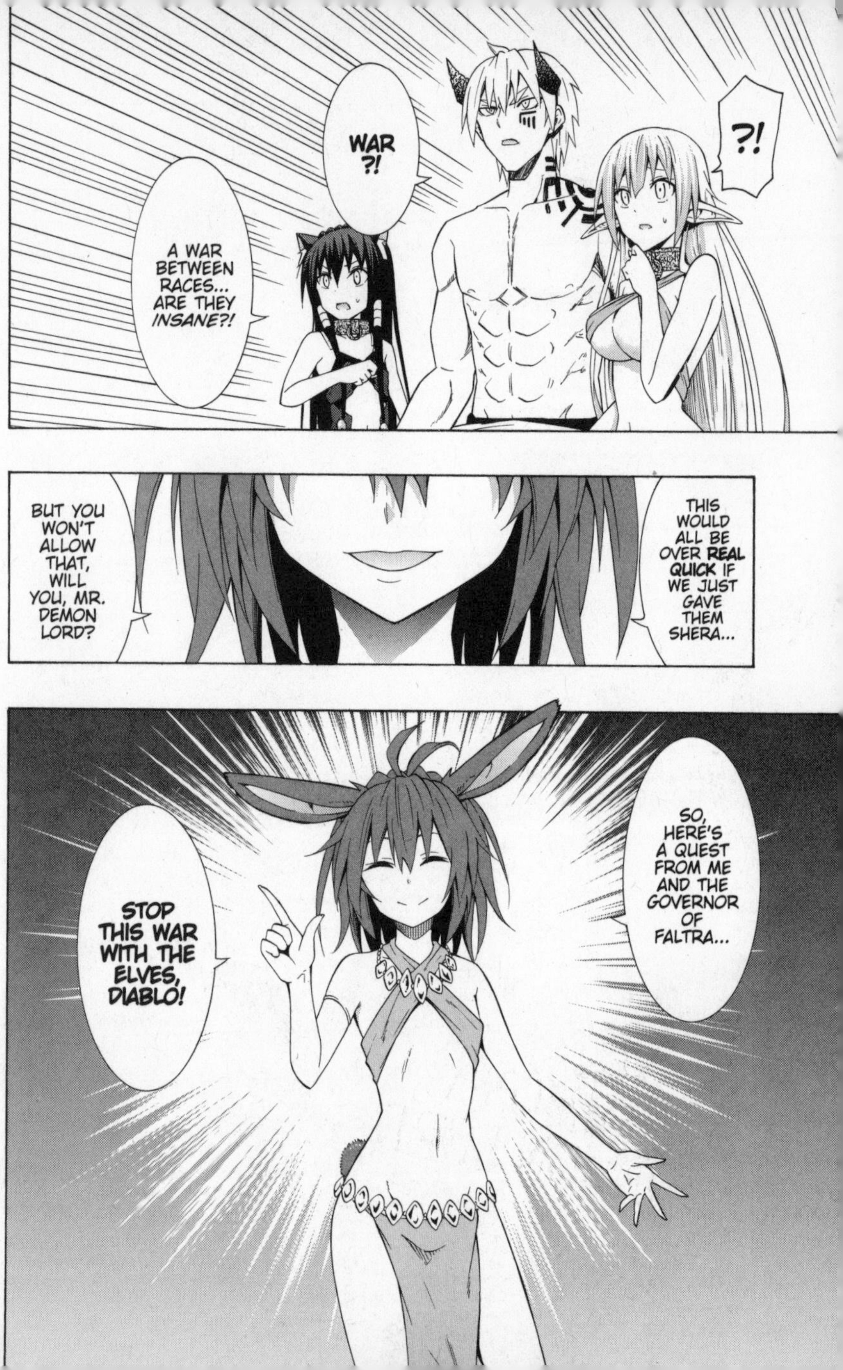
?!
WAR ?!
A WAR BETWEEN RACES... ARE THEY *INSANE?!*
THIS WOULD ALL BE OVER **REAL QUICK** IF WE JUST GAVE THEM SHERA...
BUT YOU WON'T ALLOW THAT, WILL YOU, MR. DEMON LORD?
SO, HERE'S A QUEST FROM ME AND THE GOVERNOR OF FALTRA...
STOP THIS WAR WITH THE ELVES, DIABLO!

HOW NOT
TO SUMMON A
DEMON LORD

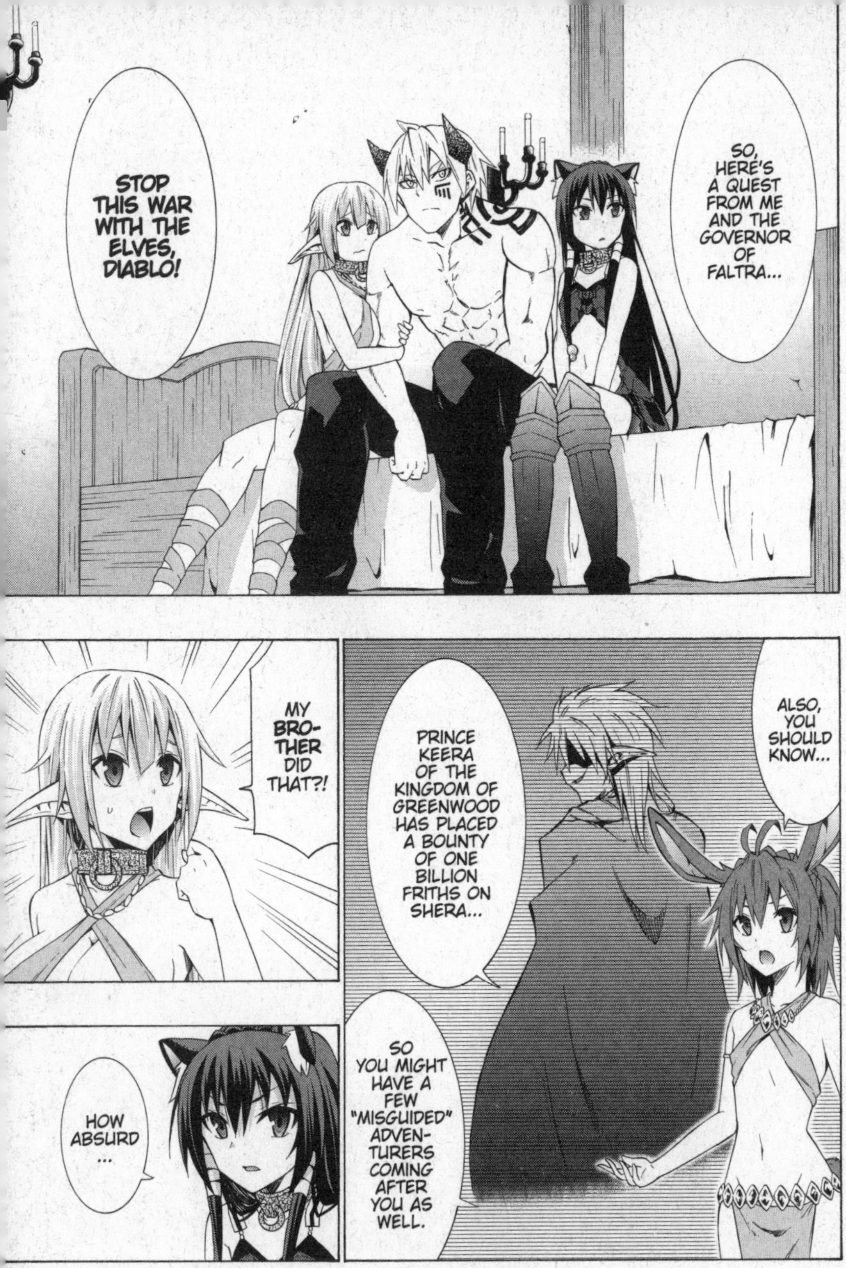
SO, HERE'S A QUEST FROM ME AND THE GOVERNOR OF FALTRA...
STOP THIS WAR WITH THE ELVES, DIABLO!
ALSO, YOU SHOULD KNOW...
PRINCE KEERA OF THE KINGDOM OF GREENWOOD HAS PLACED A BOUNTY OF ONE BILLION FRITHS ON SHERA...
SO YOU MIGHT HAVE A FEW "MISGUIDED" ADVEN-TURERS COMING AFTER YOU AS WELL.
MY BRO-THER DID THAT?!
HOW ABSURD...

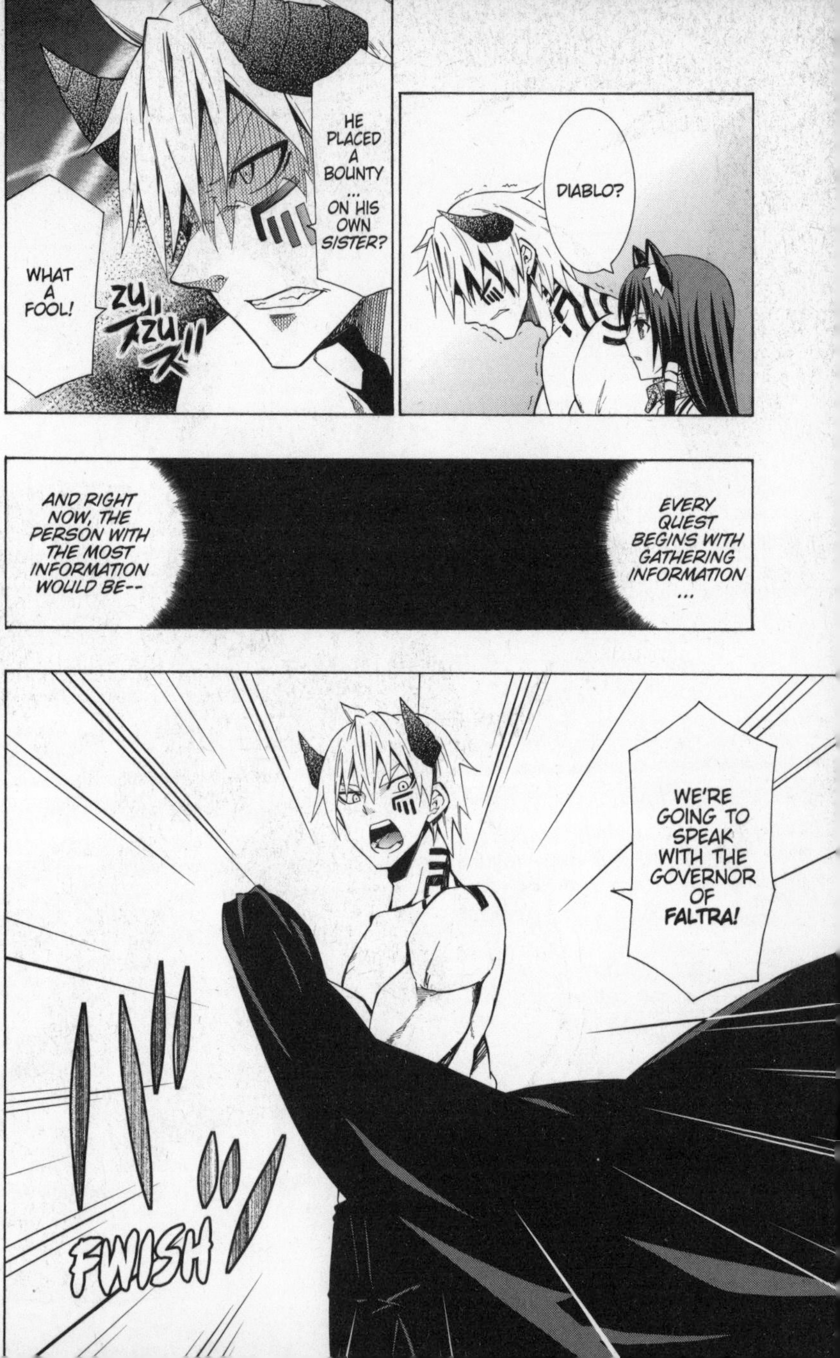
DIABLO?
HE PLACED A BOUNTY ... ON HIS OWN SISTER?
WHAT A FOOL!
ZU ZU
EVERY QUEST BEGINS WITH GATHERING INFORMATION ...
AND RIGHT NOW, THE PERSON WITH THE MOST INFORMATION WOULD BE--
WE'RE GOING TO SPEAK WITH THE GOVERNOR OF FALTRA!
FWISH

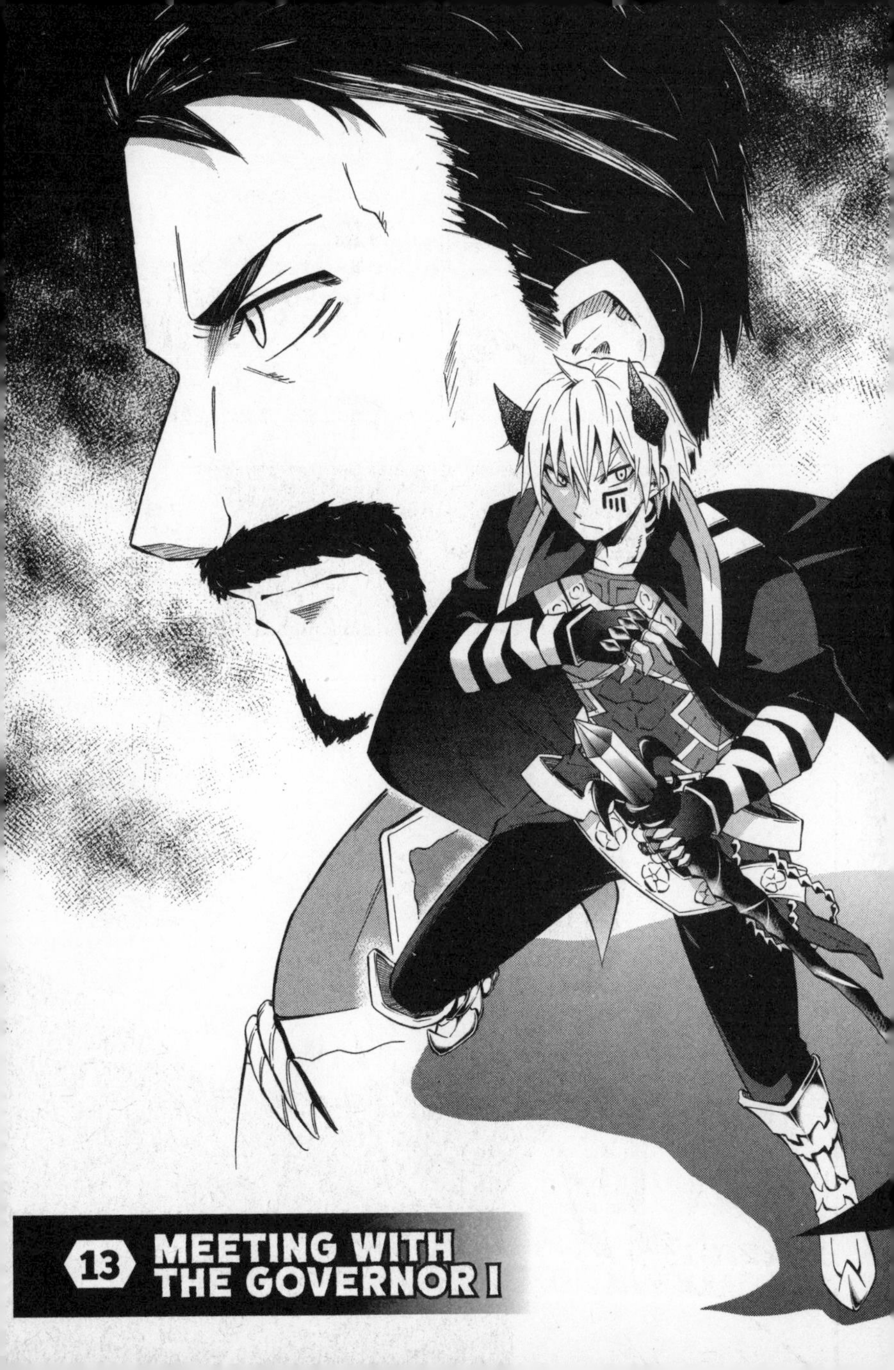

13 MEETING WITH THE GOVERNOR I

BEFORE WE GET TO THE GOVERNOR, I'M GOING TO TALK ABOUT HOW IMPORTANT **FALTRA** IS, OKAY?

CHATTER

CHATTER

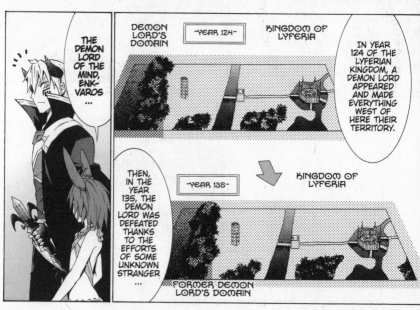

THE DEMON LORD OF THE MIND, ENKVAROS...

DEMON LORD'S DOMAIN

~YEAR 124~

KINGDOM OF LYFERIA

IN YEAR 124 OF THE LYFERIAN KINGDOM, A DEMON LORD APPEARED AND MADE EVERYTHING WEST OF HERE THEIR TERRITORY.

THEN, IN THE YEAR 135, THE DEMON LORD WAS DEFEATED THANKS TO THE EFFORTS OF SOME UNKNOWN STRANGER...

~YEAR 135~

KINGDOM OF LYFERIA

FORMER DEMON LORD'S DOMAIN

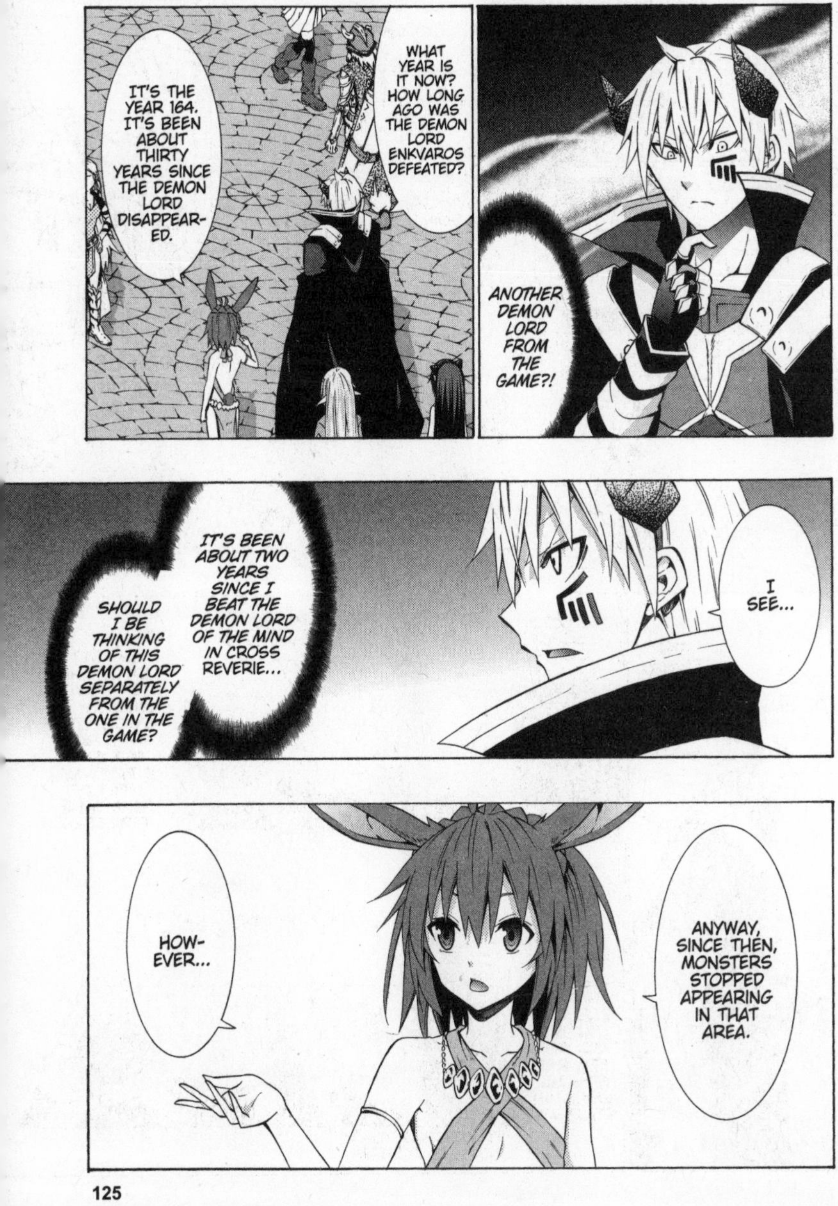
ANOTHER DEMON LORD FROM THE GAME?!
WHAT YEAR IS IT NOW? HOW LONG AGO WAS THE DEMON LORD ENKVAROS DEFEATED?
IT'S THE YEAR 164. IT'S BEEN ABOUT THIRTY YEARS SINCE THE DEMON LORD DISAPPEARED.
I SEE...
IT'S BEEN ABOUT TWO YEARS SINCE I BEAT THE DEMON LORD OF THE MIND IN CROSS REVERIE...
SHOULD I BE THINKING OF THIS DEMON LORD SEPARATELY FROM THE ONE IN THE GAME?
ANYWAY, SINCE THEN, MONSTERS STOPPED APPEARING IN THAT AREA.
HOW-EVER...

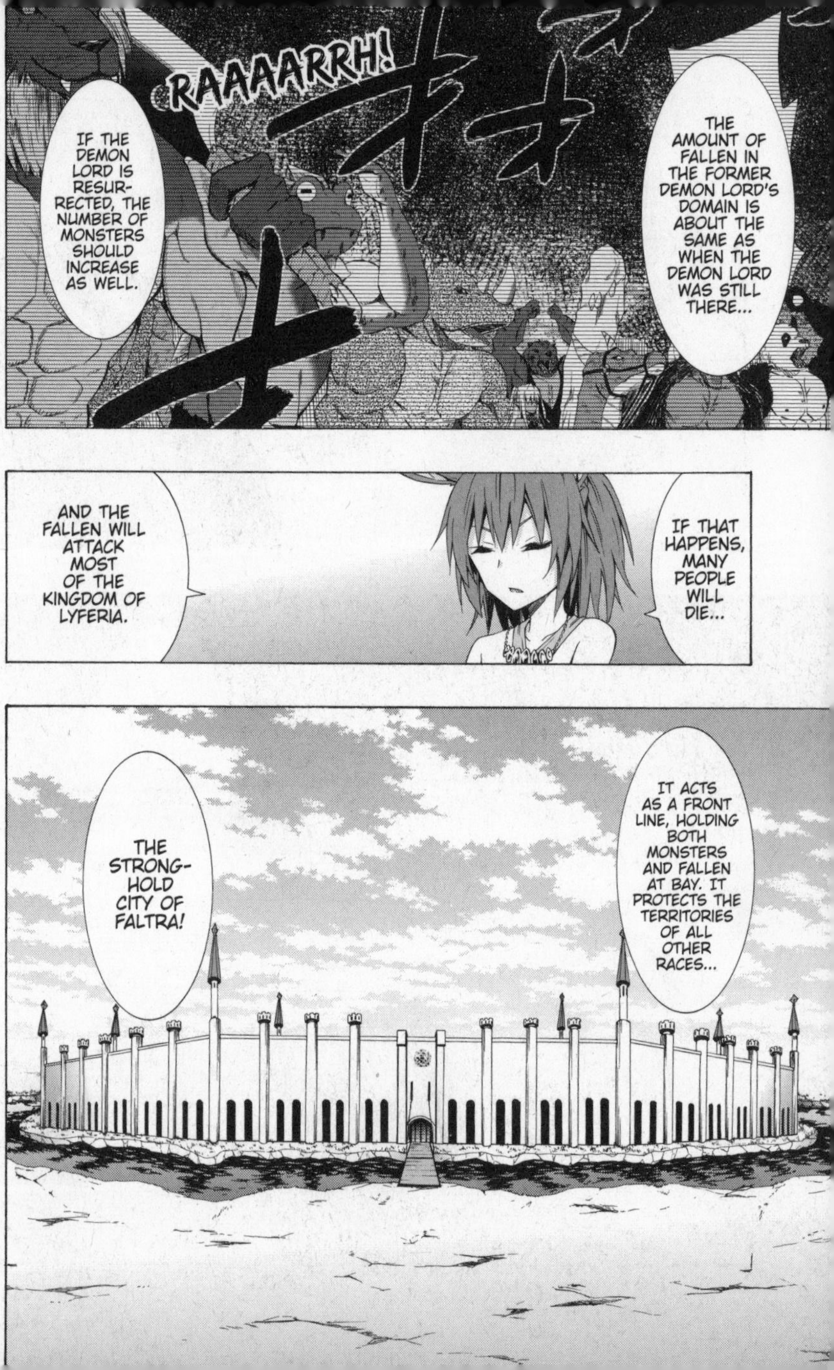
THE AMOUNT OF FALLEN IN THE FORMER DEMON LORD'S DOMAIN IS ABOUT THE SAME AS WHEN THE DEMON LORD WAS STILL THERE...
RAAAARRH!
IF THE DEMON LORD IS RESUR-RECTED, THE NUMBER OF MONSTERS SHOULD INCREASE AS WELL.
IF THAT HAPPENS, MANY PEOPLE WILL DIE...
AND THE FALLEN WILL ATTACK MOST OF THE KINGDOM OF LYFERIA.
IT ACTS AS A FRONT LINE, HOLDING BOTH MONSTERS AND FALLEN AT BAY. IT PROTECTS THE TERRITORIES OF ALL OTHER RACES...
THE STRONG-HOLD CITY OF FALTRA!

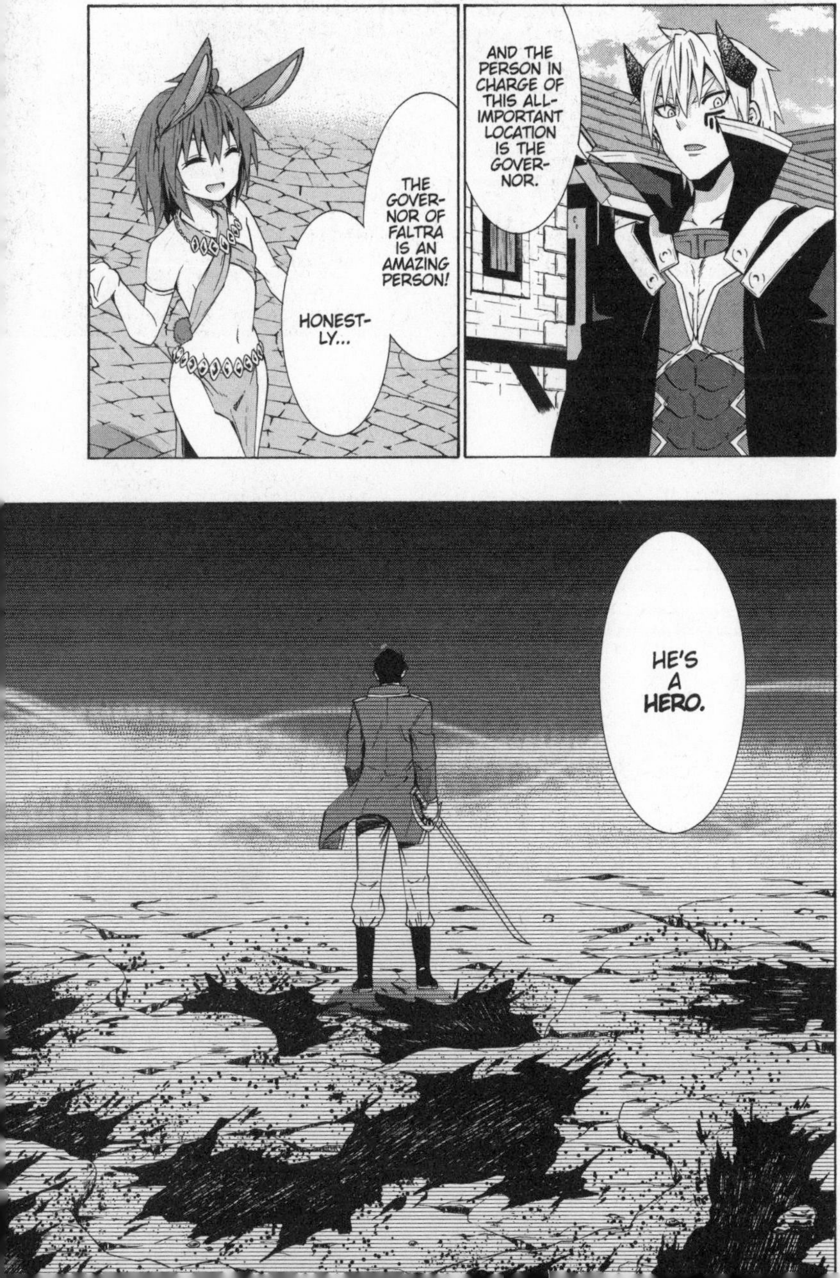
AND THE PERSON IN CHARGE OF THIS ALL-IMPORTANT LOCATION IS THE GOVERNOR.
THE GOVERNOR OF FALTRA IS AN AMAZING PERSON!
HONESTLY...
HE'S A HERO.

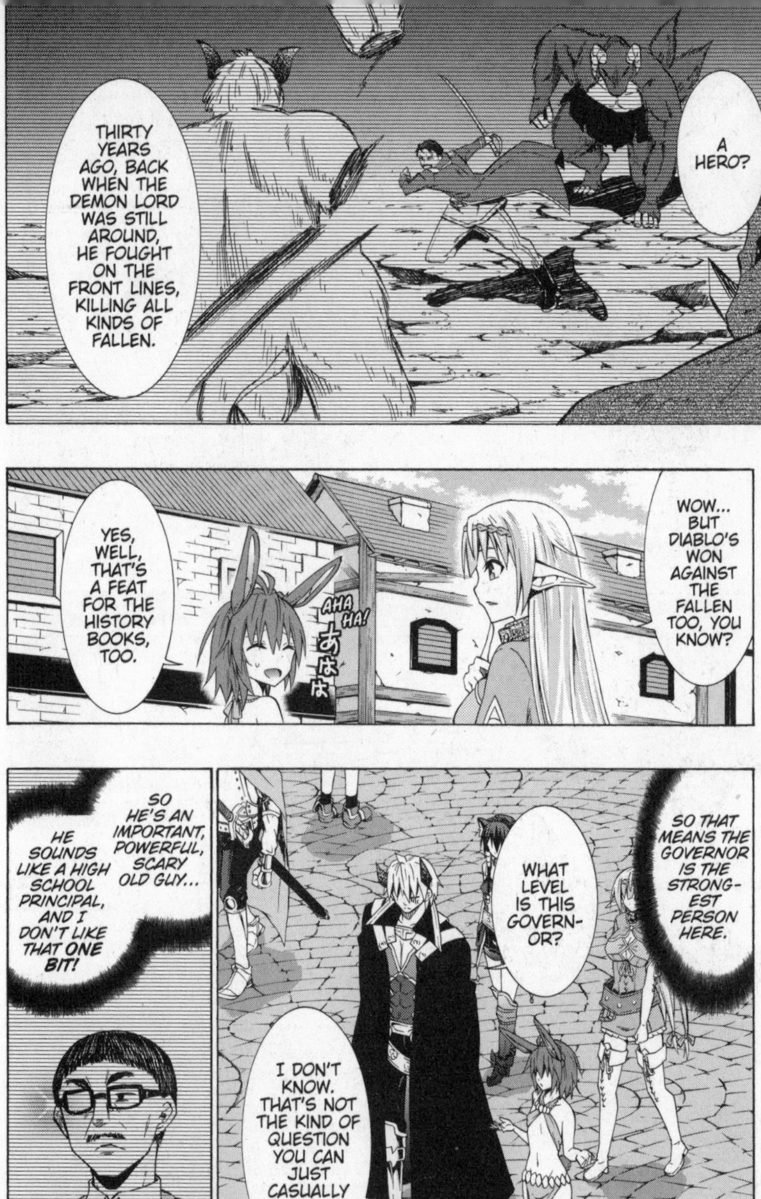
A HERO?
THIRTY YEARS AGO, BACK WHEN THE DEMON LORD WAS STILL AROUND, HE FOUGHT ON THE FRONT LINES, KILLING ALL KINDS OF FALLEN.
WOW... BUT DIABLO'S WON AGAINST THE FALLEN TOO, YOU KNOW?
AHA HA!
あはは
YES, WELL, THAT'S A FEAT FOR THE HISTORY BOOKS, TOO.
SO THAT MEANS THE GOVERNOR IS THE STRONGEST PERSON HERE.
WHAT LEVEL IS THIS GOVERNOR?
I DON'T KNOW. THAT'S NOT THE KIND OF QUESTION YOU CAN JUST CASUALLY ASK HIM.
SO HE'S AN IMPORTANT, POWERFUL, SCARY OLD GUY...
HE SOUNDS LIKE A HIGH SCHOOL PRINCIPAL, AND I DON'T LIKE THAT ONE BIT!

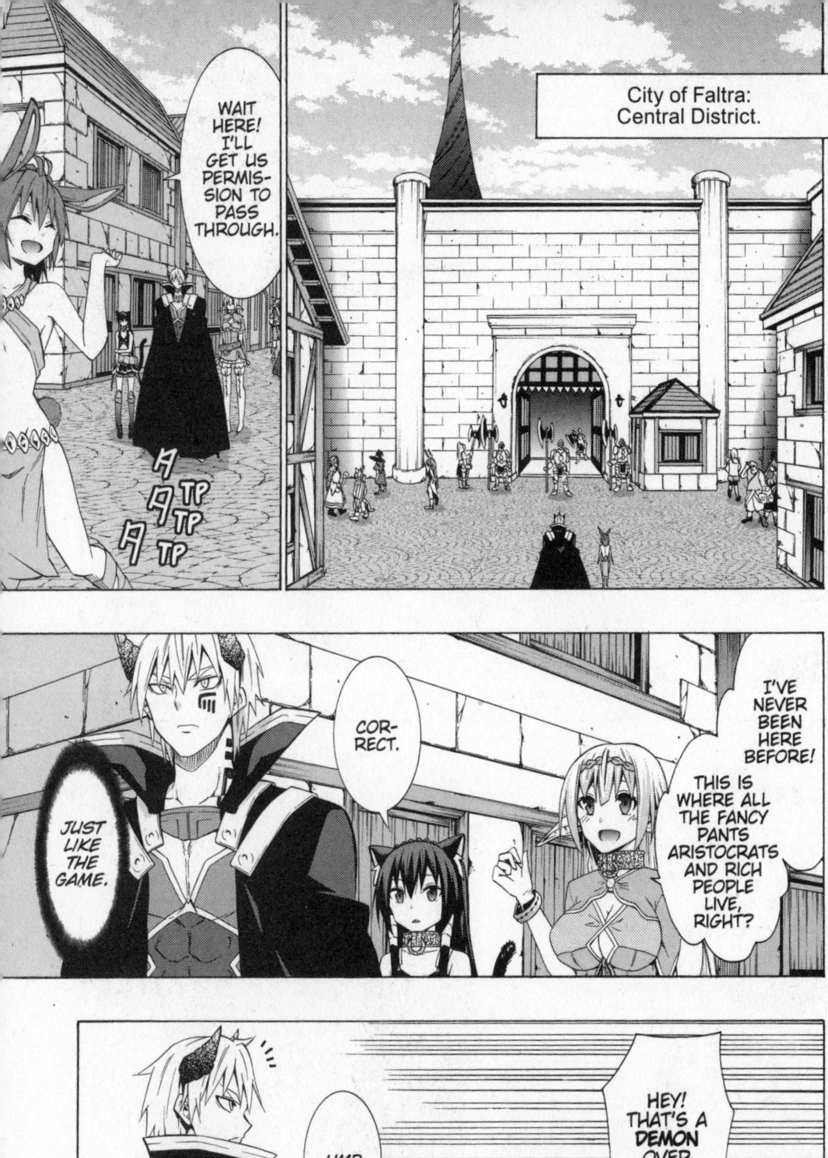
City of Faltra: Central District.
WAIT HERE! I'LL GET US PERMIS-SION TO PASS THROUGH.
TP TP TP
I'VE NEVER BEEN HERE BEFORE!
THIS IS WHERE ALL THE FANCY PANTS ARISTOCRATS AND RICH PEOPLE LIVE, RIGHT?
COR-RECT.
JUST LIKE THE GAME.
HEY! THAT'S A DEMON OVER THERE!
HM?

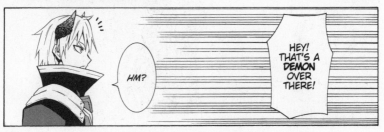

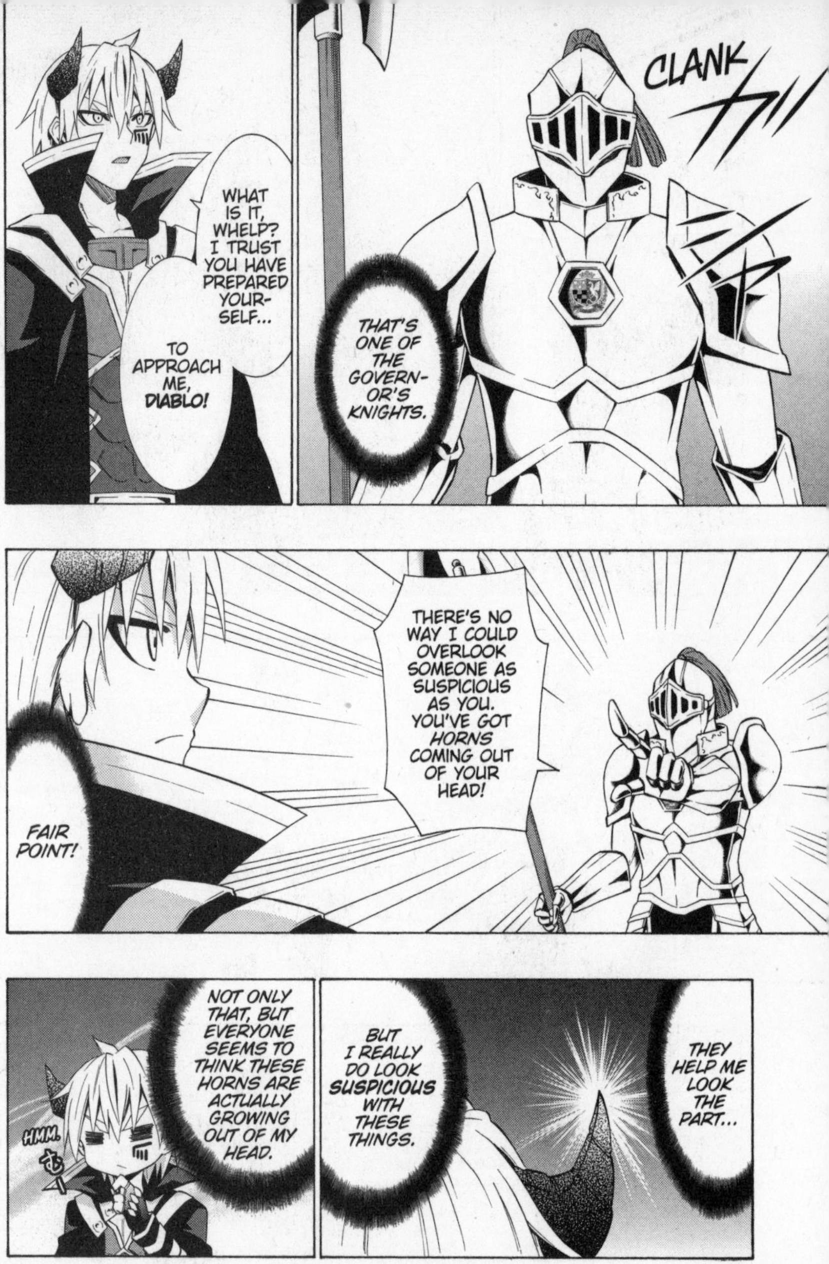
CLANK
THAT'S ONE OF THE GOVERNOR'S KNIGHTS.
WHAT IS IT, WHELP? I TRUST YOU HAVE PREPARED YOURSELF...
TO APPROACH ME, DIABLO!
THERE'S NO WAY I COULD OVERLOOK SOMEONE AS SUSPICIOUS AS YOU. YOU'VE GOT HORNS COMING OUT OF YOUR HEAD!
FAIR POINT!
THEY HELP ME LOOK THE PART...
BUT I REALLY DO LOOK SUSPICIOUS WITH THESE THINGS.
NOT ONLY THAT, BUT EVERYONE SEEMS TO THINK THESE HORNS ARE ACTUALLY GROWING OUT OF MY HEAD.
HMM.
むー

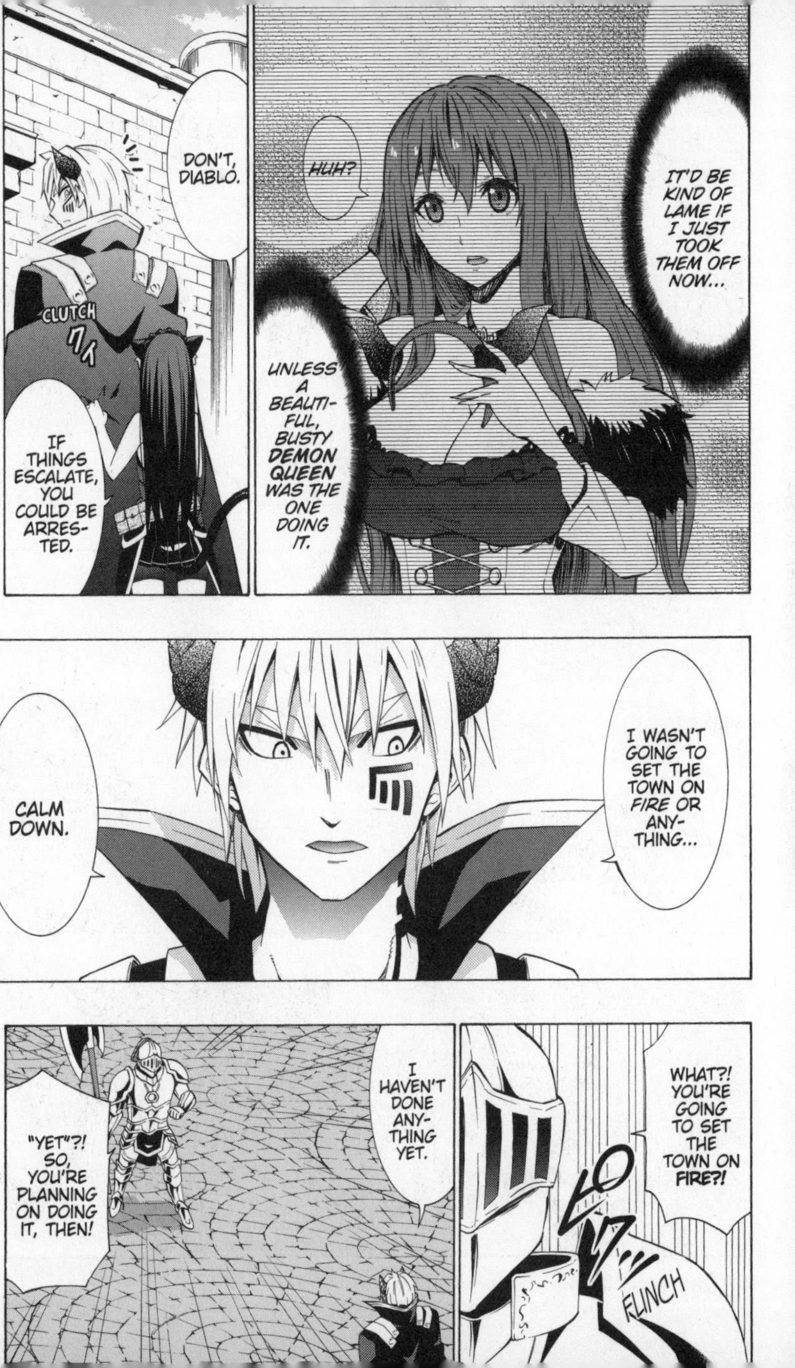
IT'D BE KIND OF LAME IF I JUST TOOK THEM OFF NOW...
HUH?
UNLESS A BEAUTIFUL, BUSTY DEMON QUEEN WAS THE ONE DOING IT.
DON'T, DIABLO.
CLUTCH
IF THINGS ESCALATE, YOU COULD BE ARRESTED.
I WASN'T GOING TO SET THE TOWN ON FIRE OR ANYTHING...
CALM DOWN.
WHAT?! YOU'RE GOING TO SET THE TOWN ON FIRE?!
FLINCH
I HAVEN'T DONE ANYTHING YET.
"YET"?! SO, YOU'RE PLANNING ON DOING IT, THEN!

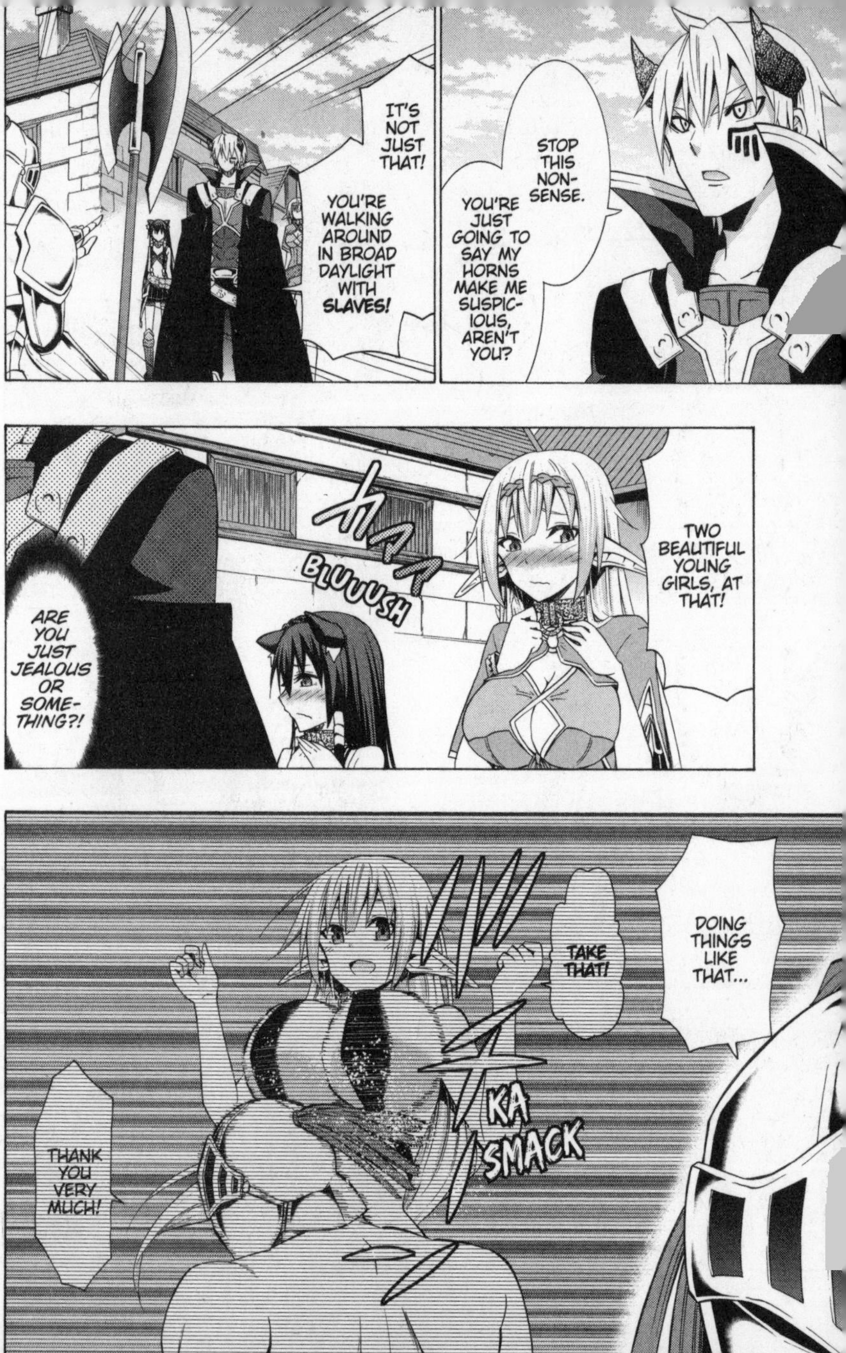
STOP THIS NON-SENSE.
YOU'RE JUST GOING TO SAY MY HORNS MAKE ME SUSPICIOUS, AREN'T YOU?
IT'S NOT JUST THAT!
YOU'RE WALKING AROUND IN BROAD DAYLIGHT WITH SLAVES!
TWO BEAUTIFUL YOUNG GIRLS, AT THAT!
BLUUUSH
ARE YOU JUST JEALOUS OR SOME-THING?!
DOING THINGS LIKE THAT...
TAKE THAT!
KA SMACK
THANK YOU VERY MUCH!

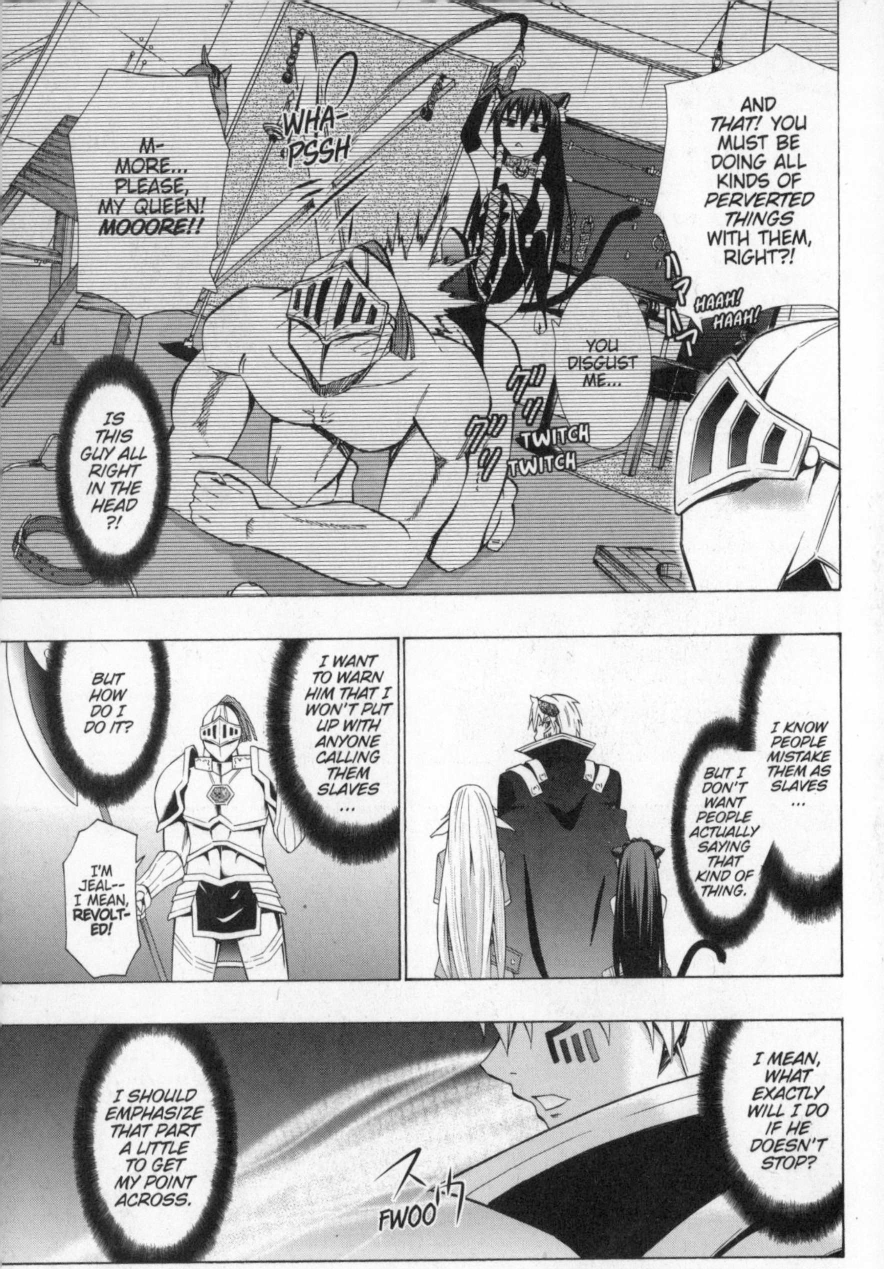
AND THAT! YOU MUST BE DOING ALL KINDS OF PERVERTED THINGS WITH THEM, RIGHT?!
HAAH! HAAH!
WHA-PSSH
M-MORE... PLEASE, MY QUEEN! MOOORE!!
YOU DISGUST ME...
TWITCH TWITCH
IS THIS GUY ALL RIGHT IN THE HEAD?!
I KNOW PEOPLE MISTAKE THEM AS SLAVES ...
BUT I DON'T WANT PEOPLE ACTUALLY SAYING THAT KIND OF THING.
I WANT TO WARN HIM THAT I WON'T PUT UP WITH ANYONE CALLING THEM SLAVES ...
BUT HOW DO I DO IT?
I'M JEAL-- I MEAN, REVOLTED!
I MEAN, WHAT EXACTLY WILL I DO IF HE DOESN'T STOP?
FWOO
I SHOULD EMPHASIZE THAT PART A LITTLE TO GET MY POINT ACROSS.

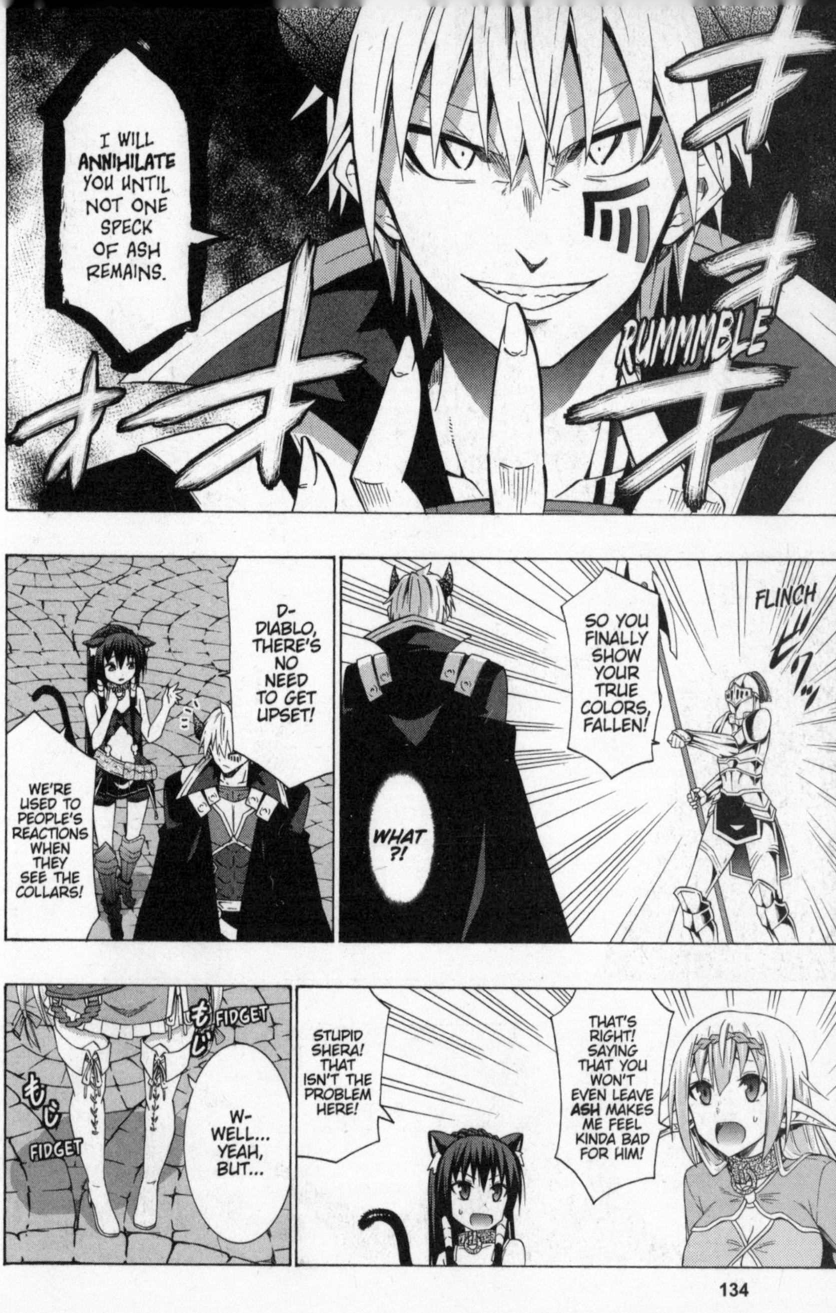
I WILL ANNIHILATE YOU UNTIL NOT ONE SPECK OF ASH REMAINS.
RUMMMBLE
FLINCH
SO YOU FINALLY SHOW YOUR TRUE COLORS, FALLEN!
WHAT?!
D-DIABLO, THERE'S NO NEED TO GET UPSET!
WE'RE USED TO PEOPLE'S REACTIONS WHEN THEY SEE THE COLLARS!
THAT'S RIGHT! SAYING THAT YOU WON'T EVEN LEAVE ASH MAKES ME FEEL KINDA BAD FOR HIM!
STUPID SHERA! THAT ISN'T THE PROBLEM HERE!
FIDGET
W-WELL... YEAH, BUT...
FIDGET

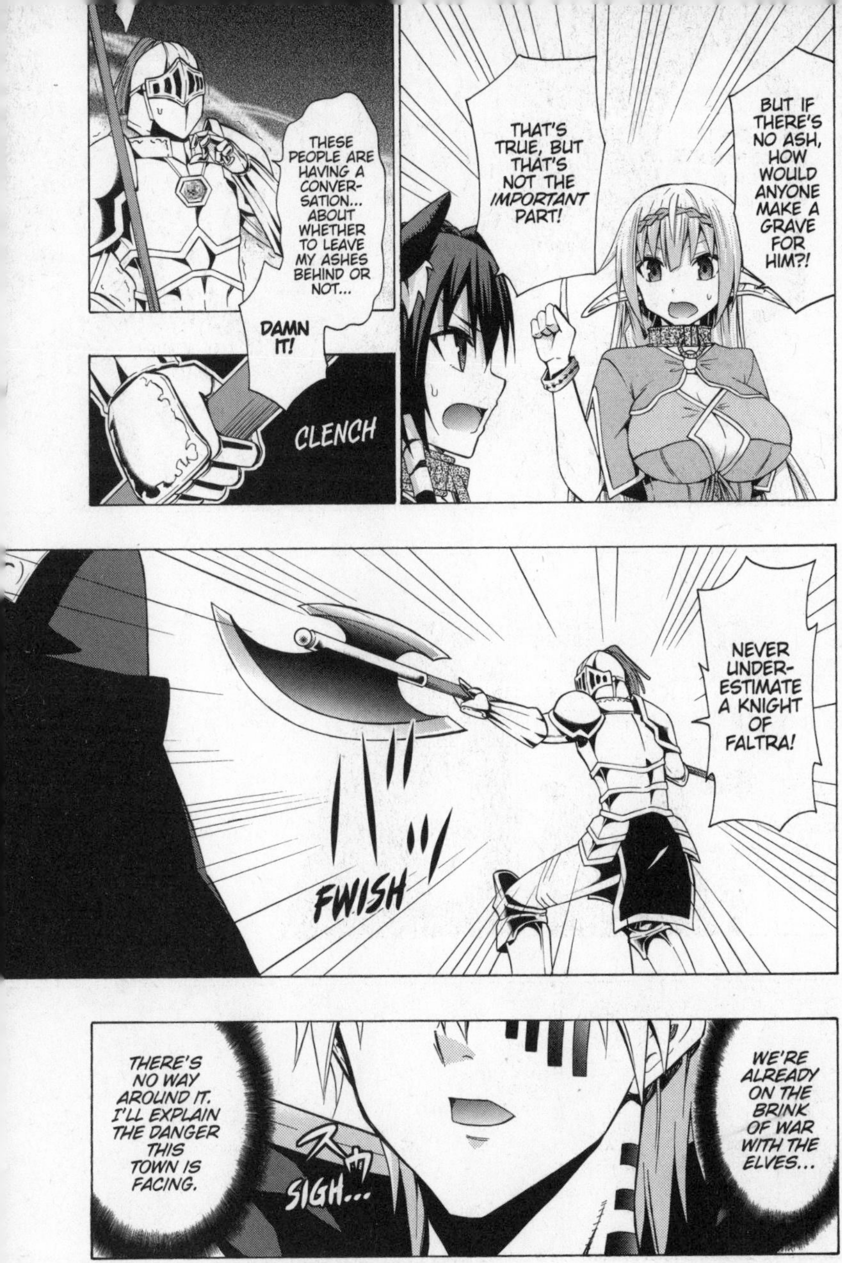
BUT IF THERE'S NO ASH, HOW WOULD ANYONE MAKE A GRAVE FOR HIM?!
THAT'S TRUE, BUT THAT'S NOT THE *IMPORTANT* PART!
THESE PEOPLE ARE HAVING A CONVER-SATION... ABOUT WHETHER TO LEAVE MY ASHES BEHIND OR NOT...
DAMN IT!
CLENCH
NEVER UNDER-ESTIMATE A KNIGHT OF FALTRA!
FWISH
WE'RE ALREADY ON THE BRINK OF WAR WITH THE ELVES...
SIGH...
THERE'S NO WAY AROUND IT. I'LL EXPLAIN THE DANGER THIS TOWN IS FACING.

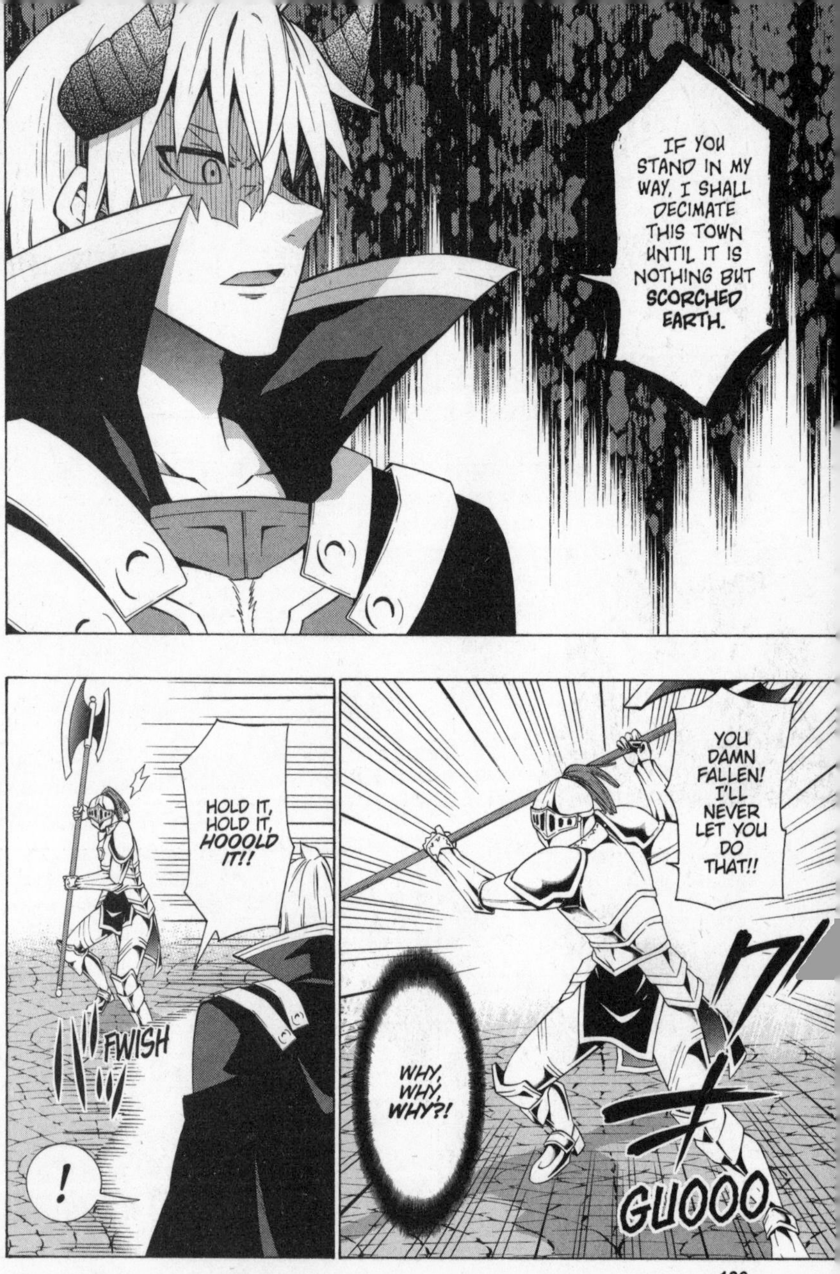
IF YOU STAND IN MY WAY, I SHALL DECIMATE THIS TOWN UNTIL IT IS NOTHING BUT SCORCHED EARTH.
YOU DAMN FALLEN! I'LL NEVER LET YOU DO THAT!!
WHY, WHY, WHY?!
GUOOO
HOLD IT, HOLD IT, HOOOLD IT!!
FWISH
!

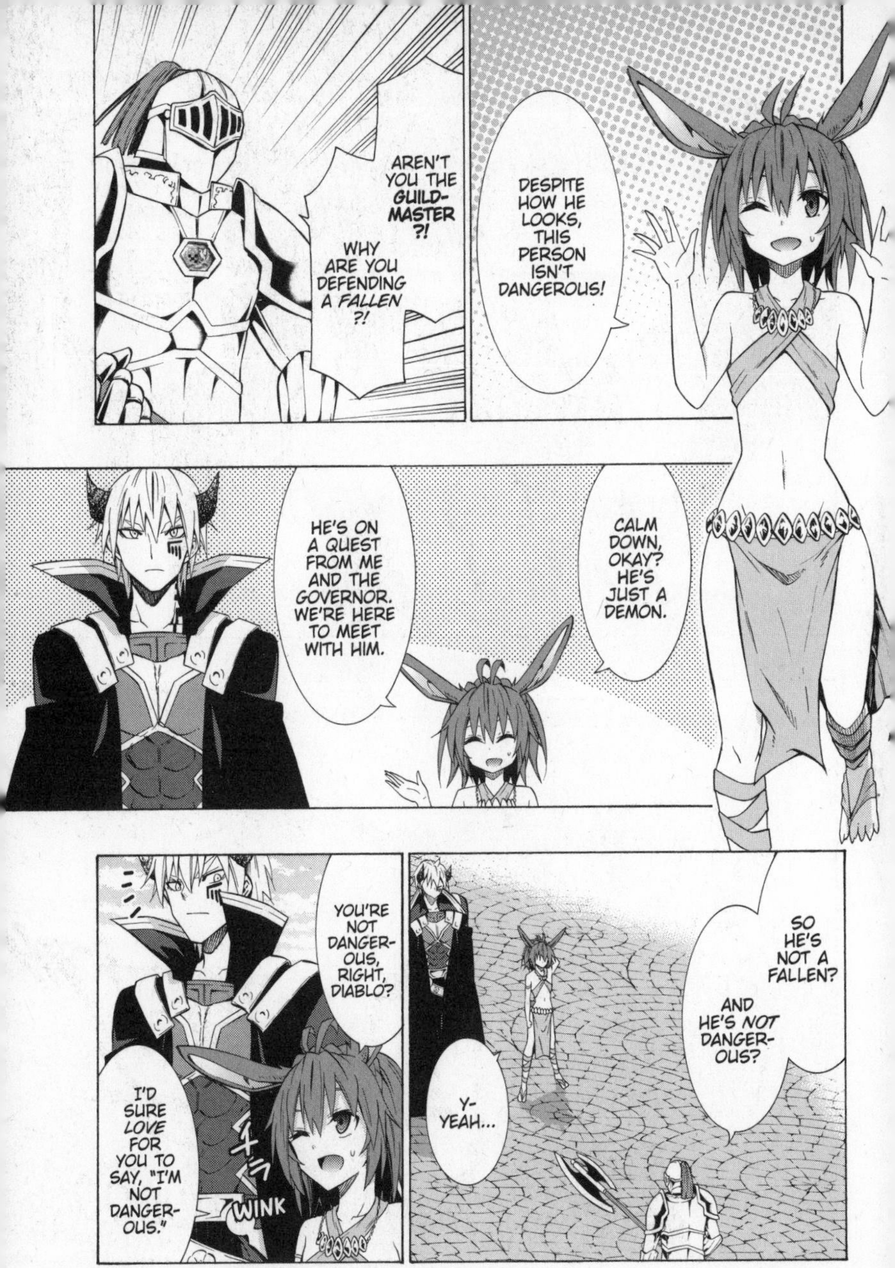
DESPITE HOW HE LOOKS, THIS PERSON ISN'T DANGEROUS!
AREN'T YOU THE **GUILD-MASTER**?!
WHY ARE YOU DEFENDING A *FALLEN*?!
CALM DOWN, OKAY? HE'S JUST A DEMON.
HE'S ON A QUEST FROM ME AND THE GOVERNOR. WE'RE HERE TO MEET WITH HIM.
SO HE'S NOT A FALLEN?
AND HE'S *NOT* DANGEROUS?
Y-YEAH...
YOU'RE NOT DANGEROUS, RIGHT, DIABLO?
I'D SURE *LOVE* FOR YOU TO SAY, "I'M NOT DANGEROUS."
WINK

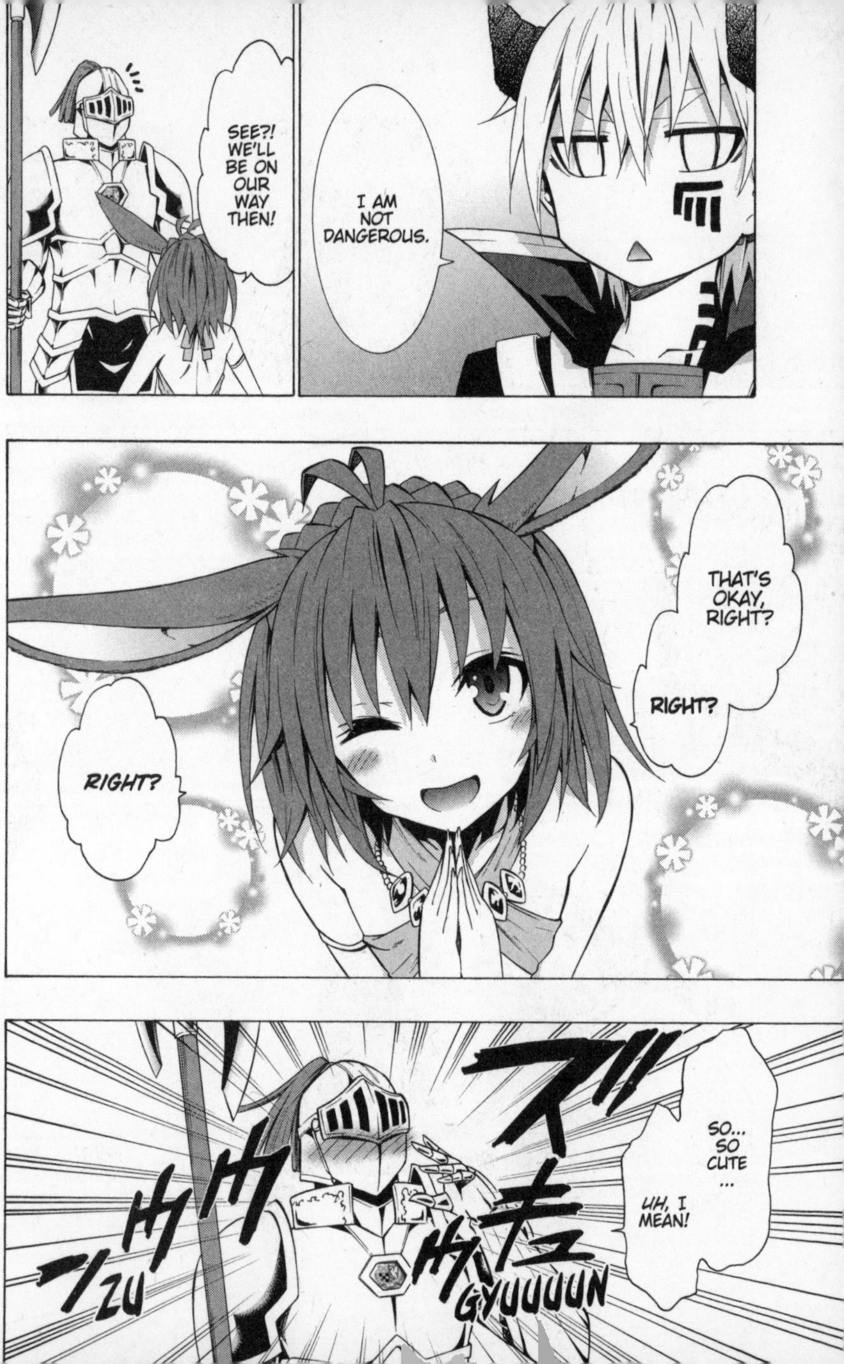
I AM NOT DANGEROUS.
SEE?! WE'LL BE ON OUR WAY THEN!
THAT'S OKAY, RIGHT?
RIGHT?
RIGHT?
SO... SO CUTE...
UH, I MEAN!
GYUUUUN
ZU

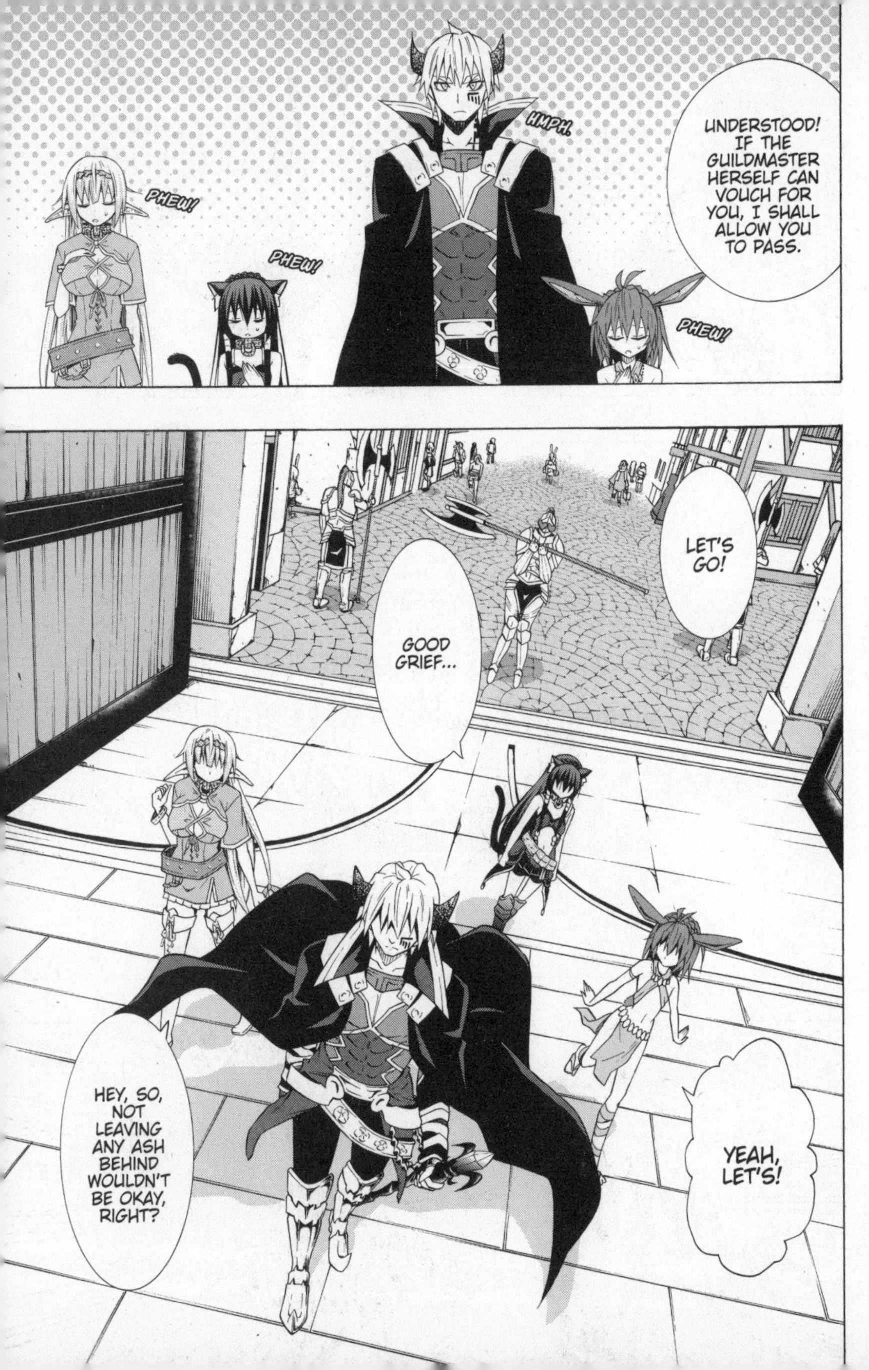
UNDERSTOOD! IF THE GUILDMASTER HERSELF CAN VOUCH FOR YOU, I SHALL ALLOW YOU TO PASS.
HMPH.
PHEW!
PHEW!
PHEW!
LET'S GO!
GOOD GRIEF...
YEAH, LET'S!
HEY, SO, NOT LEAVING ANY ASH BEHIND WOULDN'T BE OKAY, RIGHT?

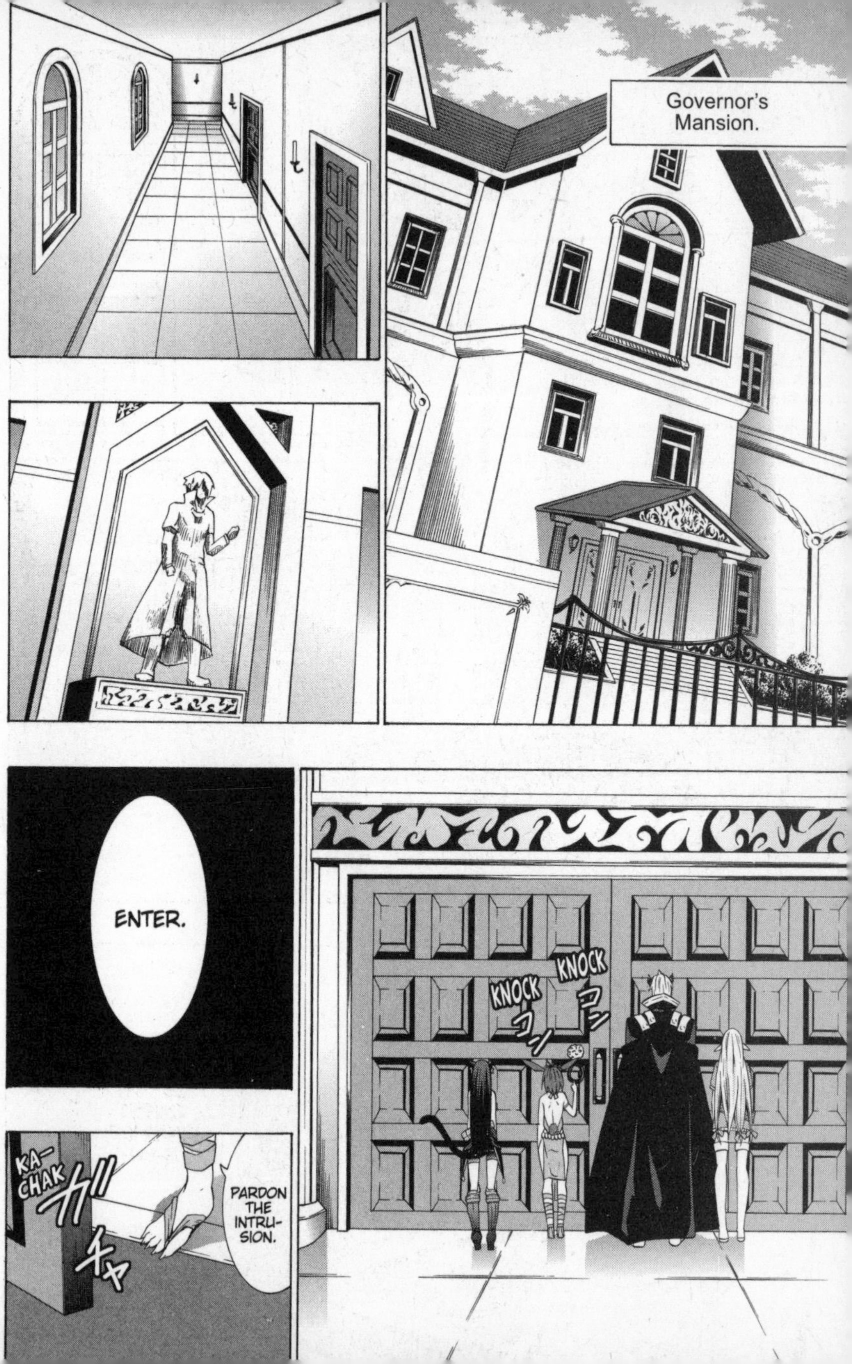
Governor's Mansion.
KNOCK
KNOCK
ENTER.
KA-CHAK
PARDON THE INTRUSION.

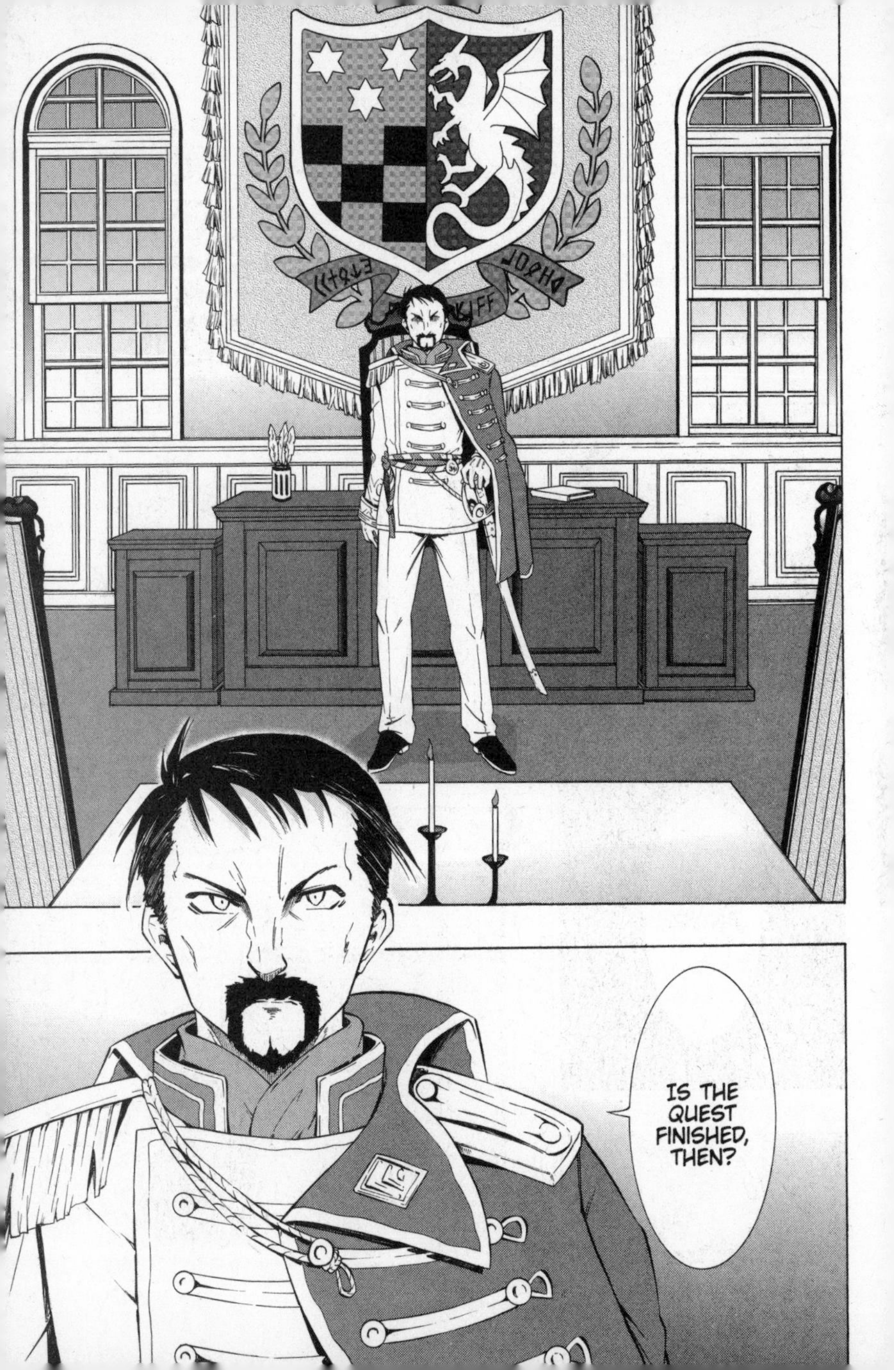
IS THE QUEST FINISHED, THEN?

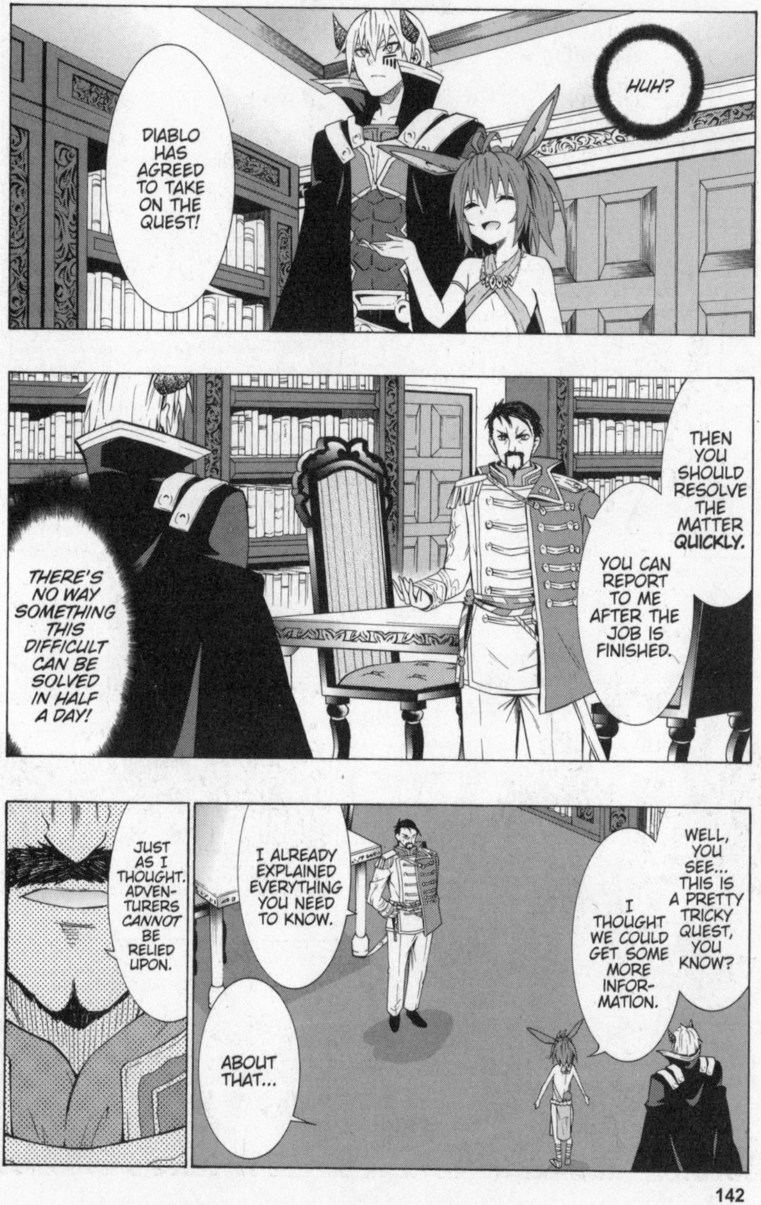
HUH?
DIABLO HAS AGREED TO TAKE ON THE QUEST!
THEN YOU SHOULD RESOLVE THE MATTER **QUICKLY.**
YOU CAN REPORT TO ME AFTER THE JOB IS FINISHED.
THERE'S NO WAY SOMETHING THIS DIFFICULT CAN BE SOLVED IN HALF A DAY!
WELL, YOU SEE... THIS IS A PRETTY TRICKY QUEST, YOU KNOW?
I THOUGHT WE COULD GET SOME MORE INFORMATION.
I ALREADY EXPLAINED EVERYTHING YOU NEED TO KNOW.
ABOUT THAT...
JUST AS I THOUGHT. ADVENTURERS *CANNOT* BE RELIED UPON.

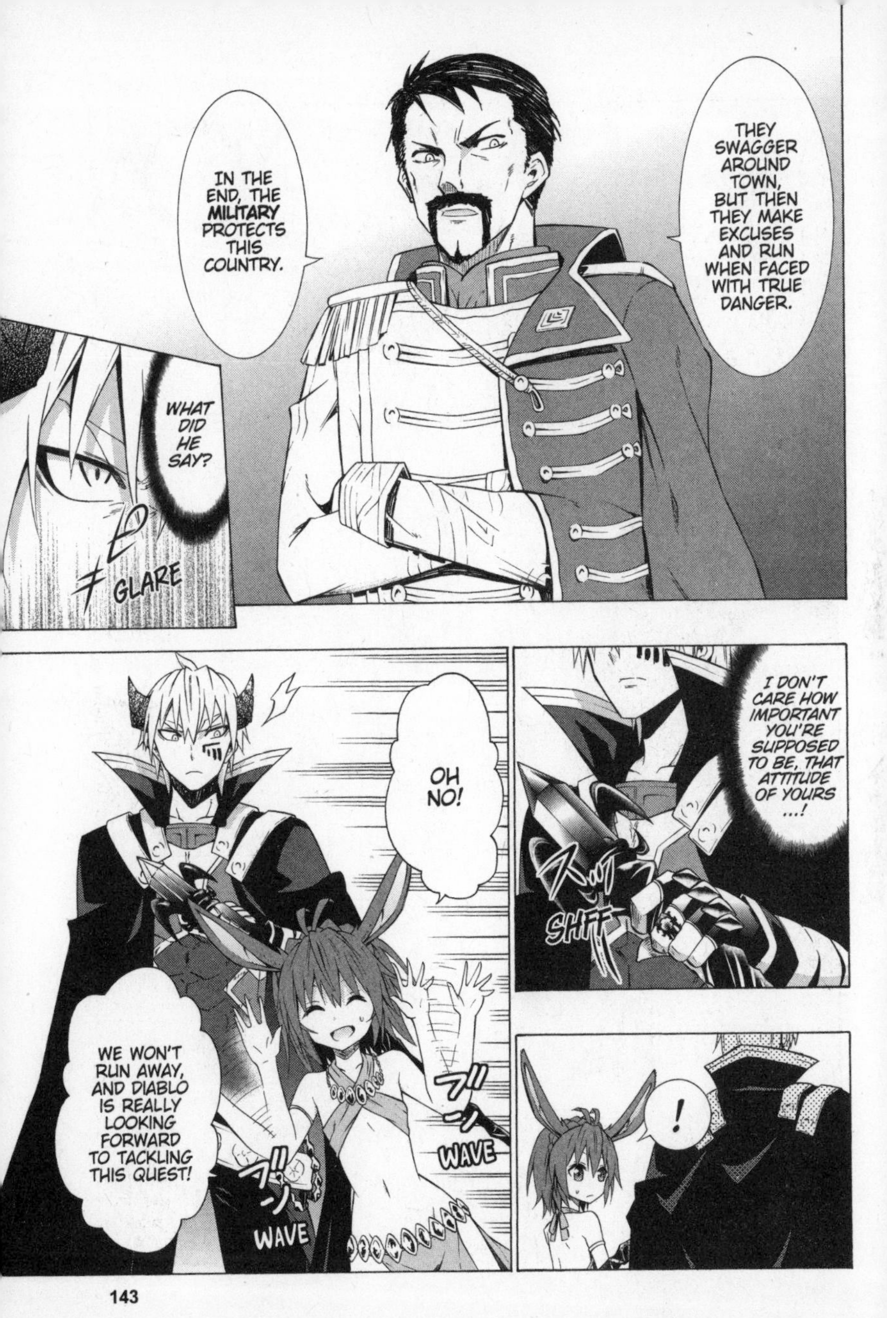
THEY SWAGGER AROUND TOWN, BUT THEN THEY MAKE EXCUSES AND RUN WHEN FACED WITH TRUE DANGER.
IN THE END, THE MILITARY PROTECTS THIS COUNTRY.
WHAT DID HE SAY?
GLARE
I DON'T CARE HOW IMPORTANT YOU'RE SUPPOSED TO BE, THAT ATTITUDE OF YOURS ...!
SHFF
!
OH NO!
WE WON'T RUN AWAY, AND DIABLO IS REALLY LOOKING FORWARD TO TACKLING THIS QUEST!
WAVE
WAVE

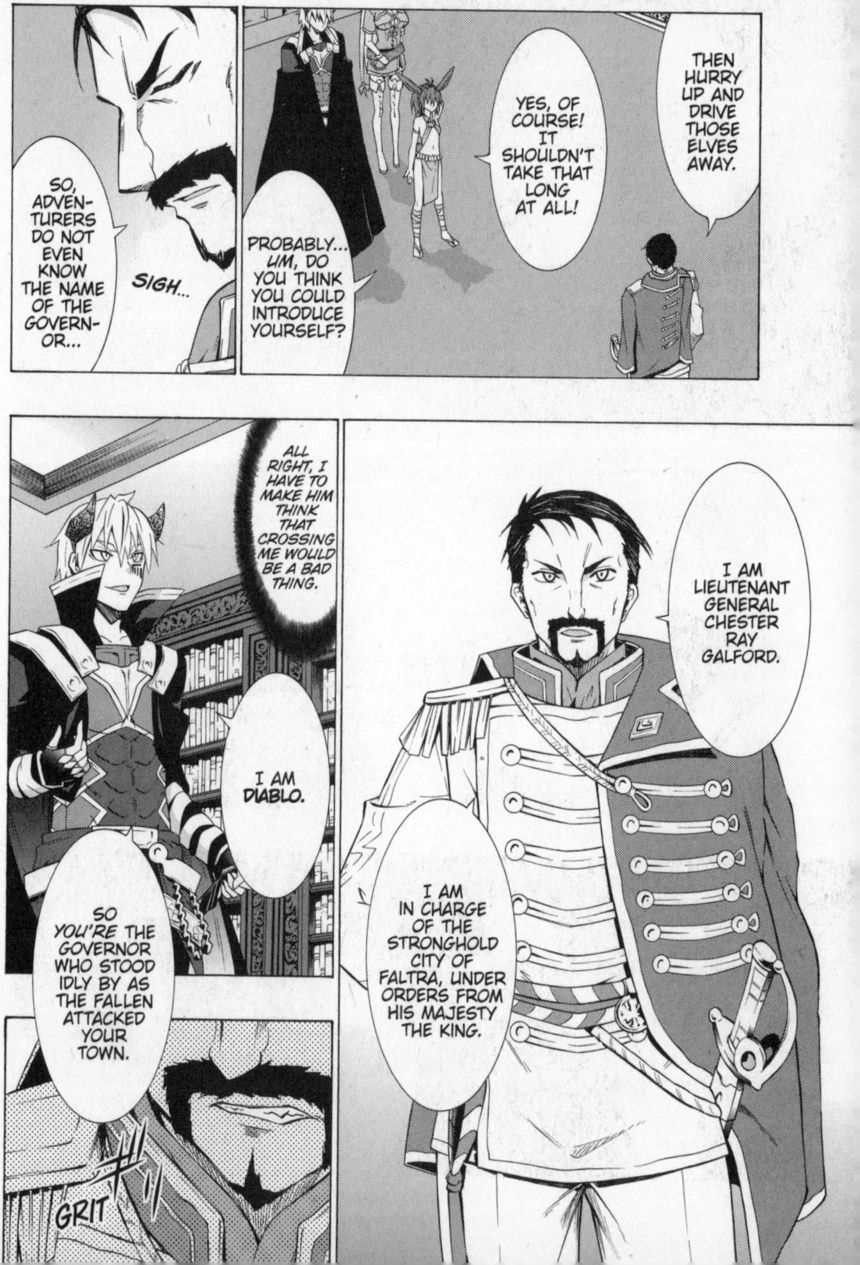
THEN HURRY UP AND DRIVE THOSE ELVES AWAY.
YES, OF COURSE! IT SHOULDN'T TAKE THAT LONG AT ALL!
PROBABLY... UM, DO YOU THINK YOU COULD INTRODUCE YOURSELF?
SO, ADVENTURERS DO NOT EVEN KNOW THE NAME OF THE GOVERNOR...
SIGH...
I AM LIEUTENANT GENERAL CHESTER RAY GALFORD.
I AM IN CHARGE OF THE STRONGHOLD CITY OF FALTRA, UNDER ORDERS FROM HIS MAJESTY THE KING.
ALL RIGHT, I HAVE TO MAKE HIM THINK THAT CROSSING ME WOULD BE A BAD THING.
I AM DIABLO.
SO YOU'RE THE GOVERNOR WHO STOOD IDLY BY AS THE FALLEN ATTACKED YOUR TOWN.
GRIT

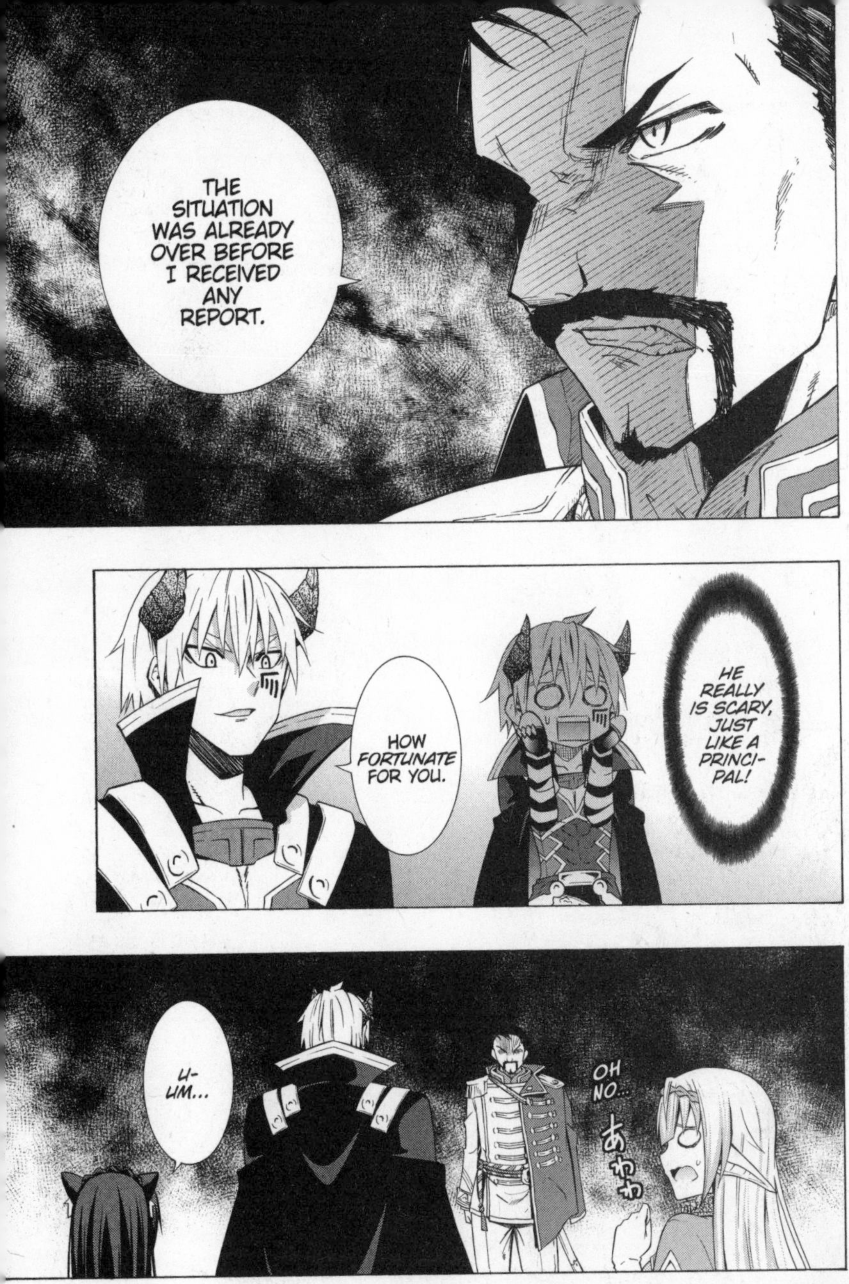
THE SITUATION WAS ALREADY OVER BEFORE I RECEIVED ANY REPORT.
HE REALLY IS SCARY, JUST LIKE A PRINCI-PAL!
HOW FORTUNATE FOR YOU.
OH NO...
あわわ
U-UM...

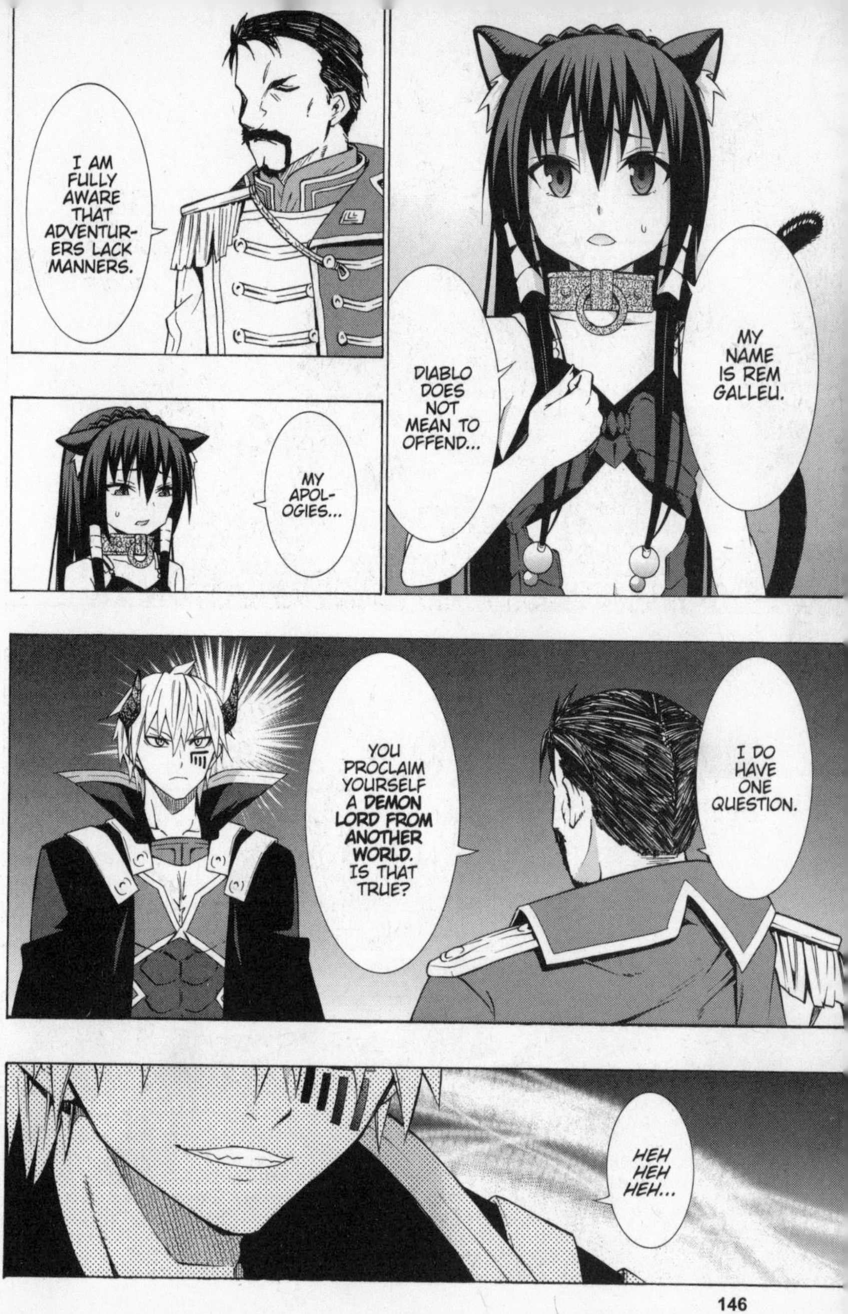
MY NAME IS REM GALLEU.
DIABLO DOES NOT MEAN TO OFFEND...
I AM FULLY AWARE THAT ADVENTURERS LACK MANNERS.
MY APOLOGIES...
I DO HAVE ONE QUESTION.
YOU PROCLAIM YOURSELF A DEMON LORD FROM ANOTHER WORLD. IS THAT TRUE?
HEH HEH HEH...

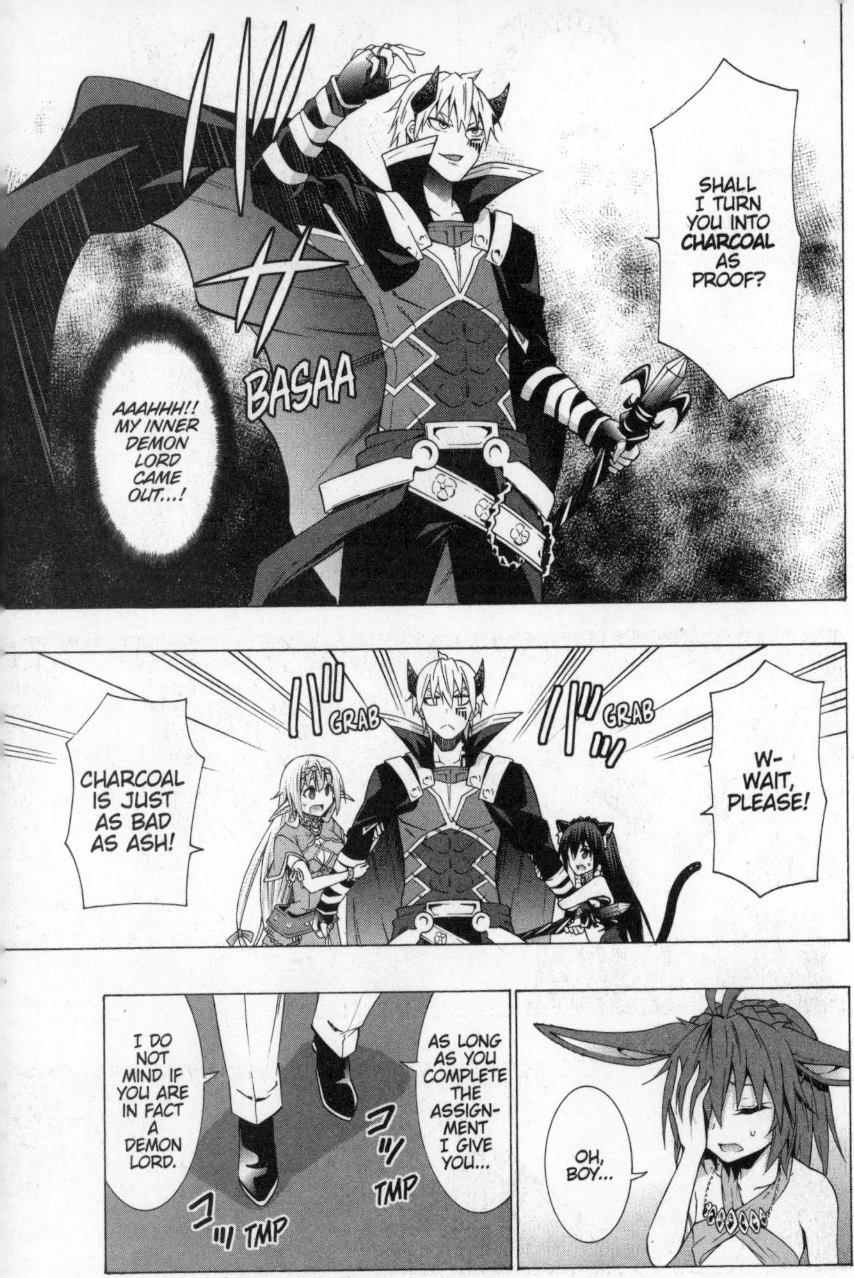
SHALL I TURN YOU INTO CHARCOAL AS PROOF?
BASAA
AAAHHH!! MY INNER DEMON LORD CAME OUT...!
W-WAIT, PLEASE!
GRAB
GRAB
CHARCOAL IS JUST AS BAD AS ASH!
OH, BOY...
AS LONG AS YOU COMPLETE THE ASSIGNMENT I GIVE YOU...
I DO NOT MIND IF YOU ARE IN FACT A DEMON LORD.
TMP
TMP

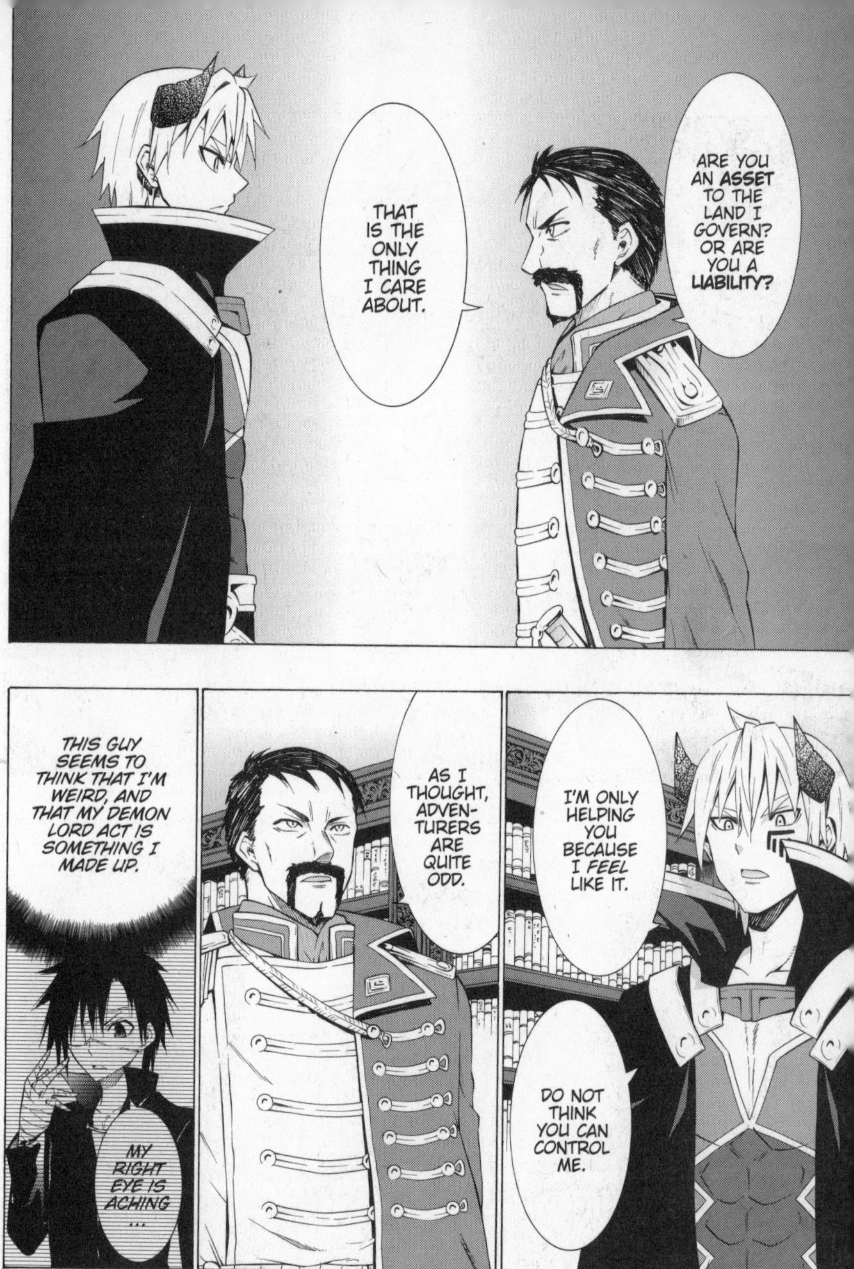
ARE YOU AN ASSET TO THE LAND I GOVERN? OR ARE YOU A LIABILITY?
THAT IS THE ONLY THING I CARE ABOUT.
I'M ONLY HELPING YOU BECAUSE I FEEL LIKE IT.
DO NOT THINK YOU CAN CONTROL ME.
AS I THOUGHT, ADVENTURERS ARE QUITE ODD.
THIS GUY SEEMS TO THINK THAT I'M WEIRD, AND THAT MY DEMON LORD ACT IS SOMETHING I MADE UP.
MY RIGHT EYE IS ACHING ...

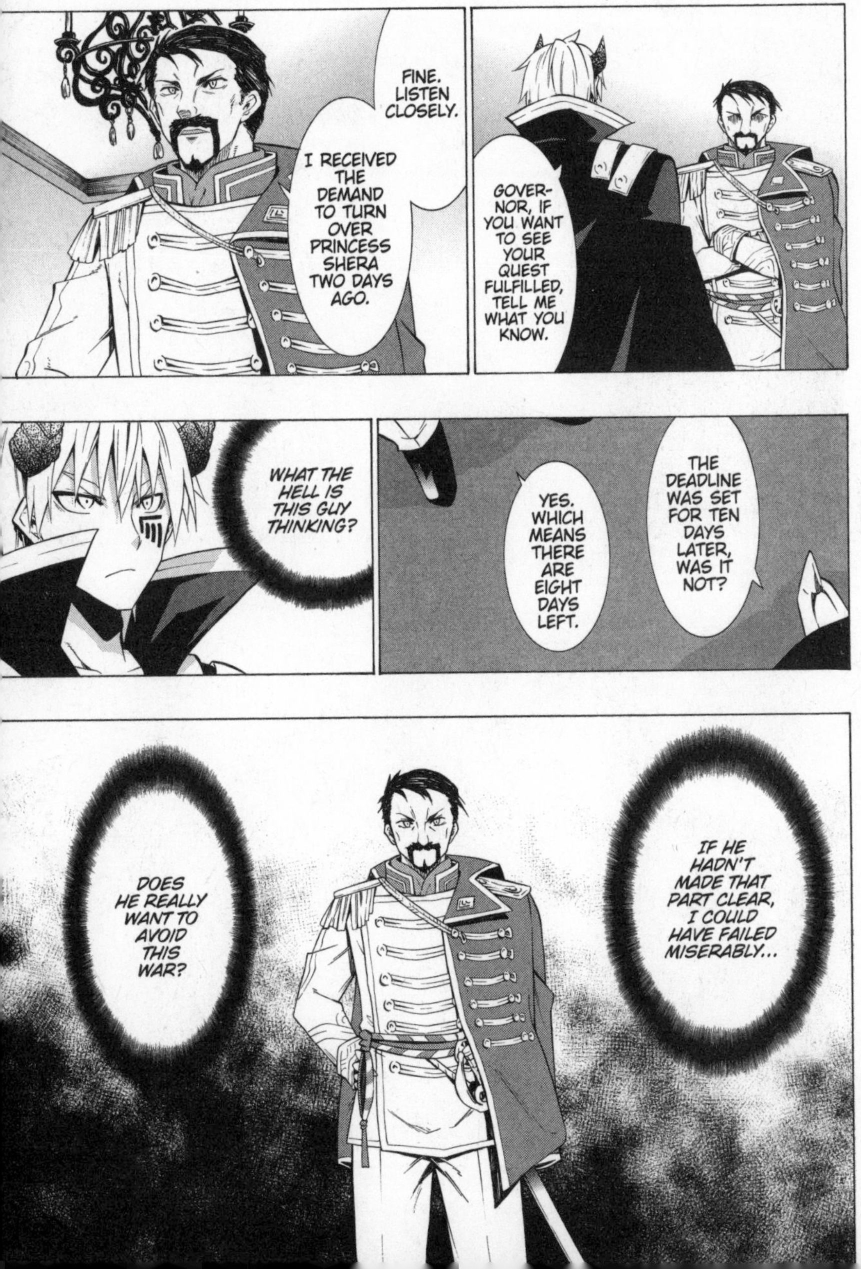
GOVERNOR, IF YOU WANT TO SEE YOUR QUEST FULFILLED, TELL ME WHAT YOU KNOW.
FINE. LISTEN CLOSELY.
I RECEIVED THE DEMAND TO TURN OVER PRINCESS SHERA TWO DAYS AGO.
THE DEADLINE WAS SET FOR TEN DAYS LATER, WAS IT NOT?
YES. WHICH MEANS THERE ARE EIGHT DAYS LEFT.
WHAT THE HELL IS THIS GUY THINKING?
IF HE HADN'T MADE THAT PART CLEAR, I COULD HAVE FAILED MISERABLY...
DOES HE REALLY WANT TO AVOID THIS WAR?

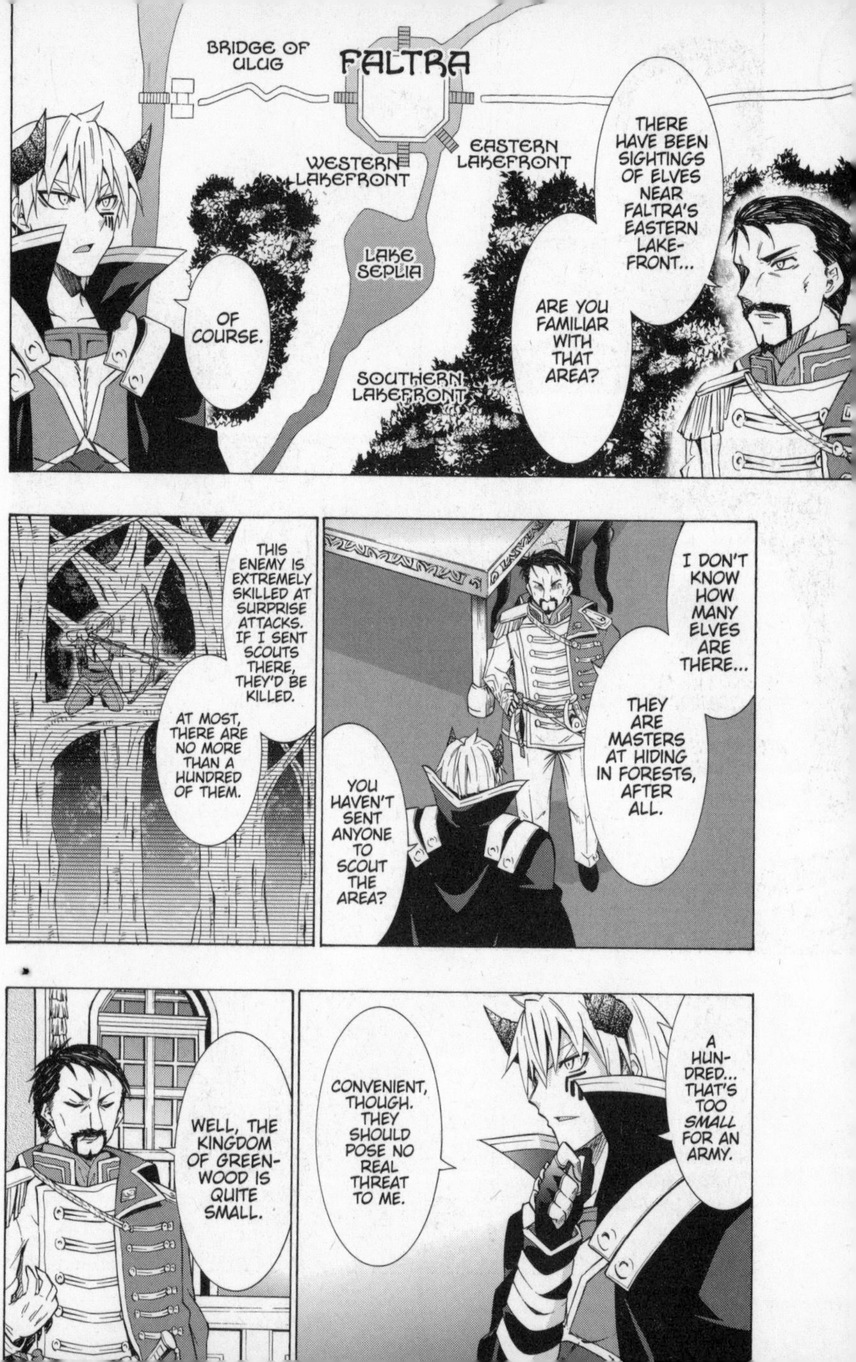
BRIDGE OF ULUG
FALTRA
WESTERN LAKEFRONT
EASTERN LAKEFRONT
LAKE SEPLIA
SOUTHERN LAKEFRONT
THERE HAVE BEEN SIGHTINGS OF ELVES NEAR FALTRA'S EASTERN LAKE-FRONT...
ARE YOU FAMILIAR WITH THAT AREA?
OF COURSE.
I DON'T KNOW HOW MANY ELVES ARE THERE...
THEY ARE MASTERS AT HIDING IN FORESTS, AFTER ALL.
YOU HAVEN'T SENT ANYONE TO SCOUT THE AREA?
THIS ENEMY IS EXTREMELY SKILLED AT SURPRISE ATTACKS. IF I SENT SCOUTS THERE, THEY'D BE KILLED.
AT MOST, THERE ARE NO MORE THAN A HUNDRED OF THEM.
A HUN-DRED... THAT'S TOO *SMALL* FOR AN ARMY.
CONVENIENT, THOUGH. THEY SHOULD POSE NO REAL THREAT TO ME.
WELL, THE KINGDOM OF GREEN-WOOD IS QUITE SMALL.

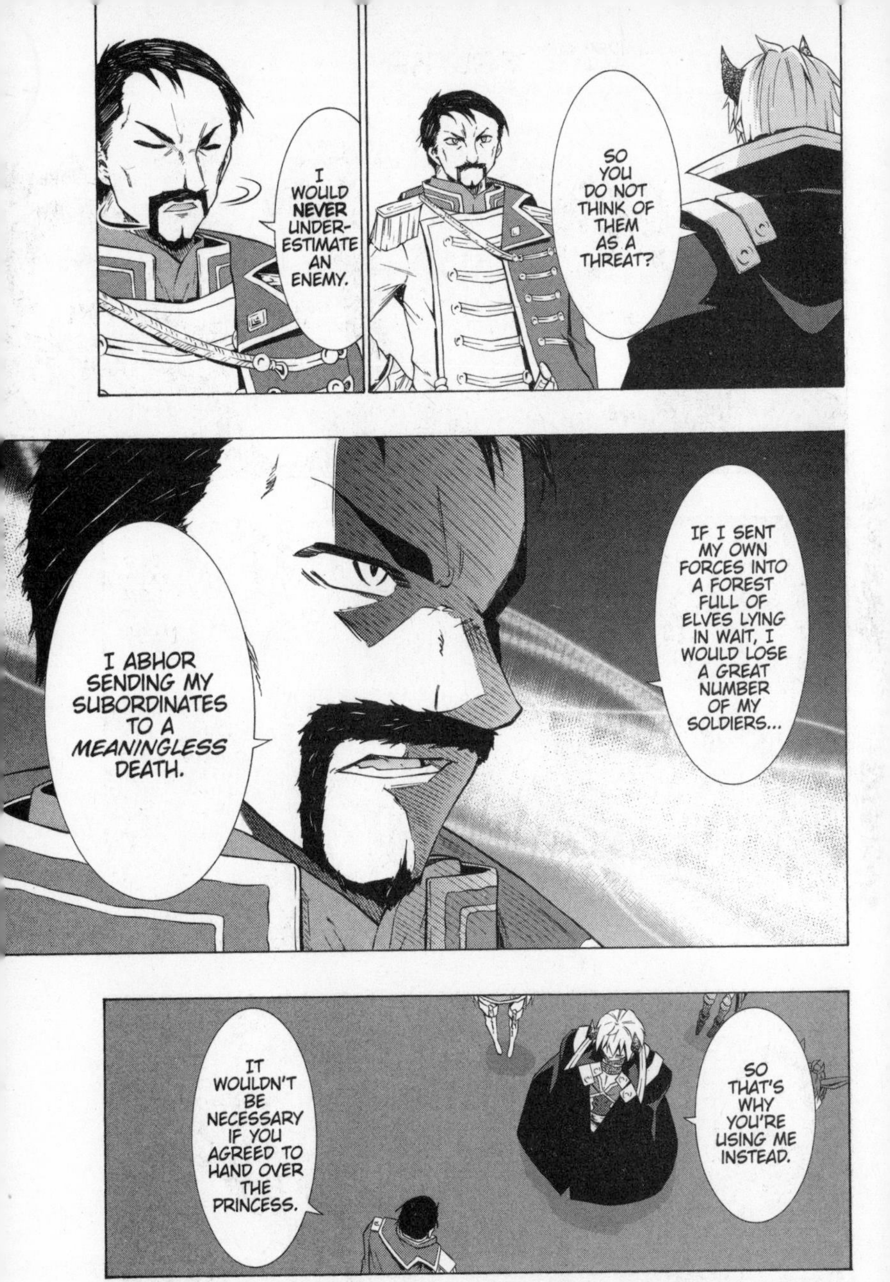
SO YOU DO NOT THINK OF THEM AS A THREAT?
I WOULD NEVER UNDER-ESTIMATE AN ENEMY.
IF I SENT MY OWN FORCES INTO A FOREST FULL OF ELVES LYING IN WAIT, I WOULD LOSE A GREAT NUMBER OF MY SOLDIERS...
I ABHOR SENDING MY SUBORDINATES TO A MEANINGLESS DEATH.
SO THAT'S WHY YOU'RE USING ME INSTEAD.
IT WOULDN'T BE NECESSARY IF YOU AGREED TO HAND OVER THE PRINCESS.

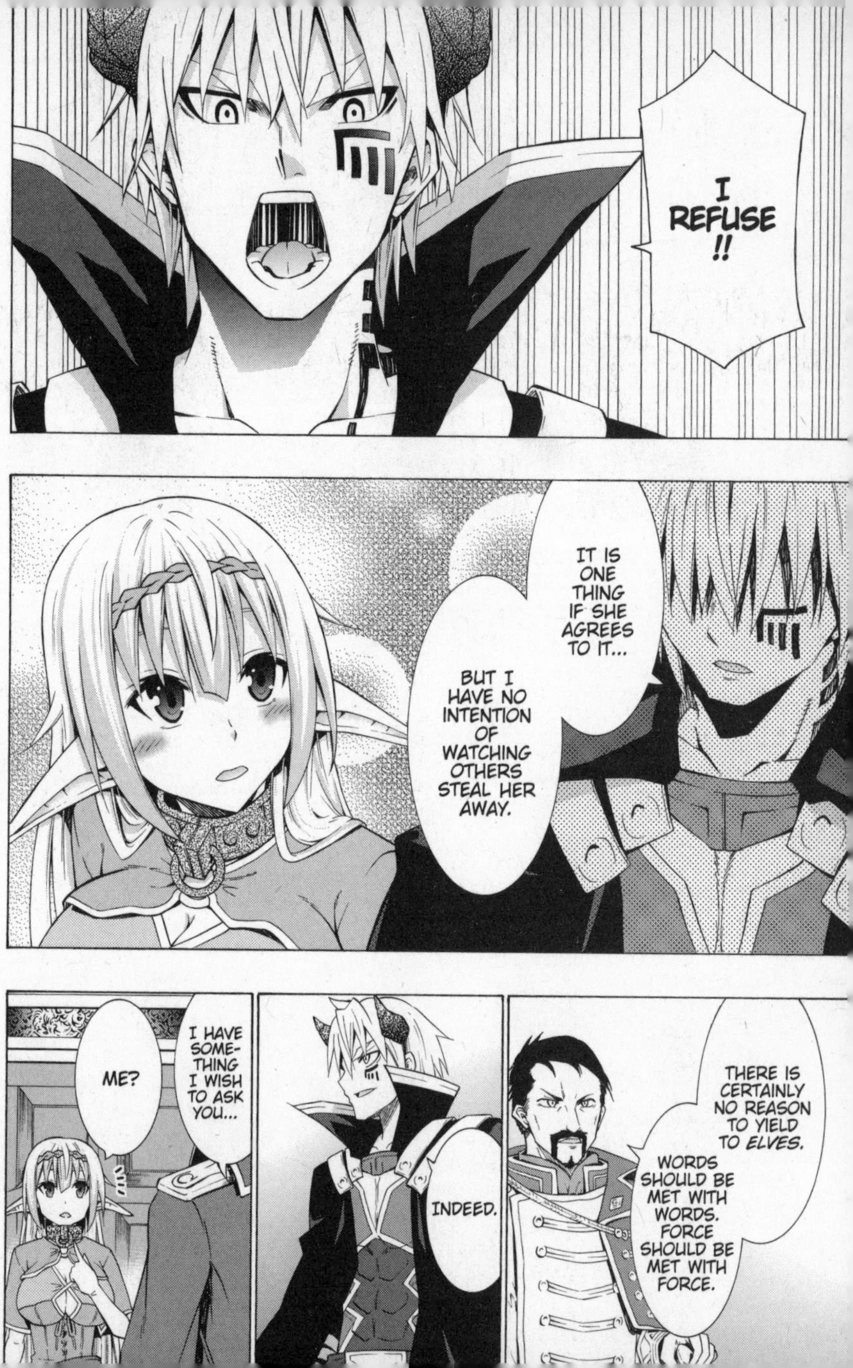
I REFUSE!!
IT IS ONE THING IF SHE AGREES TO IT...
BUT I HAVE NO INTENTION OF WATCHING OTHERS STEAL HER AWAY.
THERE IS CERTAINLY NO REASON TO YIELD TO *ELVES.*
WORDS SHOULD BE MET WITH WORDS. FORCE SHOULD BE MET WITH FORCE.
INDEED.
I HAVE SOMETHING I WISH TO ASK YOU...
ME?

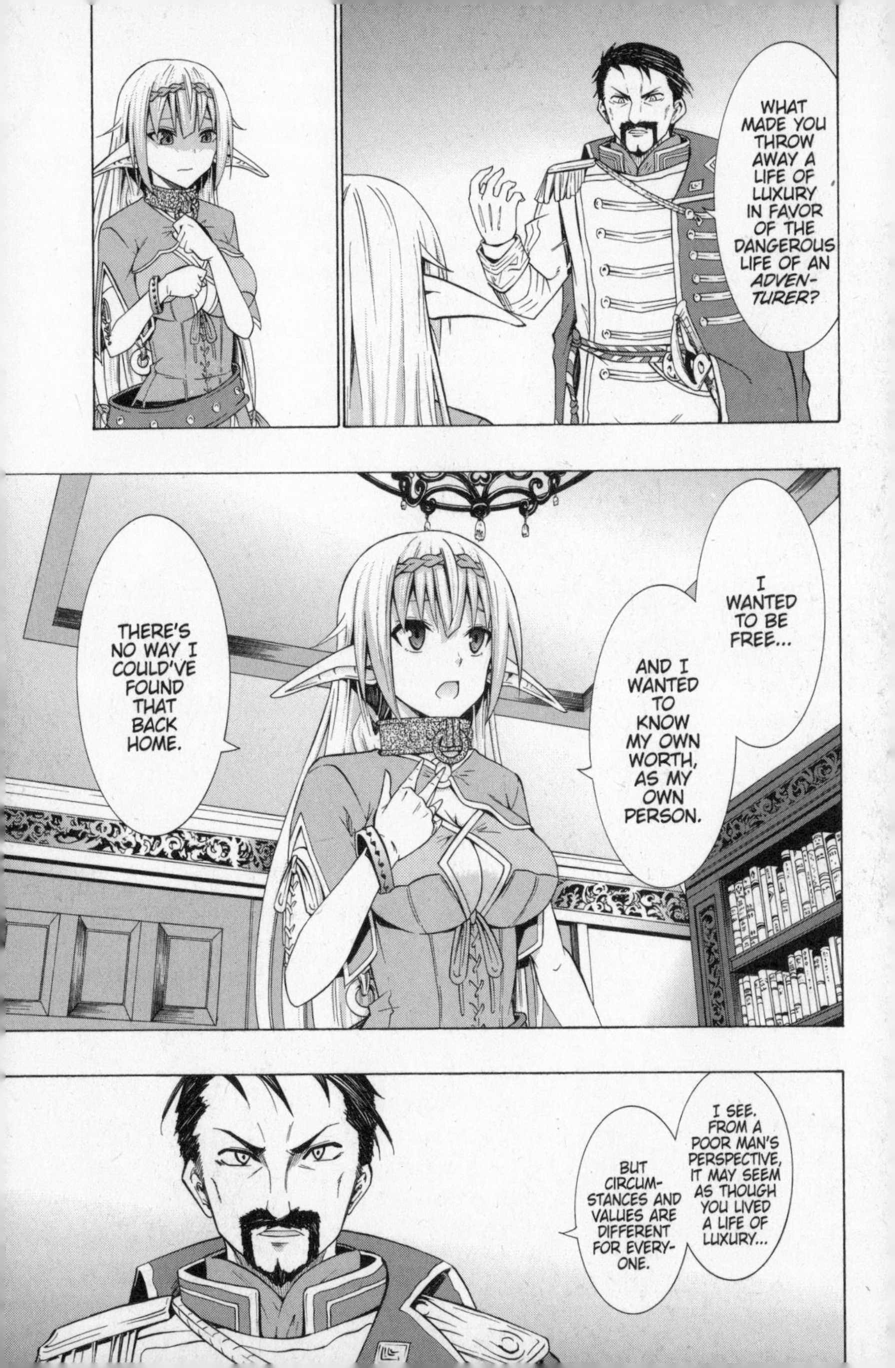
WHAT MADE YOU THROW AWAY A LIFE OF LUXURY IN FAVOR OF THE DANGEROUS LIFE OF AN *ADVENTURER?*
I WANTED TO BE FREE...
AND I WANTED TO KNOW MY OWN WORTH, AS MY OWN PERSON.
THERE'S NO WAY I COULD'VE FOUND THAT BACK HOME.
I SEE. FROM A POOR MAN'S PERSPECTIVE, IT MAY SEEM AS THOUGH YOU LIVED A LIFE OF LUXURY...
BUT CIRCUM-STANCES AND VALUES ARE DIFFERENT FOR EVERY-ONE.

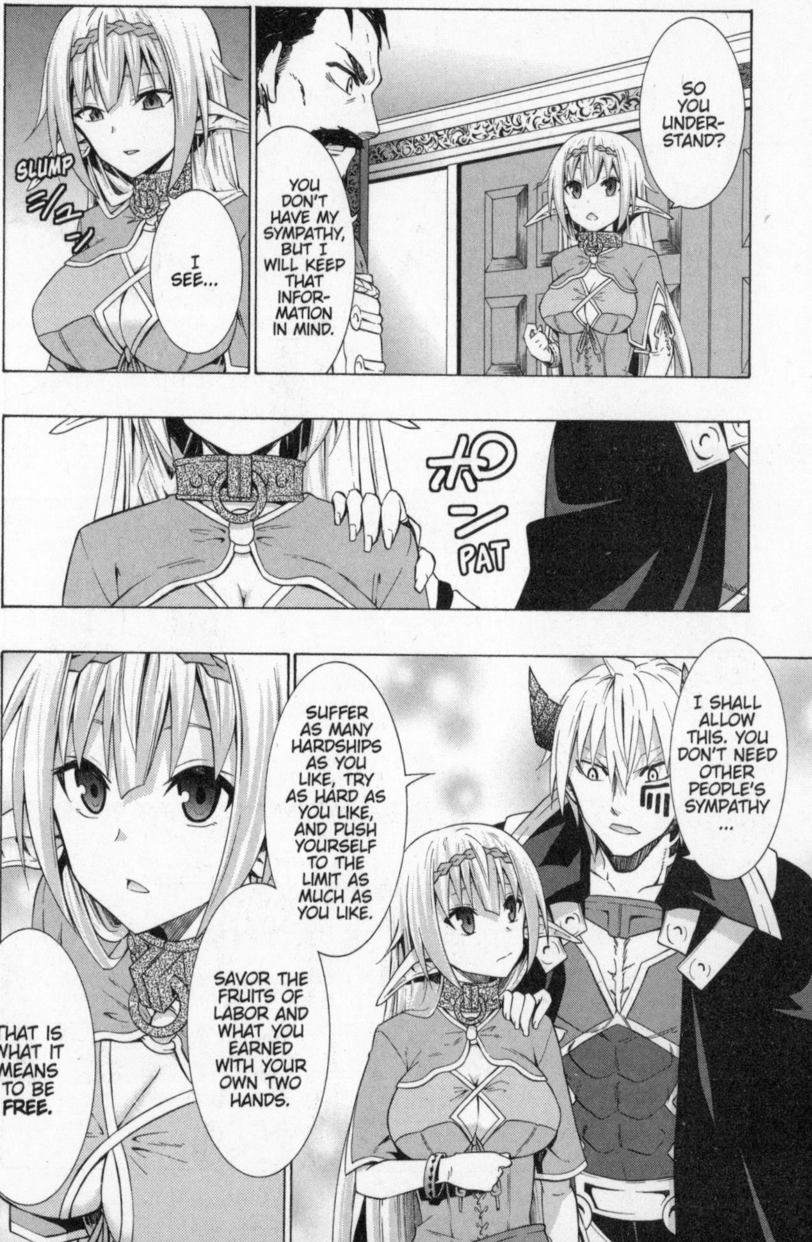
SO YOU UNDER-STAND?
YOU DON'T HAVE MY SYMPATHY, BUT I WILL KEEP THAT INFORMATION IN MIND.
SLUMP
I SEE...
PAT
I SHALL ALLOW THIS. YOU DON'T NEED OTHER PEOPLE'S SYMPATHY...
SUFFER AS MANY HARDSHIPS AS YOU LIKE, TRY AS HARD AS YOU LIKE, AND PUSH YOURSELF TO THE LIMIT AS MUCH AS YOU LIKE.
SAVOR THE FRUITS OF LABOR AND WHAT YOU EARNED WITH YOUR OWN TWO HANDS.
THAT IS WHAT IT MEANS TO BE FREE.

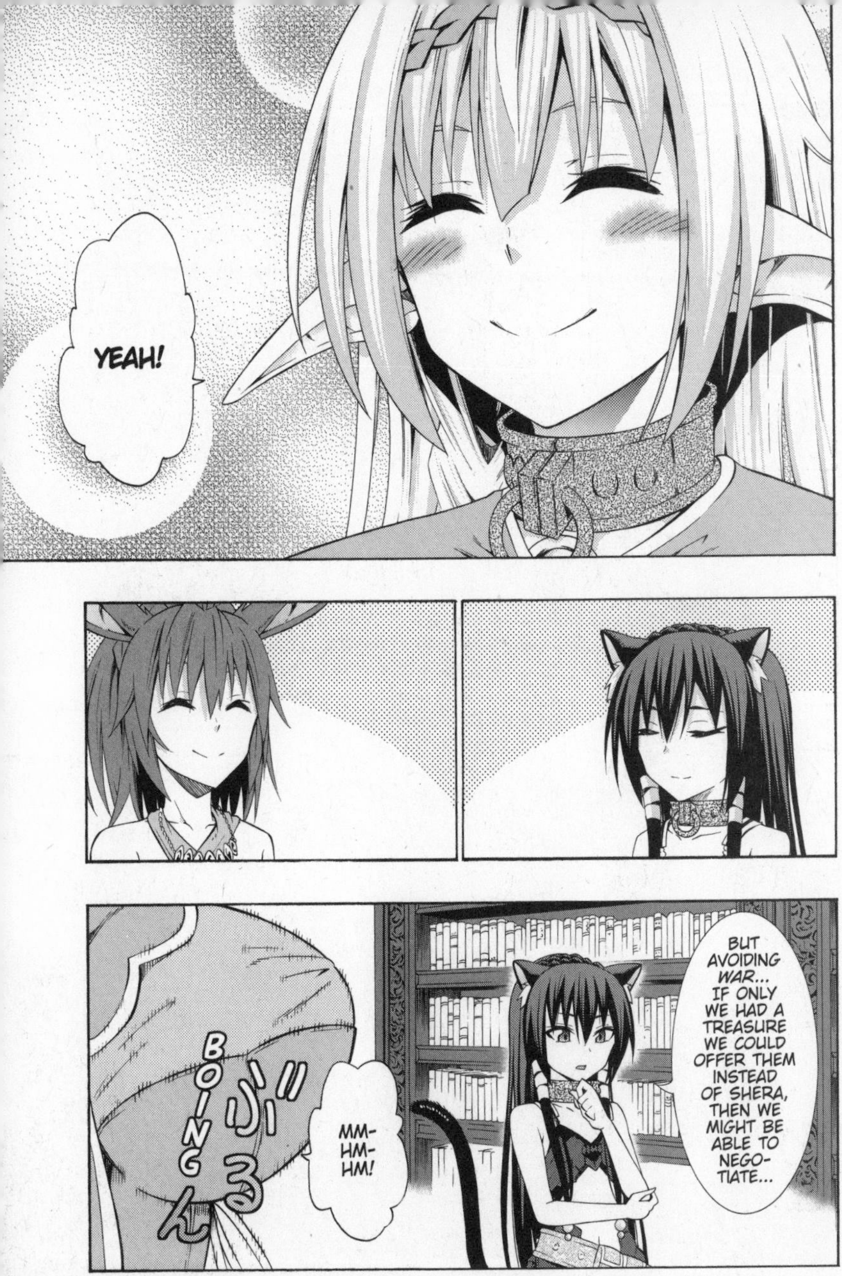
YEAH!
BUT AVOIDING WAR... IF ONLY WE HAD A TREASURE WE COULD OFFER THEM INSTEAD OF SHERA, THEN WE MIGHT BE ABLE TO NEGO-TIATE...
MM-HM-HM!
ぷるん
BOING

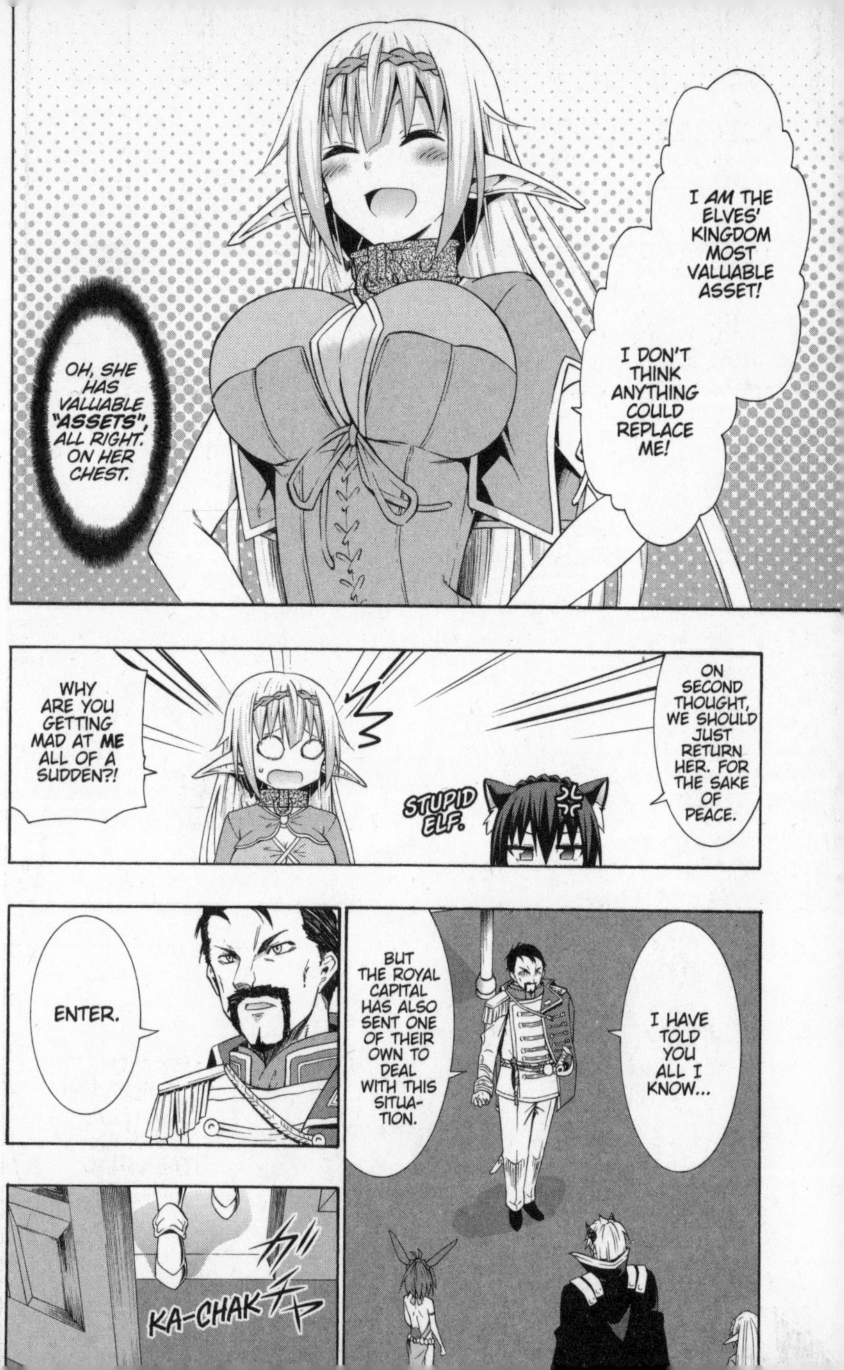
I AM THE ELVES' KINGDOM MOST VALUABLE ASSET!
I DON'T THINK ANYTHING COULD REPLACE ME!
OH, SHE HAS VALUABLE "ASSETS", ALL RIGHT. ON HER CHEST.
ON SECOND THOUGHT, WE SHOULD JUST RETURN HER. FOR THE SAKE OF PEACE.
STUPID ELF.
WHY ARE YOU GETTING MAD AT ME ALL OF A SUDDEN?!
I HAVE TOLD YOU ALL I KNOW...
BUT THE ROYAL CAPITAL HAS ALSO SENT ONE OF THEIR OWN TO DEAL WITH THIS SITUATION.
ENTER.
KA-CHAK

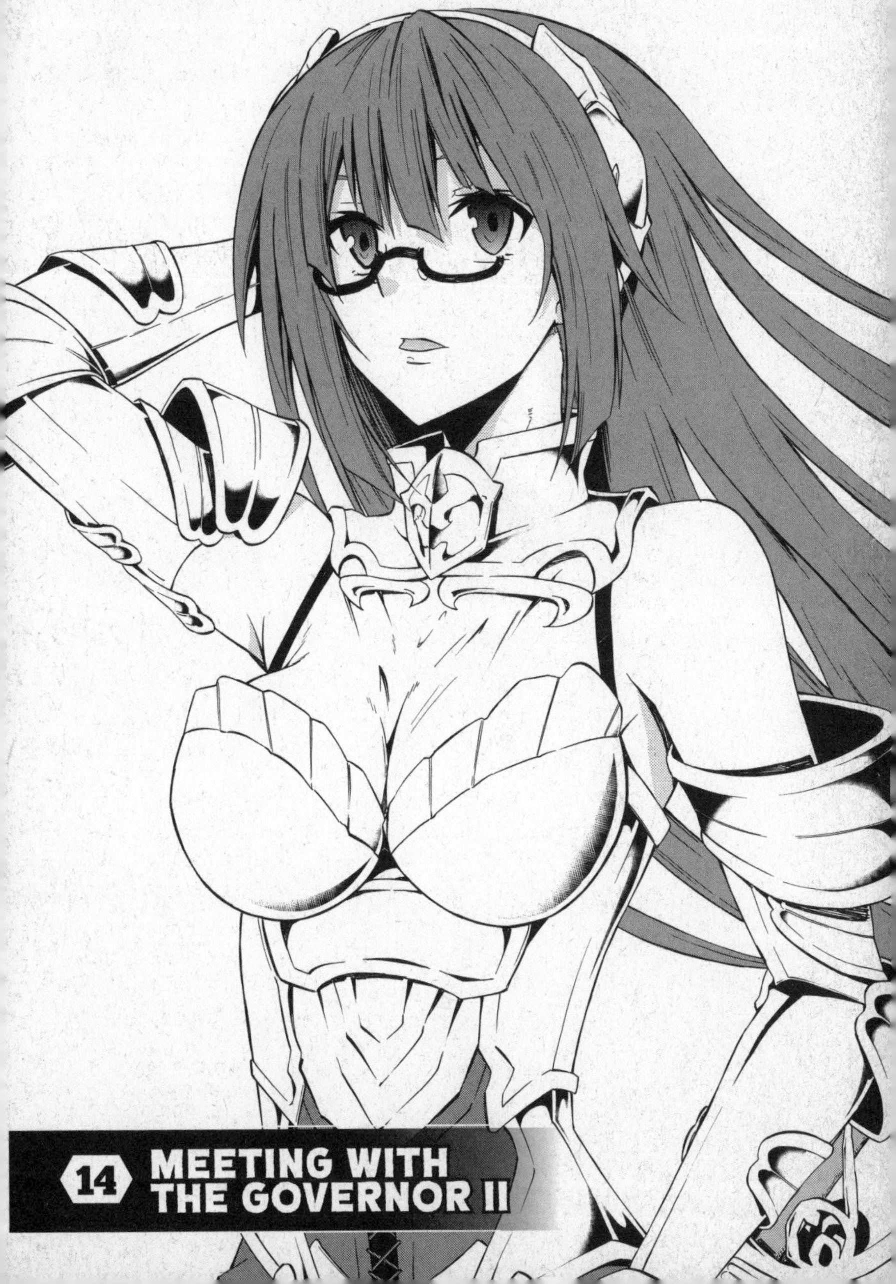
14
MEETING WITH
THE GOVERNOR II

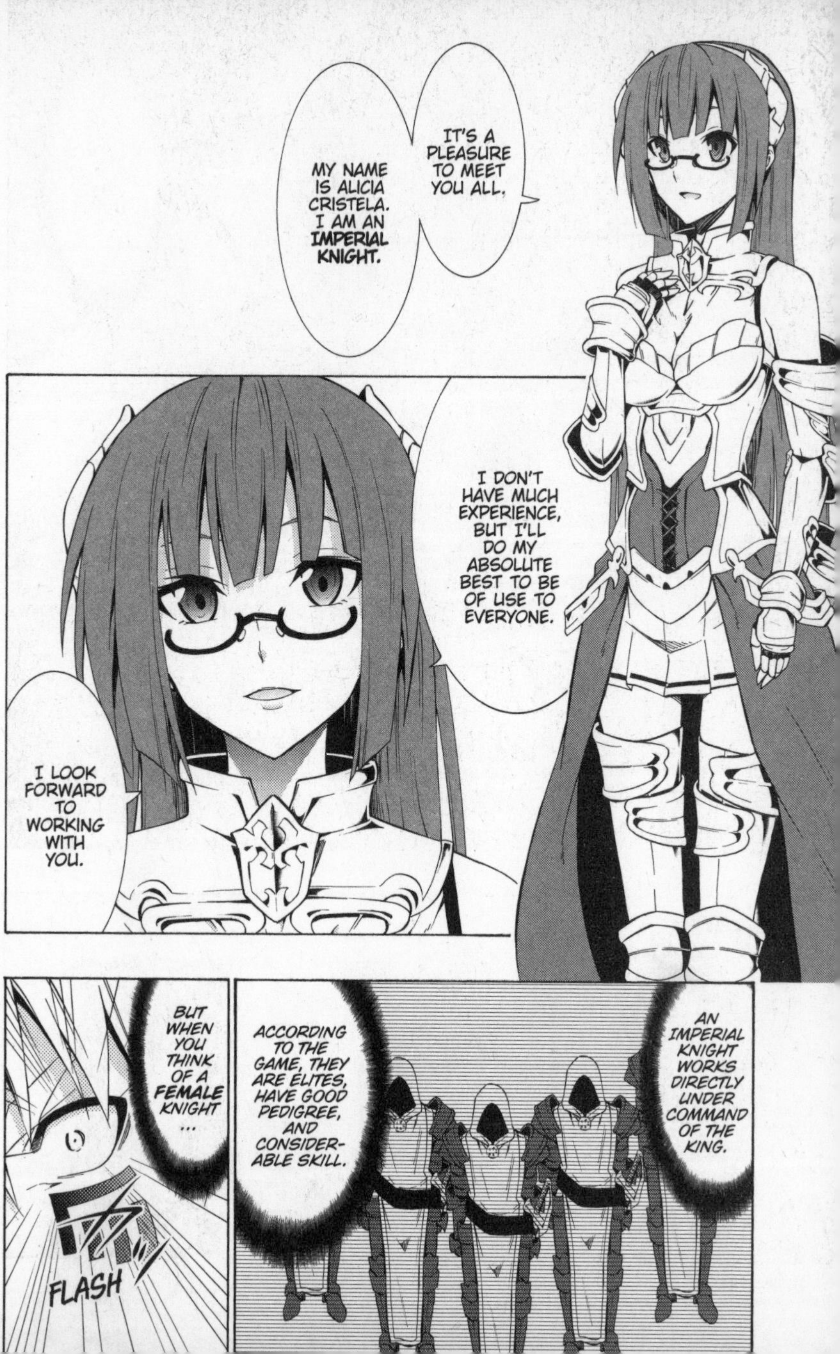
IT'S A PLEASURE TO MEET YOU ALL.
MY NAME IS ALICIA CRISTELA. I AM AN IMPERIAL KNIGHT.
I DON'T HAVE MUCH EXPERIENCE, BUT I'LL DO MY ABSOLUTE BEST TO BE OF USE TO EVERYONE.
I LOOK FORWARD TO WORKING WITH YOU.
AN IMPERIAL KNIGHT WORKS DIRECTLY UNDER COMMAND OF THE KING.
ACCORDING TO THE GAME, THEY ARE ELITES, HAVE GOOD PEDIGREE, AND CONSIDER-ABLE SKILL.
BUT WHEN YOU THINK OF A FEMALE KNIGHT ...
FLASH

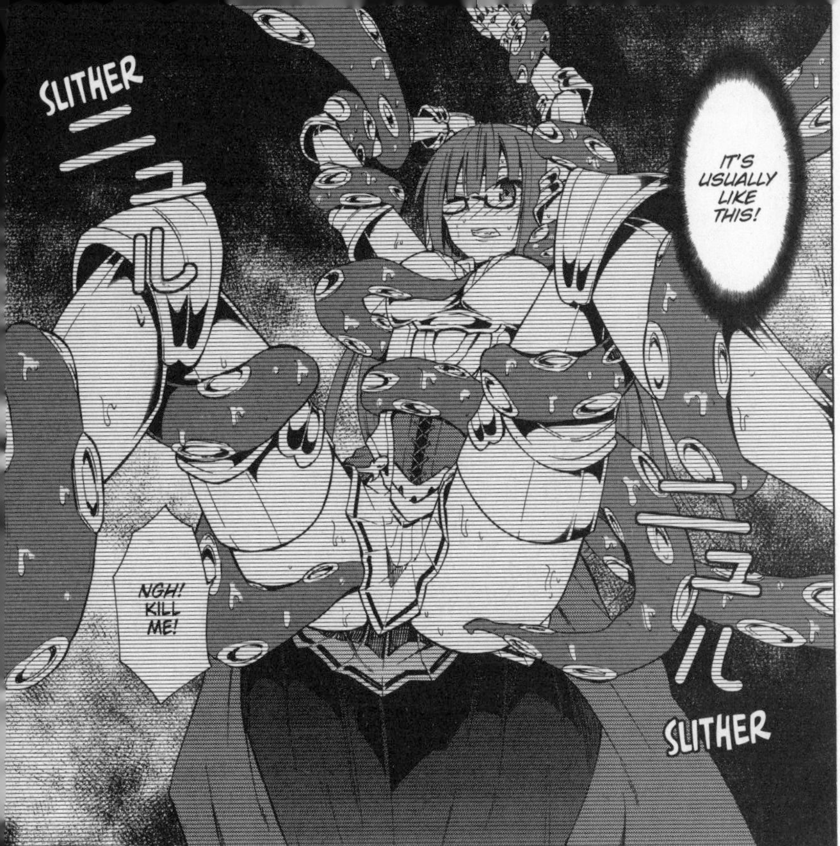
IT'S USUALLY LIKE THIS!
SLITHER
NGH! KILL ME!
SLITHER

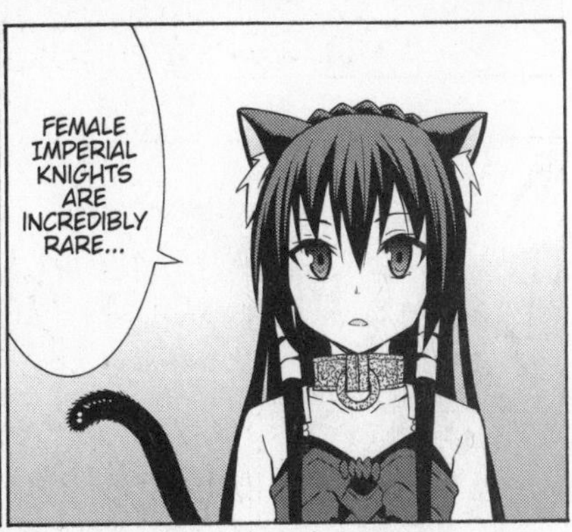
FEMALE IMPERIAL KNIGHTS ARE INCREDIBLY RARE...

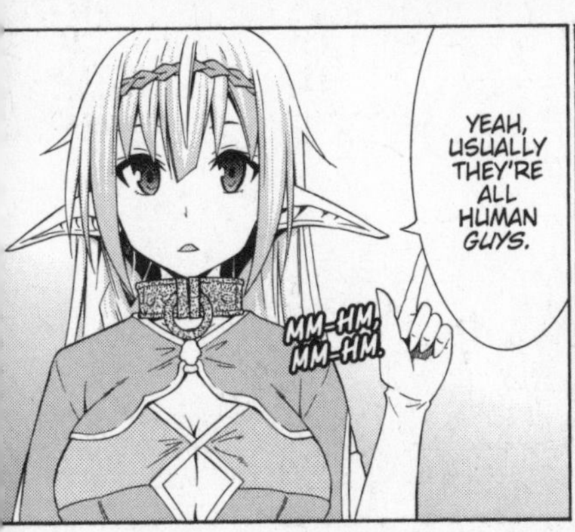
YEAH, USUALLY THEY'RE ALL HUMAN GUYS.
MM-HM, MM-HM.

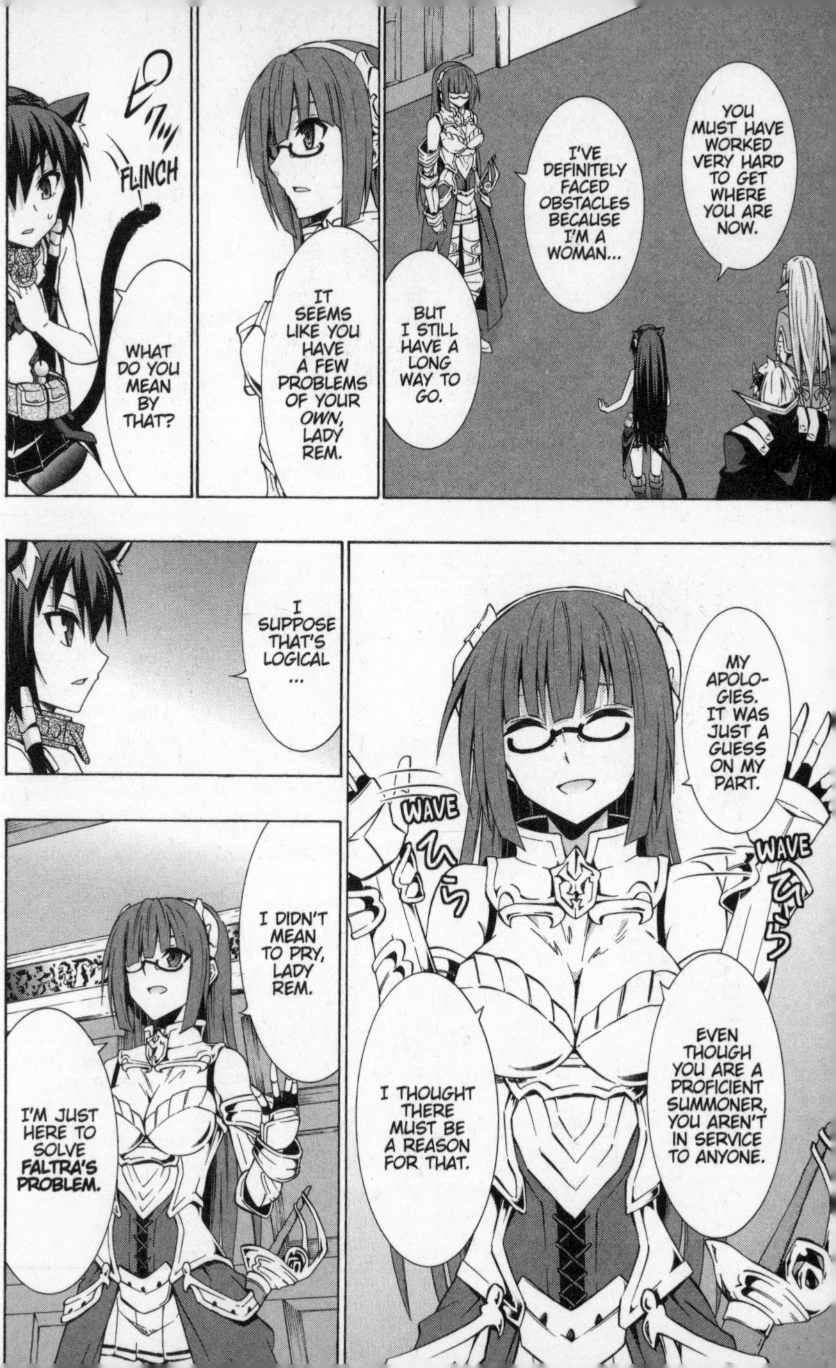
YOU MUST HAVE WORKED VERY HARD TO GET WHERE YOU ARE NOW.
I'VE DEFINITELY FACED OBSTACLES BECAUSE I'M A WOMAN...
BUT I STILL HAVE A LONG WAY TO GO.
IT SEEMS LIKE YOU HAVE A FEW PROBLEMS OF YOUR *OWN*, LADY REM.
FLINCH
WHAT DO YOU MEAN BY THAT?
MY APOLOGIES. IT WAS JUST A GUESS ON MY PART.
WAVE
WAVE
EVEN THOUGH YOU ARE A PROFICIENT SUMMONER, YOU AREN'T IN SERVICE TO ANYONE.
I THOUGHT THERE MUST BE A REASON FOR THAT.
I SUPPOSE THAT'S LOGICAL...
I DIDN'T MEAN TO PRY, LADY REM.
I'M JUST HERE TO SOLVE FALTRA'S PROBLEM.

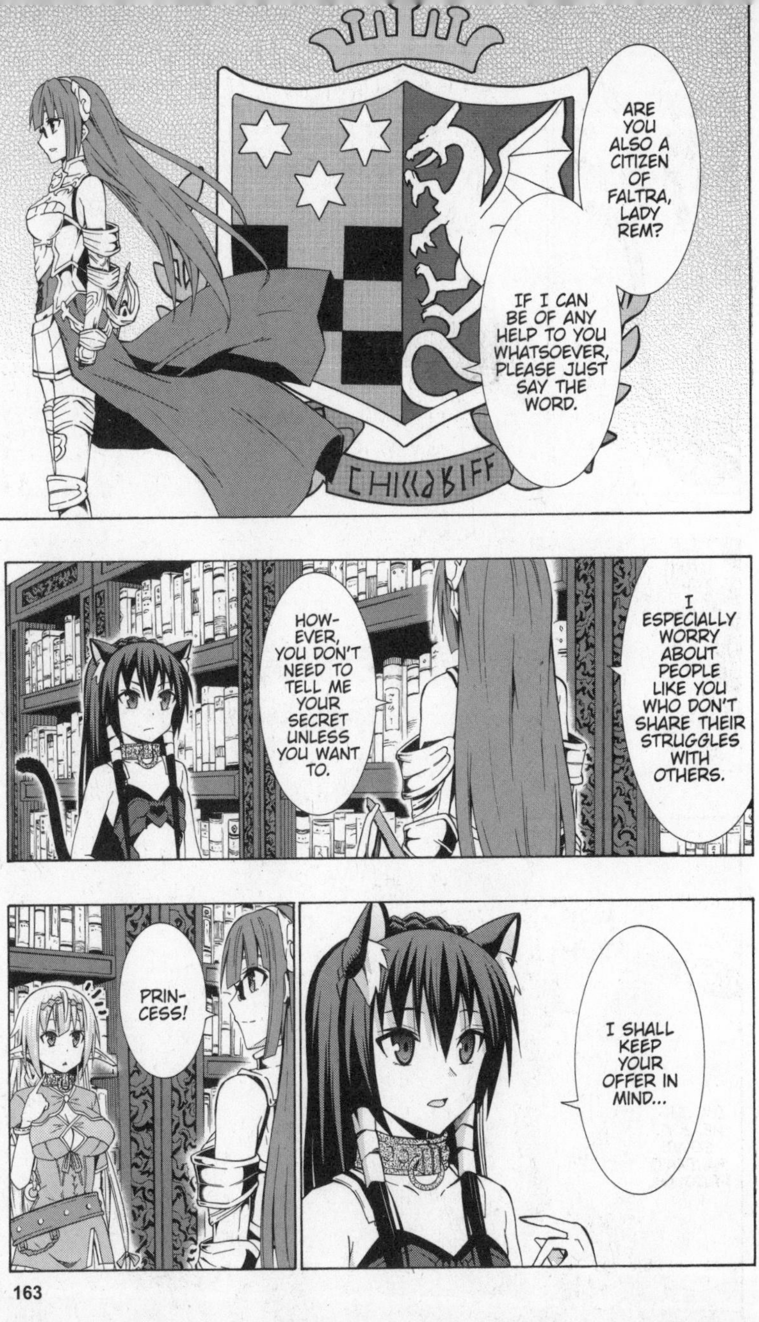
ARE YOU ALSO A CITIZEN OF FALTRA, LADY REM?
IF I CAN BE OF ANY HELP TO YOU WHATSOEVER, PLEASE JUST SAY THE WORD.
I ESPECIALLY WORRY ABOUT PEOPLE LIKE YOU WHO DON'T SHARE THEIR STRUGGLES WITH OTHERS.
HOW-EVER, YOU DON'T NEED TO TELL ME YOUR SECRET UNLESS YOU WANT TO.
I SHALL KEEP YOUR OFFER IN MIND...
PRIN-CESS!

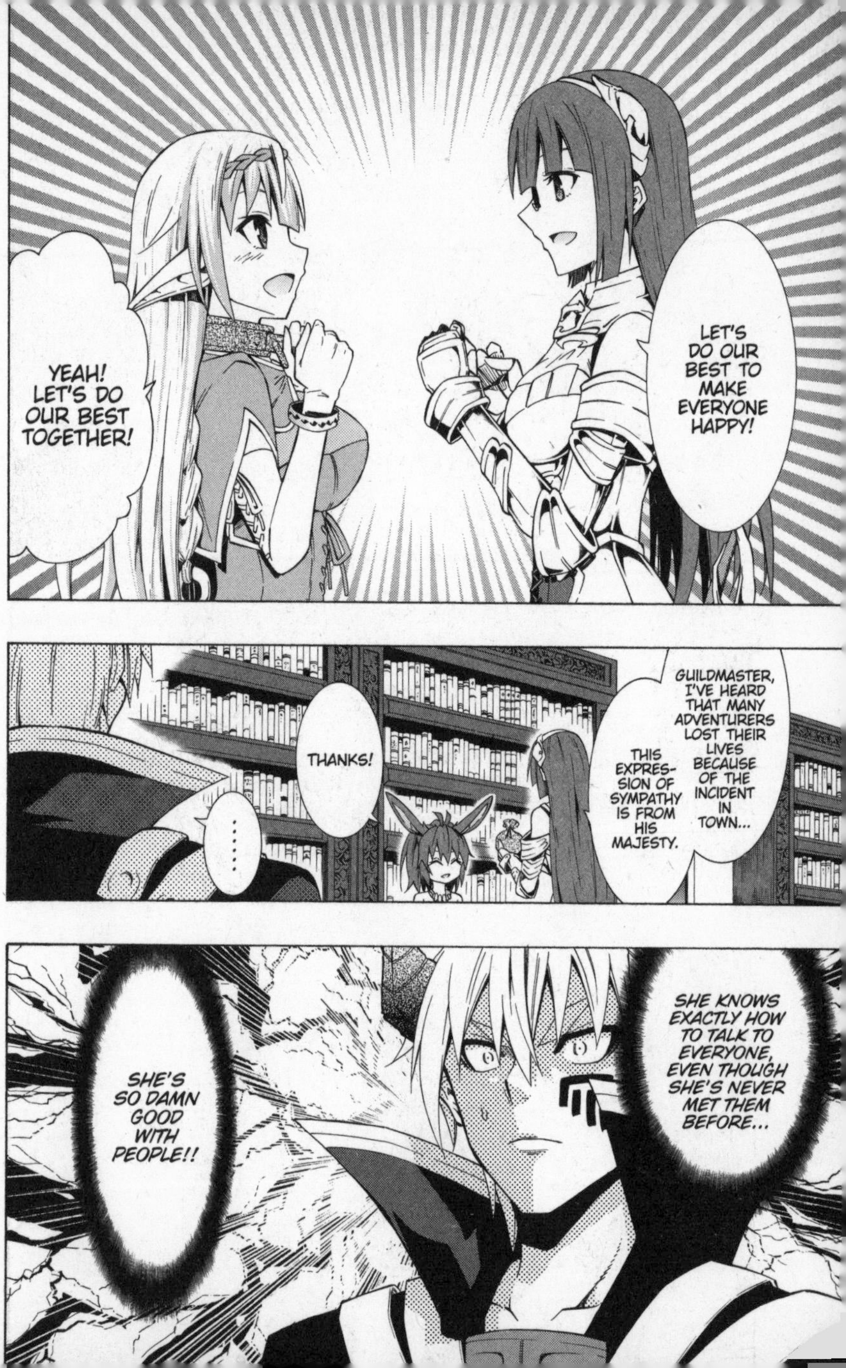
LET'S DO OUR BEST TO MAKE EVERYONE HAPPY!
YEAH! LET'S DO OUR BEST TOGETHER!
GUILDMASTER, I'VE HEARD THAT MANY ADVENTURERS LOST THEIR LIVES BECAUSE OF THE INCIDENT IN TOWN...
THIS EXPRES-SION OF SYMPATHY IS FROM HIS MAJESTY.
THANKS!
......
SHE KNOWS EXACTLY HOW TO TALK TO EVERYONE, EVEN THOUGH SHE'S NEVER MET THEM BEFORE...
SHE'S SO DAMN GOOD WITH PEOPLE!!

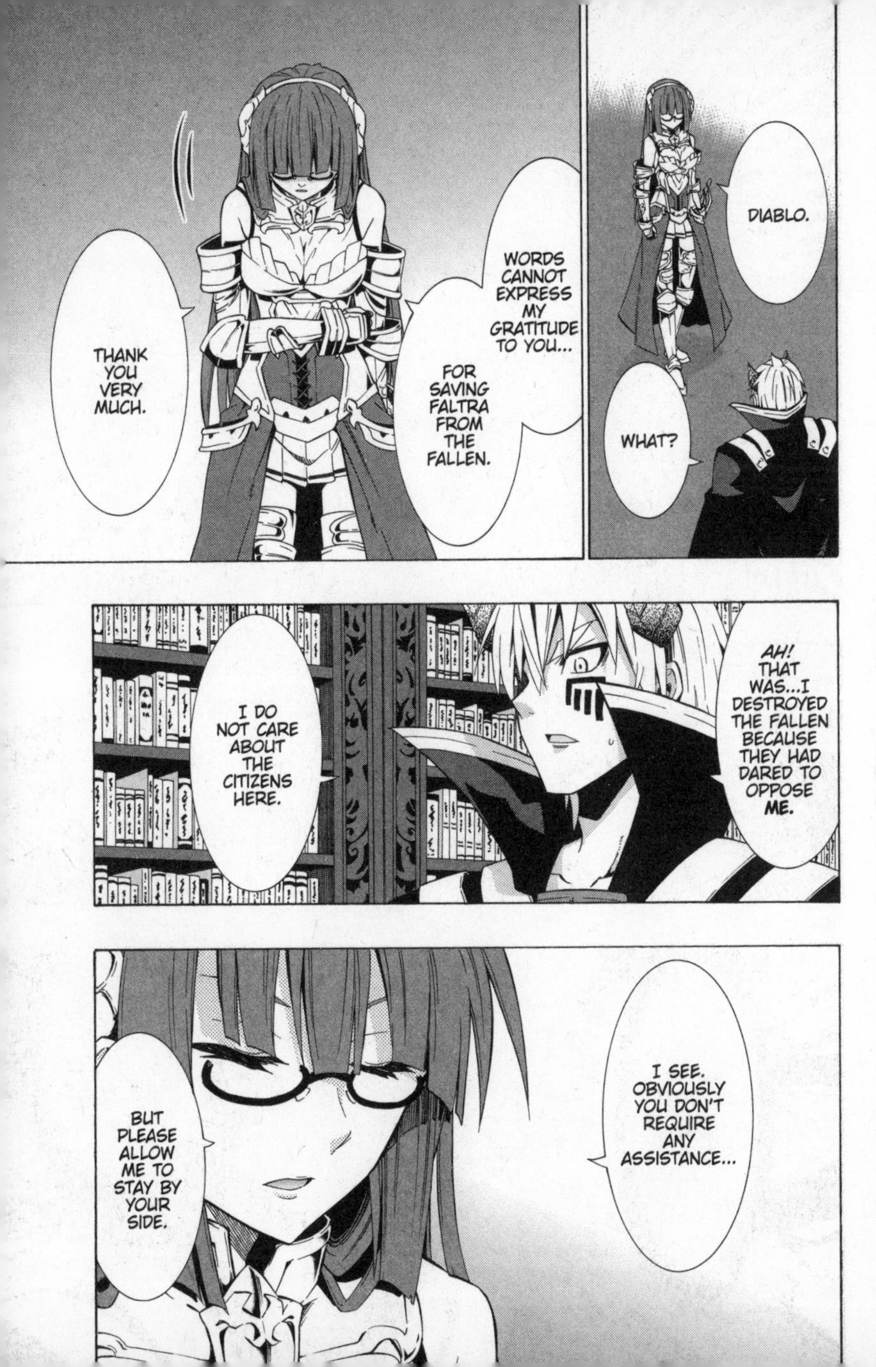
DIABLO.
WHAT?
WORDS CANNOT EXPRESS MY GRATITUDE TO YOU...
FOR SAVING FALTRA FROM THE FALLEN.
THANK YOU VERY MUCH.
AH! THAT WAS...I DESTROYED THE FALLEN BECAUSE THEY HAD DARED TO OPPOSE ME.
I DO NOT CARE ABOUT THE CITIZENS HERE.
I SEE. OBVIOUSLY YOU DON'T REQUIRE ANY ASSISTANCE...
BUT PLEASE ALLOW ME TO STAY BY YOUR SIDE.

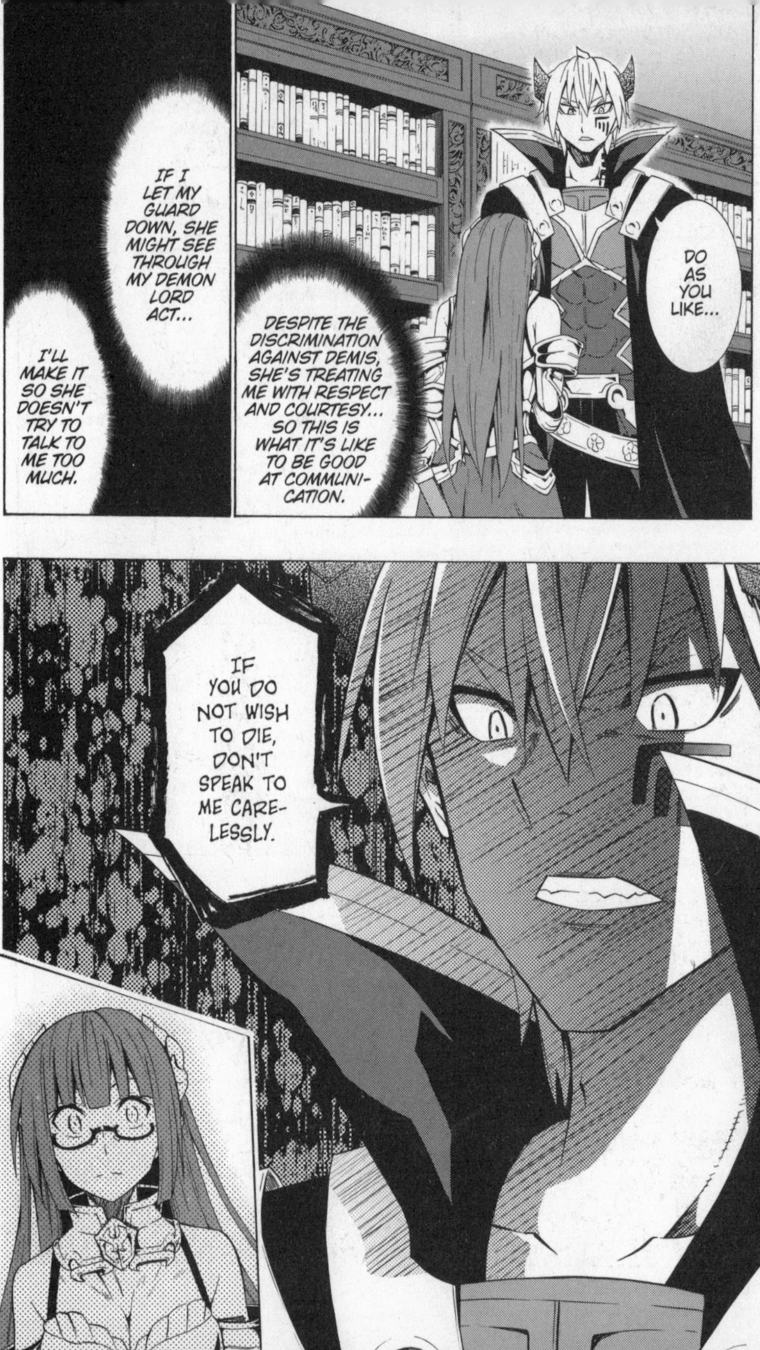
DO AS YOU LIKE...
DESPITE THE DISCRIMINATION AGAINST DEMIS, SHE'S TREATING ME WITH RESPECT AND COURTESY... SO THIS IS WHAT IT'S LIKE TO BE GOOD AT COMMUNI-CATION.
IF I LET MY GUARD DOWN, SHE MIGHT SEE THROUGH MY DEMON LORD ACT...
I'LL MAKE IT SO SHE DOESN'T TRY TO TALK TO ME TOO MUCH.
IF YOU DO NOT WISH TO DIE, DON'T SPEAK TO ME CARE-LESSLY.

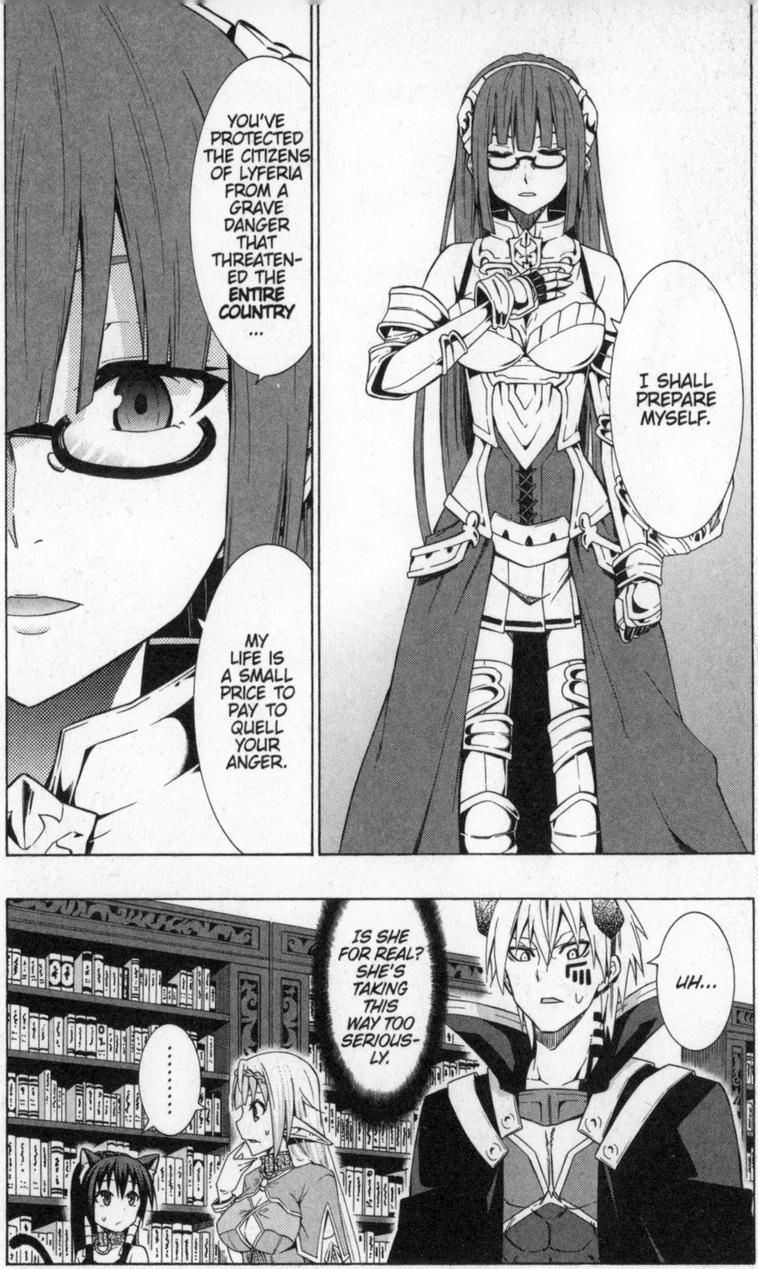
I SHALL PREPARE MYSELF.
YOU'VE PROTECTED THE CITIZENS OF LYFERIA FROM A GRAVE DANGER THAT THREATEN-ED THE ENTIRE COUNTRY ...
MY LIFE IS A SMALL PRICE TO PAY TO QUELL YOUR ANGER.
UH...
IS SHE FOR REAL? SHE'S TAKING THIS WAY TOO SERIOUS-LY.
......

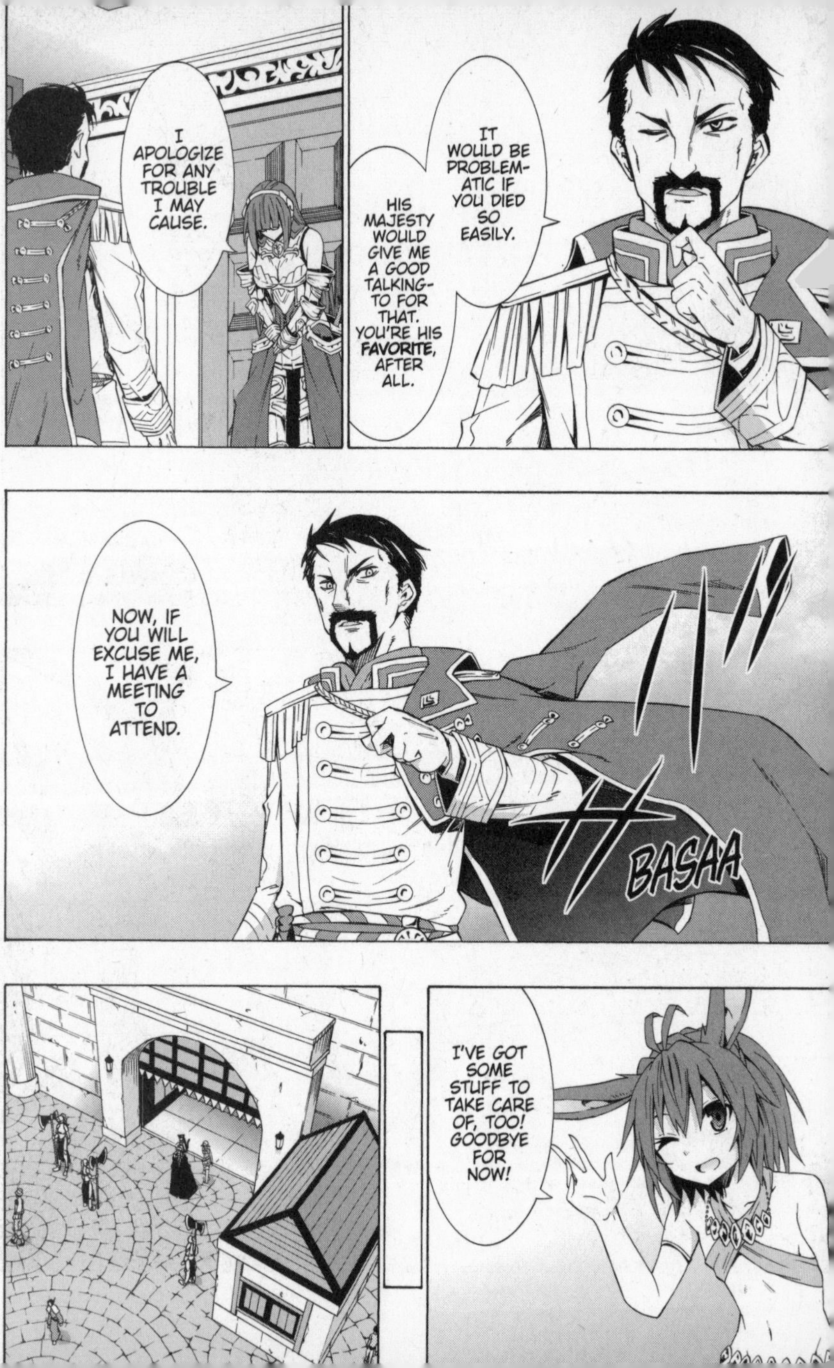
IT WOULD BE PROBLEM-ATIC IF YOU DIED SO EASILY.
HIS MAJESTY WOULD GIVE ME A GOOD TALKING-TO FOR THAT. YOU'RE HIS **FAVORITE**, AFTER ALL.
I APOLOGIZE FOR ANY TROUBLE I MAY CAUSE.
BASAA
NOW, IF YOU WILL EXCUSE ME, I HAVE A MEETING TO ATTEND.
I'VE GOT SOME STUFF TO TAKE CARE OF, TOO! GOODBYE FOR NOW!

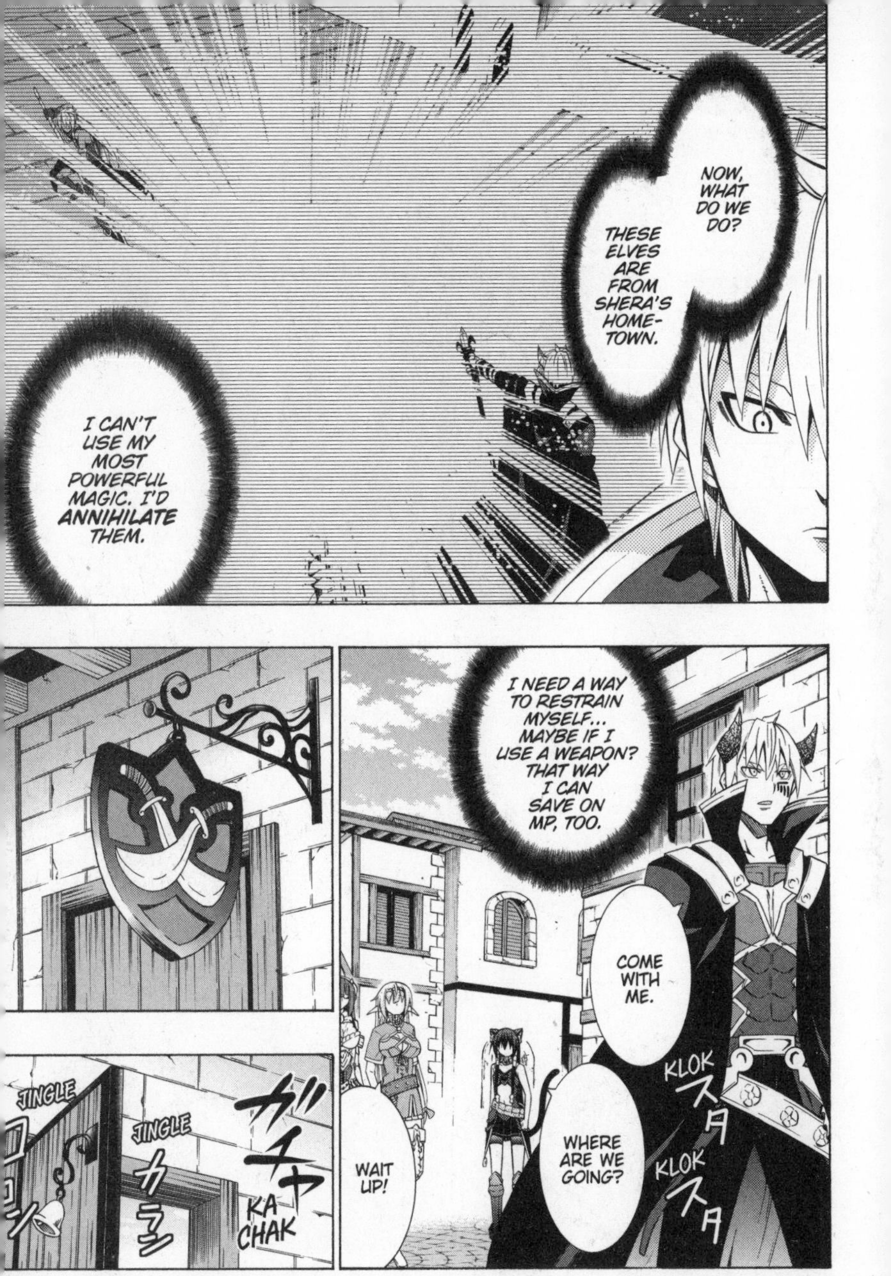
NOW, WHAT DO WE DO?
THESE ELVES ARE FROM SHERA'S HOME-TOWN.
I CAN'T USE MY MOST POWERFUL MAGIC. I'D ANNIHILATE THEM.
I NEED A WAY TO RESTRAIN MYSELF... MAYBE IF I USE A WEAPON? THAT WAY I CAN SAVE ON MP, TOO.
COME WITH ME.
KLOK
KLOK
WHERE ARE WE GOING?
WAIT UP!
JINGLE
JINGLE
KA CHAK

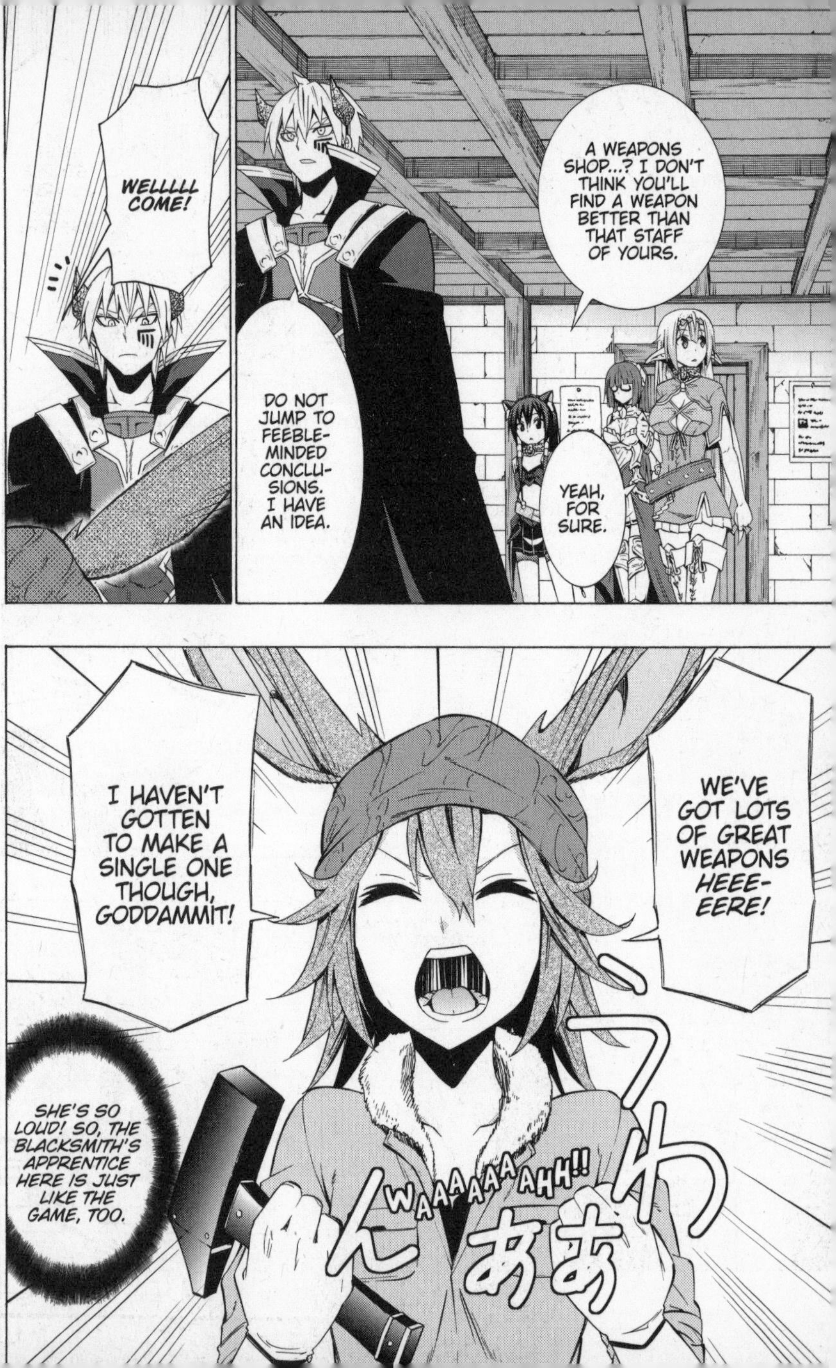
A WEAPONS SHOP...? I DON'T THINK YOU'LL FIND A WEAPON BETTER THAN THAT STAFF OF YOURS.
YEAH, FOR SURE.
DO NOT JUMP TO FEEBLE-MINDED CONCLUSIONS. I HAVE AN IDEA.
WELLLLL COME!
WE'VE GOT LOTS OF GREAT WEAPONS HEEEEERE!
I HAVEN'T GOTTEN TO MAKE A SINGLE ONE THOUGH, GODDAMMIT!
WAAAAAAAHH!!
わああん
SHE'S SO LOUD! SO, THE BLACKSMITH'S APPRENTICE HERE IS JUST LIKE THE GAME, TOO.

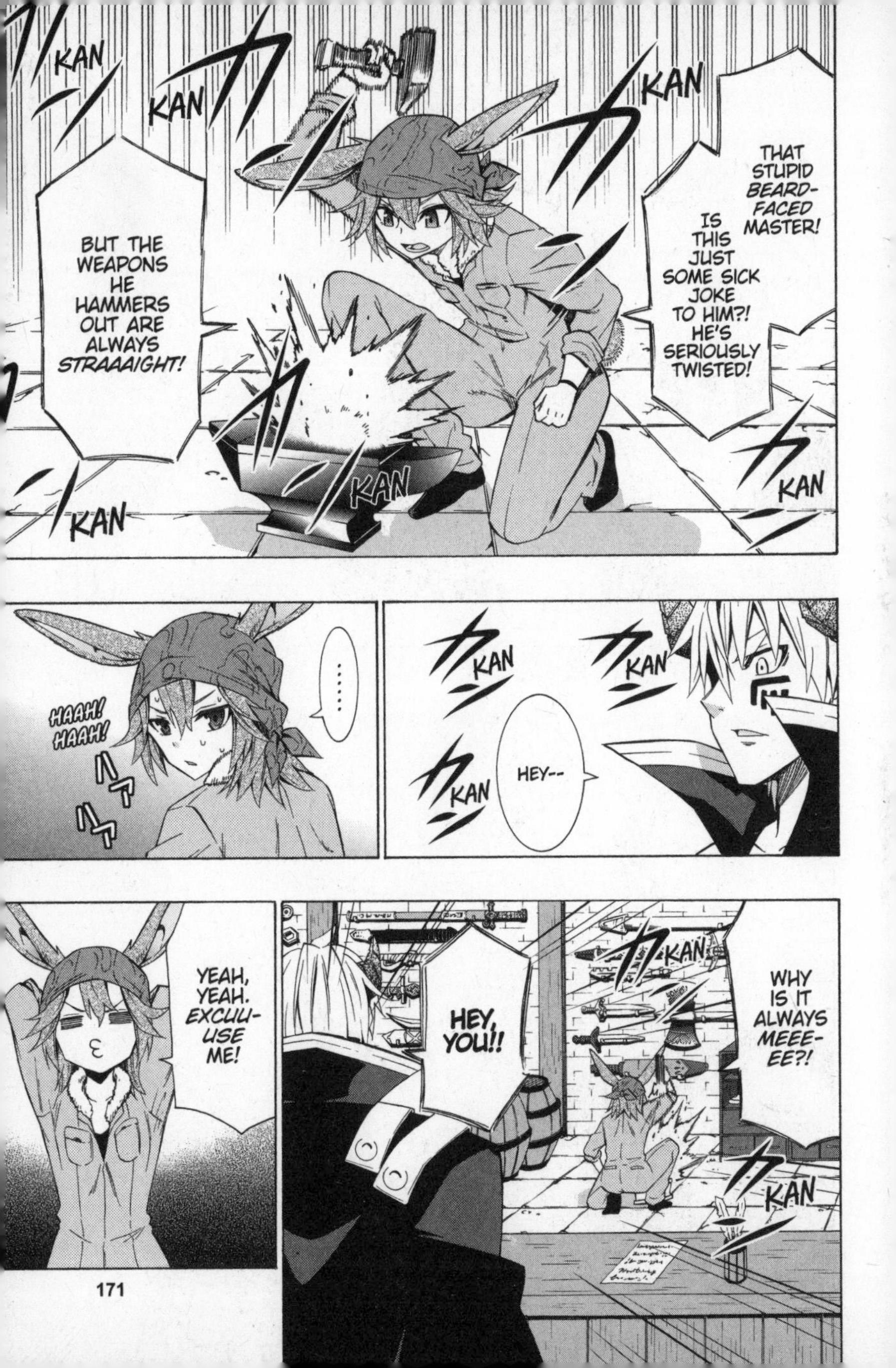
KAN
THAT STUPID BEARD-FACED MASTER!
IS THIS JUST SOME SICK JOKE TO HIM?! HE'S SERIOUSLY TWISTED!
KAN
KAN
BUT THE WEAPONS HE HAMMERS OUT ARE ALWAYS STRAAAIGHT!
KAN
KAN
KAN
KAN
KAN
KAN
HEY--
......
HAAH! HAAH!
WHY IS IT ALWAYS MEEEE-EE?!
KAN
HEY, YOU!!
KAN
YEAH, YEAH. EXCUU-USE ME!

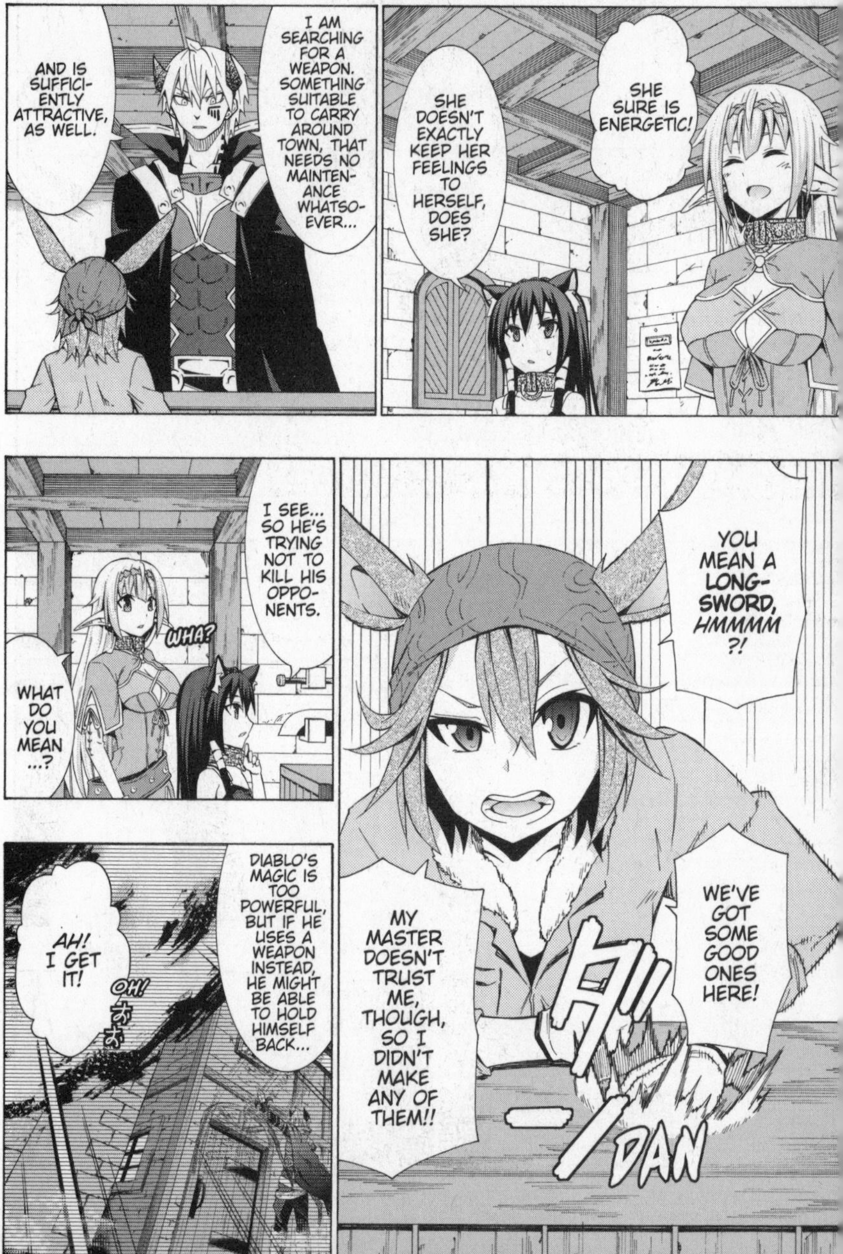
SHE SURE IS ENERGETIC!
SHE DOESN'T EXACTLY KEEP HER FEELINGS TO HERSELF, DOES SHE?
I AM SEARCHING FOR A WEAPON. SOMETHING SUITABLE TO CARRY AROUND TOWN, THAT NEEDS NO MAINTEN-ANCE WHATSO-EVER...
AND IS SUFFICI-ENTLY ATTRACTIVE, AS WELL.
YOU MEAN A LONG-SWORD, HMMMM?!
WE'VE GOT SOME GOOD ONES HERE!
MY MASTER DOESN'T TRUST ME, THOUGH, SO I DIDN'T MAKE ANY OF THEM!!
DAN
I SEE... SO HE'S TRYING NOT TO KILL HIS OPPO-NENTS.
WHA?
WHAT DO YOU MEAN ...?
DIABLO'S MAGIC IS TOO POWERFUL, BUT IF HE USES A WEAPON INSTEAD, HE MIGHT BE ABLE TO HOLD HIMSELF BACK...
OH! おお
AH! I GET IT!

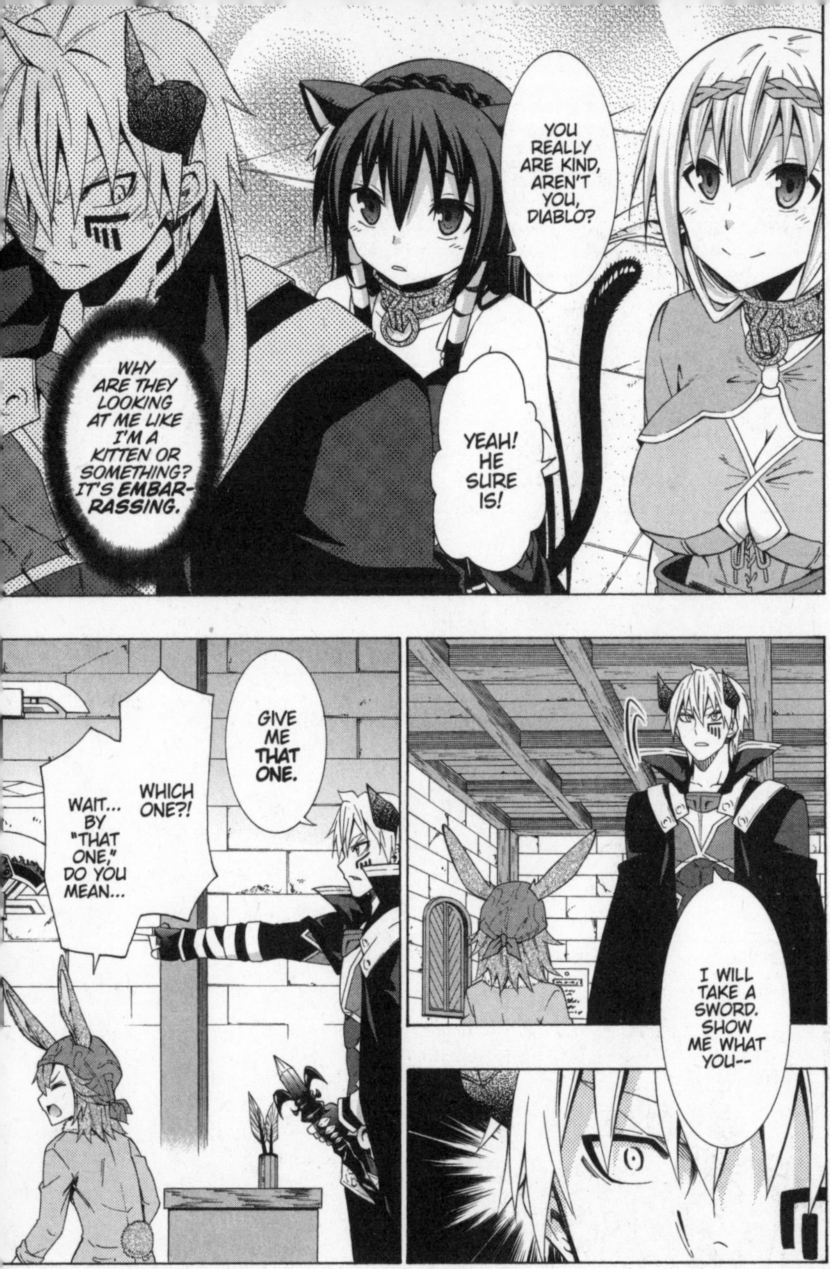
YOU REALLY ARE KIND, AREN'T YOU, DIABLO?
YEAH! HE SURE IS!
WHY ARE THEY LOOKING AT ME LIKE I'M A KITTEN OR SOMETHING? IT'S EMBARRASSING.
I WILL TAKE A SWORD. SHOW ME WHAT YOU--
GIVE ME THAT ONE.
WHICH ONE?!
WAIT... BY "THAT ONE," DO YOU MEAN...

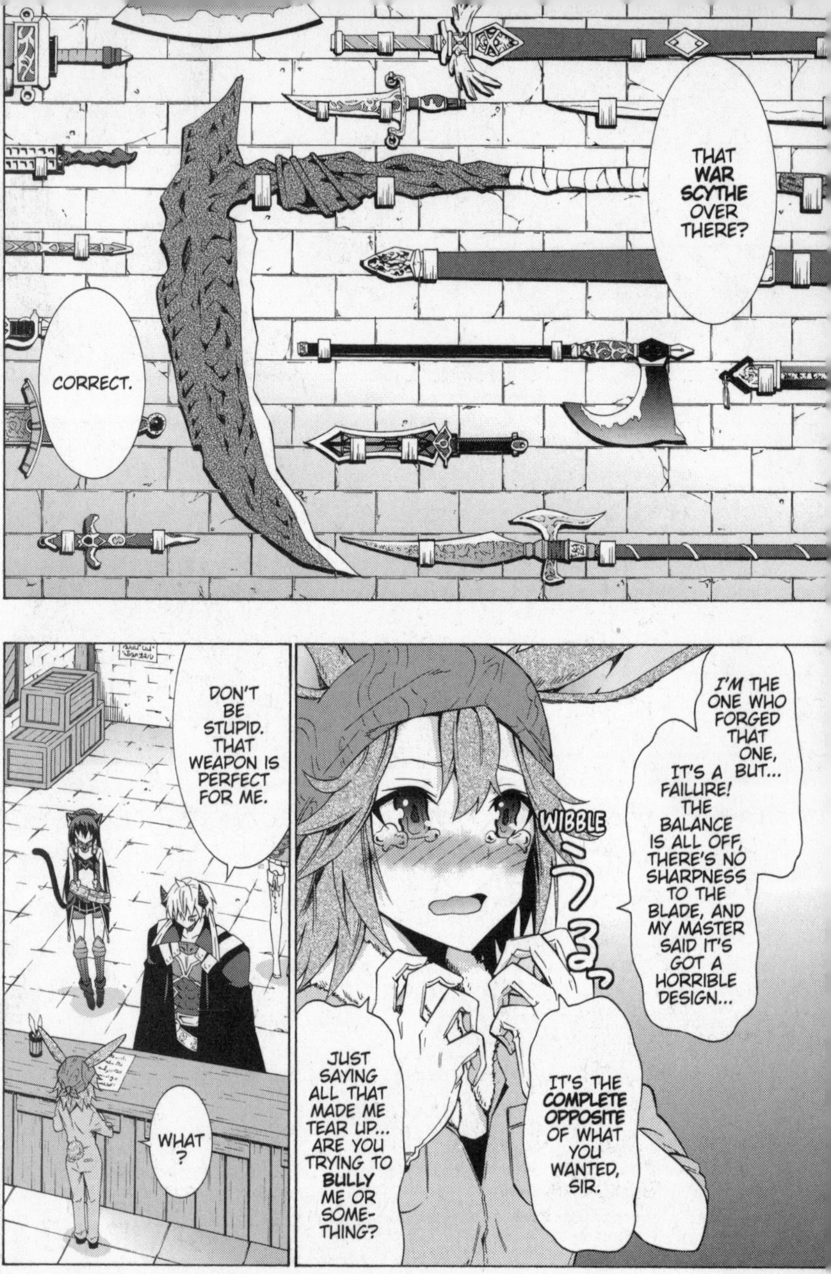
THAT WAR SCYTHE OVER THERE?
CORRECT.
I'M THE ONE WHO FORGED THAT ONE, BUT... IT'S A FAILURE! THE BALANCE IS ALL OFF, THERE'S NO SHARPNESS TO THE BLADE, AND MY MASTER SAID IT'S GOT A HORRIBLE DESIGN...
WIBBLE
うるっ
IT'S THE COMPLETE OPPOSITE OF WHAT YOU WANTED, SIR.
JUST SAYING ALL THAT MADE ME TEAR UP... ARE YOU TRYING TO BULLY ME OR SOME-THING?
DON'T BE STUPID. THAT WEAPON IS PERFECT FOR ME.
WHAT?

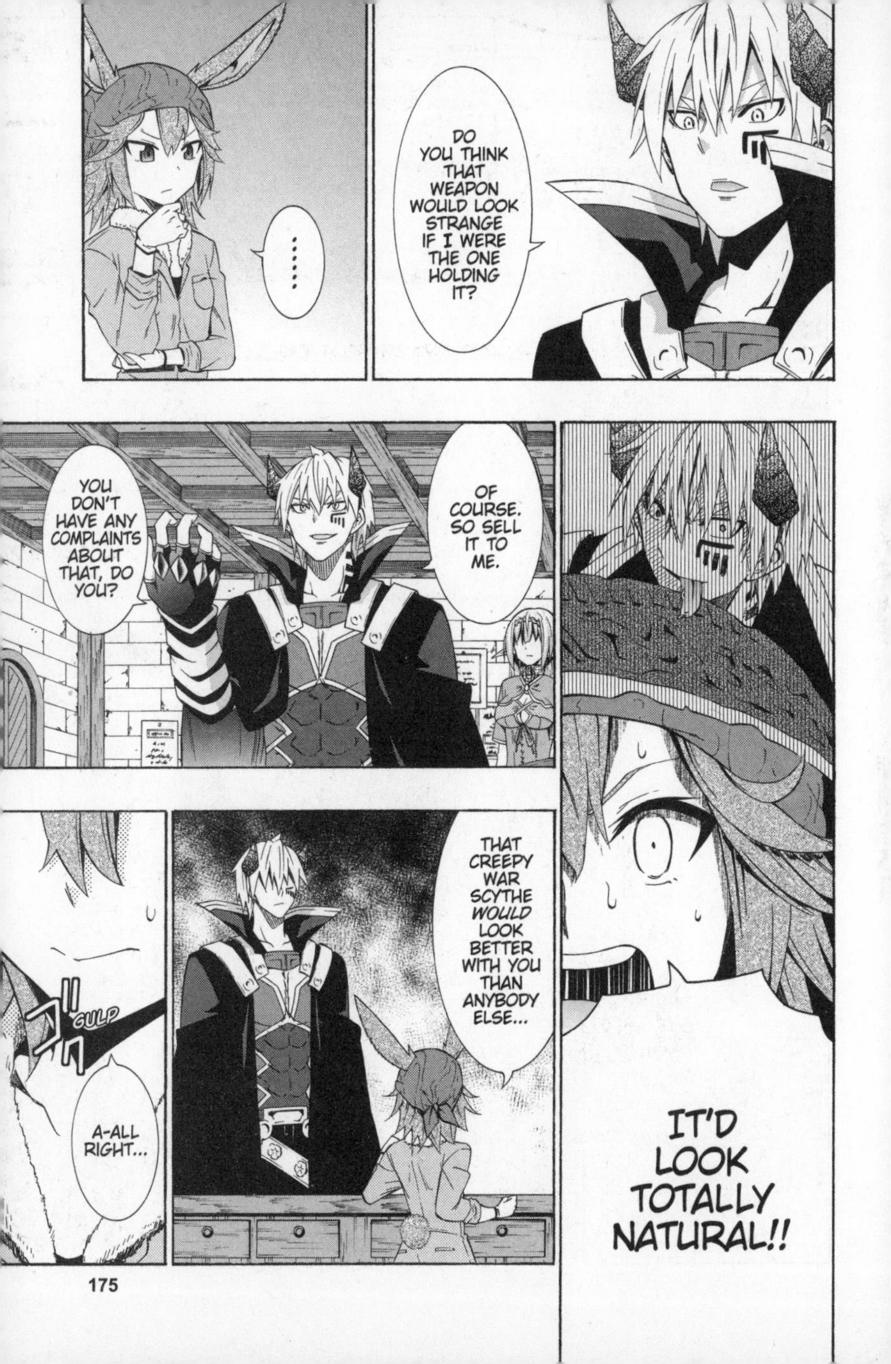
DO YOU THINK THAT WEAPON WOULD LOOK STRANGE IF I WERE THE ONE HOLDING IT?
......
IT'D LOOK TOTALLY NATURAL!!
OF COURSE. SO SELL IT TO ME.
YOU DON'T HAVE ANY COMPLAINTS ABOUT THAT, DO YOU?
THAT CREEPY WAR SCYTHE *WOULD* LOOK BETTER WITH YOU THAN ANYBODY ELSE...
GULP
A-ALL RIGHT...

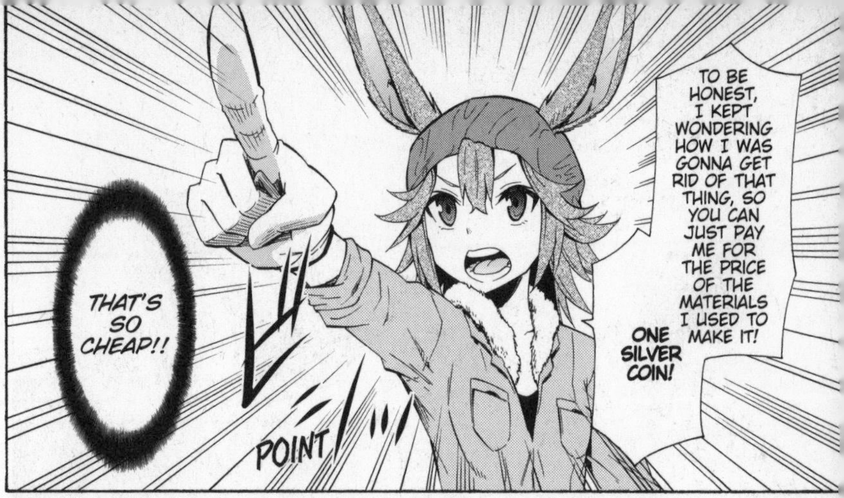
TO BE HONEST, I KEPT WONDERING HOW I WAS GONNA GET RID OF THAT THING, SO YOU CAN JUST PAY ME FOR THE PRICE OF THE MATERIALS I USED TO MAKE IT!
ONE SILVER COIN!
POINT
THAT'S SO CHEAP!!

※One silver coin = 4,000 friths.

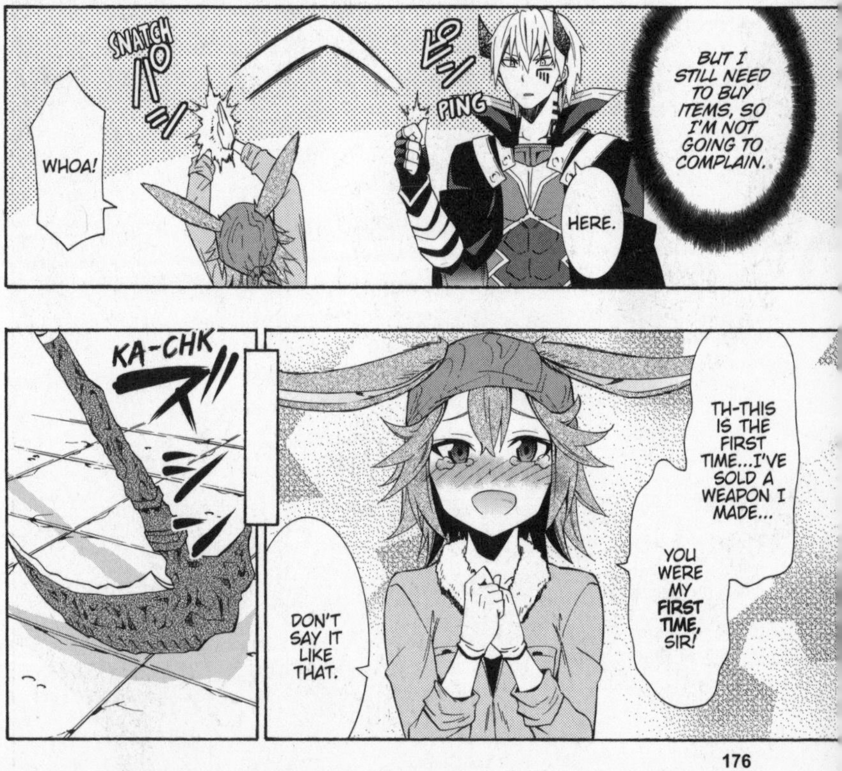
BUT I STILL NEED TO BUY ITEMS, SO I'M NOT GOING TO COMPLAIN.
HERE.
PING
SNATCH
WHOA!
TH-THIS IS THE FIRST TIME...I'VE SOLD A WEAPON I MADE...
YOU WERE MY FIRST TIME, SIR!
DON'T SAY IT LIKE THAT.
KA-CHK

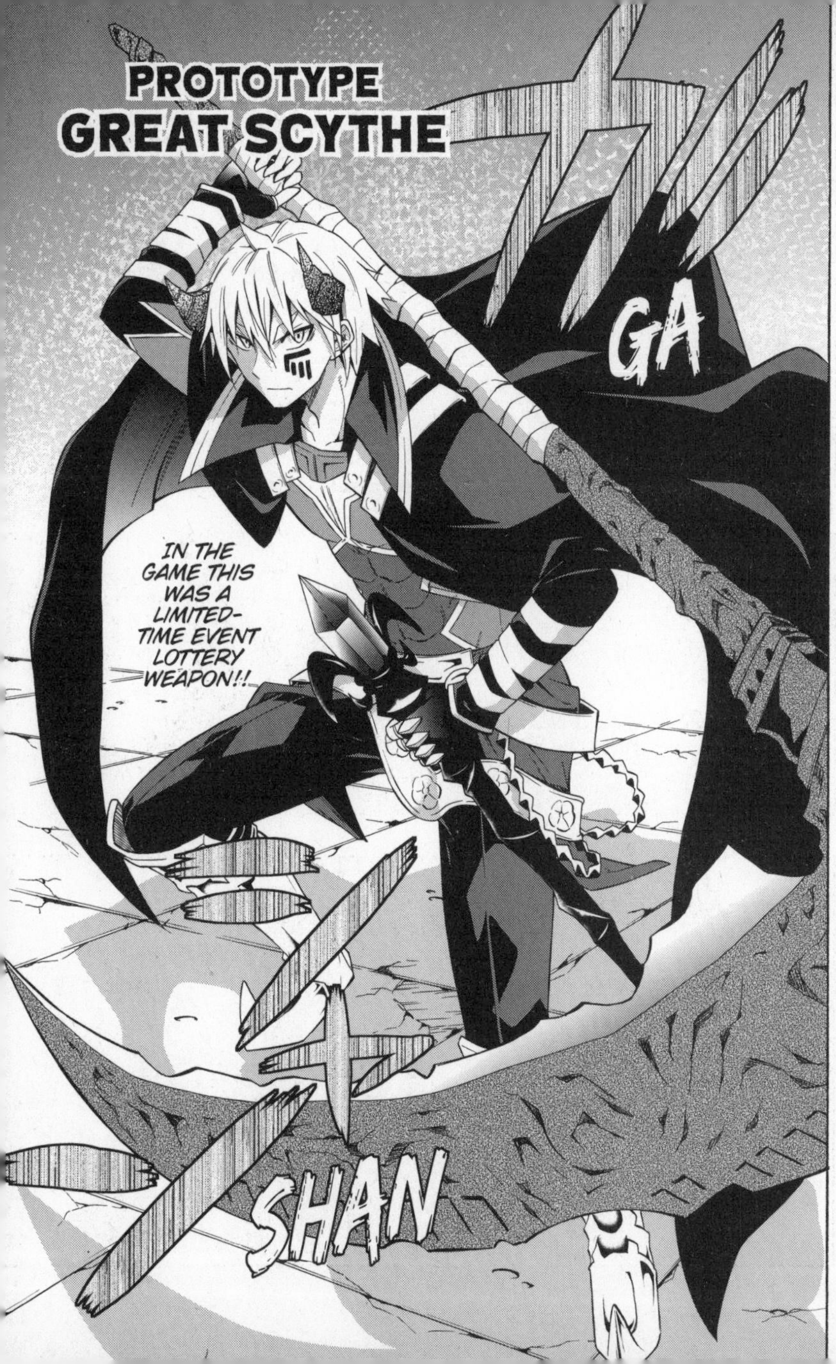
PROTOTYPE GREAT SCYTHE
GA
IN THE GAME THIS WAS A LIMITED-TIME EVENT LOTTERY WEAPON!!
SHAN

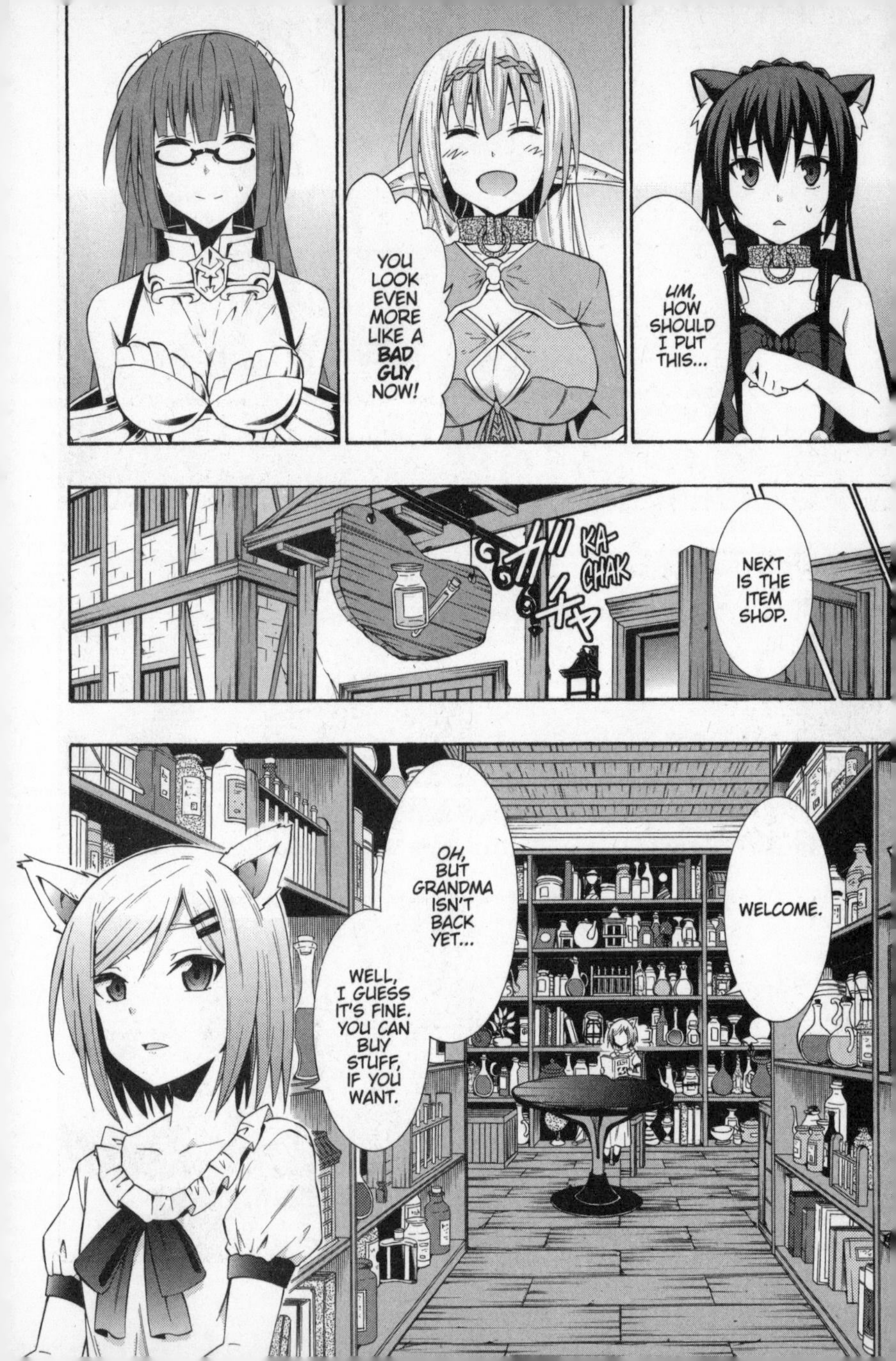
UM, HOW SHOULD I PUT THIS...
YOU LOOK EVEN MORE LIKE A BAD GUY NOW!
NEXT IS THE ITEM SHOP.
KA-CHAK
WELCOME.
OH, BUT GRANDMA ISN'T BACK YET...
WELL, I GUESS IT'S FINE. YOU CAN BUY STUFF, IF YOU WANT.

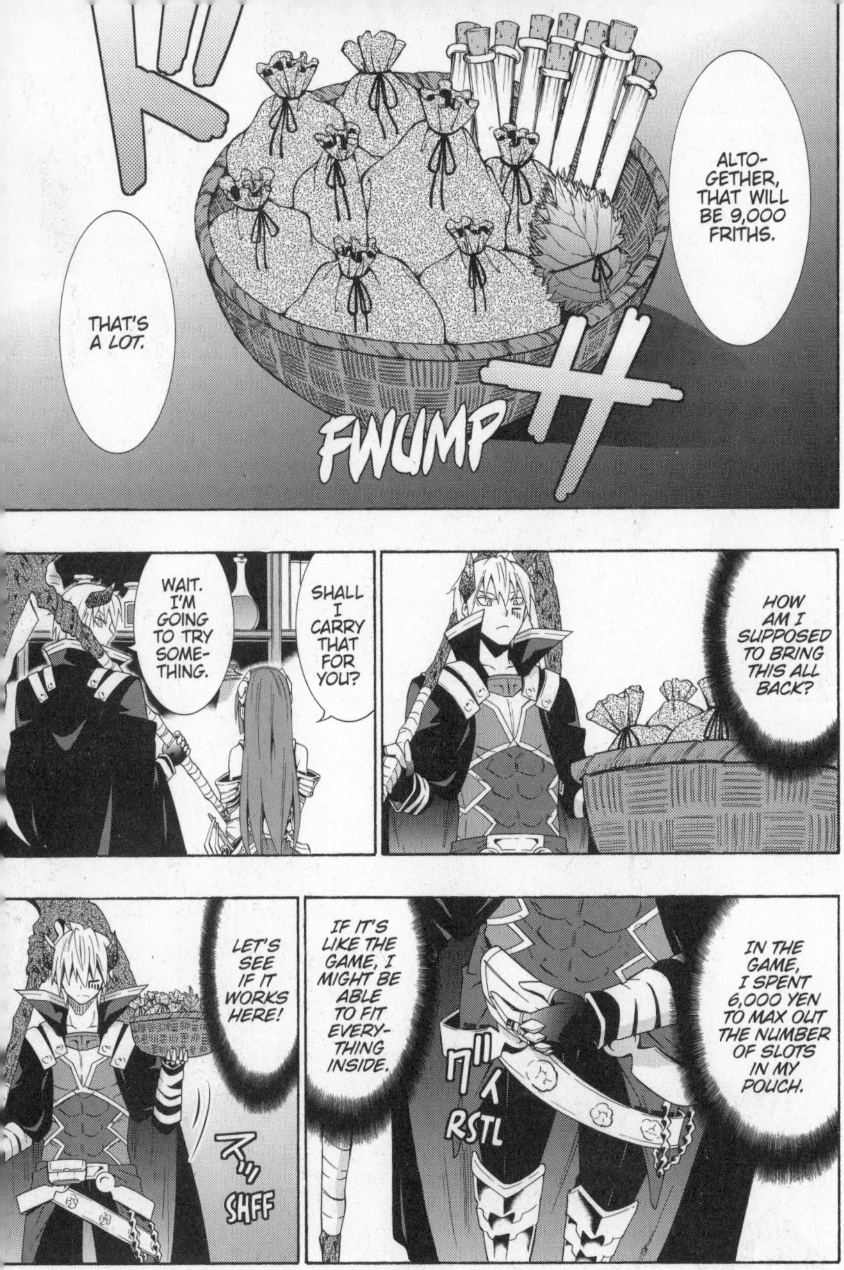
ALTO-GETHER, THAT WILL BE 9,000 FRITHS.
THAT'S A LOT.
FWUMP
HOW AM I SUPPOSED TO BRING THIS ALL BACK?
SHALL I CARRY THAT FOR YOU?
WAIT. I'M GOING TO TRY SOME-THING.
IN THE GAME, I SPENT 6,000 YEN TO MAX OUT THE NUMBER OF SLOTS IN MY POUCH.
IF IT'S LIKE THE GAME, I MIGHT BE ABLE TO FIT EVERY-THING INSIDE.
RSTL
LET'S SEE IF IT WORKS HERE!
SHFF

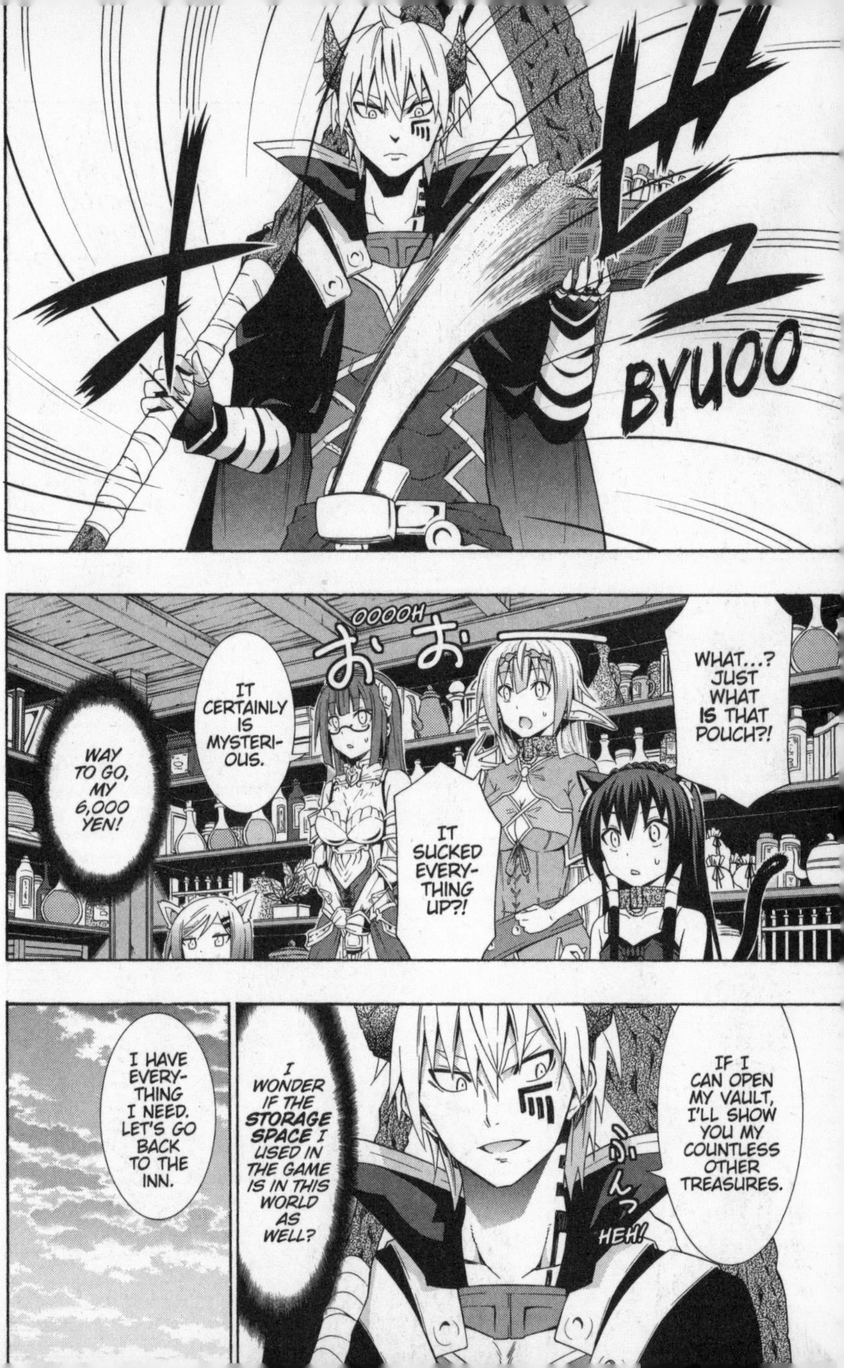
BYUOO
WHAT...? JUST WHAT IS THAT POUCH?!
おお
OOOOH
IT SUCKED EVERYTHING UP?!
IT CERTAINLY IS MYSTERIOUS.
WAY TO GO, MY 6,000 YEN!
IF I CAN OPEN MY VAULT, I'LL SHOW YOU MY COUNTLESS OTHER TREASURES.
ふんっ
HEH!
I WONDER IF THE **STORAGE SPACE** I USED IN THE GAME IS IN THIS WORLD AS WELL?
I HAVE EVERYTHING I NEED. LET'S GO BACK TO THE INN.

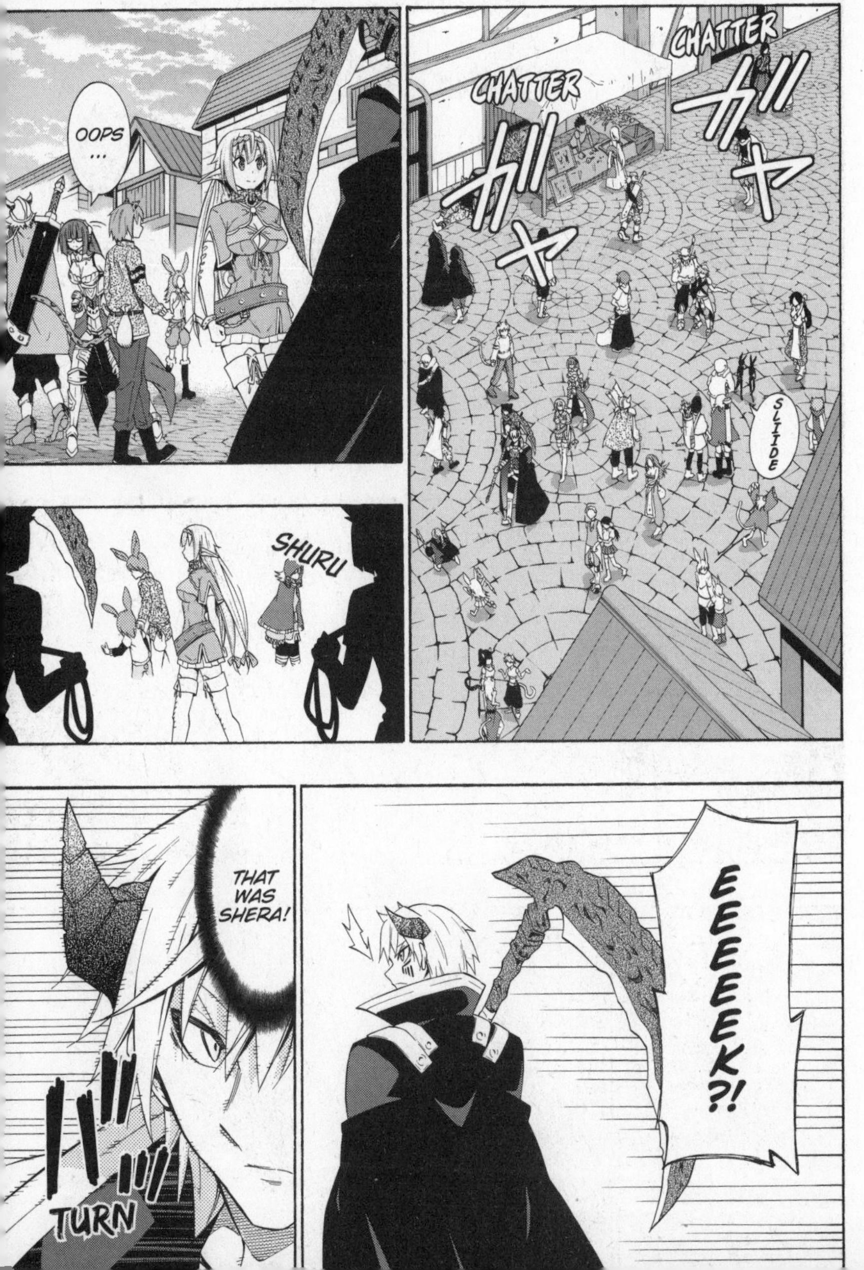

CHATTER
ガヤ
CHATTER
ガヤ
SLIIDE
OOPS ...
SHURU
EEEEEEK?!
THAT WAS SHERA!
TURN

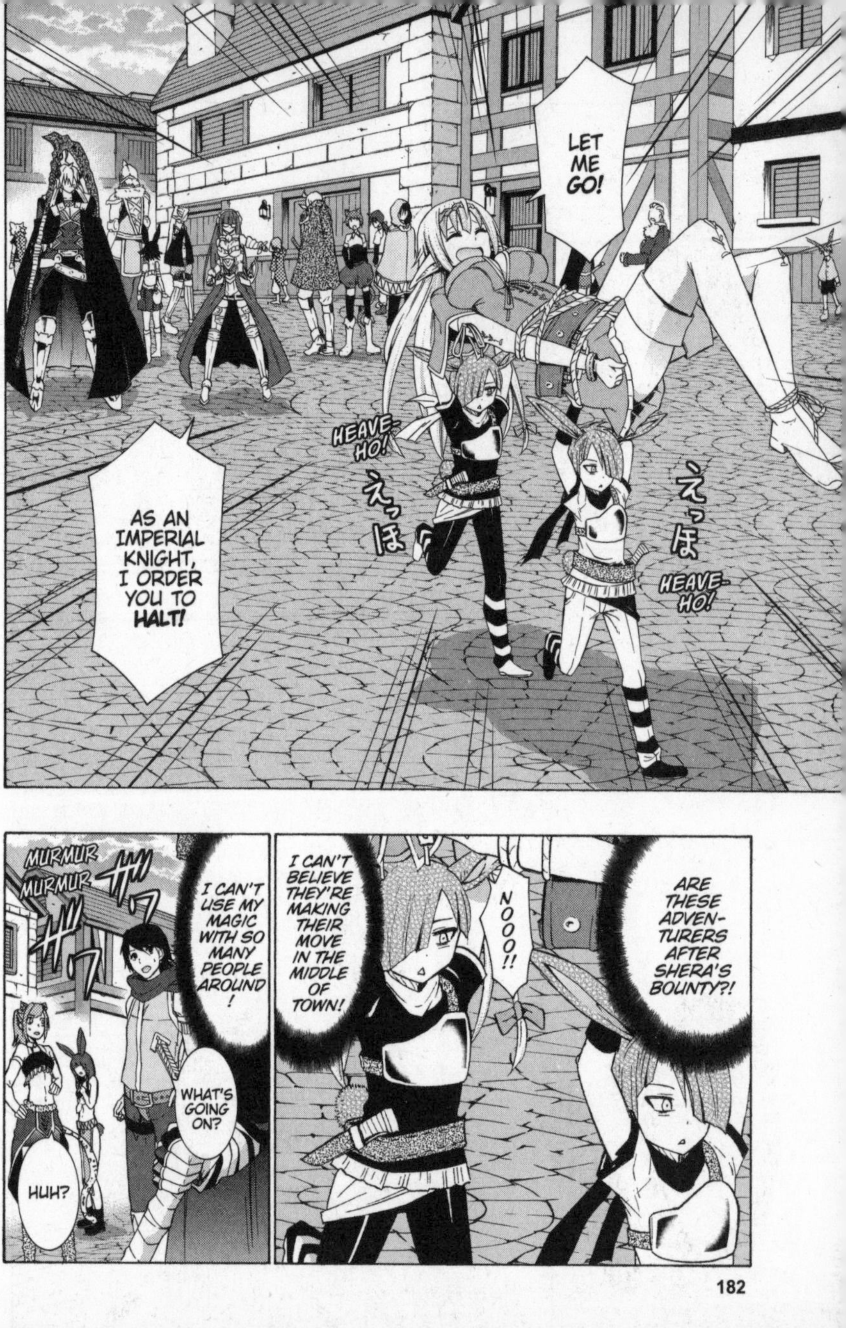
LET ME GO!
えっほ
HEAVE-HO!
HEAVE-HO!
えっほ
AS AN IMPERIAL KNIGHT, I ORDER YOU TO **HALT!**
ARE THESE ADVENTURERS AFTER SHERA'S BOUNTY?!
NOOOO!!
I CAN'T BELIEVE THEY'RE MAKING THEIR MOVE IN THE MIDDLE OF TOWN!
I CAN'T USE MY MAGIC WITH SO MANY PEOPLE AROUND!
ザワ
ザワ
MURMUR MURMUR
WHAT'S GOING ON?
HUH?

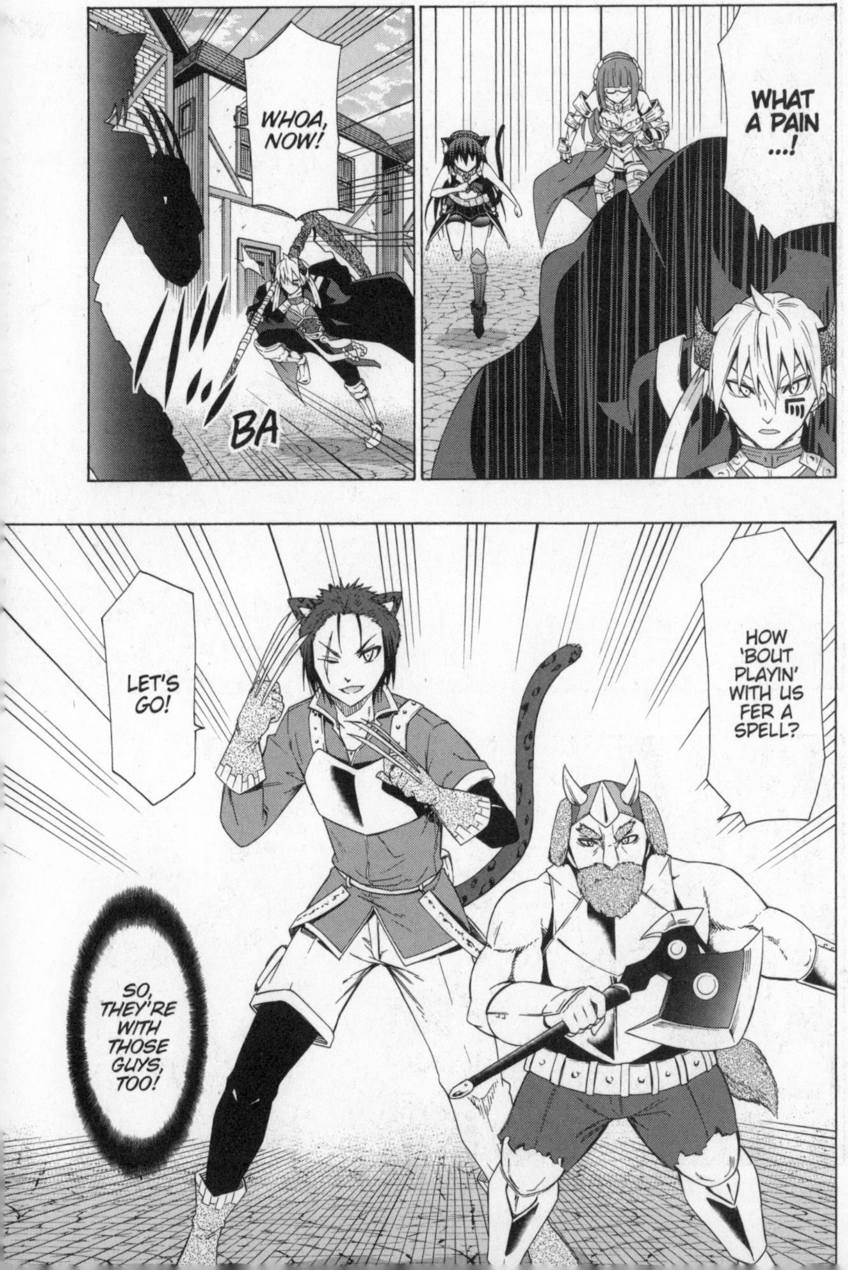
WHAT A PAIN ...!
WHOA, NOW!
BA
HOW 'BOUT PLAYIN' WITH US FER A SPELL?
LET'S GO!
SO, THEY'RE WITH THOSE GUYS, TOO!

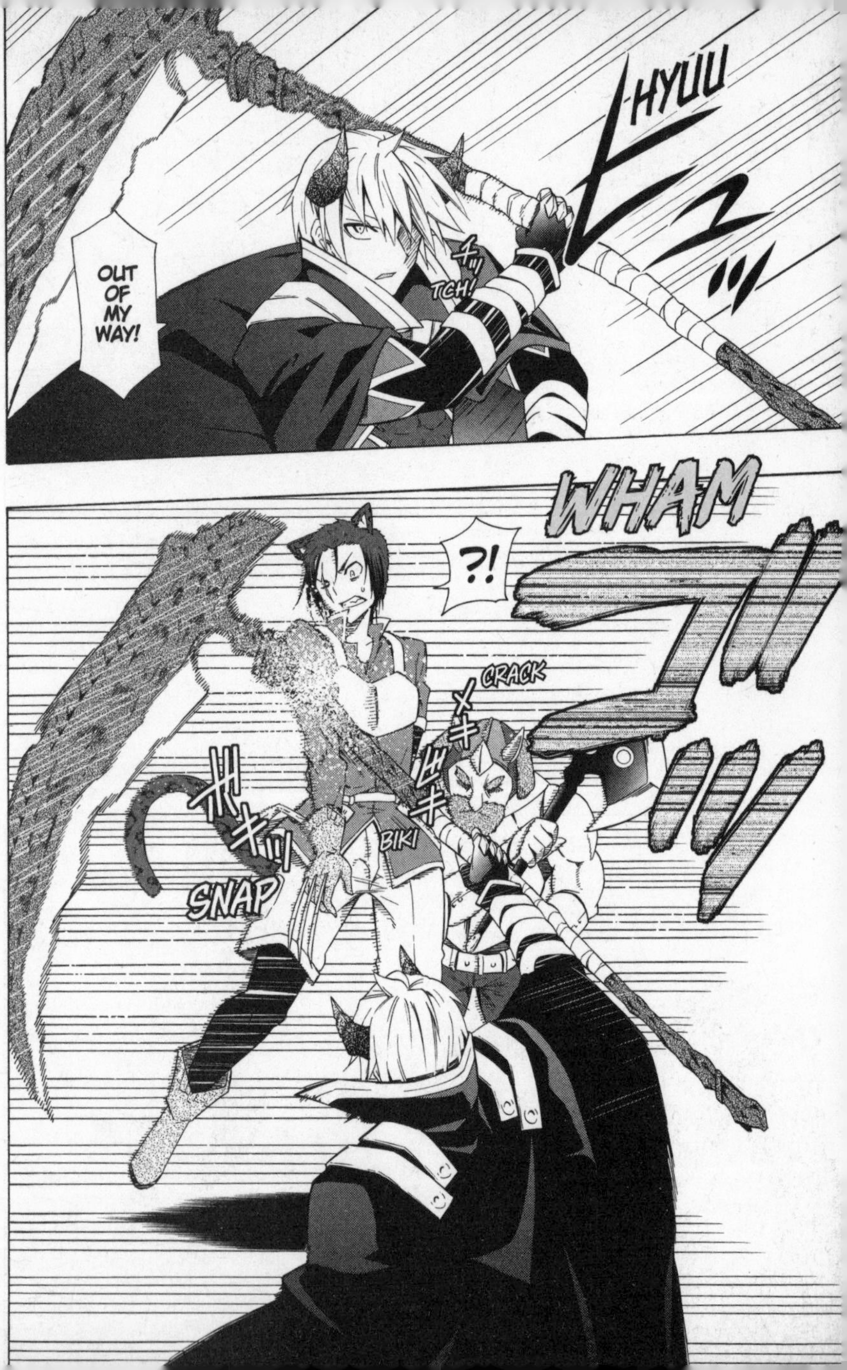
HYUU
TCH!
OUT OF MY WAY!
WHAM
?!
CRACK
BIKI
SNAP

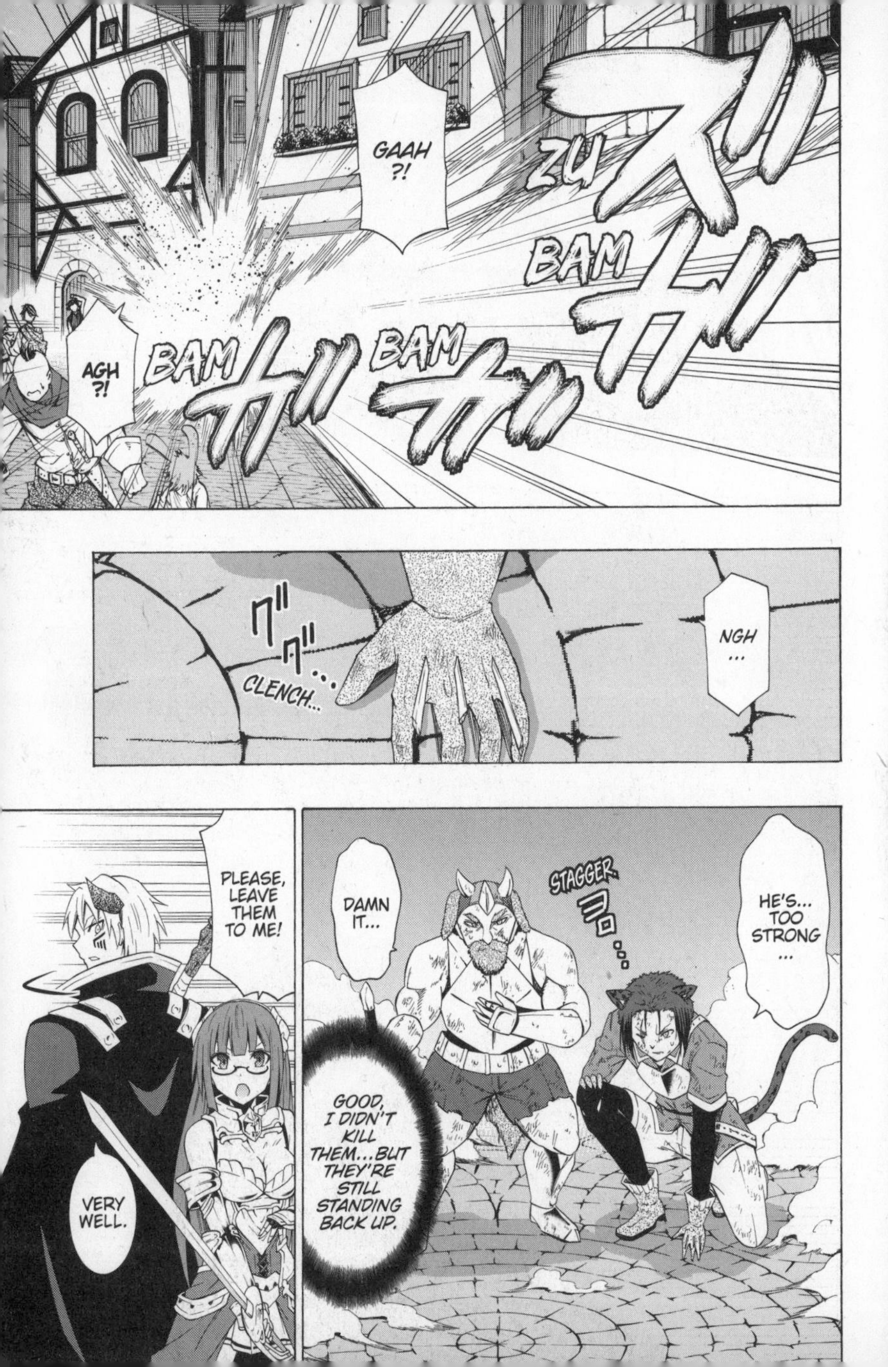
ZU
BAM
GAAH ?!
BAM
BAM
AGH ?!
NGH ...
CLENCH...
HE'S... TOO STRONG ...
STAGGER.
DAMN IT...
GOOD, I DIDN'T KILL THEM...BUT THEY'RE STILL STANDING BACK UP.
PLEASE, LEAVE THEM TO ME!
VERY WELL.

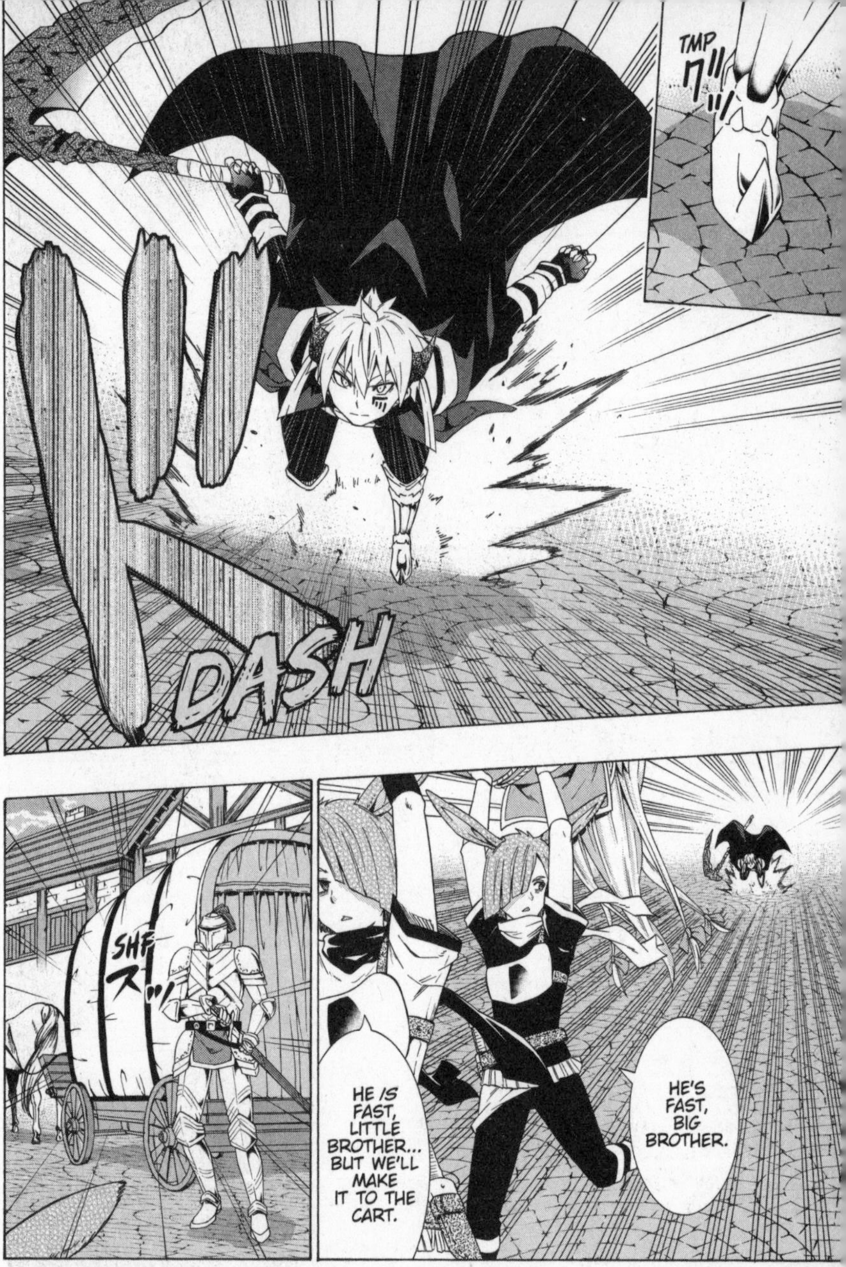
TMP
DASH
HE'S FAST, BIG BROTHER.
HE IS FAST, LITTLE BROTHER... BUT WE'LL MAKE IT TO THE CART.
SHF

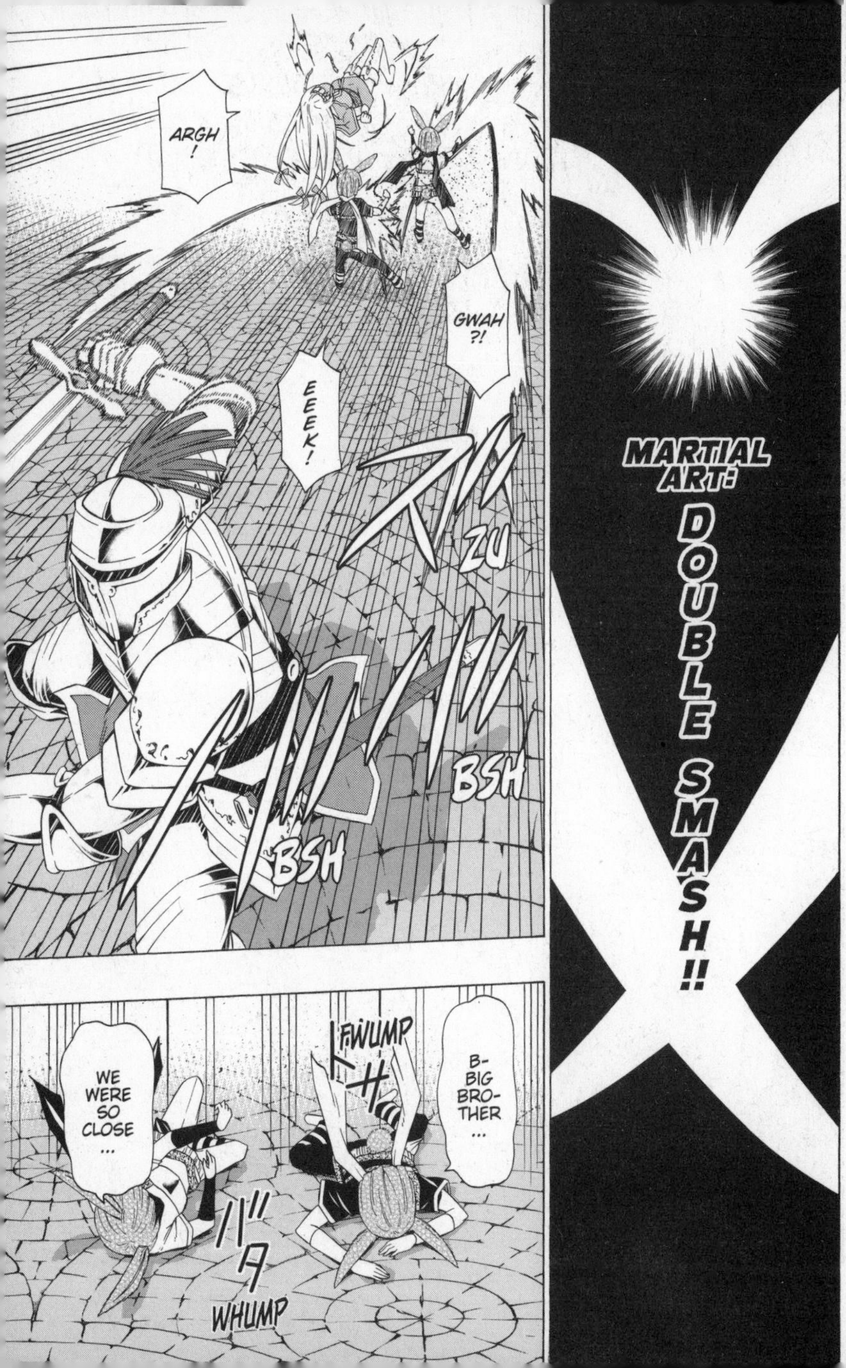
MARTIAL ART: DOUBLE SMASH!!
ARGH!
GWAH?!
EEEK!
ZU
BSH
BSH
B-BIG BROTHER...
FWUMP
WE WERE SO CLOSE...
WHUMP

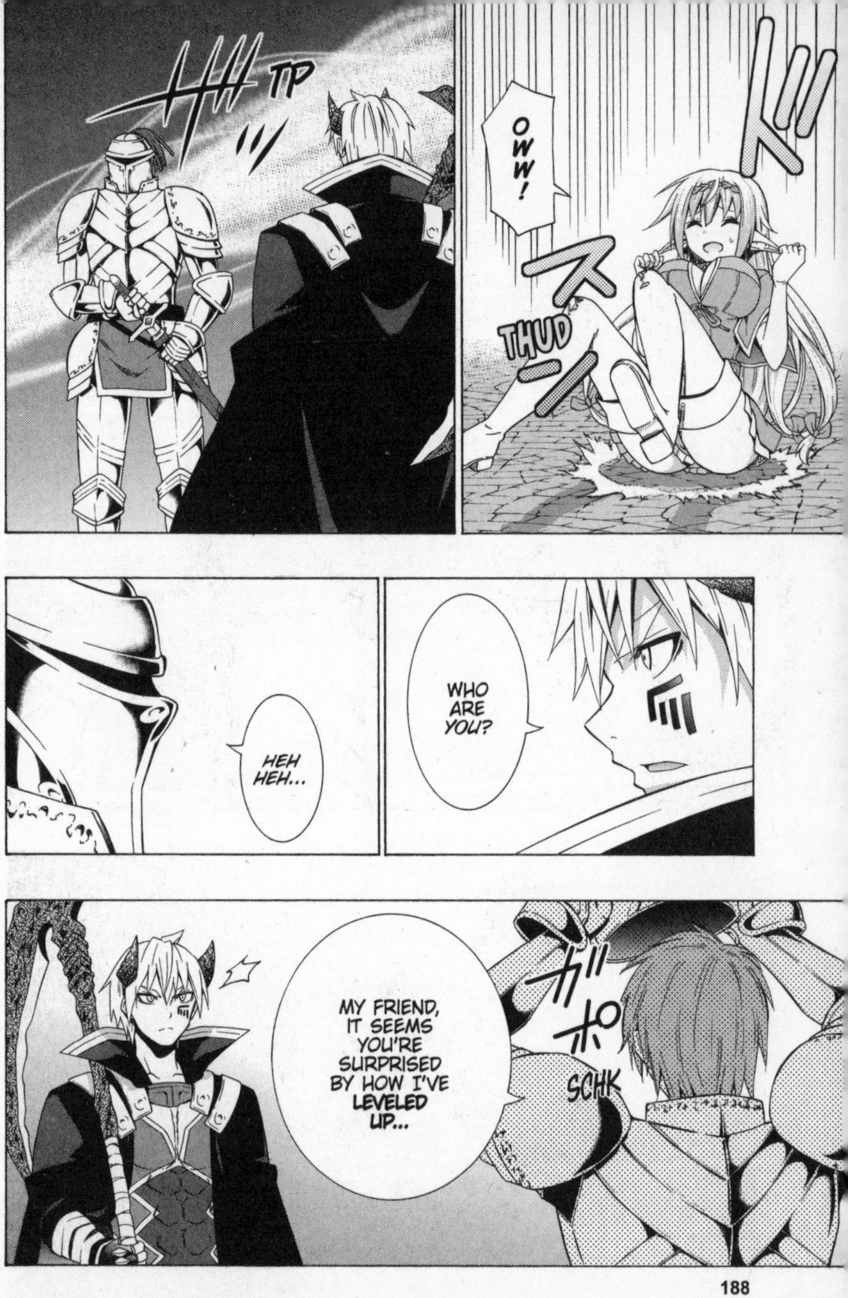
OWW!
THUD
TP
WHO ARE YOU?
HEH HEH...
MY FRIEND, IT SEEMS YOU'RE SURPRISED BY HOW I'VE **LEVELED UP**...
SCHK

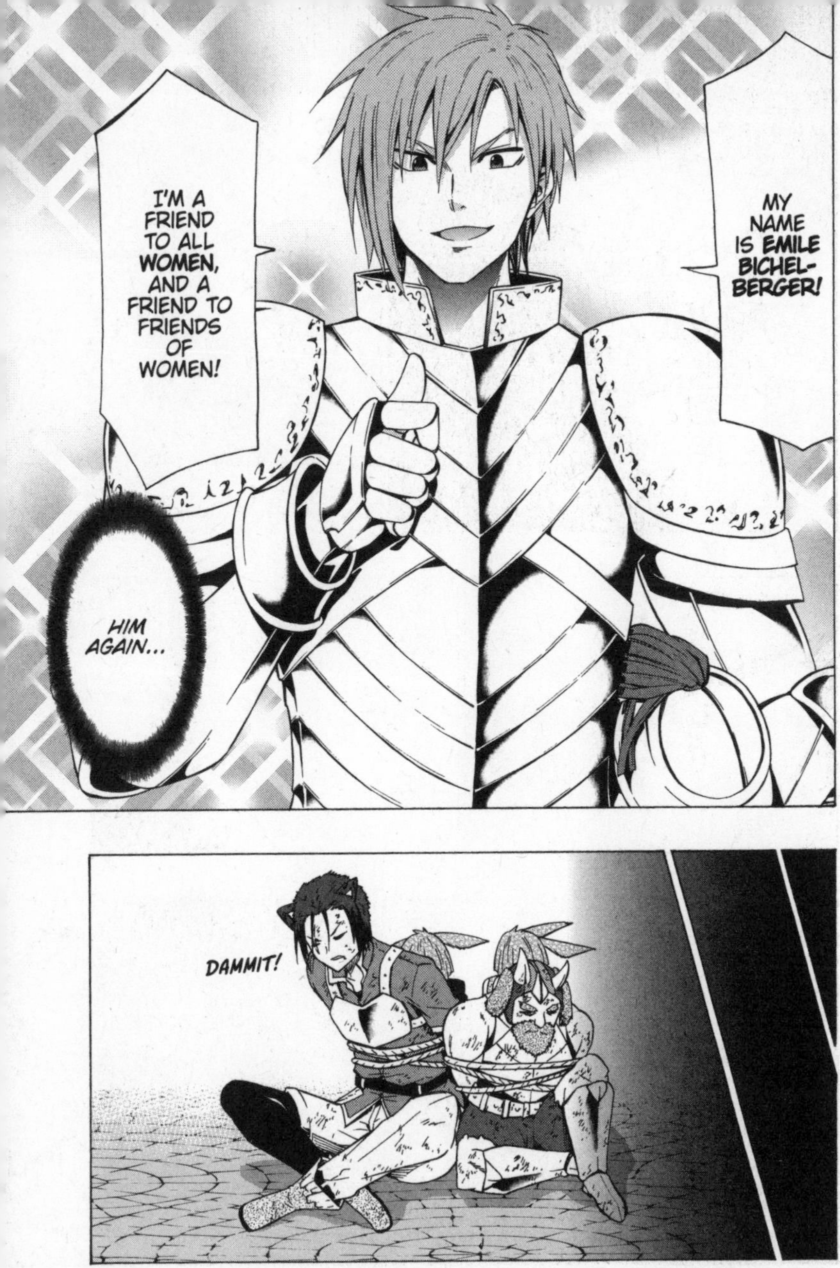
MY NAME IS EMILE BICHEL-BERGER!
I'M A FRIEND TO ALL WOMEN, AND A FRIEND TO FRIENDS OF WOMEN!
HIM AGAIN...
DAMMIT!

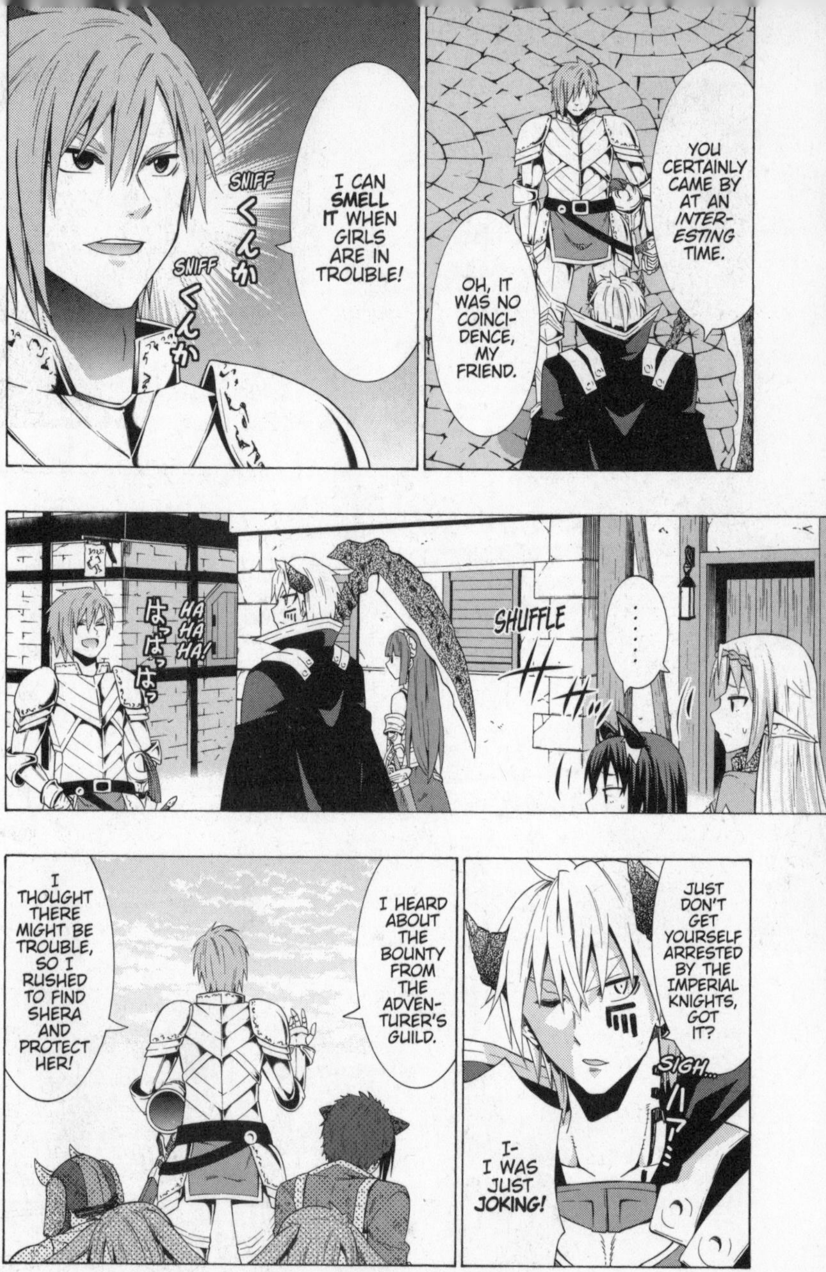
YOU CERTAINLY CAME BY AT AN INTERESTING TIME.
OH, IT WAS NO COINCIDENCE, MY FRIEND.
I CAN SMELL IT WHEN GIRLS ARE IN TROUBLE!
SNIFF くんか
SNIFF くんか
......
SHUFFLE ザッ
HA HA HA! はっはっはっ
JUST DON'T GET YOURSELF ARRESTED BY THE IMPERIAL KNIGHTS, GOT IT?
SIGH... はァー
I- I WAS JUST JOKING!
I HEARD ABOUT THE BOUNTY FROM THE ADVENTURER'S GUILD.
I THOUGHT THERE MIGHT BE TROUBLE, SO I RUSHED TO FIND SHERA AND PROTECT HER!

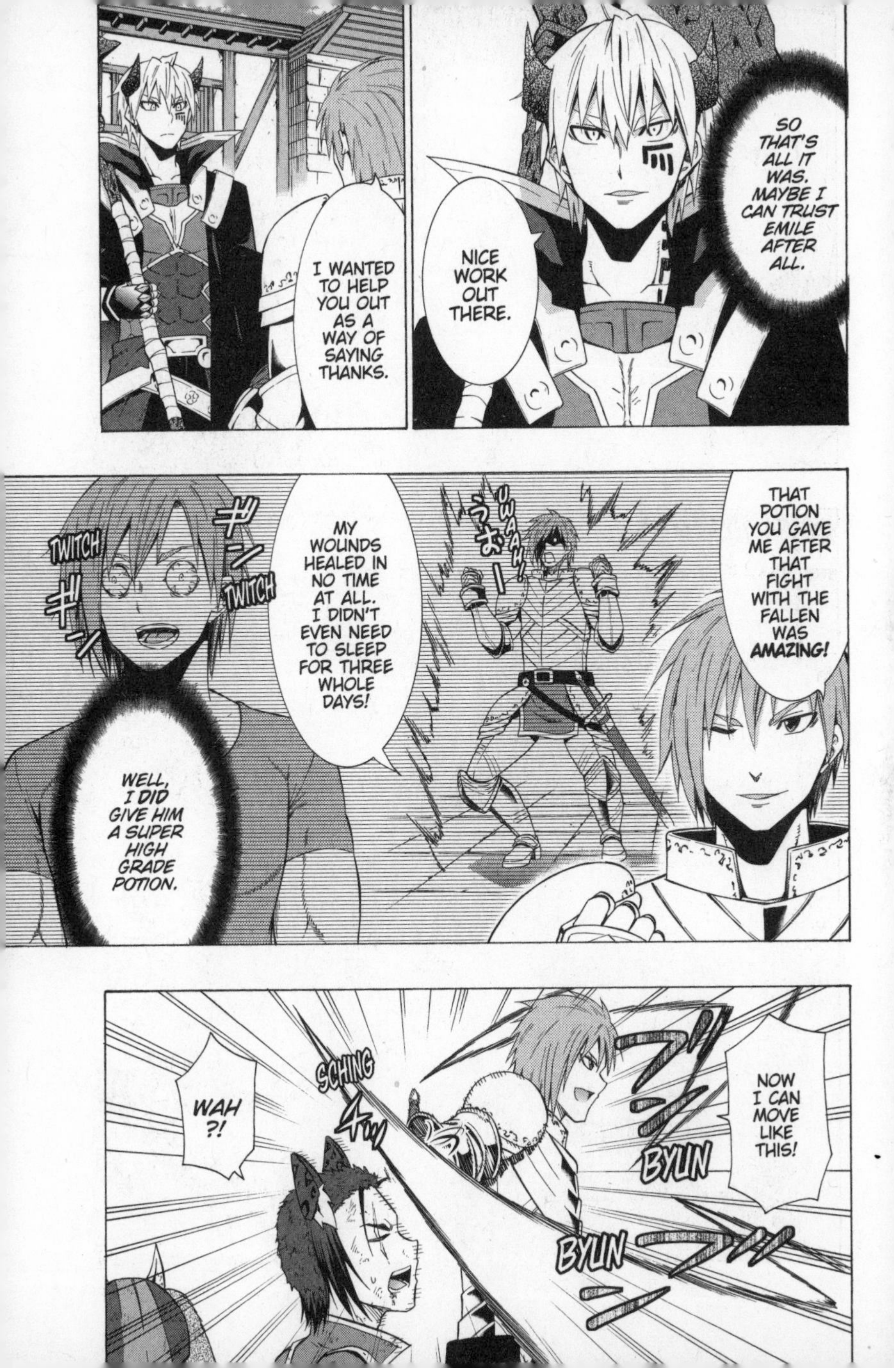
SO THAT'S ALL IT WAS. MAYBE I CAN TRUST EMILE AFTER ALL.
NICE WORK OUT THERE.
I WANTED TO HELP YOU OUT AS A WAY OF SAYING THANKS.
THAT POTION YOU GAVE ME AFTER THAT FIGHT WITH THE FALLEN WAS AMAZING!
UWAAH!
MY WOUNDS HEALED IN NO TIME AT ALL. I DIDN'T EVEN NEED TO SLEEP FOR THREE WHOLE DAYS!
TWITCH
TWITCH
WELL, I DID GIVE HIM A SUPER HIGH GRADE POTION.
NOW I CAN MOVE LIKE THIS!
BYUN
BYUN
SCHING
WAH ?!

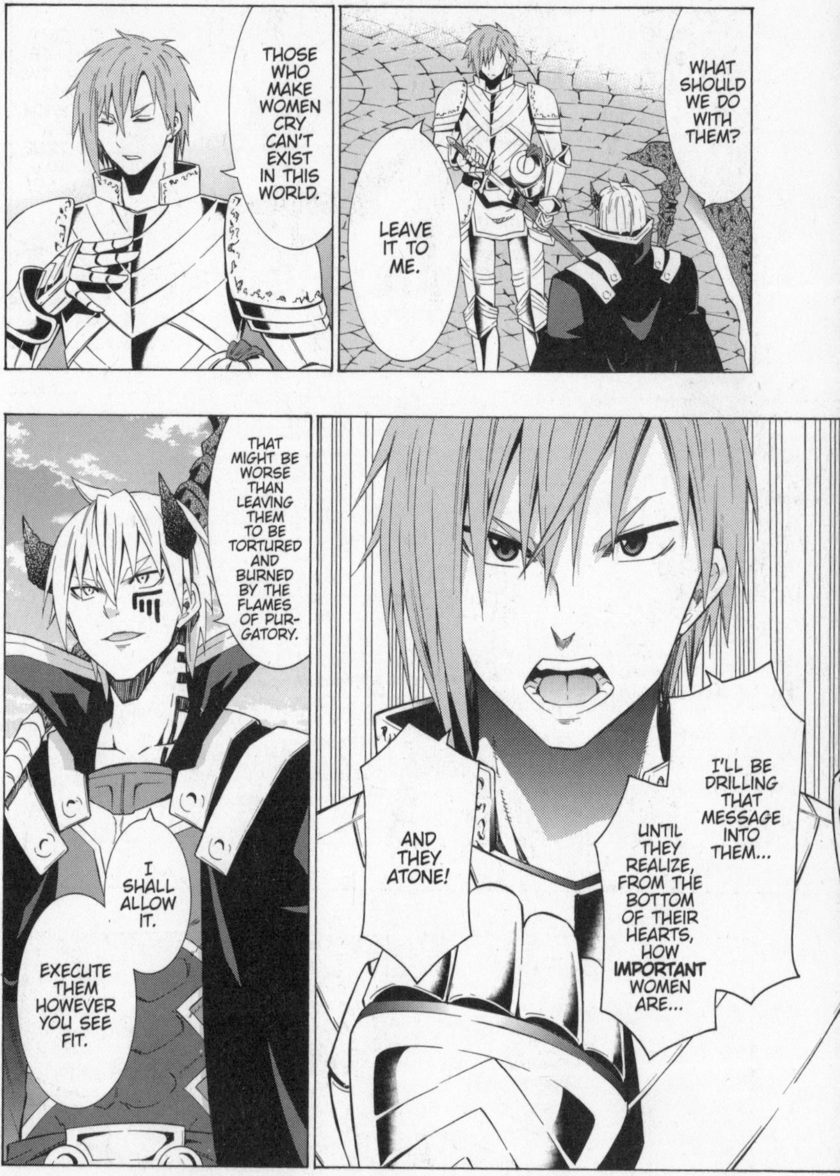
WHAT SHOULD WE DO WITH THEM?
LEAVE IT TO ME.
THOSE WHO MAKE WOMEN CRY CAN'T EXIST IN THIS WORLD.
I'LL BE DRILLING THAT MESSAGE INTO THEM...
UNTIL THEY REALIZE, FROM THE BOTTOM OF THEIR HEARTS, HOW **IMPORTANT** WOMEN ARE...
AND THEY ATONE!
THAT MIGHT BE WORSE THAN LEAVING THEM TO BE TORTURED AND BURNED BY THE FLAMES OF PURGATORY.
I SHALL ALLOW IT.
EXECUTE THEM HOWEVER YOU SEE FIT.

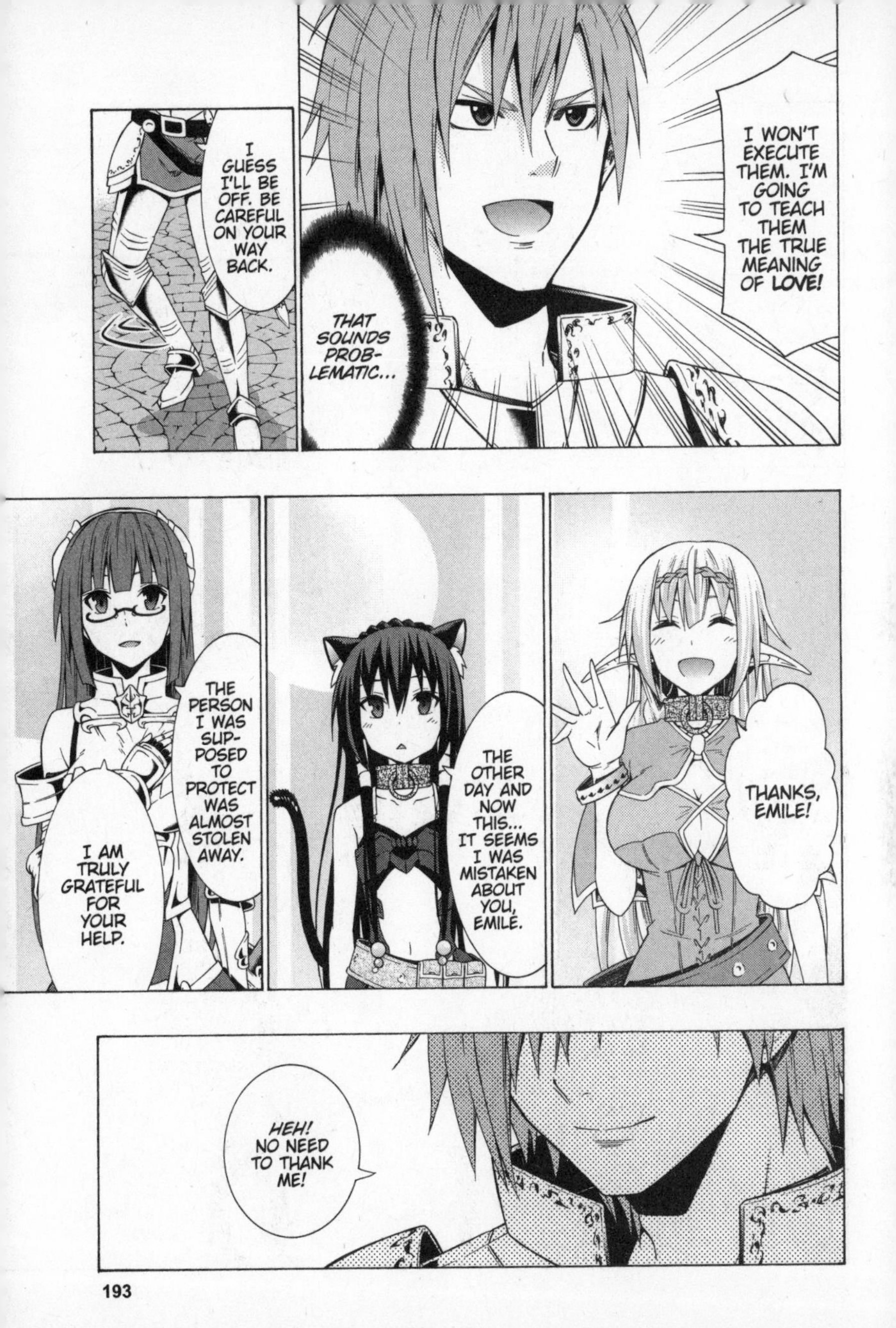
I WON'T EXECUTE THEM. I'M GOING TO TEACH THEM THE TRUE MEANING OF LOVE!
THAT SOUNDS PROB-LEMATIC...
I GUESS I'LL BE OFF. BE CAREFUL ON YOUR WAY BACK.
THANKS, EMILE!
THE OTHER DAY AND NOW THIS... IT SEEMS I WAS MISTAKEN ABOUT YOU, EMILE.
THE PERSON I WAS SUP-POSED TO PROTECT WAS ALMOST STOLEN AWAY.
I AM TRULY GRATEFUL FOR YOUR HELP.
HEH! NO NEED TO THANK ME!

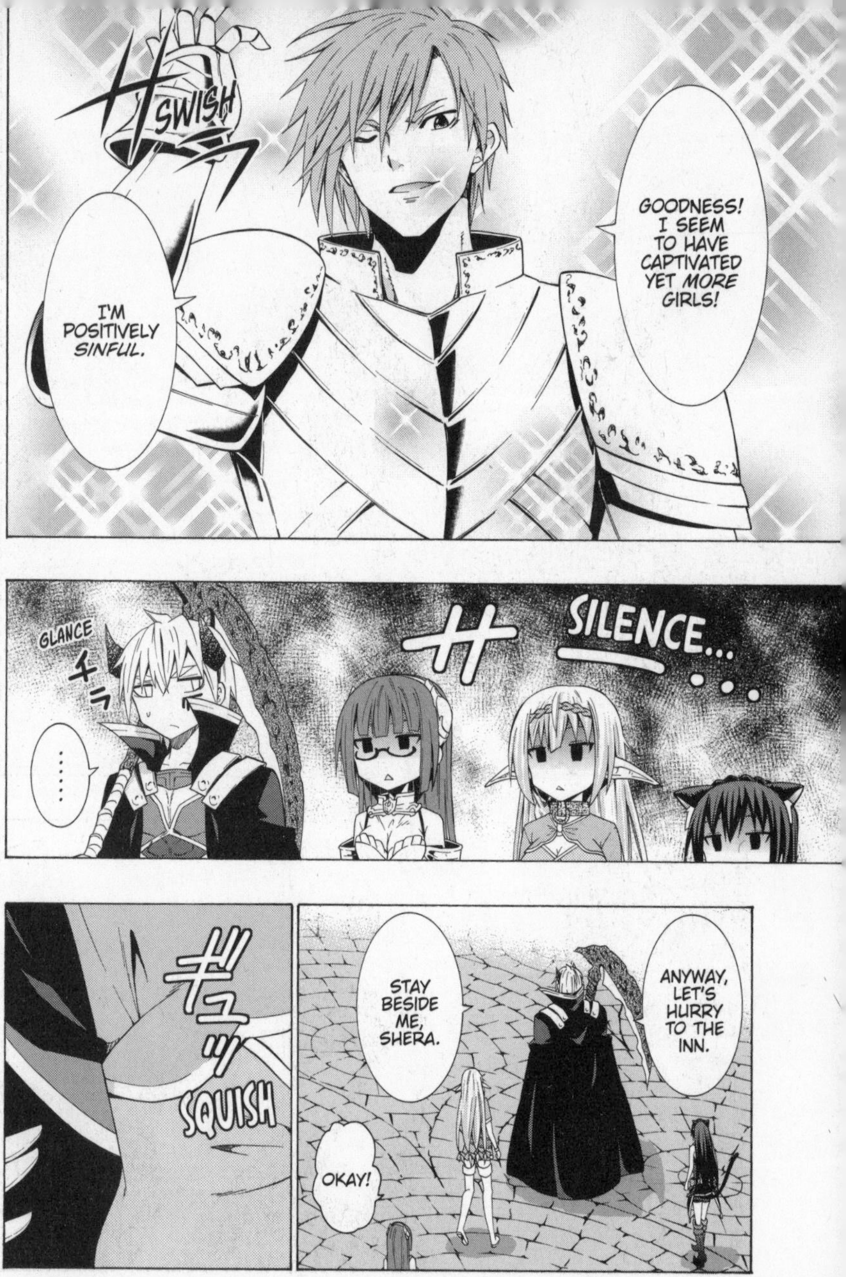
SWISH
GOODNESS! I SEEM TO HAVE CAPTIVATED YET MORE GIRLS!
I'M POSITIVELY SINFUL.
SILENCE...
GLANCE
チラ
......
ANYWAY, LET'S HURRY TO THE INN.
STAY BESIDE ME, SHERA.
OKAY!
ギュッ
SQUISH

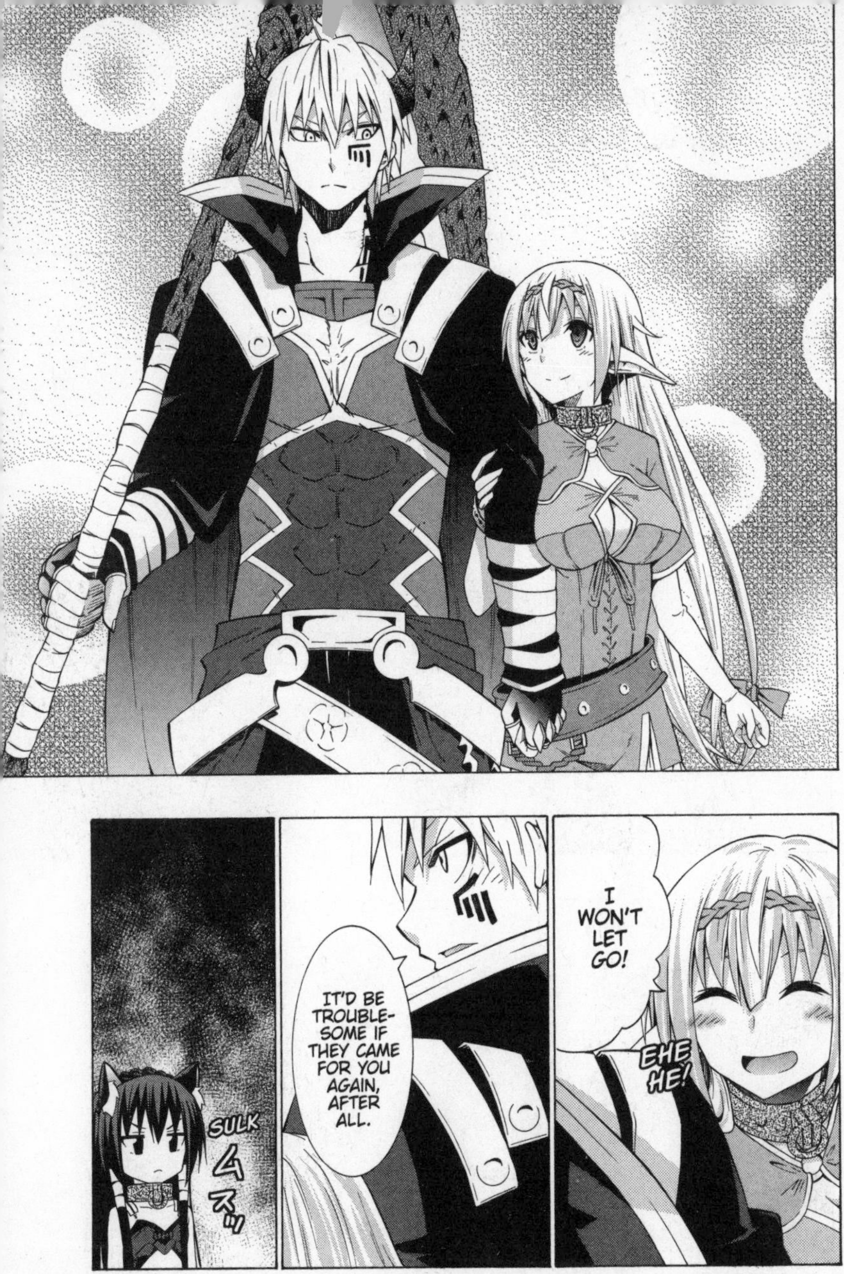
I WON'T LET GO!
EHE HE!
IT'D BE TROUBLE-SOME IF THEY CAME FOR YOU AGAIN, AFTER ALL.
SULK
ムスッ

HOW *NOT*
TO SUMMON A
DEMON LORD

to be continued...

SPECIAL THANKS FOR VOLUME 3

YUKIYA MURASAKI

TAKAHIRO TSURUSAKI

<<ASSISTANTS>>
YOSHITSUGU OHARA
TAKUYA NISHIDA
DAIKI HARAGUCHI
YUU TAKIGAWA
AKARI MATSUURA
CHITOSE SAKURA
NAGISA
ISSEI

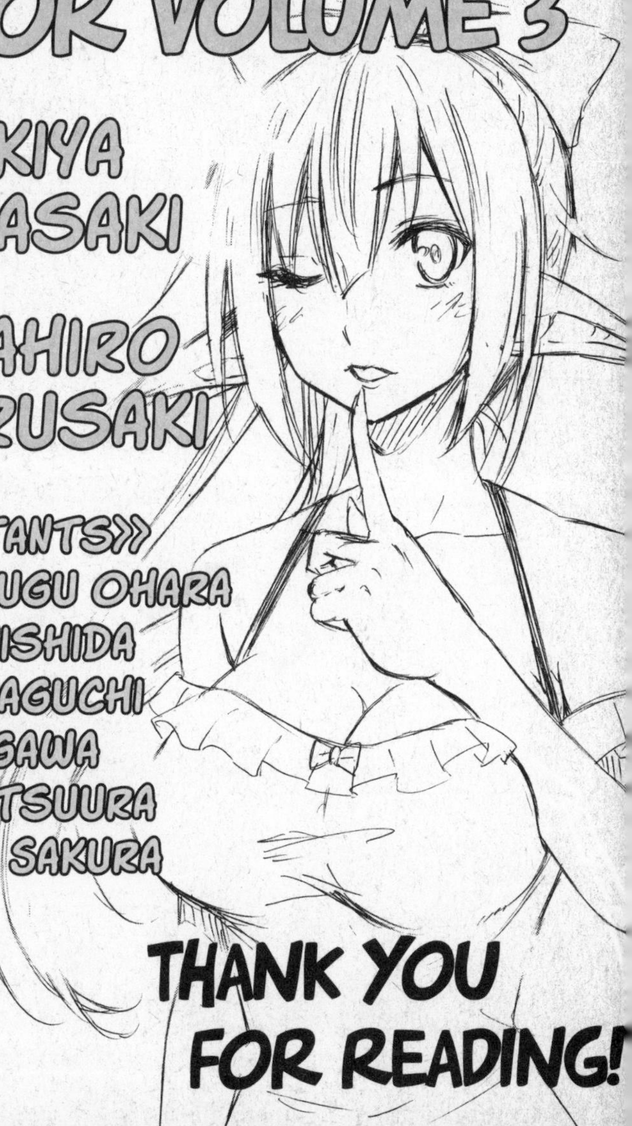

THANK YOU FOR READING!

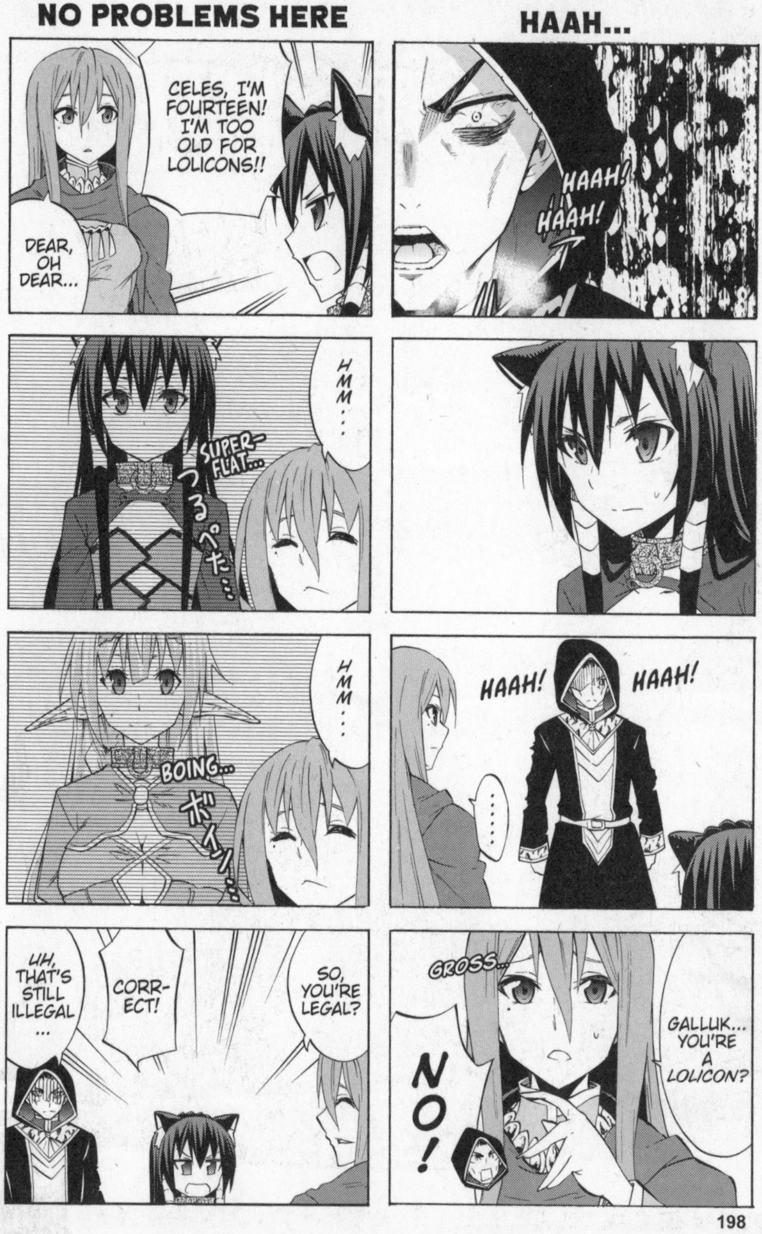
HAAH...
HAAH! HAAH!
HAAH!
HAAH!
......
GALLUK... YOU'RE A LOLICON?
GROSS...
NO!
NO PROBLEMS HERE
CELES, I'M FOURTEEN! I'M TOO OLD FOR LOLICONS!!
DEAR, OH DEAR...
HMM...
SUPER-FLAT...
つるぺた…
HMM...
BOING...
ボイ〜ン…
SO, YOU'RE LEGAL?
CORR-ECT!
UH, THAT'S STILL ILLEGAL...

SEVEN SEAS ENTERTAINMENT PRESENTS

HOW NOT TO SUMMON A VOLUME 3 DEMON LORD

story by YUKIYA MURASAKI   art by NAOTO FUKUDA

TRANSLATION
Garrison Denim

ADAPTATION
Lora Gray

LETTERING AND RETOUCH
Charles Pritchett

COVER DESIGN
KC Fabellon

PROOFREADER
Danielle King
Cae Hawksmoor

EDITOR
Shannon Fay

PRODUCTION ASSISTANT
CK Russell

PRODUCTION MANAGER
Lissa Pattillo

EDITOR-IN-CHIEF
Adam Arnold

PUBLISHER
Jason DeAngelis

Seven Seas books may be purchased in bulk for promotional, educational, or
business use. Please contact your local bookseller or the Macmillan Corporate
and Premium Sales Department at 1-800-221-7945, extension 5442, or by
e-mail at MacmillanSpecialMarkets@macmillan.com.

Seven Seas and the Seven Seas logo are trademarks of
Seven Seas Entertainment, LLC. All rights reserved.

ISBN: 978-1-626929-65-4

Printed in Canada

First Printing: February 2019

10 9 8 7 6 5 4 3 2 1

FOLLOW US ONLINE: *www.sevenseasentertainment.com*

READING DIRECTIONS

This book reads from *right to left*, Japanese style. If this is your first time reading manga, you start reading from the top right panel on each page and take it from there. If you get lost, just follow the numbered diagram here. It may seem backwards at first, but you'll get the hang of it! Have fun!!

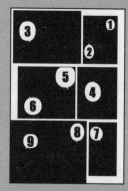